CHANNELING

C·H·A·N·N·E·L·I·N·G

INVESTIGATIONS ON RECEIVING INFORMATION FROM PARANORMAL SOURCES

JON KLIMO

JEREMY P. TARCHER, INC.
Los Angeles
Distributed by St. Martin's Press
New York

Library of Congress Cataloging in Publication Data

Klimo, Jon.
   Channeling : investigations on receiving information from paranormal
sources.

   Bibliography.
   Includes index.
   1. Spiritualism.   2. Mediums.   3. Extrasensory perception.   I. Title.
BF1286.K58   1987   133.9'1   87-11525
ISBN 0-87477-431-4

Jeremy P. Tarcher, Inc.
9110 Sunset Blvd.
Los Angeles, CA 90069

Design by Rosa Schuth

Manufactured in the United States of America
10   9   8   7   6   5   4   3

For Jane VanderVeer

CONTENTS

ONE
THE PERSONALITIES

ACKNOWLEDGMENTS

I especially owe my dear Jane the deepest acknowledgment for her loving support of me throughout the making of this book. She has continually worked for my productivity and fulfillment, teaching me along the way through the example of her loving and unselfish spirit. I want to thank my mother, who has always believed in me and what I am to do in this lifetime. And I thank my daughter, Elizabeth, for her love.

Willis Harman deserves my thanks for suggesting in 1981 that I write down some of my ideas on channeling. A copy of what I had written found its way into the hands of Mineda J. McCleave in Davenport, Iowa, and I have Mineda to thank for passing it on to John White. My appreciation to John for becoming my agent and matching me up with Jeremy Tarcher as publisher. I have felt John's support and understanding throughout.

I wish to acknowledge the people who consented to be interviewed by me for this book. Their contributions have been of great value. They include: Ralph B. Allison, Earl Babbie, Margo Chandley, Armand Di-Mele, James Fadiman, Marilyn Ferguson, Philip Goldberg, Jean Houston, Stanley Krippner, "Lazaris," Robert Masters, Jeffrey Mishlove, Robert Monroe, Tam Mossman, Michael Murphy, Karl F. Pribram, Jach Pursel, Shawn Randall, Pat Rodegast, D. Scott Rogo, Jack Schwarz, Judith Skutch, Huston Smith, Jose Stevens, Hal Stone, Charles Tart, Marcello Truzzi, Frances Vaughan, and Ken Wilber.

I am indebted to the various expert readers who have given me much-needed feedback: Ernest Hilgard and Steven Feinberg in hypnosis; William Tiller and Robert Shacklett in physics; James Brown in brain synchrony and psychophysiology; Justine Owens in cognitive psychology and state-specific learning; Matt Erdyie on Freud; and Frank Barr on his melanin model. I especially wish to thank Margo Chandley for her careful reading of the entire manuscript and for her numerous valuable suggestions.

I want to acknowledge the help Jonas Bastys and Joshua have provided me with resource materials. Special thanks to Silver for his friendship and for our crystalline coffee conversations. Ernest Pecci has

ACKNOWLEDGMENTS

aided my thinking as well. In addition, many others have helped me throughout the research and writing of this book, and I only wish there were space to list them all. I think they know who they are. They have my gratitude.

I wish to thank Connie Zweig, the editor who worked with me for most of this book. She took the obtuse, idiosyncratic poet-philosopher that I was in my writing, and patiently taught me to think and write clearly and succinctly. I wish also to thank Kip Hargrove, John White, and Hank Stine, who came in later as editorial readers to help wrest a final shape and size from the manuscript. Hank Stine's enthusiasm and expertise were especially helpful. And finally, I wish to say what an absolute pleasure and extraordinary education it has been working throughout with my publisher, Jeremy Tarcher. No author could ask for wiser, more witty, or more supportive circumstances for writing a book than Jeremy has provided. He is an artist among publishers, and it has been an honor for me to have worked with him.

FOREWORD

Who am I?

The question is an eternal one. If you don't answer it, you will never be able to distinguish between what your essential self wants and what other people manipulate you to want. Each of us must answer it for himself or herself, as no one else's answer will really do. Yet the answers given by others do affect the way we approach (or avoid) this question. Several general types of answers have been offered.

The most traditional answer in Western culture is that you are a creature, a creation of God, a creation that is flawed in vital ways. Conceived and born in original sin, you are someone who must constantly struggle to obey the rules laid down by that God, lest you be damned. It is an answer that is depressing in many ways: on one hand, it leads to low self-worth and the expectation of failure; on the other, to the rigid, conceited arrogance of being one of the "elect." Further, this view doesn't really encourage you to think about who you really are, as the answer has already been given from a "higher" source.

The modern answer to "Who am I?" is that you are a meaningless accident. Contemporary science is associated with a view of reality that sees the entire universe as totally material, governed only by fixed physical laws and blind chance. It just happened that, in a huge universe, the right chemicals came together under the right conditions so that the chemical reaction we call life formed and eventually evolved into you. But there's no inherent meaning in that accident, and no spiritual side to existence.

I believe that this view is not really good science, but rather what we *believe* to be scientific and factual. More important, it's a view that has strong psychological consequences. After all, if you're just a mixture of meaningless chemicals, your ultimate fate—death—is clear, and you might as well get yours while you can. Don't worry too much about other people, as they are just meaningless mixtures of chemicals, too. In this view, it doesn't really matter if you think about who you really are—whatever conclusions you arrive at are just subjective fancies, of no particular relevance in the real physical world.

Psychologically speaking, this physicalistic view of our ultimate nature leaves as much to be desired as does the born-in-original-sin view.

As a psychologist, I stress the psychological consequences of these two views of your ultimate identity because your beliefs do shape your reality. Modern research has shown that, in many ways, what we believe affects the way our brain constructs the world we experience. Some of these beliefs may be conscious—you know you have them. Many are implicit—you act on them, but don't know you have these beliefs. If you think life in general is a meaningless accident, your perceptions of the complex world around you will be biased toward more readily seeing the meaningless and the absurd. Seeing them will in turn reinforce your belief in the meaninglessness of things. If you believe in original sin and the great difficulties of finding salvation, your perceptions will be biased toward seeing your own and others' failures, again reinforcing your belief. Our beliefs about who we are and what our world is like are not mere beliefs—they strongly control our lives. So we had better find out what we believe and how those beliefs affect us.

Between these traditional religious and materialistic views of who you are, there are a variety of ideas that embrace elements of each, but include possibilities for personal and social growth. The common element in these other views is that the universe is inherently spiritual and that each of us shares in that spiritual nature. Yet they also recognize that something has gone wrong somewhere. We have "temporarily" lost our way; we have forgotten the essential divine element within us and have become psychologically locked into a narrow, traditional, religious or materialistic view.

There is an old Eastern teaching story that illustrates this—the story of the Mad King. Although he is the ruler of vast dominions, the Mad King has forgotten them. He has gone into the dankest cellar storeroom of the palace and lives in the dark among rats and rags, brooding on his misfortunes. His ministers try to persuade him to come upstairs where it is light and beautiful, but the Mad King regards them as madmen and will not listen. He will not be taken in by fairy tales of kings and palaces! Just an old Eastern story, but we have a lot of evidence in modern psychology to show how little of our natural potential we use, how much of our suffering is self-created, clasped tightly to our bosoms in crazed fear and ignorance.

Yet the ministers do carry a light with them when they come down into the cellar, and they do bring good food to the Mad King. Even in his madness he must sometimes notice this. In the real world, events keep occurring that don't fit into our narrow views, no matter how tightly we hold them, and sometimes these events catch our attention.

So-called psychic phenomena are like that. They certainly don't fit into a materialistic view, and they constantly challenge the traditional religious view that the only unusual phenomena happened thousands of years ago and are to be believed, not pondered. The phenomena we call channeling are particularly compelling.

Jon Klimo's book plunges us into phenomena that are disturbing to both the traditional religious and the materialistic views of who we are. It is one thing to consider abstractly that our true identity may be more than we conceive, or that we may live in a universe filled with other, more spiritual intelligences. It is quite another thing when the ordinary looking person sitting across from you seems to go to sleep, but suddenly begins speaking to you in a different voice, announcing that he is a spiritual entity who has temporarily taken over the channel's body to teach you something! Now you have to really look at what's going on. Who is that so-called "entity"? Who is that person who channels? If someone else can have his or her apparent identity change so drastically, am I sure about who I am? If you have been conditioned to believe that who you are is meaningless or inherently bad or sinful, you might not welcome the stimulation that the phenomena of channeling gives to the question "Who am I?"

We have many ways of psychologically defending ourselves against dealing with things that don't fit into our organized and defended world. You could just say, "This person is crazy! Or maybe even deliberately faking this stuff!" It's a good defense, for of course there are some people known as channels who are probably just crazy or are deliberately faking it. The best lies always contain a very high proportion of truth.

You could just naively accept whatever the ostensible channeled entity says. "Yes, you are the Master Shananagans from the 17th planet of the chief divine galaxy Ottenwelt, teach me Master, I hear and obey!" This overenthusiastic acceptance can be just as much a defense against thinking as overenthusiastic rejection.

Channeling is having a great impact on our culture today, and we can use this impact for personal and social growth if we think about what it means and examine the things we take for granted about our inherent nature. If we just believe or disbelieve without really looking at channeling, this opportunity will be lost.

Klimo has pulled together many fascinating facts and ideas about channeling in a comprehensive way that has never been done before. Read, reflect, examine, argue, go meet some channeled entities. Perhaps you will decide they are "real." Perhaps you will decide they are not "real" in the ordinary sense of the word but are psychologically or spiritually "real" or important. Perhaps you will decide that some (or most or all) of this stuff is really crazy. But in the process you will learn a lot about who you (and we) are!

Charles T. Tart
Professor of Psychology
University of California, Davis

INTRODUCTION
SETTING THE SCENE

In the trance session [Elwood] Babbitt, sitting upright in a straight-backed chair, appears gradually to fall into a deep sleep. This "sleep" is sometimes brief, sometimes prolonged. Changes in breathing occur, and the expressions of his face also change. After a while there are movements of the lips and other muscles of his face that suggest the efforts of the incoming entity to gain control of them. Finally the entity greets the sitter and starts to talk.

Today we are hearing increasingly about something called channeling. It is a phenomenon in which otherwise ordinary people seem to let themselves be taken over by, or in other ways receive messages from, another personality who uses them as a conduit, medium, or channel for the communication—hence the term *medium* or *channel*. Such personalities usually purport to be from some other dimension or level of reality, often claiming to be more highly evolved that we on earth are. Much of their information seems intended to hasten personal and planetary growth.

Cases of channeling have become pervasive. An increasing number of people are now seeking and following the guidance provided through channeling. Accounts of the phenomenon are sweeping the media. Dozens of new books said to be channeled are cropping up in bookstores. Millions of readers have been introduced to the phenomenon through actress Shirley MacLaine's recent best-selling books featuring her own dramatic, positive experiences with channels. All of this activity and visibility points to the fact that something very interesting and unusual is going on, and on a wide scale. Exactly *what* is going on, however, remains open to question.

Often the channeled personalities have names such as "Seth," "Ramtha," the "Invisibles," "Jesus," and "Archangel Michael," imparting a mythic quality complete with biblical, Egyptian, and other ancient overtones or an otherworldly flavor. Does this mean that channeling is simply the stuff of fantasy and wishful thinking, of myth devoid of objective reality? Or, as with spiritual practice throughout history, might something real, though transcending our normal reality, be involved?

Other questions arise: questions regarding the honesty of the channels; questions regarding whether currently understood mechanisms of the brain and mind can adequately account for the phenomenon. And given how many people are now allowing themselves to be guided by this channeled material with an almost religious type of fervor, we must also inquire into the benefits or dangers of this phenomenon and the information it provides. Because of all of these concerns and questions, and because of the sheer scope of channeling today, a serious examination of the phenomenon has become necessary.

Let me begin with my definition of channeling: *Channeling is the communication of information to or through a physically embodied human being from a source that is said to exist on some other level or dimension of reality than the physical as we know it, and that is not from the normal mind (or self) of the channel.* Although the human mind might be considered nonphysical, I want to rule out by my definition not only communication from one's own normal mind as source, but communication from fellow physically embodied minds. Jeffrey Mishlove, author of *The Roots of Consciousness,* points out that a great deal rests on the phrase "is said to" in this definition.[1] Clearly, it is the channels, their alleged sources, and the various followers of the phenomenon who comprise the rapidly growing worldwide channeling subculture, who say that the sources being channeled come from another level of reality.

Although channeling as just defined may seem far out to many of you, it will be presented in this book as part of a spectrum that includes not only spirits of the deceased, alien disembodied intelligences, the higher Self, and the Universal Mind, but also such familiar concepts as intuition and creativity. I will also argue that, just as intuition and inspiration are potentials we all have, so is channeling. I will even offer a number of techniques that will allow you to explore this potential for yourself.

I want this to be an exploration that you and I share page by page. And although we are venturing into relatively unknown territory, I intend for this book to be a balanced and objective treatment of the phenomenon of channeling so that you the reader can make your own judgments. Toward this end, I have done my best to keep out my own feelings and opinions that are unargued or unsupported by evidence. This has not been easy to do, both because of who I am—basically a creative person full of feelings and intuitions—and because of the nature of the subject.

This book has been written for three reasons. The first is to clarify thinking about channeling—to attempt definitions and a general understanding—and in the process to clarify thinking about related phenomena. These phenomena are as various as current information-processing models in cognitive science, recent interest in multiple-personality disorder in clinical psychology, and the age-old mysteries of intuition and creativity, self-transcendence, spiritual experience, and afterlife.

Although, as we shall see, channeling has been around since the beginning of recorded history, it is enjoying a remarkable resurgence today. Hundreds of thousands of people are being confronted with a kind of experience—be it their own or others'—that is forcing them to reexamine what they once held to be the limits of the universe and of human nature.

My second reason for writing this book is to address the experience that an ever-increasing number of people seem to be having of communication with beings from levels of reality beyond the physical as we know it. A 1980 Gallup Poll found that 71 percent of Americans believe in an afterlife. In a more recent poll, the University of Chicago's National Opinion Research Council found that nearly half of American adults, 42 percent, believe they have been in contact with someone who has died. Of these, 78 percent said they saw, 50 percent heard, and 18 percent talked with the departed. Thirty percent of Americans who say they don't believe in life after death still claim to have had personal contact with someone departed. As we'll see in chapter 5, the largest category of reported channeling cases involves supposed communication from human spirits who have survived physical death.[2]

Clearly, a great many people are experiencing a hunger for personal meaning in their lives, for deeper—some say spiritual—connectedness and fulfillment. Add to this the fact that recent attempts by scientific inquiry to understand the universe are beginning to lose their traditional objectivity and precision. Many of us find ourselves, like many of the scientists, in a shadowland where unarguable public evidence is no longer possible; unprovable, often unsharable private experience and belief are all that remain in its place. Channeling lies at the heart of this territory.

This suggests the third reason for writing this book: to expand your view of reality, both the nature of the self and the nature of physical reality, and to awaken you to the greater possibilities of being human.

In light of this third reason, consider the following analogy. *Lucid dreaming* occurs when the dreamer becomes aware that he or she is dreaming and is then able to continue dreaming consciously. Lucid-dream researchers, such as Stephen LaBerge at Stanford University, tell us that a normal dreamer usually becomes lucid when something anomalous takes place within the dream that alerts the dreamer to the fact that it *is* a dream and not reality that he or she is experiencing. Perhaps some aspects of channeling are the anomalies that could awaken us to a kind of lucidity within the waking dream of earthly existence, resulting in conscious wakefulness of a kind higher than normal waking. Other possibilities of human experience, other realms of information, may lie in store for us.

And even if the analogy is not true, the material in this book challenges our deepest beliefs and values. It is intended to provide everyone with food for thought because it deals with the very essence of what constitutes human identity. It raises fundamental questions about the nature of the self and the nature of reality. This book will attempt to demonstrate that the realms of the psyche and spirit may be more real and run more deeply than most of us believe.

WHAT IS CHANNELING?

Given the fact that many consider the mind to be nonphysical, I should explain further the part of my definition of channeling that says channeling does not include information received from one's own or from another embodied person's mind (at least as usually defined). The mind of the ordinary self includes conscious and assorted altered states like daydream and dream, as well as memories and the personal unconscious. We need to exclude such ordinary, embodied mind from being a channeling source if we are to separate the study of channeling from disciplines already established to investigate versions of simply "talking to oneself" (clinical and cognitive psychology) and telepathy and ESP communication between minds of embodied persons (parapsychology). (However, these related perspectives will be brought to bear upon channeling as part of our exploration of possible explanations in chapter 7.)

Variations on my definition of channeling have been formulated by fellow researchers; the field of channeling studies has yet to arrive at a consensus. Fellow channeling researcher Arthur Hastings, president of the California Institute of Transpersonal Psychology in Menlo Park, California, shares my definition. He defines channeling as "the process in which a person transmits messages from a presumed discarnate source external to his or her consciousness."[3] William Kautz, a pioneer in working with channels at his Center for Applied Intuition in San Francisco, has a more open definition of channeling with regard to possible sources of information. Using the term *trance channeling,* he defines it as "one form or aspect of mediumship" that "is a mental process in which an individual (the channel) partially or totally sets aside waking consciousness, to allow knowledge that lies beyond conscious awareness to flow into the mind."[4]

But what if our own respective minds are really part of some vast impersonal sea of mind (or energy) with which we interact to give birth to further, seemingly separate minds or personalities (or energy systems) that are the "entities" being channeled? This is but one of many related hypotheses that might help expand the definition of channeling beyond the stereotype that it is always some entity—autonomous and at a distance (or dimension) from us and our minds—that is communicating, and that we are each a bounded and autonomous entity as well, albeit an incarnate one. Maybe everything *is us*—all a hydra-headed choral interaction of the "I" of one being—a single creative source generating, sustaining, and merging the endless possible subentities or subpersonalities of itself. And the more we move into the experience of this, the more we know it to be a blending of what once appeared as separate minds, entities, and energies. Sheer fantasy? For some, this concept is less bizarre than the prospect that there are totally separate beings living outside the physical universe as we know it who are communicating with us. Perhaps an expanded notion of "it's all in the mind" or "it's all one sea of energy" is no more farfetched than notions of disembodied intelligences or an other-dimensional afterlife. I include such possibilities within my definition of channeling.

Beverly Hills, California, researcher Margo Chandley, who recently completed her doctoral dissertation on contemporary channels, holds a view of channeling similar to the one just mentioned. Chandley believes that "we're going to find that this nonphysical energy is a part of all of us, and the reason that we label it entities and outside of us is that it's the only way we can communicate with it right now . . . My research shows me that if we're one part physical and then the rest of us—the other 506 or however many dimensions of us—is nonphysical, then we're going to attract whatever nonphysical energy system is out there not focusing in physical reality." She adds, "Our belief system will attract this energy." Therefore, for Chandley, the developing, integrating personality of the channel is key to the nature and quality of the channeling process.[5] As you are perhaps beginning to sense, the old inner/outer and self/other designations may have to be reexamined as we continue our exploration.

California parapsychologist D. Scott Rogo, author of numerous books, including *Exploring Psychic Phenomena* and *Mind Beyond the Body,* does not consider the terms *mediumship* and *channeling* to be synonymous, as so many other researchers do. In addition, his definition of channeling is more open, like Kautz's. According to Rogo, "Mediumship is the art of bringing through spirits of the dead specifically to communicate with their relatives. Channeling I define as bringing through some sort of intelligence, the nature undefined, whose purpose is to promote spiritual teachings and philosophical discussion."[6]

Educated at Harvard and the University of California, Berkeley, sociologist Earl Babbie was for twelve years professor at the University of Hawaii. Author of some of the leading textbooks used today in social-science research, Babbie has recently undertaken his own study of channeling. Based on his understanding of research methodology, he says, "I'm not concerned with rigid definitions of things . . . I'm comfortable for now at least having a rather loose set of boundaries for what is and isn't channeling. It's something that's continually under review and advisement."[7]

As we shall see in later chapters, several kinds of channeling fall under the definition I have given. There are also different kinds of sources involved as well as different kinds of subject matter reportedly communicated. In chapters 3 through 6, I will define terms and present the issues fundamental to an understanding of the subject. First, however, we will survey the most recent examples of channeling (chapter 1), as well as its earlier historical panorama (chapter 2), to give an idea of the rich legacy of material on which the conclusions and classifications in this book are based. Our exploration will continue in chapters 7 and 8 with a series of possible explanations for the channeling phenomenon, based on ideas from the fields of psychology, physiology, and physics. In chapter 9 we will examine the relationship of channeling to intuition, creativity, the arts, and spiritual experience. Finally, in chapter 10 we'll look at some of the ways in which you can explore your own channeling potential, including suggestions from contemporary channels.

Because of its subjective and relatively unverifiable nature, channeling is an inherently difficult phenomenon to research. Consider the parallel between our attempt to understand channeling and the attempts by philosophers and theologians to understand the mystical experience. In both cases there appears to be a paranormal contact with a presence that exists beyond our normal reality. C. D. Broad in his book *Religion, Philosophy and Psychical Research* and W. T. Stace in *Mysticism and Philosophy* are just two of the contemporary philosophers whose careful approach to studying mysticism has provided sound procedures that may help us think clearly about channeling. In order to highlight the similarity, I have replaced "mystical" with "channeling" in the following from Stace:

We start with a psychological fact the denial of which could only proceed from ignorance. Some human beings do occasionally have unusual experiences which could be distinguished as [channeling]. These are recorded, or at least referred to, in the literatures of most advanced peoples in all ages . . .

Since the term [channeling] is utterly vague, we must first examine the field empirically to determine what types and kinds of experience are called [channeling], to specify and classify their main characteristics, to assign boundaries to the class, and to exclude irrelevant types. We then ask whether these experiences, or these states of mind, so selected and described, throw any light on such problems as the following: whether there is in the universe any spiritual presence greater than man; and, if so, how it is related to man and to the universe in general; whether we can find in [channeling] any illumination on the questions of the nature of the self, the functions of language, the truth or untruth of human claims of immortality . . .

The question is raised whether [channeling] experience is objective or subjective. Does it reveal the existence of anything outside the [channel's] own mind and independent of his consciousness? If so, what sort of existence does it reveal? . . . [Also] What *truths*, if any, about the universe does [channeling] yield which the mind could not obtain from science and the logical intellect?[8]

Stace presents the "argument for unanimity," or "argument from analogy," that must lie at the heart of any attempt to make a case for the objective reality of basically subjective phenomena such as mysticism and channeling. The argument contends "that there is an analogous agreement among mystics [and channels] everywhere about what they experience, and that this supports belief in the objectivity of the experience." This requires the assumption "that the witnesses are telling the truth . . . [and] that in their reports of their experiences they have not unintentionally misdescribed the nature of their experiences."

From this premise, according to Stace, the conclusion would appear to be that "it is more likely than not that the mystic [channel] in his experience comes in contact with some reality or some aspect of reality with which men do not come in contact in any other way."

Stace then counterargues that "an experience may be universal and yet illusory." For example, "The fact that all men who push one eye on one side correctly report the experience of double vision does not afford any evidence of any actual duplication of objects." And "hallucinatory perception of rats and snakes . . . shared by innumerable drunkards" does not lead to proof of the objective existence of these things beyond the mind of those experiencing them.[9] We are left, then, with no clear resolution.

INTRODUCTION: SETTING THE SCENE

Channeling, like mysticism, is a phenomenon that has been part of human experience as far back as human records go. It appears to be an essential element in the origins of virtually all of the great spiritual paths. It is not just a curiosity of current interest based on a resurgence of inner voices, visions, trance seances, and automatic writing. Rather, the phenomenon is an important aspect of human consciousness, a crucial experience for human beings in all cultures and times, even though we do not yet understand its origins or mechanisms.

As old as the phenomenon of channeling is, however, it has always been controversial. Some topics in this book will arouse a wide range of response, because in examining channeling we are dealing with our underlying and often unconscious assumptions about the nature of reality. This study will touch you where you live, for it will challenge basic beliefs.

Our common sense may sometimes be utterly wrong, but nonetheless we are used to relying on it in evaluating our experiences. Be forewarned that there are things in this book that are *not* commonsensical, that fly in the face of what we think we know about life and human nature.

We will call into question the notion of objective reality and the dimensions of subjective reality. We will ask what it means to trust someone else's experience. We will deal with the possibility of disembodied intelligence and with the related possibility that human personality can survive physical death. We will explore the idea that the universe is really a hierarchy of inhabited dimensions, only one of which is physical as we know it. We will ask uncomfortable questions: Are there other beings that are as far evolved beyond human beings as we adults are beyond infants? Are we collectively awakening to a spectrum of consciousness that defies the notion of one objective reality? Does each altered state of consciousness reflect a discrete realm of experience that possesses its own objective reality?

If we accept *any* of the accounts of channeling to follow, we have to accept that human beings are much more complex and creative than previously imagined and are much more open systems than previously believed. This is a mystery of awesome proportions. Whatever the ultimate nature of the channeling phenomenon may turn out to be, we must first acknowledge that there is something here worthy of examination.

The best stance is to remain open to all possibilities, without forsaking a clear and careful mind. As one of the world's leading parapsychologists, Stanley Krippner, puts it:

Talking about the channels both in this country and abroad whom I run into, some of them give very sophisticated explanations of these other levels of reality. In this field, I don't have many problems with taking an indeterminate stand and living with ambiguity. I think that that comes with the territory. So I simply don't know. I'm open to these possibilities as more evidence, or as more conviction, comes in.[10]

Consciousness researcher John White adds that having an open mind is not the same as having a hole in the head. Reason, discrimination, and analysis provide the difference. Or, as contemporary philosopher and author Jacob Needleman puts it, "You should be open-minded, but not so open-minded that your brains fall out.[11]

EXCLUSIONS AND INCLUSIONS

As we have seen, what channeling is and is not is a question on which there is not yet unanimity. Some constrict the definition to a narrow band of behavior and experience, while others see it as including almost any information-processing of an apparently self-transcending nature. In this book, I exclude two aspects that are sometimes included; on the other hand, I include two aspects that are sometimes left out.

First, I make a distinction between energy and information, and so I do not include "channeling" energy (without information) as part of my definition. To do so would require including the realms of physical mediumship (manifestation, ectoplasm, levitation, and so on) and some types of paranormal healing. Added to the current enterprise, these would be too much to handle in a single volume. I do agree, however, that so far as we presently understand it, there can probably be no information, or communication of information, without some kind of carrier wave of energy on which it rides or from which it is made. Also, in chapter 8, for the purpose of better exploring certain possible scientific explanations, I will take the stance that perhaps everything that exists which is a subjective and mental nature—thoughts, feelings, knowing, and consciousness itself—might be composed entirely of the kind of substance that physicists recognize as real: energy in the form of wave systems. From this perspective, all aspects of channeling would involve energy interactions only.

A second exclusion: telepathy (or anomalous thought transference) in particular, and extrasensory perception (ESP) in general, will not be considered part of channeling in this book, though they are clearly related phenomena. The terms *telepathy* and *ESP* have been defined and used extensively to denote somewhat different phenomena or processes, primarily nonsensory or paranormal information transmission and reception *between two physically embodied persons* (telepathy), or *between one person and the physical environment* (clairvoyance or remote viewing). In my definition of channeling, the sender or source is experienced as residing on some level of reality other than the one on which the receiver resides. While we may eventually conclude that aspects of channeling are some kind of *interdimensional* telepathy or ESP, I nevertheless leave these phenomena to the parapsychologists for now. I should point out that some see telepathy as *the* process involved in channeling. For example, in her dissertation, Margo Chandley has chosen to define channeling simply as "the method of transmitting information through a telepathic system of communication."[12] And a variety of allegedly discarnate authorities have communicated their telepathy-type explanation of channeling through Durango, Colorado, channel Tuella in her book *The Dynamics of Cosmic Telepathy.*[13]

So, though I begin this study by excluding the traditional concept of telepathy as it regards *embodied* minds as the information sources, we may eventually find that we are dealing with an extended notion of telepathy that involves *disembodied* beings as information sources communicating to *embodied* beings.

The first of two areas I will explicitly *include* in channeling is the Supreme Spiritual Being, or God, as a possible source of channeling. The Hebrew prophets of the Old Testament and Muhammad, the founder of the Islamic faith, claimed to hear the voice of a nonphysical God in a language-like manner that provided specific, repeatable information. This experience falls squarely within our definition of channeling. As we shall see in chapter 2, I will include as channeling most major recorded spiritual communication between physical and nonphysical beings throughout history. Most, if not all, of the early prophets and saints of the world's religious traditions can be considered channels of extraordinary spiritual import.

If there is to be a quarrel over definitions, it would appear to lie with the issue of whether channeling is *mediating* information from a nonphysical source by way of the instrument of the human channel, as we have defined the phenomenon, or whether it is an expression of unity with the source. For example, those who claim that Jesus Christ was not only the son of God but was and is God in the flesh, would not be likely to agree that Christ was a channel through whom God spoke. In addition, if channeling is necessarily a *mediated* process of transferring information from one mind to another, then the *direct knowing* associated with mystic experience and with intuition in general would not be channeling. I will, however, be treating them as channeling.

The second area I will explicitly *include* is the phenomenon I call open channeling. This category includes what has variously been called intuition, insight, inspiration, and aspects of creativity and imagination. Open channeling is included in our study because it involves receiving material that seems to come from some level of reality different from the physical one of the channel and different from his or her own mind, even though we cannot identify a specific extradimensional individual or personality as the source. Rogo's, Kautz's, and Chandley's definitions of channeling in general seem to fit what I am calling open channeling in particular. I will devote an entire chapter (9) to a study of open channeling, because I see it as touching all of us, whereas some of the other kinds of channeling we will be exploring may not.

CONSTRUCTIVE SKEPTICISM

It is the point of view of this book that, whatever the resolution of their ultimate nature, these channeling experiences are meaningful and useful to the majority of those having them and are potentially meaningful to the rest of us as well. However, there is another point of view about the phenomenon: that it is only nonsense, an entirely self-generated phenomenon, which very often involves conscious or unconscious fakery. It is true that the claims of some channels have been found to be without merit. We must keep in mind, therefore, that this subject is fraught with possibilities of deception and misunderstanding.

Professor Marcello Truzzi is a sociologist of "maverick science" at East Michigan University and one of the leading critics of exorbitant claims made on behalf of paranormal phenomena. His interests led him to co-found the Committee for Scientific Investigation of Claims of the Paranormal and to set up the Center for Scientific Anomalies Research. Truzzi's stand is that "until someone comes forward with channeled information that is evidential" (that can prove the source of the material is who or what it says it is), he prefers to maintain what he calls constructive skepticism. He does find it curious, however, that "the channeled material capturing the most attention, and the channels and their followers, seem least interested in providing evidence that is scientifically verifiable."[14] Research psychologist Charles Tart has noticed the same thing. But even if evidence became available, Truzzi adds, "I would examine those materials while remaining skeptical. Evidence is a matter of degree, and even evidential materials would have to be very strong to balance so extraordinary a claim."

John Searle, philosophy professor at the University of California at Berkeley, recalls an experience that took place while he was a young student at Oxford University. The great British philosopher Bertrand Russell was engaged in disputing with his students about the philosophical issues regarding evidence that we survive the death of our bodies. As Searle recalls the story, someone asked, "Lord Russell, suppose that the Christian story was really true. You came to your natural end, and you're facing St. Peter. What would you say?" And Russell replied: "I would say to him: 'You didn't give us enough evidence.' "

The more closed-minded contemporary skeptics of channeling say that there will never be sufficient evidence to prove the objective reality of reported deceased human spirits, because there is no survival of physical death. Others leave open the possibility that such survival, and other equally unusual channeling possibilities, may be true, but, like Russell, they say there has been little or no convincing evidence thus far to persuade them to believe the claims involved. And for many, it is no help at all to have the alleged sources themselves tell us, as does "Lazaris" at the end of chapter 1, that they are indeed real but we are not to be given conclusive proof of this, so that each of us has to cross the bridge of personal belief or faith with regard to the truth of the matter.

Since much of the channeled material purports to be of a religious or spiritual nature, emanating from transcendent sources, skepticism is necessarily strongly exercised by those charged by our culture with what might be called the quality control of interaction with these realms. Speaking of many of the channeled sources being reported today, noted Harvard University theology professor Harvey Cox says, "They're so cuddly and friendly. They seem to be yuppified versions of the demons and spirits of another time." Representing the view of dozens of other theologians and clinicians today, Eugene d'Aquili, associate professor of psychiatry at the University of Pennsylvania, points to the resurgence of channeling as a manifestation of the declining influence of traditional religion. D'Aquili claims that "people reach out for a sense of transcendent meaning." The question is whether there is objective reality to what is reached out for, other than the wishes, desires, and fantasies of those doing the reaching.[15]

Throughout its long history, channeling has had as many or more critics providing one kind of evidence and interpretation of it, as it has had advocates presenting another kind. We can go as far back as the ancient Greek playwright Euripides, who wrote, "I perceived how seer's craft is rotten and full of falsehood . . . The best mantis [oracle] is brains and good judgement."[16] Or we can find someone such as contemporary Brown University philosopher C. J. Ducasse, who reported finding "one of the most remarkable factories in the world":

Here is everything a medium [channel] needs to perform a spiritualist seance, and false mediums from all over the world place orders through this firm. These false mediums, who operate in most countries, then appear to make contact with the "other side," and let the ingenuous, faithful, mourning people believe that they are meeting dead relatives, while in fact the manifestations were bought by postal order from a firm in the USA . . . <u>We sent for material for an hour-long trick seance and can assure you that the effects are fantastic.</u>[17]

David Marks and Richard Kamman, in their book *The Psychology of the Psychic,* write:

The first thing we suggest is to reverse the negative connotations that are placed on skepticism. We should argue that skepticism is an adaptive, creative, liberating, and positive mental attitude, and that we need to develop *the art of doubt* to get unstuck from some of our self-defeating practices.

They remind us that, through a natural process of subjective validation, we open only to those data or situations that will help us uphold our beliefs. This can give rise, for example, to the pseudoscience best-seller, for which the formula is to "choose an exciting hypothesis and then assemble all the facts or quotes that agree with it, and ignore any that don't."[18] In the words of the late Alan Watts, author, scholar of Zen Buddhism, and consciousness researcher, "If we are only open to those discoveries which will accord with what we already know, we might as well stay shut."[19]

Esalen Institute co-founder Michael Murphy prefers to combine wonder with analysis in his own research on "supernormal" physical abilities. "If those realms suggested by channeling exist," he says, "they probably exceed our ability to conceive them." He sees himself being meticulous about degrees of evidentiality in any data confronting him. "I find such exploration more exciting," he says, "if I honor the scientific approach and embrace a multileveled empiricism with testable hypotheses."[20]

Professional magician, author, and debunker of the paranormal, James ("the Amazing") Randi provides a particularly spirited version of the skeptical stance with regard to channeling. He reports his experience with "several wild-eyed persons who ranted about entities who they said were 'speaking through channels into this world' . . . I could extract not one bit of sense from them about evidence for the reality of these 'entities' other than one lady's enthusiastic observation that 'if it happens in my head, then it's *real!*' That was a statement I could hardly accept." Randi believes channeling is "the latest supernatural fad" that "offers only the imaginative babblings of self-appointed 'gurus' supported by the need-to-believe of a certain segment of our population." For him, channels "are able to attract those amateur intellectuals who . . . in the spirit of what they believe to be 'science,' have no problems at all with critters from 'other dimensions.' "[21]

"It's basically unprovable," Mark Plummer, of the Committee for Scientific Investigation of Claims of the Paranormal, remarks of channeling. Ray Hyman, a committee colleague and professor of psychology at the University of Oregon at Eugene, claims of channels:

> Ninety-five percent are not conscious frauds. Some are split personalities. Everyone has the potential. People have enough information to act out hundreds of personalities with details. Creative artists and writers have learned to tap this. Most of us haven't. It comes out under severe conditions when hypnotized, when sick or deprived, or in some mystical ritual.[22]

As another committee member, Paul Kurtz, philosophy professor at the State University of New York at Buffalo, puts it, psychics (including channels) "are either deluding themselves, or the public, or both. The evidence for psychic phenomena is very dubious."[23]

Many believe in the inherent dangers that may be involved. Louis J. West, director of UCLA's Neuropsychiatric Institute, speaks of "New Age confidence games" that can aggravate psychiatric illness: "Trance channeling may be a harmless diversion for one person, but for the next person it might be a force drawing him further away from his already poorly grasped relationship with reality."[24]

If these channels are, in fact, in touch with something like Universal Mind or with more evolved beings who exist on other levels of reality, skeptics often ask, then why aren't more of the channels "healthy, wealthy, and wise"? Why do we often see an apparent lack of personal enlightenment and achievement among channels and their followers? I will attempt to address this issue in chapter 3.

In addition, a disturbing lack of agreement can often be found among the channels and their material, giving rise to mutually contradictory claims. Intellectual limitations, grammatical incompetence, and historical and scientific inaccuracies also appear in the expressions of the channels and of their purported sources. All of this makes it much more difficult—if not impossible—for the logical mind to accept channeling outright, or to believe that authentic channeling is actually taking place on all the fronts where it is reported.

Trickery and lies have clearly been exposed in many who claimed the channel's skills. However, channeling seems to be a phenomenon of

such overwhelming presence, character, and utility that we cannot ignore the entire field because of some falseness. Material throughout this
book, especially involving historical examples, the testimonies of contemporary channels, and the contributions of open channeling, points to
the need to take the phenomenon of channeling seriously and to evaluate the many positive claims made on its behalf.

The following principles or laws may help to establish a set of
guidelines that could prove helpful to the serious investigator of channeling. In the introduction to his 1900 study of channel Helene Smith,
From India to the Planet Mars, University of Geneva research psychologist
Theodore Flournoy offered "the 'Principle of Hamlet' and the 'Principle of La Place,' the former being, *'All things are possible,'* the latter, *'The
weight of the evidence ought to be proportioned to the strangeness of the
facts.'* "25

Colin Wilson, British author of more than a dozen books on the
paranormal, paraphrases "James's Law" from the words of the great
turn-of-the-century American psychologist William James, who spent
considerable time investigating the channels of his day. According to
Wilson, James's Law states "that we are given just enough and only
enough to convince the convincable, but to leave the skeptics still skeptics."26 "Clarke's Law," named by science fiction writer and futurist
Arthur C. Clarke, is that "any scientifically advanced technology is indistinguishable from magic" by those less advanced.

British philosopher Gilbert Ryle warns us about committing what
he calls a category mistake. This involves erroneously and confusingly
trying to treat one kind of thing in terms of another. Author Dean Inge
notes what might be such a mistake in dealing with channeling—a concern many have about trying to explain in physics-type terms the channeling of messages from what are held to be metaphysical or spiritual
entities. Inge writes, "The moment we are asked to accept scientific
evidence for spiritual truth, the alleged spiritual truth becomes neither
spiritual nor true. It is degraded into an event in the phenomenal
world."27

Geologist John W. Harrington, in his book *Dance of the Continents,*
presents what he calls the "principle of least astonishment." This may
prove useful to us as we sift through the variety of possible scientific
explanations for channeling in chapters 7 and 8. Harrington writes:

Understanding is a sport of participation and therefore something
of a game . . . The game has only one rule: draw the least astonishing conclusion that can be supported by the known set of facts
. . . Every least astonishing conclusion is a winner, judged to be
the most probable choice of all available competitors.28

Marcello Truzzi adds to Harrington's position the criteria of likelihood and parsimony (or elegant simplicity): "The least extraordinary explanation is that channeling is from the unconscious—the complex anomalous psychological processes from within that person. This would be the most parsimonious theory." Although Truzzi holds out the possibility that "reality could be *more* extraordinary than this," he states that on the whole he is "inclined to think that the most *likely* explanation is the best." For example, he says, "in some cases like 'Ramtha' [a source channeled through contemporary channel J. Z. Knight], where the channeled entity acts like a third-rate impression of Yul Brynner in a road tour of *The King and I,* the more parsimonious explanation may simply be that Mrs. Knight is faking."[29]

ENTITIES, PLANES, STATES, AND STAGES

Several terms will help build a conceptual framework, within which we will be working for the remainder of our exploration. Four interrelated concepts in this study—entities, planes, states, and stages—are at the heart of the beliefs of most channels and of the claims of their sources. These concepts also are central to our attempt to understand the phenomenon.

According to the glossary, an *entity* is *"the core identity of any individual living being said to exist; especially refers to a being that exists on a level of reality other than the physical . . . and that operates as a source in the channeling process."* By this definition, you and I are entities, and we would remain entities if we were to survive our own physical deaths. Spirits of deceased humans (if there are such things) are entities. If they reincarnated they would again become *embodied* entities such as we are. Entities can also be beings said not to be human; for example, extraterrestrial "space brothers" or angels.

As we move even farther away from what we are used to, as well as moving toward greater abstraction, it may be harder to retain a sense of discrete entities. Nonetheless, I would consider the kind of sources known as group beings to be conglomerate entities. Archetypes of the Jungian collective unconscious, or timeless thoughtforms in the Universal Mind, may be channeled, and may operate as entities by reason of their enduring, identifiable individuality.

Philosopher Huston Smith prefers to use the term *psychic centers,* rather than entities, to cover a variety of kinds of possible living, individual beings that could function as communicators by way of the channeling process.[30] Los Angeles educator and neurophysiology researcher Valerie Hunt; Albion, California, psychotherapist Hal Stone; and Margo

Chandley are among those who speak of individual energies, energy systems or patterns which they believe underlie what others term entities, beings, or sources in channeling. The source known as "Seth," for example, channeled by Jane Roberts, referred to himself as an "energy essence personality."

But, once more, there is no censensus among researchers on key terms. It is important for now to agree that the use of the term *entity* need not imply the existence of such discrete beings. My own preference throughout this book will be to use, instead of *entity*, the term *source*, which I define in the glossary as *"the generic term for anyone or anything occupying the transmitting end, or comprising the informational origin, in the channeling process."*

A fairly good consensus exists throughout the channeling literature that there are levels, dimensions, or *planes* of reality, the physical plane being only one of them—and the lowest (or one of the lowest) at that. Tracing the ascending, ever-finer levels away from the physical as we know it, the occult literature (for example, H. P. Blavatsky's Theosophical, Alice A. Bailey's Arcane, Rudolf Steiner's Anthroposophical, and Rosicrucian) and the channels associated with it contend that there is an *etheric* (or higher-physical) subtle-energy plane that acts as a template for the organization of physical structures like our bodies. There is an *astral* plane within which emotional reality is located. The *mental* plane is the arena for all forms of thought. The initiation of intentionality takes place on the *causal* plane (although the source "Lazaris," for example, defines the causal plane differently and places it below the mental plane). And there are, depending on one's viewpoint, a number of ever-more spiritual planes beyond the causal, involving will, wisdom, power, and love, approaching the source of All That Is. We are told that all of these planes operate and interact in a superimposed, coherent manner, with causal succession flowing from higher to lower planes.

One thing left unresolved is what *physical* means, since only the lowest plane of this hierarchy is said to be physical. Until this is discussed in greater detail in chapter 8, consider for now that whenever the term *physical* (or *nonphysical*) is used in this book, it is used according to the glossary definition as "the realm of matter and energy that is agreed on as objectively real by a consensus of contemporary physicists." Therefore, *physical,* for now, simply means "physical as we currently understand it."

Again, there is a lack of complete consensus among those writing, teaching, and doing research in the broad areas of the occult, paranormal, and mystic. Not all of them, nor all of the sources in the literature, concur with the above-mentioned hierarchical system, its order, or its terms. Some recent scientific researchers and theoreticians, for example, find the possibilities even much more complex. Berkeley, California, physicist Saul-Paul Sirag and parapsychologist and medical researcher Andrija Puharich speak of *hundreds* of dimensions that may well exist beyond the spatio-temporal reality with which we are familiar. Still, on the way to eventual consensus, we can agree that the concept of planes (or levels or dimensions) is important to our discussion because one of our primary models for channeling explains how beings on other planes are able to communicate through channels on our plane.

Also central to the theme of this book is the concept of a spectrum composed of discrete *states of consciousness.* This is an ancient notion—as old as the Indian Vedas and Plato. Its modern expression was pioneered by transpersonal psychologists such as Ken Wilber and Charles Tart. Normal waking consciousness, sleep, and dreams are only three possibilities out of a wide range of states. As we shall see in chapter 7, channeling may occur within, or as the result of, a discrete altered state of consciousness.

A state of consciousness can also be seen as a lens or frame of reference. Shift the state of consciousness, and you shift the frame of reference. Shift the frame of reference, and you shift what can be referenced and experienced by way of, or within, that frame. The dream state provides the dreamer with a very different experiential environment, perhaps with a different level of reality entirely, than does the ordinary waking state disposed to focus on, or reference, the normal physical reality.

This notion may provide us with grounds for a *relativistic* view of different states of consciousness in relation to the different realities experienceable by them. There may be as many separate realities that can be experienced as there are states of consciousness as frames of reference by which to experience them. The "real" or "true" reality, then, may be simply the one being experienced at the time by the most similar states of consciousness. In our exploration, we will want to hold open the possibility that there may be realities other than the ones with which we are currently most familiar that are entered into and experienced as a function of altering consciousness. This may turn out to be what is happening in channeling.

Also, depending upon slight shifts in frames of reference within the larger frame shared by ordinary, awake consciousness, some may interpret channeled sources as only the concoctions of the channel's own creative unconscious, or as separate subpersonalities of the channel, or as the voice of the higher Self, or as material from the collective unconscious or the Universal Mind drawn forth by the channel in interaction with it. Or the sources may be deemed to be the totally separate entities and personalities that the channels (and the sources themselves) claim them to be. For the moment at least, each of these perspectives can claim to be the all-encompassing truth of the matter only for the ones using it. The final truth about channeling may remain as relative as the nature of what is "real." If we can agree on this at the outset, then we will be able to keep an open mind capable of discerning and judging a variety of possibilities.

To entities (or sources), planes, and states must be added a fourth concept: *stages* of consciousness. Is channeling a discrete, passing *state* of consciousness, or is it instead a *stage* in the development or evolution of consciousness for the individual or the species, leading to some kind of optimum fulfillment? And if we entertain the idea of such a hierarchy of evolutionary stages, we must ask whether channeling is a regression from the current stage of waking consciousness or an advance. Are channels the harbingers of human behavior and experience that lie ahead for the rest of us? Michael Murphy offers a metaphor for what may be occurring: "We are amphibians coming ashore in a multidimensional world. And I propose that some of the channeled intelligences are like fishermen. They're fishing for us, as it were. They're tantalizing us, drawing us along toward a larger life."[31]

A PERSONAL, SUBJECTIVE JOURNEY

The subject of channeling is imbued with associations as varied as fakery and showmanship, the psychic and paranormal, mysticism and the occult, delusions and madness, and arguments for the survival of death and the existence of a multidimensional populated universe. The mention of channeling, therefore, can evoke responses ranging from bemused skepticism to harsh ridicule, from threatened beliefs and heated denial to fascination, nonrational affirmation, and intuitive right-feeling. I've already shared with you the reasons *why* this book is being written. Given the personal, even polarizing, nature of the subject, I think it is important, before we embark on our exploration, to share with you also *who* has written it.

In his book *King Solomon's Ring,* the physician turned ethologist Konrad Lorenz wrote, "The truth about nature is far more beautiful than what our great poets sing of it." I think I know what he means. Poet and scientist have been married within me all my life. This book has evolved out of my awe in the face of the unknown. Beginning in childhood and continuing now into my forties, under the star-filled sky, feeling ultimately estranged from yet at one with it all, I've ached with wonder. And whenever I've turned within, I've experienced the same vastness, the same wonder, as if *outer* and *inner* were really somehow the same; as if the outer world was really psychic and subjective at its heart, and the inner was a place at least as real and large as the physical cosmos. The wonder became mixed with a yearning to know the larger truth, with a homesickness for an ineffable, placeless something. My relation to this something, which was at the same time both breathtakingly present and yet not understood by me, deepened.

Under what seemed, for lack of a better phrase, the inspiration of the muse, I first found myself able to translate these powerful feelings and intimations of knowing into artwork and poetry. But always underneath my production of surface images and colors, symbols and metaphors, lay the search for the truth.

Soon my hunger to know, my intuitive response to the tugging on my heart and mind from beyond, expanded beyond the creative arts into philosophy, metaphysics, and along the branches of science. By college and graduate school, I was a firmly entrenched interdisciplinarian. For eight years I was a university professor (Rutgers, in New Jersey), designing and running a large graduate program that focused on creativity, the arts, intuition, imagination, and alternative learning approaches in education and the other helping professions. During the last five years I've continued my teaching, research, and administrative work at a small graduate school of integrative psychology (Rosebridge, in Walnut Creek, California). Here my colleagues and I have attempted to add both "new science" and ancient psychospiritual tools to mainstream approaches to training counselors and clinical psychologists. Throughout, my inquiry into human nature and how it interacts with a larger reality than itself has continued to generate more questions than answers.

To be true to an increasing sense of guidance, I can no longer keep the spiritual part of the search separate from the creative or the scientific. They are all parts of an emerging unity in me, which yearns to understand the oneness that feels beyond me at the same time it feels within me. In turn, this unity at the deepest level envelops all, erasing for me traditional distinctions of inner and outer, subject and object, self and other. Yet I consider myself to be neither a mystic nor a psychic. Each week now, I meet more people who claim to be experiencing the same thing. Many of you reading this know what I mean.

I have experienced thirty years as a poet and artist, and twenty as an educator and researcher, exploring ways of working with my own potential and that of fellow human beings who are faced, like me, with personal yearning and the need to solve very real problems. As part of my professional research, I have learned that we can harvest beautiful and meaningful things that were apparently not in our selves or in our world until they emerged through us by means of inspiration, intuition, and the creative process. And I have learned that this process can be developed in anyone. This has helped draw me into the study of channeling and to see us all as channels to varying degrees.

I find myself, like so many others today, working at the frontiers of human understanding. Few phenomena I can think of contain quite the variety of frontier components or associations as channeling. Studying it balances us at the very edge of scientific knowing: a realm of the paranormal and the abnormal, parapsychology and psychopathology, the nonphysical and the mystic. It is where I most love to be.

Recent science, such as the "new physics," attempts to maintain its tradition of empirical evidence, objective verification, corroboration, and replication, even as the material under its analytic lenses seems to shade off into realms of the subjective and nonphysical. I find myself asking, are our traditional ways of thinking adequate to what now confronts us? Are the understandings and methods of either old or new science appropriate and useful for examining channeling? If not, what must be done to learn and to know? Must the laboratory be traded in for the church, and scientific evidence traded for personal belief, or could aspects of the laboratory be brought into the church? Are there ways to interrogate the echo-chamber self-mystery of consciousness? These are some of the questions that my study of channeling has aroused in me. Hopefully, similar questions will be aroused in you by reading this book. But they are not questions I can answer for you. Perhaps no one can—or should—do this for you.

So, there may be times in the journey through this book, when I as writer and you as reader may respond more as poet than scientist to some of the mind-expanding possible truths about nature that move in and out of focus within what remains still basically unknown. For my part, I will agree at the outset that because of who I am and what I'm exploring, I will allow my wonder, creativity, and feelings—both negative and positive—to accompany me through this work. For me to do otherwise would be hypocritical. I hope that you too will do your version of this. At the same time, I will do my best not to let my feelings and personal idiosyncrasies place blinders on a mind that I want to keep open to all competing points of view regarding the phenomenon of channeling. I will work to keep clear and use carefully the lenses of my analytical objectivity and critical intellect. Again, I ask that you try to do the same. Given human nature, and the terrain, it will not be easy for us.

Criteria for Language Selection

Having shared what I think are some of the inevitably personal and subjective aspects of a project of this kind, I wish to include some brief comments about the tone and language used in this book. I don't wish to burden you with an excess of qualifying phrases that could be included to ensure a tone of critical objectivity. Some might think that words such as "purported," "alleged," "supposed," or "is said to" should be used at every turn. I have chosen throughout, however, to report what already exists as description without any judgments of truth. For instance, when I write a phrase such as "The 'space brothers' have told us," it may sound as if I am accepting that such entities objectively exist as described by those who claim to be in contact with them. Ideally such a phrase should read: "Those who report that they are communicating with extraterrestrial, nonphysical beings claim to have been told by these alleged beings . . . " To hedge each such statement would make the text unwieldy. Therefore, when you come to a phrase like "The 'space brothers' have told us," please remember that I am neither affirming nor denying the truth of such statements; I am simply reporting the claims of others. What you make ultimately of these reports is up to you. To help you decide for yourself, this objectively presented material will be subjected to a variety of critical viewpoints in chapters 7 and 8.

In the development of a discipline to investigate any new specialized area, a specialized language tends to be generated. In our case, it comes from channels, sources, and investigators alike. Therefore I have included a glossary at the end of the book. It is not offered as definitive, but as my contribution to a growing effort on the part of many to help establish a consensus with regard to terms and meanings that will be necessary for future dialogue and research in this field. (Besides referring to the glossary as you proceed, you may also find it helpful during the reading of the first two chapters to refer ahead on occasion to aspects of chapters 3 through 6 which attempt to provide different kinds of categorization for the phenomenon of channeling.)

In addition, you may note a foreign or archaic quality to the language of some of the excerpted material. There are obscure passages, metaphysical abstractions, and grand statements purporting to be "the truth" that have been channeled. The material, like poetry, may prove more evocative than obviously or objectively meaningful. Many of the channeled messages deal with areas in which precision is difficult and verification impossible. Yet, as with poetry, it may not be appropriate to reject such material simply because it cannot be measured with the yardstick of hard science. I simply ask you, the reader of this book, to sift and weigh the channeled material for whatever meaning it may evoke and for whatever usefulness it may provide.

SELECTING EXAMPLES OF CONTEMPORARY CHANNELING

A rich set of cases, contemporary and historical, faces anyone who researches the channeling story. In the next chapter, we will look at the extraordinary proliferation of channeling that has taken place throughout the world in the last ten years and brought itself so much into the public eye. (Some even speak bittersweetly of channeling's "epidemic proportions" in the mid-1980s.) By turning our attention to a kind of selected Who's Who of contemporary channels, we will see how channeling operates in real life.

To begin our story of modern channeling, where should the line be drawn separating historical from modern? Some think it should be drawn at the beginning of the last great cycle of activity prior to the current one, known as the Spiritualist era, over a century ago. Others would deem this to be early history. There are those who would begin modern times with the story of Edgar Cayce as the father of modern channeling; yet for many today who are immersed in the very latest names, Cayce is old news.

I have decided to begin the modern era of channeling with the American channel Jane Roberts and her source "Seth." It can be argued that the publication and widespread distribution of millions of copies of the assorted "Seth" books, beginning in the early 1970s, brought channeling to broader public attention than had anything or anyone in this century until then except for Edgar Cayce. The many books about the Cayce material began to surface in the 1960s, although Cayce's work had ceased with his death in 1945. Roberts's channeling spanned from the 1960s until her death in 1984.

Sometimes the individuals involved in New Age activities like channeling operate at the edges of the mainstream culture. Their behavior, as well as their beliefs and values, are often quite different from that of the rest of the population. Honest people, well intentioned and believing in who they are and what they experience, can often make exaggerated claims, or claims that turn out to have no basis in fact (at least in the estimation of those who decide for others what is fact and what is not). There are true and phony people in every profession and activity. It is not unexpected, therefore, to find this is the case in the field of channeling. Yes, there are those who have become especially visible who appear to misuse their position. In the face of this rather uncertain, or relativistic, situation, I have not made selection judgments on the basis of who I personally like and don't like among contemporary (as well as historical) channels. This allows the case for or against channeling to rest on no individual channels in particular. And it helps you avoid being biased by my viewpoint.

The chief criterion for the selections in chapters 1 and 2 is simply the degree of visibility and recognition enjoyed by the channels and their work—how well known they are among those who constitute the ever-growing subculture that is aware of channeling. They have become known by the publication and distribution of what they have channeled (including audio- and videotapes), by mention of them in the media and by word of mouth, and by their appearances at workshops and other channeling presentations.

There is obviously no way in chapter 1 to present all of the contemporary channels who are being published, mentioned, or are in other ways "going public." By many estimates, there are tens of thousands of channels throughout the world today, with as many as a thousand in Southern California alone. One rule of thumb I have followed is that the channels included here have some degree of national, if not international, recognition or reputation. Thus many local or regional channels, well known to their followers but unknown outside of them, who lack sufficient widespread distribution of their material, are left out.

Let us now turn to the channeling story in detail, beginning with the recent past.

ONE
THE PERSONALITIES

1
CHANNELING AS A MODERN PHENOMENON

Currently there is an extraordinary upswing in public interest in the phenomenon we now call channeling. In the last few years, tens of thousands of people have sought out channels privately or in workshop situations, while millions more have read material or have listened to or viewed tapes said to be channeled. The "Seth" material, the "Findhorn" books, and *A Course in Miracles,* with which we will begin this chapter, are some of the recent major bodies of work that are either channeled or based on channeling. They have enjoyed a remarkable following among people of varied personalities, world views, and walks of life.

There have been times in history when channeling and related phenomena have been accepted and in keeping with the mainstream world view and notion of what a human being is and can be. At other times, phenomena such as channeling have been deemed unusual or paranormal and have been treated as fads or voguish—which may be the case today. And at other times, such phenomena have been devalued, ignored, or considered a type of confidence game or even a punishable crime. Why has channeling sometimes been accepted and sometimes not?

During the late 1960s and 1970s, many were preoccupied with a questioning and a searching for something beyond the material realm, giving rise to what has become known as the New Age movement. Then, to many observers, that era seemed to have run its course, and it was back to work in the vineyards of materially oriented consensus reality. So what kind of changing cultural climate now allows material like the *Seth* books and *A Course in Miracles* to be received so enthusiastically? Is this a sign of deep and lasting cultural and psychological changes to come, or just another passing fad? Considering that channeling, in some form or another, has been with us throughout recorded history and in all cultures, fad doesn't seem to fit the longer-range facts. But why this widespread reemergence of the phenomenon and interest in it today? What unmet needs does channeling hold out the promise of fulfilling?

The answer may lie in a need for personal meaning in life that cannot be satisfied by material existence alone. Perhaps as a species we can go only so long at a stretch adhering to a strictly material interpretation of reality. We may be too imaginative and creative to stick for long only to the facts of the five senses for the basis of ultimate reality. Or, conversely, we may be able to wander away into the mythic realm of lone and shared subjective realities only for so long before we bring ourselves back into line with the underlying truth of the five senses. Or maybe there is some kind of cycle that runs through human history so that periodically we experience a sort of shrinkage or shutdown of a larger world view and the accompanying extrasensory experience of being in the universe.

With the current renaissance of channeling activity and interest, we appear to be in the midst of yet another round of experiences that seem to transcend (and, for some, to threaten) the usual consensus reality. We are forced to face some powerful issues: What is the nature of the individual? Where do we draw the line between self and not-self? Once we draw it, what kinds of interaction can take place across it? How open or closed is the individual system in this interaction? And what is the unconscious mind? To begin to address these kinds of questions, we need to take a good look at some of the major contemporary channeled voices that have caught the attention of, and given meaning to, an ever-growing number of people.

JANE ROBERTS AND THE "SETH" BOOKS

We begin with the entity "Seth" that was said to come through the trance channel Jane Roberts. What does "Seth" have to tell us? He claims that we are not dependent on physical matter. We are multi-dimensional in nature, existing outside of time and space as beings projected into local space-time situations as part of a larger, evolving being in turn within "All That Is" (the universe at large, or God). This All That Is originally separated out into portions of itself. We, as those portions, look longingly and lovingly back at our source; at the same time, we glory in our unique individualities. We create our own reality by projecting energy outward to form the physical world, to which we then react and from which we learn and nurture both ourselves and the larger entities of which we are an aspect. Creative expression, for "Seth," mirrors in our private realities the way the universe was and is constantly created. To change our personally experienced world, we must change ourselves in order to change what we express or project. Our beliefs act like a hypnotist; as long as the particular directions are given, our experiences conform automatically.

The idea of reincarnation is central to the "Seth" material as well. While he sees us encompassing many physical embodiments as relatively immortal beings, his view is more complex than the traditional linear notion of reincarnation. From "Seth's" perspective, all is taking place simultaneously in an eternal and infinite Now. Hence it is possible, as the multidimensional personalities that we each are, to affect our own past and future actual or probable selves by our here-and-now activity. The point of power, as "Seth" puts it, is in the experienced present. Consider the following excerpts from the various "Seth" books as a continuation on these basic themes:

> The soul can be considered as an electromagnetic, energy field, of which you are a part . . . a powerhouse of probabilities or probable actions, seeking to be expressed . . . Your reality exists in a particular area of activity in which aggressive qualities, thrusting-outward characteristics, are supremely necessary to prevent a falling back into the infinite possibilities from which you have only lately emerged. Yet from this unconscious level of possibilities you derive your strength, your creativity . . . In your terms, the inner world does represent Idea Potential as yet unrealized—but those ideas and those potentials do not exist outside of consciousness. They are ideals set in the heart of man, yet in other terms, he is the one who also put them there, out of the deeper knowledge of his being . . . Existence is wise and compassionate, so in certain terms consciousness, knowing itself as man, sent future extensions of itself out into the time scheme that man would know, and lovingly planted signposts for itself to follow "later" . . . You are given the gift of the gods; you create your reality according to your beliefs; yours is the creative energy that makes your world; there are no limitations to the self except those you believe in . . . The unconscious mind is growing toward a realization of the part it has to play in such multidimensional reality.[1]

On an early September day in 1963, in her apartment in Elmira, New York, thirty-four-year-old aspiring poet and novelist Jane Roberts first encountered channeling. It was to remain at the center of her life until her death in 1984. As she recalls, it was "as if someone had slipped me an LSD cube on the sly." Having had no more than a couple of fleeting psychic experiences before then, she was overwhelmed by the new phenomenon: "A fantastic avalanche of radical, new ideas burst into my head with tremendous force, as if my skull were some sort of receiving station, turned up to unbearable volume."

She found herself face-to-face with an adjacent level of reality more real than the one she had known: "It was as if the physical world were really tissue-paper thin, hiding infinite dimensions of reality, and I was suddenly flung through the tissue paper with a huge ripping sound. My body sat at the table, my hands furiously scribbling down the words and ideas that flashed through my head." Her ideas about the nature of reality were turned upside down, as more than one hundred pages of a manuscript titled *The Physical Universe as Idea Construction* poured forth onto paper:

> We are individualized portions of energy, materialized within physical existence, to learn to form ideas from energy, and to make them physical (this is idea construction). We project ideas into an object, so that we can deal with it. But the object is the thought, materialized . . . Idea construction teaches the "I" what it is, by showing it its products in a physical manner. And we learn responsibility in the use of creative energy.

Shaken yet inspired by this strange episode, Jane and her painter husband, Robert Butts, decided to embark on a book about developing ESP power. They started by experimenting with the Ouija board. After a few sessions, they were able to receive messages through the board from someone who initially identified himself as "Frank Withers." Soon, however, "Withers" further described himself as a fragment of a larger entity. "I prefer not to be called Frank Withers. That personality was rather colorless. You may call me whatever you choose. I call myself Seth. It fits the me of me, the personality more clearly approximating the whole self I am, or am trying to be."[2]

And so "Seth," probably the best known, most widely published channeled entity in the twentieth century, made his debut. After only four Ouija board sessions with "Seth," Jane began to receive him in a clairaudient manner, then in light trance, and eventually in full trance. (See chapter 6 for detailed descriptions of kinds of channeling.)

"Seth" described himself as an individual consciousness, "an energy personality essence no longer focused in physical reality."[3] All beings (including himself) are basically bisexual and nonphysical in nature, he said, and he preferred to call Jane by the name of "Ruburt," which he claimed was the name of the larger entity of which Jane Roberts was a part.

The resulting material not only became the stuff of which best sellers are made, but constitutes a rich and intellectually demanding body of literature. The impressive outpouring via Jane Roberts includes a book on ESP development, two books about the beginnings of the channel's involvement with her chief entity "Seth," and five books said to be dictated by "Seth" in trance voice. In addition, Roberts wrote two books to explain her experiences, plus two novels and a volume of poetry inspired by her channeling. Three other Roberts volumes, ostensibly channeled, are attributed to nonphysical sources other than "Seth."

Throughout her twenty-year career of channeling "Seth," Jane was always questioning the true nature of the phenomenon and whether "Seth" was merely part of her own psyche. On occasion, she deferred to the extraordinary source that "Seth" represented without actually deeming him a separate being. This may shed light on our categories of higher Self (chapter 5) and open channeling (chapters 6 and 9):

> Above all, I am sure that Seth is my channel to revelational knowledge, and by this I mean knowledge that is revealed to the intuitive portions of the self rather than discovered by the reasoning faculties . . . Such revelational information is available to each of us, I believe, to some degree. From it springs the aspirations and achievements of our race . . . As to who or what Seth is, his term "energy essence personality" seems as close to the answer as anyone can get. I don't believe he is a part of my subconscious, as that term is used by psychologists, or a secondary personality. I do think that we have a supraconscious that is as far "above" the normal self as the subconscious is "below" it . . . It may be that Seth is the psychological personification of that supraconscious extension of my normal self.[4]

In the introduction to her second "Seth" book, *Seth Speaks,* Roberts discusses the distinction she made between material emanating from her self and that from beyond, distinctions that call on her sensitivities as a creative writer.

> I do not believe that I could get the equivalent of Seth's book on my own. This book is Seth's way of demonstrating that human personality is multidimensional, that we exist in many realities at once, that the soul or inner self is not something apart from us, but the very medium in which we exist . . . Seth may be as much a creation as his book is. If so, this is an excellent instance of multidimensional art, done at such a rich level of unconsciousness that the "artist" is unaware of her own work and as much intrigued by it as anyone else.[5]

In *Adventures in Consciousness: An Introduction to Aspect Psychology,* Roberts tries to provide a more specific explanation.

Our present personalities . . . are Aspects of a far greater consciousness of which our individual awareness is but a part, though an inviolate one. Our personalities are composed of other Aspects, each dominant in other realities.

If activated—like Seth—they would have to communicate through the psychic fabric of the focus personality. They would have to appear in line with our ideas of personhood, though their own reality might exist in quite different terms. I think that I always sensed this about Seth. It wasn't that I mistrusted the Seth personality, but I felt it was a personification of something else— and that "something else" wasn't a person in our terms.[6]

In her introduction to *The Nature of Personal Reality,* Roberts continues with this theme: "I think that the selves we know in normal life are only the three-dimensional actualizations of other source-selves from which we receive our energy and life."[7]

And, continuing her speculation on the limits of identity, she writes in her introduction to *The Unknown Reality:*

Maybe our idea of identity is like a magic circle we've drawn around our minds, so that everything outside seems dark and alien, unselflike. There may be other psychic fires lighting up that inner landscape with a far greater light than ours; other aspects of consciousness to which we're connected.[8]

As we shall see in chapter 7, psychologists often explain channeling in terms of dissociation. By this process, the channel's mind forms an offshoot of itself that it is not consciously aware of and does not identify as part of itself. "Seth" seems to be familiar with this phenomenon when he speaks through Roberts:

I do depend upon Ruburt's [Seth's name for Jane Roberts's larger identity] willingness to dissociate. There is no doubt that he is unaware at times of his surroundings during sessions. It is a phenomenon in which he gives consent, and he could, at any time, return his conscious attention to his physical environment.

His [Ruburt's/Jane's] intuition is the gateway that relaxes an otherwise stubborn and domineering ego . . . It is true that a state of dissociation is necessary . . . You *can* have two doors open at once. In the meantime you must turn down the volume of the first channel while you learn to attune your attention to the second. This process you call dissociation.

If I succeed in convincing you of my reality as a separate personality, I will have done exceedingly well. It should be apparent that my communications come through Ruburt's subconscious. But as a fish swims through water, but the fish is not the water, I am not Ruburt's subconscious.[9]

On a few occasions, Roberts channels an entity she later refers to as "Seth Two." It appears that "Seth Two" is a group entity that contains "Seth." Here the sense of the identity shifts and seems to expand:

This evening you have reached somewhat beyond the personality by which I usually make myself known to you . . . The Seth personality, again, is legitimate and independent and is part of my identity . . . Our entity is composed of multidimensional selves with their own identities . . . but we are always one.[10]

Besides "Seth" and "Seth Two," Roberts also claimed to channel two other sources: the nineteenth-century French impressionist painter Paul Cezanne and the American psychologist and philosopher William James. In both cases, she was equally cautious with regard to their final identities.

While *The World View of Paul Cezanne: A Psychic Interpretation* was being channeled, Roberts recalls that "I didn't ask if this was really Cezanne . . . the sentences were not natural for me; they had an unaccustomed feel to them . . . a 'translated' feel."[11]

"Seth's" explanation of the source of the Cezanne material seems to involve concepts such as the akashic records (discussed in chapter 5) and the Universal Mind.

In that infinite gallery there exists a unique individual view of the world as seen through the eyes of each person ever graced to follow the paths of physical experience . . . If there were a sign outside it would read, "The Gallery of the World's Mind."

Certain elements of Cezanne's world view were attracted to the "canvas" of the Roberts mind because of the elements it found there. In the same way, certain purposes, abilities, and intents of the Roberts mind searched out particular kinds of information from the Cezanne world view and ignored other data.[12]

Roberts again confronted the enigma of her situation in *The Afterlife Journal of an American Philosopher: The World View of William James,* one of the last books completed before her death. Roberts received it "automatically" on the typewriter.

> The usual questions annoyed me like a swarm of bees. Was this manuscript supposed to originate with the historic William James? Was the material my creative version of the man instead, or was something else happening—some commingling of consciousness in which valid knowledge from unofficial levels of reality expressed itself in a form that I could understand?
> The personality I sense as James is a construct, I believe; unconsciously formed as an automatic process when my consciousness tunes in to his reality—and it stands for or represents whatever James's reality "really is" now.[13]

In sum, the subject matter of the "Seth" literature is extraordinary. "Seth's" chief contribution, repeated throughout, is that we each create our own reality by our beliefs and desires. We do this as one of many expriencing personalities, each within its own respective level of reality, and each part of a larger that is also learning and evolving.

THE FINDHORN CIRCLE: DOROTHY MACLEAN, EILEEN CADDY, DAVID SPANGLER, AND ANNE EDWARDS

In the middle of an otherwise normal, rather unquiet day in Glasgow, Scotland, at the beginning of the 1960s, Eileen Caddy found herself growing very quiet. She then heard an inner voice saying, "Be still . . . and know that I am God. You have taken a very big step in your life. Listen to Me, and all will be well. Let not your heart be troubled. Know who I am. I am closer than your breath, than your hands and feet. Trust in me."[14] Soon the entire Caddy family—Eileen, Peter, and their three children—were on their way, guided by this voice.

In this way, a remarkable community began when the Caddys parked their trailer on the grounds of a desolate corner of an abandoned Royal Air Force base in Findhorn on the north coast of Scotland in 1962. Soon they were joined by their friend Dorothy Maclean, followed by Dorothy's teacher, Sheena Govan, Lena Lamont, David Spangler, and his colleague Myrtle Glines. Anne Edwards ("Naomi") and R. Crombie Ogilvie ("Roc"), a retired Edinburgh educator, came soon after. Each of the adults was a channel; they had been brought together by inner guidance to form the spiritual community of Findhorn.

What is the nature of the material said to be received by this band of people? What it shares is a common source: the realm of Nature, particularly the *devas,* spirits or angels said to be responsible for the unique patterns of emergence and manifestation of the plant kingdom into our physical level of reality. As Dorothy Maclean claimed to hear in 1970 from the inner voice of the "Rue" plant deva: "There is the pattern, held in consciousness by us on what you call the higher levels where energy is particularly clear and powerful, dedicated to the mighty purposes of life of which a planet is the outcome. Then on the lower levels are the results of these different energy patterns: each leaf distinct and beautiful." The theme, over and over throughout the Findhorn material, is the hope for cooperation of humans with the forces of Nature, which are operating more "naturally" than we are—that is, more in alignment and at one with unadulterated Universal principles and processes. As the "Landscape Angel" expressed to "Roc":

There is a world to be redeemed, and all forces are needed for that purpose. Unity and cooperation are the keynotes. We are with you as you are aligned to God, and the forces we deal with are absolutely essential to your life . . . Man can no longer rape his worlds . . . or the whole cannot continue. Life is a whole. Harmony has been ordained throughout the Universe. Man will play his unique part . . . You join us in your wider-ranging fields so that His will be done on Earth to create God's finest fruits.[15]

What has most characterized the Findhorn experience, therefore, is the degree of communication and cooperation established between these channels and the alleged forces and beings of the Nature world. Eileen Caddy's inner voice directed participants in just how to do the planting, fertilization, and cultivation. We have not only the subject matter of the mmaterial as evidence, but the bigger-than-life fruits, vegetables, and flowers that grew in that otherwise forlorn and arid seaside. Botanists and farmers are forced to consider the channeled explanation that these plant prodigies are the result of human cooperation with the spiritual truths of Nature. Rich details of Caddy's work are available in a number of books, especially *God Spoke to Me*.[16]

Today, although its founders are gone, Findhorn is a self-sufficient community numbering in the hundreds, with full-fledged facilities, a school, a printing plant, and other cottage industries. The central theme of Findhorn is openness to new ways of communication with the rest of Nature, which is contained within one living spiritual Source.

The sources for channeling sessions were varied and colorful. Sheena and Lena apparently had suprahuman spiritual sources. Both

Dorothy and Eileen claimed to channel God. Dorothy specialized in Nature spirits. Roc was reported to have a special link to fairies, elves, and Pan. Naomi, as we shall see, received information from "transformed" Russian prisoners about how to spiritually interact with Nature.

Dorothy Maclean speaks of her channeling experiences:

> Yes, I talk with angles, great Beings whose lives infuse and create all of Nature. In another time and culture I might have been cloistered in a convent or a temple, or, less pleasantly, burnt at the stake as a witch. In our skeptical time and culture, such a claim is more likely to be met with scoffing disbelief or as the ramblings of a dreamy female . . . Yet, when this communication began to occur, it did so in a way that I could not dispute.[17]

After years of supposed communication from angels or plant devas, Maclean believes she can make some generalizations about this experience. Like many other channels, she says, "It is true that the message, even from the highest levels, is colored by the person who receives it, by that person's beliefs, vocabularly, sub-conscious, etc."[18]

Bearing this precaution in mind, she proceeds:

> It took me quite a few years to conclude that these beings and I were communicating only because we were sharing the same spheres, that of the human soul, or higher self, and that naturally everyone, in attuning to his or her higher self, was also attuning to the angels.

By "angels" Maclean generally means plant devads, who are supposed to be her chief source. The devas are the "builders of our world":

> Embodiments of creative intelligence, they wield or transmute what me might call energy (vibratory waves or particles in patterns) into increasingly more "physical" structures (including emotional and mental structures) and finally into what we call matter (which is pattern in space). They build vehicles for the expression of life on many levels.

For example, in the following, Maclean hears clairaudiently an anonymous deva:

> You cannot bring weights into our world. You cannot come to us unless you are free, childlike, light . . . Our consciousness is

higher than that of humans because, although we deal with matter as much as you do, we could not cut ourselves off from the divine source of power. You humans cut yourselves off from the same source by your thoughts . . . We are not imprisoned by the lower form; you need not be, and you will not be when you identify with that source.[19]

American writer and teacher David Spangler, who claims to have channeled a variety of sources since childhood, soon found his sessions becoming the intellectual focus of Findhorn. He is considered by many to be an articulate spokesman regarding the earth's increasing spiritualization. According to his sources, this process includes the evolution into a new age or millennium, probably within our lifetime.

Spangler describes both his chief entity "John" and the channeling process itself:

The contact with him is through a blending of thoughts and perspectives. In order to accomplish it, I must enter into meditation and align with my own Higher Self, my inner spirit, for it is with that level that John can communicate most effectively. What he says, though, I must translate into appropriate words, which limits the transmission to my vocabulary and, sometimes, to my state of mind and attunement in that moment. For this reason, any unclarity that may result comes from my side of the contact.[20]

Rounding out this rather remarkable group, Anne Edwards claims to have channeled transmissions from "a center of light" composed of a group of Soviet prisoners deep in a Siberian salt mine. Either very near death or already physically deceased and in an etheric-level state, they said they were able to spiritually interact with matter and alchemically transmute the rock walls by aligning intention with the newfound radiations of their own higher beings. We are told that from their new perspective everything is the light of the living mind of God, differentiated into a variety of manifestations.[21]

A COURSE IN MIRACLES

In 1965, psychologist Helen Cohn Schucman, employed at the Psychiatry Department of New York's Columbia University College of Physicians and Surgeons, began to vaguely sense and then clearly hear an inner voice. A trained psychologist, atheist, and disbeliever in the paranormal, she didn't know what to make of it. She told a colleague, "You know that inner voice? It won't leave me alone! It keeps saying, 'This is a course in miracles. Please take notes.' What am I supposed to do?" The colleague responded, "Why don't you take notes? Take them down in that shorthand you use." "But what if it's gibberish?" Helen responded. "Then I'll *know* I'm crazy."[22]

In her first clairaudient dictation session, Helen claimed to receive and record what was later to become the first introductory page of the *Text,* the first of the three volumes. It contained the central theme: "Nothing real can be threatened. Nothing unreal exists. Herein lies the peace of God." But after taking down only about fifteen lines, she grew increasingly agitated and broke it off, feeling panic in the face of the alien nature of the experience. Trying to convey what the voice was like, she recalls, "It's hard to describe. It can't be a hallucination, really, because the Voice does not come from outside. It's all internal. There's no actual sound, and the words come mentally but very clearly. It's a kind of inner dictation, you might say." When asked if it is a form of automatic writing, she replies, "It's not automatic at all; I'm perfectly aware of what I'm doing."[23]

Published in 1975, this three-volume set has now sold hundreds of thousands of copies, its reputation carried by word of mouth. Its quiet authority and sound reasoning, presented in an elegantly simple style, have affected a great many people, most of whom seem indifferent to the identity of its source. Most readers seem to feel they have been "spoken to" convincingly by the integrity of the language and the personal meaning it holds for them.

What does *A Course in Miracles* have to say to us? Whatever may turn out to be the ultimate truth regarding its source, its 1200 pages of published material provide an extraordinarily clear attempt to explain the maya, or illusionlike nature, associated with our day-to-day ego, which we are told we mistakenly take to be our true and only self. At the same time, the material pictures the larger spiritual reality within which our true identity resides and within which the ego is only an artificial, transient presence. With regard to the nature of the ego, *Volume One: Text* has this to say:

> The ego literally lives by comparisons. Equality is beyond its grasp, and charity becomes impossible. The ego never gives out of abundance, because it was made as a substitute for it. This is why the concept of "getting" arose in the ego's thought system. Appetites are "getting" mechanisms, representing the ego's need to confirm itself . . . The ego believes it is completely on its own, which is merely another way of describing how it thinks it originated. This is such a fearful state that it can only turn to other egos and try to

unite with them in an equally feeble show of strength. It is not free, however, to open the premise to question, because the premise is its foundation. The ego is the mind's belief that it is completely on its own.

Then we are given the larger scheme of things:

There is nothing outside you. That is what you must ultimately learn, for it is the realization that the kingdom of Heaven is restored to you. For God created only this, and he did not depart from it nor leave it separate from Himself. The Kingdom of Heaven is the dwelling place of the Son of God, who left not his father and dwells not apart from him. Heaven is not a place nor a condition. It is merely the awareness of perfect oneness, and the knowledge that there is nothing else; nothing outside this oneness, and nothing else within.[24]

In the following passage, we hear the theme continued, as the source seems to shift from the quality of a particularly lucid lawyer arguing a case, to the more personal and emotional tones of a poet:

You *are* a stranger here. But you belong to Him Who loves you as He loves Himself. Ask but my help to roll the stone away, and it is done according to His Will. We *have* begun the journey. Long ago the end was written in the stars and set into the Heavens with a shining ray that held it safe within eternity and through all time as well. And holds it still; unchanged, unchanging and unchangeable.

Be not afraid. We only start again an ancient journey long ago begun that but seems new. We have begun again upon a road we travelled on before and lost our way a little while. And now we try again. Our new beginning has the certainty the journey lacked till now. Look up and see His Word among the stars, where He has set your name along with His. Look up and find your certain destiny the world would hide but God would have you see.[25]

Volume Two: Workbook for Students provides 365 exercises, one for each day of the year, each planned around one central idea. The first set of exercises is for "the undoing of the way you see now," and the second set is for "the acquisition of true perceptions." The source tells us that "the overall aim of the exercises is to increase your ability to extend ideas you will be practicing to include everything." Many of the exercises parallel traditional psychotherapeutic approaches, such as working to undo "negative self-programming" acquired from past experience and learning to be "in the now." For example, in lesson 53, we are asked to meditate on phrases such as "I am upset because I see what is not there . . . My mind is preoccupied with past thoughts . . . I see nothing as it is now." Other ideas for the day include "I am one Self, united with my Creator," "I seek but what belongs to me in truth," the trans-materialist "The World I see holds nothing that I want," "All things are echoes of the Voice for God," and "The peace of God is shining in me now."[26]

Helen Schucman often wondered why she had been chosen for this work and often begrudged how central a place it took in her daily life. Robert Skutch—who, with his wife, Judith, and financial source Reed Erickson, was responsible for the eventual publication of the material—relates Helen's inner debate with her own "Voice": " 'Why me?' she asked. " 'I'm not religious; I don't understand these things; I don't even believe them. I'm about the poorest choice you could make . . .' The answer came back very clearly, 'On the contrary: You are an excellent choice. In fact, the best.' 'But why? she anguished. And then, without a hint of doubt she heard the answer: 'Because you'll do it.' "[27]

Who or what was the source of this material? A number of passages explain the contention of many that the author is "Christ":

> You cannot forget the Father because I am with you, and I cannot forget Him. To forget me is to forget yourself and Him Who created you. Our brothers are forgetful. That is why they need your remembrance of men and of Him Who created me . . . Come unto me, and learn of the truth in you.
> The name of Jesus Christ as such is but a symbol. But it stands for love that is not of this world. It is a symbol that is safely used as a replacement for the many names of all the gods to which you pray . . . This course has come from him.[28]

Some people believe that, even though professed to be an atheist, Schucman may have unconsciously tapped into her own previously dormant higher Self in this material, or into some combined universal source.

> The Holy Spirit is described as the remaining communication link between God and His separated Sons . . . The Holy Spirit abides in the part of your mind that is part of the Christ Mind. He represents your Self and your Creator, Who are one. He speaks for God and also for you, being joined with both. And therefore it is He Who proves them one. He seems to be a Voice, for in that form He speaks God's Word to you.[29]

In light of the quiet grace and occasional grandeur of *A Course in Miracles,* it comes as a marked contrast to read this description made by Schucman during the earlier years of scribing the *Course:*

Where did the writing come from? Certainly the subject matter itself was the last thing I would have expected to write about, since I knew nothing about the subject . . . At several points in the writing the Voice itself speaks in no uncertain terms about the Author (i.e., as Christ) . . . which literally stunned me at the time . . . I do not understand the events that led up to the writing. I do not understand the process and I certainly do not understand the authorship. It would be pointless for me to attempt an explanation.[30]

The following, taken from recent personal interviews in the course of this study, are interpretations of Schucman and *A Course in Miracles* by some of those who knew her and researched the material.

Psychologist James Fadiman: "Having met the people involved, I can say they didn't do it. Helen had the right psyche for it, but not enough talent." Esalen Institute co-founder and author Michael Murphy: "God knows what she could have regurgitated from the subliminal mind. I don't believe it's Christ. She was raised on that kind of literature. Her father had a metaphysical bookshop. Every single idea has been expressed before. There's nothing new in it." Publisher of the *Course,* Judith Skutch:

Those of us intimately associated with Helen Schucman over a long period of time until her death in 1981 were all aware that Helen's egoic rational mind was incapable of writing this material. I really feel that the part of Helen that was connected to the All received it in a form that was needed for today. This "part" of Helen—and indeed of all of us—is not of the physical. It is our eternal spiritual Self in oneness with the Mind of our Creator, which the course calls the Christ. In that sense, by its own definition, as stated in the *Manual for Teachers* of *A Course in Miracles:*

" . . . Christ takes many forms with different names until their oneness can be recognized. But Jesus is for you the bearer of Christ's single message of the Love of God . . . "

Therefore, I see the Christ Spirit as the source of the *Course* with Jesus as the symbol—a spokesperson—a Voice for the message of Love. In her later years Helen certainly shared this belief.

Transpersonal psychologist and author Ken Wilber:

Now, I'm not saying that there was not some transcendental insight involved and that Helen probably felt that it was certainly beyond her day-to-day self. I think that's true. But there's much more of Helen in the *Course* than I first thought. She was brought up mystically inclined. At four she used to stand out on the balcony and say that God would give her a sign of miracles to let her know that he was there. Many ideas from the *Course* came from the new thought or metaphysical schools she had been influenced by. It's not all pure information, there's a lot of noise that gets in. I found also that if you look at Helen's own poetry, you're initially very hard pressed to find any difference between that and the *Course*.

J. Z. KNIGHT, KEVIN RYERSON, AND JACH PURSEL

Three of the best-known channels in the United States today are J. Z. Knight, Kevin Ryerson, and Jach Pursel. Ryerson and Knight, and their respective sources, received a tremendous boost into the spotlight when actress-author Shirley MacLaine described them in her best-selling autobiographical books, *Out on a Limb* and *Dancing in the Light,* as being extraordinary teachers for her. Pursel and his source "Lazaris" are slated to be featured in MacLaine's next book. Critics and fans alike concur that MacLaine has done more than any other single person in recent times to soften the ground for people to believe and participate in things they once avoided for fear of being thought "flaky."

J. Z. Knight and "Ramtha"

During the past few years, a young Yelm, Washington, woman named J. Z. Knight has been channeling an entity that calls itself "Ramtha, the Enlightened One."

While playing with her husband one day, Knight recalls, she put a paper pyramid on her head, like a hat. She describes what followed:

When it fell down over my face, we started laughing until we cried. I lifted the pyramid up from over my eyes and looked toward the other end of the kitchen. Through my tears I saw what looked like a handful of gold and silver glitter sprinkled in a ray of sunshine. A very large entity was standing there . . . He looked at me with a beautiful smile and said, "I am Ramtha, the Enlightened One. I have come to help you over the ditch."[31]

Knight goes into a deep or cataleptic trance, claiming to leave her body so that "Ramtha," a powerful male presence, can enter. "Ramtha" speaks in a somewhat archaic, stylized manner, claiming to have been incarnated 35,000 years ago as a spiritual and political leader known as "The Ram" who came from fabled Lemuria into what is now India. "Ramtha" tends to refer to each questioner as "entity" or "master," with overtures such as, "Woman, beautiful entity, what say you?" "Ramtha" also displays a rare physicality for trance channeling, striding around during sessions, "eyeballing" members of the audience, and giving hugs.

"Ramtha's" theme is that we are like gods; part of God, yet unconscious of this identity. Nonetheless, we create our own realities within which to express ourselves, against which to react, from which to learn, and in which to evolve. This is a view that is virtually identical with the "Seth" teachings as well as with many other channeled materials. And once again, as elsewhere, we are told of great changes that are about to occur on this planet as we move inevitably toward our more spiritual nature.

Knight's channeling is best known for the lively interactions between the often humorous and gruffly teasing "Ramtha" and those attending the sessions. Investigators witness a highly sophisticated, stylized form of psychological and spiritual counseling, regardless of the ultimate identity of the counselor. Many also experience in Knight/ "Ramtha" a strong quality of holding forth—postured and almost pontifical. Following her strict Christian upbringing, there is a sense of the traditional preacher liberated by "the new age" in the attractive forty-year-old blonde Knight, as she beseeches us in her lowered "Ramtha" voice to love our godly selves and to create our own reality.

"Ramtha" responds to a question regarding his true nature:

I am Ramtha, the Enlightened One, indeed, that which is termed servant unto that which is called Source, to that which is termed the Principle Cause, indeed, unto that which is termed Life, unto that which is termed Christus—God experiencing that which is termed Man, man experiencing that which is termed God—am I a servant unto also. And who be He that be divine enough to be that which is termed the tranquility of all things within His being? You![32]

Until recently, the only way to experience "Ramtha" was to attend Knight's sessions or to view videotapes of the channeling. To date, more than 900 hours of video- and audiotapes are available. In 1985 Douglass James Mahr published the first book of selected "Ramtha" channelings, which includes interviews with Knight and her followers. It is called *Voyage to the New World: An Adventure into Unlimitedness*. Since then, a second book of excerpts, *Ramtha,* edited by Steven Lee Weinberg, has been published, as well as a collection of photographs of "Ramtha" sessions with text, entitled *I Am Ramtha.*[33]

Featured in MacLaine's *Dancing in the Light* and having received strong word-of-mouth and national media attention, Knight is now one of the best-known and most financially successful channels. A staff of fourteen helps her organize her semimonthly seminars and publish her brochures and tapes. An average weekend seminar draws up to 700 participants at $400 apiece; she admits to earning millions of dollars from "Ramtha."

Recently, Knight and "Ramtha" have become the subjects of considerable speculation in the channeling and New Age community. It seems, for many, as if the more visibility and power "Ramtha" is given by others, the more problems develop. There has been a recent souring on the part of some of his followers and a darkening on the part of the star personality, as is sometimes the case in the sociology of guru-type phenomena. That is, research shows that individuals who present themselves to others as religious leaders or possessors of wisdom often attract followers who choose to abdicate personal responsibility, relying on an authority figure for thinking and decision making. In addition, the leader often becomes perverted by this process, falling prey to self-aggrandizement or to the manipulation of his or her followers. The Reverend Jim Jones, who talked his "flock" into mass suicide in Guyana, is a recent example. Susan Rothbaum, director of Sorting It Out, a counseling center in Berkeley, California, for those who leave spiritual groups, cites the trend: "The guru starts with a simple message of openness and love; then it becomes complicated, baroque, paranoid and fearful."[34] As another observer puts it, "Many people now speculate that whatever energy came through J. Z. Knight has either shifted, departed or been replaced by a less benign entity."[35] Many others, however, continue to find useful counsel in the tapes and publications of the earlier "Ramtha" material, and a large number continue to find value even in Knight's most recent channelings.

Whatever the accuracy or inaccuracy of the specific criticisms made about Knight, or about any other channels past or current, certain questions can be legitimately raised about the specific channel, about channeling in general, and about the times in which the channeling is occurring. For example, has the channel, either consciously or unconsciously, decided to take over by mimicking a process that was perhaps once genuine but whose vein has run dry? Is it the channel or the source, people ask, who has become tempted by the endless roomfuls of devotees hanging onto each word and movement? Why such reported regressions in quality of performance? Who or what is responsible for the reported increase in all-too-human-appearing displays of ego, of manipulation and *dis*empowerment of those in attendance, quite contrary to earlier channeled themes? Many are growing suspicious that the integrity once experienced in the character of sources such as "Ramtha" is gone. Could it be that all channels have the potential of burning out or souring? Are the skeptics right in concluding it's all playacting and that the channel is just an act that's gone bad? Is this a channeling-type version of how the American Dream, with all its success and publicity, can contribute to the deterioration of a situation or person? Which channels or sources can we trust, and for how long?

Kevin Ryerson

Kevin—in his mid-thirties, with a friendly, rumpled look—is one of the most articulate channels operating today. In lectures, channeling demonstrations, and interviews, he clearly and intelligently discusses the process and its context as well as a wide range of other paranormal topics and philosophical issues. His sources are said to have amassed a track record of about 75 to 80 percent accuracy over the years with regard to material amenable to verification. Ryerson has appeared on dozens of radio and television programs. Anyone wishing to have a private channeling session with him must reserve time months in advance. He has enjoyed a healthy financial return for his gift.

The content of Ryerson's channeling closely parallels that of other historical and contemporary channeled material. Although the messages vary somewhat according to which of his sources they supposedly come from, they generally concur on certain themes. The descriptions place our earthly existence within a vast hierarchical, spiritual universe. Within this view, the material aims to assist the individual in empowering his or her Self. It reminds us that, beneath the appearance of the limited physical reality, we are essentially spiritual and immortal in nature, at one at the deepest levels with the universe, or God. From this relationship, we derive our power and our possibilities. Through a kind of co-creation with our Source identity, we can exercise our creative potential and decision-making birthright in order to access the fertile ground of Being to bring forth what we wish for ourselves and for one another on earth, in this lifetime or in any other. Reincarnation is a recurrent theme as well.

Ryerson remembers always having been interested in the psychic side of life. At twenty-two, with a fledgling graphic-arts career not meeting his deeper needs, he joined a meditation group organized around the teachings of Edgar Cayce. As many others have found, it was through experimentation in mediation with his own altered states of consciousness that Ryerson first experienced a breakthrough into channeling. Within six months, he had his first experience of an entity spontaneously appearing. It took another six months before he could develop techniques to ensure the control and predictable results associated with intentional, rather than spontaneous, channeling.

When going unconscious in order to channel, he says, "I set aside the limited responses and personality of Kevin Ryerson and in this trance state become sensitive to the universal mind." For him, the "sensation of going into the trance channeling state is identical to that of someone falling asleep—rather like falling backwards into sleep." On awakening, he says, "I have no conscious recall of the dialogue that has taken place with Spirit."[36]

He describes his sources: "The guides and teachers who speak through me are primarily energy, and I act not unlike a human telephone or radio receiver." More specifically, "The spirits who speak through me are human personalities who lived in another historical period. They are no different from you or me. They are merely in a discarnate state." According to Ryerson, "Their motivation to speak when I'm in the trance state is to help facilitate both individual and collective well-being." Many feel that since he has risen to prominence by way of his channeling, Ryerson has given himself permission to be an open channel when not in trance, allowing a lucidity and wisdom to come through him simply as the thoughts and words of Kevin Ryerson—no less impressive than the material from his sources.

But the sources, after all, are his bread and butter.

One of Ryerson's chief entities is "John," supposedly a member of the Essene Hebrew sect who was last incarnate at the time of Christ. One can almost imagine his soft, almost whispery, rapid-fire biblical-style rhetoric coming from some hooded monkish figure speaking aside in his bare stone cell. "John" comes across as a gentle and wise spiritual presence. "Hail! Please identify thyself and state purpose of gathering," tends to be "John's" opening line each time he appears. In contrast, the highly independent "Tom McPherson" speaks in a strong brogue of his last life in Elizabethan Ireland. Though more folksy, boisterous, and joking, "McPherson" can still display the same provocative insights as the scholarly, pious "John." Less frequent sources include "Obadiah," a booming West Indian–accented Haitian versed in herbal lore, and sages from ancient Egypt and Japan. Over the years, each of these characters has appeared to maintain and reflect its own internally consistent cultural and personality traits. Ryerson has concluded, "I've been able to validate for myself that these entities are who they claim to be."

Shirley MacLaine fondly refers to Ryerson as "one of the telephones in my life." Recently, as part of preparing a nationally broadcast television production of her book *Out on a Limb*, MacLaine asked Ryerson if he would play himself as a trance channel in the reenactment of her first session with him. MacLaine and the director found themselves with a show-business first when they decided against faking the scene. Rather than have Ryerson pretend to portray his own entities in order to follow the script, they had him go into trance, and they asked "John" and "Tom" if they would be able to repeat later in front of the cameras what they had said in the years-earlier situation recounted in the book and TV script. Sure enough, according to Ryerson and MacLaine, what millions saw on television was the real channel playing himself and going into a real trance and his "real" entities playing themselves! The skeptic, of course, needs only to point out that all this was merely a case of acting within acting; "All the world's a stage, and all the men and women merely players," as "Tom's" contemporary, Will Shakespeare, would say.

Jach Pursel and "Lazaris"

Jach Pursel was a regional insurance supervisor in Florida—virtually without a metaphysical bone in his body—when he began dabbling in meditation, during which times he would find himself just dozing off. In October of 1974, however, his wife, Peny, had an intuitive feeling that Jach should try to meditate. So far as Jach's awareness went, he fell asleep . . . but Peny found herself talking to an entirely different entity, an entity whom Jach would later name "Lazaris." Peny was astonished, but had the presence of mind to grab a pad and pencil and start asking questions—which "Lazaris" answered in a strangely accented voice. Peny and Jach repeated the process a number of times over the next several weeks, and finally a session was taped.

Pursel recalls first hearing his own voice being used as "Lazaris" while he remain unconscious. It had a strange Chaucerian Middle English quality. No one has been able to pin down the accent, which has stayed impeccably consistent throughout thousands of hours of channeled talking, as has the personality supposedly doing the talking, for the past fourteen years. "As soon as I heard this voice," Pursel recalls, "I shut off the machine. I walked for about an hour. I was scared. I did not understand. I cried for awhile. Then, somehow, it became all right."[37]

"Lazaris's" themes should by now seem quite familiar to us, since they closely echo what we have already found in the "Seth," *Course in*

Miracles, "Ramtha," and Ryerson material. It is a basically spiritual, united universe, "Lazaris" says, with us as essentially evolving, spiritual, immortal beings within and at one with it. Self-empowerment includes the causal, creative, intuitive ability to access what we need from our higher Selves and from the universe as "God/Goddess/All That Is." And to realize the prior two truths, we must work to overcome our negative programming, our debilitating self-image, and our limited world view.

A sense of the basic themes expressed by "Lazaris" can be gained by considering a selection of topics of recent videotapes of channeling sessions. Besides a lecture format, each usually includes "Lazaris" taking the participants on some form of experiential journey to further process the material, such as guided relaxation, meditation, and mental imagery. Recent topics include: Awakening the Love; Forgiving Yourself; The Secrets of Manifesting What You Want; Personal Power and Beyond; Achieving Intimacy and Loving Relationships; Unconditional Love; Releasing Negative Ego; Unlocking the Power of Changing Your Life; Spiritual Mastery: The Journey Begins; Personal Excellence; and Developing a Relationship with Your Higher Self.

Over time, Pursel has learned how to efficiently enter the particular type of unconscious state that has always led to "Lazaris" appearing. He closes his eyes, takes a few deep breaths, relaxes, and imagines himself descending a ten-rung ladder, rung by rung, counting backward. Reaching the bottom, he begins a second round of imagining ten slow-motion backward circling somersaults. Usually by around the sixth of these, all becomes dark. It seems like only a moment later, he says, when he opens his eyes and finds himself back in the room, the entire intervening session lost to him.[38]

Asked if he is ever concerned that "Lazaris" might not appear, he replies, "I used to worry about that. I used to have this image of sitting in front of a group, closing my eyes and doing the whole thing and opening my eyes and having people say, 'Well, when is it going to start?'"[39] Eventually, however, he came to realize that "Lazaris" would always be there for him. Indeed, "Lazaris" has said on numerous occasions that he has never before communicated through anyone else on this planet besides Pursel and never will again.

Pursel now spends as much as forty nonsleeping hours a week unconscious in order to offer "Lazaris" for an ever-growing number of private readings, public talks, and weekend workshops run by his highly successful and profitable corporation, Concept: Synergy. The enterprise is managed by Pursel, ex-wife Peny, and her new husband, Michael, from a location in Fairfax, California. The garage has been turned into a mailroom, and a row of computer workstations and telephones are manned by staff members each day, as channeling comes of age as big business. Two successful New Age art galleries are also part of the enterprise.

The "Lazaris" material is soon to appear in book form, having earlier been available only through personal or telephone appointment, attendance at live presentations, or through the myriad attractively packaged audio- and videocassette tapes distributed by way of a highly sophisticated marketing effort utilizing more than 500 metaphysical bookstores worldwide. "There's a group of Mennonites, for example," Pursel points out, "that just love the tapes. And it's unbelievable the number of Mormons in Salt Lake City wanting them . . . And there's a group of nuns out East coming into the bookstores, and they just love the tapes. They rent them all the time."[40]

While heightened media attention has brought a two-year waiting list to personally speak with him, "Lazaris" commands an increasingly large following among those already familiar with other channeled literature. His sessions are reported to provide exceptional clarity, wisdom, detail, opportunities for personal experience, and methods that seem to work. "Trustworthy," "loving," and "helpful" are words often used to describe "Lazaris." Concept: Synergy calls him "the consummate friend."

Because Pursel claims never to know at the time or remember later what occurs while he is in his unconscious trance state channeling, he has had to relate to "Lazaris" as others have, by hearing tapes and viewing videos of the sessions. From them, he has grown to care about and respect the personality that expresses itself as "Lazaris." On a recent nationally televised "Merv Griffin Show," Pursel said of "Lazaris," "He seems to know incredible things—much more than I do. So it is wonderfully helpful to me." In response to the question, "Why is 'Lazaris' so special?" he replies:

> First, because he teaches us *how* to be powerful . . . it [the material] has always been about giving power back . . . Second, Lazaris tells us *how* to change our lives and then teaches us specific techniques to accomplish the change . . . Thirdly, [he] offers us a beautiful gift of choice . . . [he] shows us the alternatives. He teaches us new ways of seeing the problems and then new ways of finding solutions . . . Fourthly, he respects and loves us as individuals.[41]

But how does "Lazaris" describe himself? He claims that he is not now and never has been physical or human. Nor is he a person as we would define it, but rather a group being living in another dimension from ours where time and space as we know it do not exist. On the "Merv Griffin Show," he said, "We refer to ourselves in the plural, most definitely—not out of any imperialness, that's for sure, but rather we are aware of the multiplicity of ourselves." (This chapter will conclude with an extended interview with "Lazaris.")

MESSAGES FROM "MICHAEL"

In 1970, the alleged entity "Michael" first made its presence known to a thirty-three-year-old San Francisco Bay Area woman. The channel is called Jessica Lansing (a fictitious name) in the best-selling books by Chelsea Quinn Yarbro, *Messages from Michael* and *More Messages from Michael*. These books have made "Michael" one of the best known of the channeling cases that have come to prominence in the last few years.[42]

Recently, more than half a dozen others in the San Francisco area have been claiming to channel the same "Michael" by various means, including automatic writing, light trance, and full trance. This multi-channeled manifestation of the same supposed source makes the "Michael" material of special interest to us.

Much in the same way as Jane Roberts and her husband, Robert Butts, were said to have discovered "Seth," Jessica and her husband, Walter (also a fictitious name), decided to play with their Ouija board after dinner one evening. "Who is this?" they asked, and the letters emerged, "You may call us anything you wish." They pressed further and received, "The last name a fragment of this entity used was Michael." As one of their guests wryly observed, "It's a kind of astral guru." The purported entity corrected him: "We are of the mid-causal plane. The astral plane is accessible to the physical plane. We are not."[43]

"Michael" indicated that it was a "recombined entity," made up of more than a thousand "old soul" fragments. Each of us, "Michael" says, is one of a thousand fragments of an entity like itself. According to "Michael," "all that is" is contained within the "Tao" rather than "God," as "Michael" wished to avoid the use of male gender and human connotations. The essence of this Tao separates into entities and fragments, which then go through a complex evolutionary path until they once again rejoin the Tao to realize their identity with it.

Human beings, then, are fragments, each containing the essence of the one all-embracing Tao, as well as the essence of the parent entity. First the fragments must rejoin their entity and then the entities must rejoin the Tao. In the vast journey out of and back to the Tao, souls must ascend through seven planes of existence. (This seven-tiered system is found in the work of Blavatsky, Bailey, Steiner, and others.)

"Michael" also describes a rather elaborate personality system. One must go through seven basic soul stages, each with a minimum of seven reincarnated lives: infant, baby, young, mature, old, transcendental, and infinite. There are assorted "overleaves," or personality characteristics, that one chooses for any incarnate lifetime. One of these overleaves is the "role," which is kept the same throughout one's lifetimes through the Tao. Roles include the sage, artisan, priest, slave, king, warrior, and scholar.

For example, in October 1982, "Michael" was asked what lay behind the lack of harmony between the USSR and the United States. Referring to the personality system described above, "Michael" replied:

The communication between the leaders is made worse because of overleaves: one country is run by a fourth-level young sage in the aggressive mode with a goal of acceptance, a pragmatist in the emotion part of intellectual center with a marked chief feature of greed. The other country is run by a fifth-level mature scholar in the observation mode with a goal of dominance, a realist in the moving part of intellectual center with a chief feature of arrogance exacerbated by failing health.[44]

To those who gather at his sessions, "Michael" refers to channeling as one of the chief methods for growth "by which your false personality is set aside so that there may be inner dialogue with the essence."[45] Yet he often is reported to grow impatient with the petty, private questions of those who seek his counsel, reminding them, at one point, "We are not the Ann Landers of the Cosmos." Apparently wishing to set a more serious and responsible tone, "Michael" added, "We would like to point out to you at this time that many of you are dabblers . . . you dabble in spiritual growth as well . . . Stop for a moment and ask yourself why it is that you search and for what."[46]

After years of channeling "Michael," Jessica asks herself: "Do I believe it? The only answer I can give is: sometimes."[47]

FROM HEAVEN TO EARTH: THE "RETURNS" SERIES

In 1973, Robert R. Leichtman, a psychiatrist with considerable psychic and channeling abilities, became interested in the nature of genius and what we might learn from studying geniuses. Most of those he wished to interview, however, were no longer alive. Undaunted, he decided to use channeling. "The basic idea," he recalls, "was not mine alone—but had been 'suggested' to me by the spooks themselves.[48] ("Spooks" is the affectionate name he gives to discarnate human spirits.) He soon settled on his longtime friend, painter and trance channel David Kendrick Johnson, rather than himself, for the project.

To date, the *From Heaven to Earth . . . Returns* series includes two sets, each of a dozen small paperback books. Those who supposedly have been channeled include William Shakespeare, Carl Jung, Sigmund Freud, and Thomas Jefferson. Of special interest to us are some of the chief luminaries of the channeling literature whom we will look at in our next chapter: Sir Oliver Lodge, Charles Leadbeater, H. P. Blavatsky, Edgar Cayce, Eileen Garrett, Arthur Ford, and Stuart Edward White.

Representing the sentiments of many of these sources, the alleged spirit of the noted British physicist and channeling researcher Sir Oliver Lodge says through David Kendrick Johnson, "People might wonder why I come back and talk through a medium as I am doing now. It is because I'm still involved in life and curious about life. My perspectives are slightly different than they were, and I'm concerned with a fuller view of life than most physical people are."

By his own presence and the information he provides, he advocates the existence of life after death. As do the other sources in the series, he describes the mechanics of the channeling process as seen from his now discarnate perspective. He warns the novice of the high probability of having his or her own unconscious and wish-fulfillment activity operating through both automatic writing and the Ouija board. As the others do, he warns of the presence of negative and even harmful spirits that can be drawn in by seeking the channeling experience. He also counsels that even when the contacts are positive, "it's a real mistake to become *too* dependent on spooks [i.e., channeled sources]." And he retains the view he had on earth, amazed "that anyone could explore the psychic world without realizing that God is behind it all."

Leichtman observes, "The ideas of each spirit were translated into words by the medium's subconscious using his vocabulary and speech patterns; David's personality and voice box remained very much in evidence, even though they were being used and controlled by a different entity." Leichtman adds, "I have left in . . . lighter remarks in the hope that readers will be able to see that spooks are very much human."[49]

Leichtman addresses the chief psychological explanation for channeling: Does the subconscious mind of the medium create its own false "spirits," which appear to be channeled from outside the self?

Through Johnson, the supposed spirit of the late well-known medium Arthur Ford tells Leichtman that "anyone can close his eyes and allow his hysterical subconscious to put on a sheet and go, 'Boo, I'm a spook!' But he's only allowing his subconscious free reign."[50] And the spirit of noted psychic Eileen Garrett adds:

Your subconscious is a very willing servant . . . it will essentially do whatever we ask it to do. If you want to pretend to be a medium . . . it will play ghost for you. It will tell you, "I'm William the Conqueror" . . . Only the person who has made no effort to houseclean his subconscious can be fooled by that sort of playacting.[51]

The purported spirit of Garrett refers to her current identity, issues of proof, and the value of messages:

The personality of Eileen Garrett basically no longer exists. It is gone. The inner being of Eileen Garrett still exists, though, and that is me. I'm speaking now through this medium and am using his speech patterns, his cultural idiosyncrasies, his subconscious associations and his physical body.
    In the final analysis, I don't think it makes any difference whether I can "prove" I am Eileen Garrett or not. The key is this: Do the ideas and subjects discussed during this interview enhance what Eileen Garrett stood for and the work she did? . . . However, I really am Eileen Garrett.[52]

"SPACE BROTHERS"

One widely reported type of source is known as "space brothers" or "extraterrestrials." Records of this kind of activity date back to 1947, when pilot Kenneth Arnold registered his observation of an arrangement of nine saucer-shaped unidentified flying objects, or UFOs, flying in formation near Mount Rainier, Washington. Since then, there has been a close parallel between reported observations of UFOs and individuals claiming to receive paranormal communications from the beings associated with such craft.
    In the Mojave desert in 1952, George Adamski first met an entity who claimed to be a man from Venus. Thus began a thirteen-year communication, until Adamski's death in 1965. Bear in mind that scientists tell us that the planet Venus is hundreds of degrees centigrade and has no oxygen and no discernible life-forms. The supposed Venusians say that they come not from the physical but from the etheric plane of Venus. Much of what Adamski received, then, was supposed to have come by way of a kind of transdimensional telepathy. By the end of his life, he had shared this information with John F. Kennedy, received the Golden Medallion from Pope John XXIII, and been given honors from eighteen nations.[53]

Besides Adamski, numerous others have similar stories to tell. Engineer Daniel Fry claimed communications from similar beings and told his story in *To Men of Earth*. George Van Tassel reported receiving the following message from an unseen "space brother" in 1952:

> Hail to you beings of Shan [their name for Earth]. I greet you in love and peace. My identity is Ashtar, commandant quadra sector, patrol station Schare, all projections, all waves. Greetings. Through the Council of the Seven Lights you have been brought here, inspired with the inner light to help your fellow man.[54]

"Ashtar" proceeds to warn the human race about what lies in store for us, given our emphasis on material rather than spiritual reality and your recent initiation into nuclear weaponry. He also stresses the imminent shift of frequency level for the entire planet, which will cleanse the old vibrations and usher in a new, more spiritual millennium. We find these themes recurring throughout the "space brothers" literature. In addition, the same sources keep cropping up through the years up to the present from dozens of channels. So do references to the same "Confederation of Planets," "Saturn Tribunal (or Council)," and "Intergalactic Confederation," for example. We even find the same or similar forms of greeting and farewell being used by the alleged communicators.

Material from "space brothers" can be classified as channeling because these beings are reputed to be from another level of reality and, therefore, must communicate with earthbound channels in a manner similar to other sources. The majority of "space beings" are said to be from a dimension above but close to our own. This is often called the etheric realm, situated below the astral domain, within which discarnate human spirits are supposed to dwell. The "space brothers" are, for the most part, similar to human beings but more spiritually and technologically evolved. Their technologies, they claim, permit them to modulate the vibratory rate of their own bodies and spacecrafts, which operate in the same range as their home dimension. When they lower their frequencies, they claim, they can occasionally be seen by us.

Here is a sample passage clairaudiently channeled by author Aleutia Francesca from a being named "Orlon" in the 1950s in Oregon, which again contains the theme of a new age coming:

> My brothers, my sisters in Light, I, Orlon, communicate with you from the craft stationed above your mountain locality. As the midnight hour approaches for change upon your planet, we state to you categorically: WE come in PEACE. Our mission with your peoples is one of enlightenment, is indeed, one of rescue from the morasses

of the lower mind of Earthman: Rescue in the sense of bringing that enlightenment which gives release, which gives evolvement into that greater self which Man, in essence, IS. We speak of a midnight hour; we speak of changes, changes vast and tremendous on the face of planet Earth: Changes in frequency, of density, of consciousness of being.[55]

One of the most extensive cases of channeling from "space brothers" is the multivolumed collection produced by Guardian Action Publications, now in Durango, Colorado. The primary channel for this work has been a gentle, unassuming woman who chooses to go by the spiritual name of Tuella.

She too speaks of the liaison between the earth's traditional spiritual teachers and the "space brothers." In *Project World Evacuation,* by "the Ashtar Command" through Tuella, we are given in detail the picture of pending catastrophe and "harvest."[56] Harvest is the term they use to represent their intended aid to those of us who are more spiritually evolved, during the upcoming planetary changes they prophesy.

Carla Rueckert, in her book *Secrets of the UFOs* (with Don Elkins; privately published; distributed by L/L Research, Louisville, Kentucky, 1977), provides passages from her years of channeling "space brothers." The following echoes the "Seth" and "Michael" notions of group entities and provides a clear picture of the relation of vibration to spirituality.

[Your] vibration or frequency is the only important part of your being, since it is an index of your consciousness with respect to the original thought. When an individual is aware of life in its infinite sense, he is also aware of the benefits of matching this vibration with the vibration of the original thought (of the Creator). It is our effort to match our vibration with that of the original thought. This is the reason that we of the Confederation of Planets in the Service of the Infinite Creator are here now . . . We are attempting to give instructions to those of planet Earth who would seek the instructions for how to produce within themselves the vibration that is more harmonious with the original thought.[57]

In 1981, L/L Research began publishing the channelings, through Rueckert, Elkins, and others, of a group being calling itself "Ra." This multivolume material, together with dozens of other materials like it through other channels and from other similar "extraterrestrial" sources, will deserve the scrutiny of future researchers because of its often highly technical "unearthly science" nature.

"J.W.," purporting to be a "being from Jupiter through the instrument of Gloria Lee," as recorded in *Why We Are Here,* offers a note of caution with its explanation:

> When the message I wish brought to you is given her [Lee], I merely project this thought to her mind where the highest chakra of the body is. The crown chakra or the pineal gland is your channel for communicating with Higher Beings . . . We shall now come to many of you with this same type of thought, but if you create illusion in your mind then we cannot come to you with Truth.

Enough of these "space brothers" messages have been amassed over thirty-five years to fill many volumes; there is not room here to begin to do justice to them. Of particular interest, however, is the relatively high degree of correlation across the content of this material. For example, physician/researcher Andrija Puharich, Israeli psychic Uri Geller, Texas channel Ray Stanford, and numerous others have separately experienced channeling from "Spectra," which is said to be an "extraterrestrial higher intelligence *from the future,*" possibly computerized. The being known in Egyptian times as the hawk-headed god Horus has also been implicated. After having been in the thick of such activity, psychologist and author Robert Anton Wilson wonders if "there really is an interstellar ESP channel to which you can tune in by metaprogramming your nervous system."[58]

MARK AND ELIZABETH CLARE PROPHET

The Prophets have had their own community in Southern California, known as Camelot, complete with publishing house (Summit University Press), newsletter (*Pearls of Wisdom*), and school. Recently, however, plans have been made to move all operations to Oregon to escape impending natural upheavals that Elizabeth's sources have warned of. The upheavals will signal the shift into a new age, the sources say.

Assuming mythic proportions, channels Mark and Elizabeth are called the "Twin Flames" by their followers. Mark, who died in 1973, also is supposedly channeled by his widow. Elizabeth claims to have been invested by "ascended master Saint Germain" with the title and responsibility of "Mother of the Flame," or "Mother" for short.

The sources channeled by both Prophets, and in the past fifteen years by Elizabeth alone, are said to be "ascended masters," spiritually advanced beings no longer residing on the physical plane. Among those most extensively channeled are "Saint Germain"; "Kuthumi," or

"Koot Hoomi," also known as "the Master K.H."; "Djwal Kul," or "the Master D.K."; and "the Master El Morya." The last three are said to be the same entities—the "Mahatmas" and "The Tibetan"—who had worked earlier with H. P. Blavatsky and Alice A. Bailey (discussed in chapter 2). "The ascended masters," Elizabeth believes, "are contacting mankind today in a very real way. Through the power of the spoken Word, they are reaching . . . all who will hear the true message . . . of the individual Christ Self." The material she has supposedly channeled from them now comprises dozens of volumes.

Even though there may be off-putting aspects to it (or to her), Elizabeth Prophet's material seems to contain enough originality and even profundity to attract both the intellect and heart of a wide range of people.

Here she purports to channel "Djwal Kul" (or "Khul"), "the Master D.K.":

I come to you in the company of the heart, your own Christ self. I come as a teacher; and yet I bow before your own mentor of the Spirit, the mediator who is Christ the Lord. For as I instruct the outer consciousness according to the precepts of the inner law, it is the Christ, the light of the manifestation which you call your self, who releases inspiration, intuition . . . to become receptacles of God's light.[59]

KEN CAREY, MEREDITH LADY YOUNG, AND PAT RODEGAST

During a snowy eleven days in 1979, a young Missouri postal employee turned farmer, Ken Carey, began to channel for the first time. The result, *The Starseed Transmissions,* would later be called by philosopher and psychologist Jean Houston "perhaps the finest example of 'channeled knowledge' I ever encountered."[60]

The *Transmissions* are rich with elegantly phrased reminders that we are spiritual beings who are awakening, in the last part of this century and the beginning of the next, into the organic unity of a planetary species operating in harmony with the larger Creation, as was always meant to be. The material speaks of the fact that we are the bridge between spirit and matter, Creator and Creation, between the spirit and the forms through which spirit flows. At the same time, we are learning to identify ourselves not as the form, but as the force that flows through and gives life to the form. "Feel me rising up within," the source says, "reflect me in all that you are." As the transmutation from material disorder to spiritual order occurs, we are told, "You are not to act upon my information in the future, you are to be my information." The reader is beseeched to awaken to the inevitable changes at hand and to come into alignment with, and so join, the loving forces at work, rather than to hold back within the outmoded forms of matter and selfishness that are to be transformed by the work.

Of the channeling experience, Carey writes:

> The messages came first in non-verbal form, on waves or pulsations, that carried the concise symbolic content of what I term "meta-conceptual information." Automatically, it would seem, the nearest approximating words or phrases from the English language would be assigned to ride, as it were, the fluctuations of the non-verbal communications. Often it was the case that the only human conceptual system with approximating terminology was religious. Hence, the occasional use of "Christian" words and phrases . . .
> The communications that are presented seem to have been transmitted neurobiologically. As I communed with these spatial intelligences, our biogravitational fields seemed to merge, our awarenesses blend, and my nervous system seemed to become available to them as a channel for communication.[61]

Through Carey, "Raphael" (some say the "Archangel Raphael"), the entity said to be responsible for *The Starseed Transmissions,* says:

> I come from the Presence where there is no time but the eternal now . . . My individual identity comes into being only as I enter the context of my relationship with you. When I am no longer needed in this capacity, I will merge back into the Being behind all being. There I remain in unity and fulfillment until the next impulse comes to send me on another mission.[62]

"Do you want to know more about extraterrestrials?" the source asks. "Do you want a definition of angels? We are you, yourself, in the distant past and distant future. We exist in a parallel universe of non-form, experiencing what you would have experienced had you not become associated with the materializing processes."

Two-thirds of the way through the eleven-day transmission, the identity of the reputed source seems to shift (as seemed also to occur in *A Course in Miracles*):

> I am Christ. I am coming this day through the atmosphere of your consciousness. I am asking you to open the door of your reason, to

allow me into your heart . . . I am the bridegroom, spoken of old. I came to you first through a man named Jesus . . . Rejoice! The millennia of your fasting is over, the bridegroom returns . . . Whoever will come after me will have to die to all definitions of self, take up my spirit, and follow along the lines of my vibrational field.[63]

Carey recalls, in the introduction to his second book, *Vision*: "Everything was so still. I felt something, a low humming, an energy field, a Presence. When I first heard the voice, I cried."[64] A growing number are finding his books among the most moving and beautiful of all channeled literature.

Agartha, the name given to Meredith Lady Young's higher Self by her source "Mentor," helped form the title of the widely distributed volume, *Agartha: A Journey to the Stars*. Young, who is co-founder of Still-Point Publishing in Walpole, New Hampshire, found herself becoming aware that "truth has a vibration of its own that is perceptible to those who can attune themselves to it." She reports that the channeling began to infiltrate her normal meditation sessions. "I had not heard voices; I had not seen the words. I had not thought words. I had *felt* them as though they grew from within me. They had a depth and dimension and like an echo reverberating through a canyon, the essence of that echo had filled me and became instantly translated into words."

A sampling from the chapter headings of *Agartha* reflects the kinds of channeled material now familiar to us: Coming from the Heart; Where Is Enlightenment?; Creating Your Own Reality; The Power Connection: Key to Earth's Survival (including Learning to Draw from the Source); Inner Space Versus Outer Space; The Experience of Healing; Death: The Need to Survive; and Man as God. "Mentor" tells us:

Your planet and its people will be exposed to an unprecedented period of harmonious realignment if the energies of more advanced realities are successful in catalytically sparking this new age of awareness. The Earth's evolving consciousness will gradually transcend those negative limitations which currently dominate your diminished and depleted world.

"Who are you?" Young asks. The response: "We are multidimensional beings from another more spiritually evolved plane. Our aim is one of positive reinforcement to further man's development."

She is told "to channel your energies in the appropriate fashion to draw in our presence. The human race must recognize its deeply buried bond with Universal Energy or no significant spiritual growth is possible. Guidance is crucial to all people of all realities."

When "Mentor" is asked if he might be a product of Young's imagination, he responds:

What is imagination except a glimpse of reality experienced and expressed in a normally unprecedented manner? We tied our collective energies into this communication and then selectively decreased the volume. The conversion of energy into thought impressions, which are then telepathically transmitted, is how we are able to communicate with you, Agartha. This is the way communication is most successfully accomplished where there is a wide variance in energy levels. This communication is simply awareness strung together creating complete thoughts; and, yes it does come through Agartha's subconscious, or as we would rather call it, superconscious.[65]

Pat Rodegast (further profiled in chapter 3) is the channel for "Emmanuel," the source said to be responsible for a widely read collection, *Emmanuel's Book: A Manual for Living Comfortably in the Cosmos.* In the introduction to this work, psychologist and spiritual teacher Ram Dass (Richard Alpert) says that "Emmanuel," through Rodegast, is one of the most influential teachers in his own life.

Regarding the ultimate nature of the source, Ram Dass writes:

From my point of view as a psychologist, I allow for the theoretical possibility that Emmanuel is a deeper part of Pat. However, experientially, I know Emmanuel as quite separate in personality, language style, and vibration from the way in which I know Pat. In the final analysis, what difference does it make? What I treasure is the wisdom Emmanuel conveys as an essence spiritual friend. Beyond this his identity doesn't matter. I see Emmanuel as a mirror, and possibly an identity with not only Pat's higher consciousness or true self, but mine as well. Thus, I feel that I am speaking to another part of my own being that I still do not have easy access to because of the blinders of attachment.[66]

"Emmanuel" first came to Rodegast during meditation, as "inner visions" that she feared were hallucinations. She then claimed to be able to clairvoyantly see "a being of golden light."

"In your spirit reality," "Emmanuel" proclaims, "you are already one with God. There is nothing in human existence that does not exist in spirit. There is divinity in all things and in order to find that divinity one must work with the material at hand." "Emmanuel" assures us, "Those of us who have been human know full well the courage it takes."[67]

INTERNATIONAL CHANNELS

The "Hilarion" Books of Maurice B. Cooke

The private world of Maurice B. Cooke, a scientifically trained, respected Toronto businessman, dramatically shifted in 1977 when he started experimenting with mental, or raja, yoga techniques. By stilling his mind, he found it "possible to receive symbolic, conceptual or verbal information which may contain insights into areas beyond those with which the mind is normally familiar." Soon, Cooke continues, "works were 'dictated' to me from a non-physical source who gives his name as Hilarion, through a process in which my conscious mind is stilled deliberately so that a form of telepathy can take place."[68]

To date, at least eleven books have been recorded and published in this manner. Some have been on specific topics. For example, *Dark Robes, Dark Brothers* (1981) purports to deal with the "negative forces which seek to hinder the spiritual progress of mankind."

In *The Nature of Reality,* "Hilarion" provides detailed, rather technical descriptions, often very much at odds with current scientific thinking, of such concepts as space, time, light, matter, magnetism, gravity, and nuclear energy. Also included are other topics as varied as the conscious mind, karma, and predestination. In *Seasons of the Spirit,* we are treated to subject matter ranging from the symbolic significance of the various parts of the body to descriptions of our prebiblical origins.

One of most curious subjects is the so-called inert gases technology. According to "Hilarion," inert gas atoms—such as helium, neon, and argon—mask certain primary points that link three-dimensional reality to higher-dimensional realities. When these elements are subjected to a certain magnetic field and pressure, they can be moved off the interdimensional points they usually cover, causing an influx of higher-dimensional energy, which can then be used, primarily for healing.

Using the inert gases under the magnetic field and pressure prescribed by "Hilarion," Cooke and two fellow Canadian scientists tested the idea with some success. The resulting story is told in *Einstein Doesn't Work Here Anymore.*[69]

Another subject associated with the "Hilarion" books is the notion of "The Tribulation," which "Hilarion" describes on many occasions as the catastrophic end-of-the-world-as-we-know-it scenario that will "sort out" those who will remain as the planet shifts into a higher, more spiritual vibratory rate. The rest will relocate, "Hilarion" says, to reincarnate on a more dense, earthlike planet to continue the needed growth experiences.

In *Seasons of the Spirit,* "Hilarion" says, "All of the souls and entities at the level from which this dictation is originating feel deeply the distress of their human brothers at this hour, as the shadows of the Great Tribulation lengthen upon the planet. We know what trials lie just ahead."[70]

Cooke holds open the possibility that "Hilarion" may be only the product of his (Cooke's) own unconscious. He also presents what seems to be a rather healthy way to relate to purportedly channeled work:

I have always felt that endless enquiries into the precise nature of such sources [as Hilarion] are of little use, since in the last analysis one can never be absolutely certain what one is dealing with. A much better test, in my view, is to examine one's feelings and impressions upon reading the transmitted material. If the general tone of the information is one of spiritual uplift and encouragement, if it presents a higher view of reality than that commonly held, then careful consideration of the material is in order.[71]

Canada has its other channels as well. Based on years of counseling, teaching, healings, and demonstrations of his channeling throughout Canada, Montreal native Joey Crinita recently brought together his experiences in *The Medium Touch: A New Approach to Mediumship.*[72] In Ontario, "the echoes" are the source that has made Clifford Preston a self-described professional medium. In Ottawa *The Channel Sourceletter* has just begun publication.

Among internationally known channels, British artist and journalist Benjamin Creme has received particular notoriety. This is not only because of his claim to be a channel for the Christ, to whom he refers as "Maitreya, head of the planet's spiritual hierarchy." More importantly, it is because he has been guided to announce specific dates when "Maitreya, the Christ"—said to have fully entered the physical body in 1977—was supposed to make himself publicly known. Each time, however, there has been no appearance. Yet Creme sticks to his role of chosen representative to pave the way for this second coming.

The messages from "Maitreya" tell of the "spiritual hierarchy of the planet and its new world order," including a new group of discarnate and incarnate "world servers" who will lead us into a spiritual age. Much of this work is available in the book *The Reappearance of the Christ and the Masters of Wisdom* and in the newsletter *Share International.*

Creme addresses topics such as "The Christ and His Reappearance," "The Masters and [Spiritual] Hierarchy," the "Effect on Existing Institutions" of Christ's return, and "The Anti-Christ: The Forces of Evil." The following are excerpts said to be from the "Maitreya," or Christ presence, channeled by Creme:

I come to tell you that you will see Me very soon, each in his own way . . . Nothing separates you from Me, and soon many will realize this. I am with you and in you. I seek to express that which I am through you; for this I come . . . My body of workers will show the world that the problems of Mankind can be solved: through the process of sharing and just redistribution the needs of all can be met . . . The greatest change will be in the hearts and minds of men, for My Return among you is a sign that men are ready to receive new life. That New Life for men do I bring in abundance. On all the planes this life will flow, reaching the hearts and souls and bodies of men, bringing them nearer to the Source of Life Itself. My task will be to channel those waters of Life through you.[73]

"No trance or mediumship is involved," Creme emphasizes, "and the voice is mine, very obviously strengthened in power and altered in pitch by the overshadowing energy of Maitreya." Continuing to describe the particular kind of channeling involved, he claims, "The messages are transmitted simultaneously on all astral and mental planes, while I supply the basic etheric-physical vibration for this to take place."

Regarding his self-proclaimed role, he says that "it is an enormous and embarrassing claim to have to make that the Christ is giving messages through oneself." But Creme believes in the existence of his sources. "For me, their existence is a fact, known through my direct experience and contact." Yet he must resign himself to "leave it to a study of the quality of the messages themselves to convince or otherwise."[74]

Carolyn Del La Hey is another of the channels in England gaining a following. Her work includes *Lifeline: Experiences of Psychic Communication.* The Ramala Centre in Glastonbury, Somerset, England, is the focus for the activities of "the Ramala teachers," sources who come through a channel who has remaind anonymous since 1970. The major material has been published as *The Revelation of Ramala.*[75] Space does not allow mentioning the dozens of others across Great Britain who are sharing their sources through private consultations, publications, and demonstrations.

One of the best-known channels in West Germany is Gabriele Wittek, who claims to channel "cherubs," "Jesus Christ," and even "God, the Father." Worldwide tours of her channeling presentations and the publication of her channeled material fall under the names Homebringing Mission of Jesus Christ and, more recently, The Christ State.[76]

In addition, hundreds of channels—usually preferring to call themselves mediums—are active today within the Spiritualist movement with its sittings, circles (once called seances), and churches scattered throughout the world. This movement, which had its roots 130 years ago in a farmhouse in upstate New York, will be examined in detail in the next chapter. Spiritualist activity, preoccupied with communications with spirits of the departed, is most heavily concentrated in the United States and Britain, although it is found in more than a dozen countries. Spiritualist communities, where the resident mediums often outnumber the visitors, include Lily Dale, New York; Cassedaga, Florida; and Camp Chesterfield, Indiana.

OTHERS

William Kautz, a senior research scientist at SRI International in Menlo Park, California, is founding director of The Center for Applied Intuition in San Francisco. Kautz has pioneered an approach to bringing together channels, whom he calls intuitives, with those who can most profit from their abilities and services. The center was founded "to help people develop, refine, and control their intuitive abilities and come to effectively apply their talents to the potential demands of a busy and increasingly complex world." To date, he has employed no less than seven "channels/intuitives" on a variety of projects as varied as ancient Egypt, future studies for the Japanese government, and how earthquakes are triggered. He employs what he calls an intuitive consensus approach. Using the information from the alleged sources of a number of channels, he attempts to find a consensus on whatever area the inquiring client is interested.

Kautz sees channeling as a "skill [that] can be gained by a variety of techniques. Fundamentally, it involves clearing out from the subconscious mind enough of the individual's fear-based incompleteness to allow information to flow from the superconscious clearly and without distortion." This process, for Kautz, is "the essence of spiritual growth, and the resulting information flow constitutes intuition."[77]

Of the various intuitives used by Kautz, probably the best known is Kevin Ryerson. Another is Jon Fox, who claims to channel "Hilarion," thought by some to be the same entity that comes through Maurice B. Cooke and Elizabeth Clare Prophet. Other channels include Verna Yater, a former consultant to federal agencies; art director Penny Peirce; Richard Ryal, who receives "Diya"; Debora Reynolds, a successful commercial designer and artist; and Richard Lavin, who first learned how to contact "Ecton" in a hypnosis course in Berkeley, California. All of these channels also operate independently of Kautz's center, as consultants, readers, and teachers.

The most recent crop of channels is drawn from every quarter—Hawaii, for example. Nancy Shipley Rubin of Honolulu, at one time a counselor in Arizona, now devotes full time to channeling "Aurorra," described in the handsome advertisements for her touring workshops as "a powerful female persona, a nonphysical entity" who refers to herself as "a pinnacle of wisdom." Fellow Hawaiian Alice Anne Parker, who has also attained the status of a professional channel, is a Phi Beta Kappa Columbia University graduate who learned to channel her source "Menos" in Great Britain, she says, while studying under the chief of an ancient order.

Jane Loomis, director of the Aquarian Center in Connecticut, and Tom Massarri of Los Angeles are just two of a number of channels who claim to receive the same "Seth" as did Jane Roberts. "Seth" groups have sprung up throughout the United States, as have groups centered around *A Course in Miracles* and around the entities "Michael," "Ramtha," "Emmanuel," and "Lazaris."

Probably the highest concentration of channels in any one area right now is in greater Los Angeles. Channeling researcher Margo Chandley recently produced a Los Angeles–area television series called "Future Classics," featuring interviews with thirteen local channels and demonstrations of their skills. Real-estate agent Elaine Rock has now turned publicity agent for at least eight channels.

One of the new Southern California stars is Penny Torres. Raised Catholic, a shy housewife in her late twenties married to a local policeman, Torres recently found herself able to channel a being calling itself "Mafu, an enlightened entity . . . from the Brotherhood of Light," last on earth as a first-century Greek. Although recent publicity has her presentations overflowing with patrons, Torres's critics accuse her of consciously or unconsciously trying to emulate the earlier and better-known channel, J. Z. Knight and her entity "Ramtha" (discussed earlier in this chapter). "Mafu's" channeling is peppered with the same repeated phrases—"indeed," "so be it," "that which is termed"—and the same stylized ways of talking to and touching those who come to her group sessions, as those displayed by "Ramtha."

Son of a Lakewood, Ohio, Congregational minister, Thomas Jacobson was, among other things, a Marine, a policeman, and a salesman before becoming, in his late thirties, a psychic counselor with his own radio program, crowded workshops, and considerable financial success. He has his source to thank for this: "Dr. Peebles," the spirit of either a nineteenth-century academic or a seventeenth-century physician, depending on whom you talk to. Jacobson was introduced to "Dr. Peebles" by his teacher, William Rainan, who is credited as the first to channel "Peebles."

Known for years as a successful psychic, lecturer, and author well versed in the paranormal, Alan Vaughan nevertheless thought channeling was nonsense until "Li-Sung" entered his life fours years ago. Vaughan, now fifty, says, "Most people can channel. It's like whistling a tune." He and his source "Li-Sung"—who claims to have been last incarnated as a small-town philosopher in eighth-century northern China—offer classes together in psychospiritual growth in North Hollywood. "I believe in a free spiritual marketplace," Vaughan says. "People have a right to believe in who they want. So long as it works in a positive way."[78]

Daryl Anka, a special-effects designer, channels a personality that calls itself "Bashar," an extraterrestrial from the planet "Essassani." "Bashar" has earned a reputation for providing some of the most analytical and technical material said to be channeled today.

As the movement spreads, channels are starting to teach, as well as demonstrate, channeling. Shawn Randall of Studio City, a free-lance writer and former children's drama teacher, has been receiving "Torah" for four years. A year ago, she felt herself guided by this being to begin offering classes in channeling, with "Torah" taking over the latter half of each session. So far, she counts more than a hundred students with whom she has succeeded. In Oakland, California, Sanaya Roman and Duane Packer (profiled in chapter 3) claim to have transformed hundreds into channels through their workshops and courses in recent years. Formerly from Berkeley, Kathryn Ridall, with a Ph.D. in counseling psychology, runs small training groups in Los Angeles, conducted by her and her entity "Diya" (said to be the same entity channeled by Richard Ryal of Kautz's group).

The Northern California Bay area has been the setting for one of the most interesting cases in all of contemporary channeling. While immersed in prayer one night in the early 1970s in Los Gatos (in the heart of Silicon Valley), scientist James J. Hurtak found himself bathed in light. Before him stood "Master Ophanim Enoch." Then Hurtak felt himself taken out of body and into regions from which he would receive information for years to come. Passing through "the star regions served by the Brotherhoods of Light," he describes being taken by "Enoch" to "Metatron, the Creator of Light in the outer universe . . . Metatron then took me into the presence of the Divine Father." The result of this initial encounter and later communications was *The Book of Knowledge: The Keys of Enoch*,[79] probably the single most scientifically rich and puzzling set of channeled material in modern times. Its mix of biblical (or Talmudic) style and highly complex scientific content drawn from many disciplines leaves readers both consternated and exhilarated.

Although an informal survey of channels in the United States finds a disproportionate number in California (a state that seems to incubate what later spreads its wings and flies off to become fashionable elsewhere), most states and dozens of foreign countries have their resident channels, sometimes in the dozens or hundreds. This emergence of new channels is reflected in the recent inception of two national journals devoted to publishing channeled material: *Metapsychology: The Journal of Discarnate Intelligence,* edited in Charlottesville, Virginia, by Tam Mossman, and *Spirit Speaks,* edited in Los Angeles by Molli Nickell. Both tend to feature previously unheard-from, up-and-coming channels. Mossman, earlier the editor at Prentice-Hall responsible for all the Jane Roberts "Seth" books, is himself a channel (see chapter 3).

To close this chapter on channeling as a modern phenomenon, I would like to provide you with the transcript of a remarkable interview that I conducted with "Lazaris," the entity reputed to be channeled by Jach Pursel. I hope that it will provide you with a sense of what it would be like for you to go to a contemporary channel and his or her entity and ask questions of them. In my choice of questions, I have tried to keep you as reader in mind. In its clarity and detail, some of this material is among the finest channeled information I have encountered—whatever the ultimate truth of its source may be.

AN INTERVIEW WITH "LAZARIS"

"Lazaris": State your name and age. We ask your name so as to tap into your vibration and your age . . . Of course, in our reality there is not time, and therefore the Jon Klimo who is twenty and the one who is sixty is right now. And therefore we tap into which vibration you are calling yourself . . . and therefore, perhaps, give you more precise and direct answers to the questions that would be more appropriate to you at this time in your early forties, as opposed to what you might hear in your sixties.

Question: What would you have to say to readers of this book?

"Lazaris": People are growing more rapidly than they've ever grown. They're opening the doors to a spirituality more profoundly than ever. ["Lazaris" briefly reviews social and spiritual awakening in the 1960s and 1970s.] We'd suggest that what was sought was an opening or an expanding spirituality, a *personal* spirituality, where people were and are

seeking a personal relationship with their God, or their God/Goddess/ All That Is. Spirituality, we would define, is simply your relationship with God. Therefore everybody is spiritual. Even the atheistic, existential people who say there is no God are still defining their relationship with the source . . . We would suggest that this spirituality is bursting forth.

And what is happening in that bursting forth is that there's a movement in two directions. There's a movement of those toward a fundamental Christian approach, and there's an unbelievable growth in that movement . . . The other direction is toward a metaphysical relationship, toward a metaphysical spirituality as opposed to a fundamentalist spirituality. In other words, people are moving in centrifugal energy away from this middle ground of nebulousness—of "we'll-just-have-to-wait-and-see, won't we" attitude—away from the intellectual noncommitment of science and of philosophy that has so long been predominant in your reality . . . We're moving into a more avant-garde sort of spirituality, a reaching out to the edge of reality, to the edge of possibility, and saying, "Is there something more?" and therefore moving in that direction. We would prefer those that are moving into that metaphysical spirituality as opposed to the fundamentalist spirituality, but we respect both.

It's an interesting matrix which is unfolding, and therefore people are interested, people are searching, people are seeking. That's why more of this channeling is happening. That's why more channels are "popping up" every day. And there are people who are reading your book, in that sense who are looking. And it is important for them to realize and get a glimpse of this sort of dynamic that we're talking about: a division and movement and pull and tug and expulsion and change that is happening in this sort of amoebic progression of this field of spirituality. And if people can put it in perspective that way, then they can realize that channeled entities can be helpful to them; and then there are those that they won't be able to relate to as well.

It's important at this time that people open themselves secondly to discernment, not just the heart but the mind as well. In your world there's such a criticism of thinking: Thinking's terrible. Thinking takes you away from your feelings. Yes, we would agree, if that means thinking alone . . . We would suggest here that feeling, alone, feeling without thought, feeling without the influence of any other part of you, similarly can lead you astray, can turn you into a spent dandelion—fluff floating in the cosmic breeze of reality, with no grounding, no understanding. No, we would suggest that what you're here to do is *combine* them to create a whole that is greater, a whole that is your intuition, a whole that is your discernment, a whole that is your ability, your inner guidance . . . And then bring these raw ingredients together to create a whole, to create a world that is your intuition, that is your creativity, that is your discernment at this particular time. As people are moving through the veil into realities that are yet unknown, it is important that they have this gyroscopic compass of beliefs, attitudes, thoughts and feelings, choices and decisions. And as people read and explore this phenomenon of channeling, don't leave these ingredients out. *Use* them.

Question: What do you have to say to the physical scientists who might read this book?

"Lazaris": Within this whole field of the paranormal—in which we would have to include ourselves—there are certain things that are provable . . . One thing that the parapsychologist can never prove absolutely, conclusively, is that there's life after death. Indeed, there can be those that experience and those that write of such experiences . . . But that is not conclusive; that's not absolute. It's important to realize that it's never been intended that life after death should be proved . . . It must be taken on inner knowledge, or faith, if you want to call it. You would prefer the term belief. The bridge from this world to that is *belief* . . . Similarly, physicists—more than ever the quantum physicists, those that are at the edge of their field—are proving, not just speculating, but proving mathematically, proving with the movement of subatomic particles, that your reality is an illusion . . . All the theories of the quantum are based on the fact that reality is a product of your thought.

The whole idea of double-blind experimentation [double-blind research requires that neither the experimenter nor the subject be allowed access to certain information critical to the experiment, in order to avoid the possible biasing of it] is proof in and of itself that you create your own reality. The concept being that because I *have* an expectation of what the results should be, because I've already made some decisions and choices, I am no longer objectively separate from the experiment. I am part of it, and therefore to protect that experiment from me, there must be a double blind. If there's not a double blind, there's not a scientist in this world who would accept the data. And yet, ask that scientist, "Do you create your own reality?" and the answer is "No." A massive contradiction.

So let's pursue love. Let's try to trap God on the blackboard. Let's try to catch him in an accelerator at Stanford. Let's try to catch God on a metal plate of lead as we smash atoms and bombard subatomic particles and as we divide light. But you won't find God in a laboratory. God, similarly, lies on the other side of belief. And the only way to get to God/Goddess/All That Is, is over the bridge of belief.

Similarly, regarding us as a consciousness, people can say, "That's just the channel. Look, that's just him. He's closed his eyes and he's talking in a funny voice. He's saying very nice things, but that's just him faking it." People can say that we are an aspect of the unconscious, or an aspect of the higher consciousness, or that we are a spirit force that indeed is communicating, that is ultimately nothing more than an enigma. Or you can say that indeed we are a part of the light, part of what is God, part of what is God/Goddess/All That Is. You can say any number of things, and you'll never be able to prove it conclusively, because truth—the channeled entity, just as God/Goddess/All That Is—lies on the other side of belief. It was never intended to be proved scientifically. You will never trap that energy in a laboratory . . . You can never catch the elusiveness of what lies on the other side of belief . . . If the thought of letting go of that life jacket is so frightening to you, then don't let go. We don't want you to believe in us. We don't want to put an arm around you and wrestle you to the ground and convince you who we are. We are there for those who are willing to cross the bridge of belief. And if, when they cross it, they find us and what we have to offer, we embrace them. If not, then we wish you well. And that's what we would suggest to the physical scientist.

Question: What are the limits of your knowledge?

"Lazaris": We don't think, we create thought. Thinking requires time, and we don't have time; and therefore we don't think, we just create thought as we go . . . We're growing as well. We're discovering ourself more and more totally. We're discovering God/Goddess/All That Is more fully, more completely. Yes, we have discovered it more than most physical beings, indeed all physical beings, but that's just a matter of position which doesn't ultimately exist at all. And therefore it's a constant expansion.

We like to work with people with questions. Come ask us questions. And part of that is that we want you to be responsible for this time we are together, and not just: "I'm going to sit here and open my heart and open my mind and let it be filled. You just do it to me, Lazaris." No, we want you to be a participant because we respect you. We don't think you're barnacles of the cosmos . . . We've not come into a position where we've been unable to talk to people, where we've come to a person who has come to us who has discussed things that we are simply unaware of . . . We may not have in your language the same vocabulary words, because we may run into certain vibratory frequencies that we have not aligned with in your reality . . . Therefore, we would suggest here that the beginning and the end of knowledge is available to us. The limit of our knowledge is really the limits of what a person would deal with. And therefore the question is not so much, "What is the limit of our knowledge," as it is "What's the limit of *your* knowledge?," and that will define ours.

Question: Can you describe a day in your life?

"Lazaris": First of all, we don't have days. But, more or less, we are always in a state of expansion. We have no boundary. We have no edge of who we are, and yet we know who we are. We know where we begin and end, although there is no form . . . We would perhaps describe ourselves as a continuous explosion and implosion of energy . . . To use the analogy, we are a speck of light. We call ourselves a spark of consciousness . . . We have always been and we will always be; and therefore, we are always constantly exploring our awareness, gathering data, gathering insight, gathering vibration and internalizing that vibration. We are always everywhere and nowhere simultaneously.

What we "do," to put it in your language, is that about one percent of our energy is devoted to interaction with the physical plane. We don't sit around on the channel's shoulder waiting to be asked questions . . . We also work with other consciousnesses that are no longer physical . . . so that they might grow, they might expand, they might continue their expression as they experience more. We also work with energy. Our "day" is filled with creating—with creating thought, attaching to that feeling, to creative feelings. And out of that we create universes, solar systems around certain galactic gases that are called stars. For the joy of it, for the expression of it, for the experience of it. We, in a sense, coagulate thought, coagulate feelings; to take these coagulated thoughts and feelings and place them somewhere in the physical plane of reality.

We also interact with others on our own levels. We are not alone in that regard. There are more nonphysical beings than there are physical beings . . . We are the only one from our level who has communicated, because our level is filled with elegance. Everything is done eloquently. There is no wasted moment . . . And so if there's one from our level communicating, there's no need for others . . . But there are others of us on our plane of reality who similarly don't have form, who don't have boundaries . . . We spend a good part of our "day" interacting, with merging one consciousness with another. We, in that sense, say, "Good morning. How are you?" We can say that in English to you: "How are you? It's good to see, Jon. How are you doing? What's happening in your reality? How's the book coming?" . . . In our reality, that interaction happens in silence. There are no mouths to speak, no words to say. There's thought to create . . . The intent is to reach out with love

. . . There are two sparks of consciousness that are everything and nothing simultaneously . . . And what happens is that there's a merging of the two and they become one for that brief "moment," and that's when the "Hello-how-are-you-what's-up?" occurs.

We "spend our time" constantly exploring joy, constantly stretching, in a sense, to see how much fun we can have today, how much joy can we experience today, how much wonder we can generate today, how much curiosity can we muster today. Doing that, we conclude the "day" with the realization: a lot! And therefore, let's do it again tomorrow, and spend the rest of eternity constantly exploring, stretching, searching for God absolutely and finally, knowing there's more to be found . . . It's not that you're searching for God and have not found it yet . . . No, you've found God, you've found pieces of God/Goddess/All That Is within you, outside of you, around you . . . Admittedly, there's always more treasure to be found. Therefore, much like you, we expand in search of God/Goddess/All That Is, in search of that full awareness of ourselves in relationship to, becoming that which is, God/Goddess/All That Is.

Question: Can you describe how communication takes place between you and the channel, Jach Pursel?

"Lazaris": We generate thoughts. We align those thoughts as bleeps and blips, which makes no sense without time . . . Basically how it works is that we create the thoughts as a mumbo jumbo, and we then project those thoughts through the planes of reality, as they're called, in whatever direction. Usually people think of "down," and so we project them "down," into denser levels. We project the conglomeration of all the thoughts and all the blips and bleeps we want to work with, and we project them down into a denser level and a denser level, and these enter in through the star system Sirius, to be quite specific with you, into the physical world.

Downstep, downstep—it's a downstep generator in electrical terminology—to downstep this specific vibration to where it reaches a certain density. Then those particular bleeps and blips, we can take that mass of energy and align it because it's dense enough to be able to be aligned. There's a concept of time that we can work with in that way. Then it enters into what we call the Mental Plane of reality, which is the highest of your lower worlds. And it goes into what we call the Causal Plane of reality, which is where cause and effect basically hang out. Not causes causing effects, but all the causes and all the effects sort of stockpiled, waiting for you to come along and hook them up . . . Sort of like going out and picking a Christmas present and wrapping it up and coming home and unwrapping it and, "Oh, I forgot what I gave myself here" . . . And it steps down to the Astral Plane into the physical. And then the antenna which is the channel—for that's what the channel is, an antenna—it comes into him, the blips and bleeps. They are amplified and they come out of here [points to Pursel's throat]. You hear the bleeps and blips and they vibrate against the ears and send a pattern of signals to the brain, and the brain is where these vibrations become words. In that sense, not a word has been spoken until the brain picks up the vibration and translates that frequency of vibration into sounds . . . We would suggest here that it is because of the particular alignment of the energy that it comes through as a particular accent.

Question: If we could understand how you interact with Jach Pursel's brain, could it help us understand how we interact with our own brains? Can you give more detail about the interaction of nonphysical consciousness with the physical plane?

"Lazaris": It's rather difficult to speak of it in those terms . . . There is an interface with light. What happens is that the vibration is down-stepped into the various planes. It comes to a certain place where it interfaces. That point might be called a conversion from love to light. Prior to the point that it is light, it is love. At a certain point that love translates into a vibrational frequency that is particle and wave simultaneously. For us to interact with you there must be a *you.* The love that we are gets downstepped to the point where it can be systematized and in sequential order, and thus is the love aligned. And then it is down-stepped further until it meets that level where it converts to light. It converts to wavelengths, wavelengths of light, where it becomes measured. It converts to particles when the frequency hits this instrument, which is what the channel is—vocal cords are an instrumentation. When the waves of light hit the instrumentation, they are converted simultaneously, instantly, into particles—particles, frequencies of vibration, which then are amplified.

And that's the quantum. That's the mysterious leap that occurs. And by the way, scientists have now seen the release of the electron without motivation. Without cause, they've seen effect . . . It's not gradually becoming and not becoming: it is and it is not. They've got conclusive evidence of the quantum. We would suggest here that what the quantum is, is the mystery . . . that's God/Goddess/All That Is. And so what happens is that the translation from love to light takes that quantum movement. It has no cause. It is pure effect, without cause . . . Then as the waves of light convert to particles, it is *caused* by observation—that's its cause, so to speak. But we would suggest the effect, and the intent is there first, and then it seeks a cause, it seeks observation. Once it finds observation, then it converts, from wave to particle, and then particle of light—which is the frequency of vibration then—one frequency comes through as sound, color, fragrance, matter. It just depends upon the harmonic that it chooses to function upon, or that you choose to experience it upon.

And therefore your participation is important in the communication in order to have it occur. Just as within yourself indeed the mechanism whereby those thoughts and energies that you pick up from your own higher Self, from your own Higher Being, get translated into words as you speak them out . . . The phenomenon that occurs is God, is that energy of conversion that is the quantum, or contained within the quantum. That's why it can never be discovered . . . The conversion requires observation by others, by yourself, in order to exist. Observation is critical to the existence of reality, the existence of communication, to the existence of interaction. That's the best answer we can give at this particular point, for there are not words to experience that particular conversion. There is only the understanding which comes beyond words, or between or under or over words. It's just an inner knowing that it does occur. And that's something where one has to get across the bridge of belief.

CONCLUSION

This first chapter has presented a brief survey of the groundswell of channeling activity and interest that has arisen in the last dozen years. In so doing, I hope some of the questions you may have brought with you to the reading of this book have been addressed. Those of you new to the phenomenon may have been wondering: What's all this I hear about channeling? What's been going on recently? Who are these characters I've been reading about in the media and seeing on television—"Seth," Findhorn, *A Course in Miracles,* Kevin Ryerson, "Ramtha," "Lazaris," "Michael"? What do they say? Is there anything to it? What about life after death? Are there other dimensions to existence than ours? And for those of you who may have had more knowledge of channeling coming into this book, I hope that this chapter enriched your understanding with greater breadth of examples and depth of detail?

In this brief perspective, I have focused only on the most visible stars in the contemporary channeling firmament. Hundreds of other channels, and their sources and messages, have had to go unmentioned. Otherwise the entire book could have been taken up with only the most recent cases. In truth, channeling is not some recent faddish phenomenon. It is as old as human nature. Throughout history, channels have gone under names as various as shamans, seers, and mediums, although the process involved appears to be the same. The channeling ability has manifested itself time and again in myriad circumstances, whether it has been the aboriginal elder, the maiden turned priestess, or the modern businessperson or homemaker. The fact that channeling, under whatever name, has taken place on this planet continually, among so many kinds of people and across so many cultures, leads to the speculation that channeling may be a potential ability we all possess.

We turn now to history to continue our exploration. In the process, we will see that the wealth of recent channeling is part of a much longer, fascinating theme that runs throughout the very heart of our human story.

2
CHANNELING AS A HISTORICAL PHENOMENON

Channeling has apparently been an essential part of the human story from its origins. It can be found in all times and across all cultures. Though it may take different forms or names in different lands, this universal, enduring, and still enigmatic phenomenon has permeated history, providing the wellsprings for virtually every spiritual path. For thousands of years, channeling has tantalized people with the prospect that physical existence is by no means all there is, and that the life of mind and spirit is more vast than most have led themselves to believe.

Throughout history and among varied peoples, channels have been named according to what they do. Besides the term *medium* and the more recent *channel*, other names have included shaman, witch doctor, healer, and medicine man in native cultures. They have also been called fortune-tellers, oracles, seers, soothsayers, savants, and visionaries. In religious contexts, they have been known as priests, gurus, prophets, saints, mystics, and holy ones. And in the esoteric schools they are called light workers, initiates, teachers, adepts, or masters. The majority of mainstream psychologists and psychiatrists would probably regard these channels as dissociated, delusional, suffering from multiple-personality disorder, schizophrenic, or simply as persons with runaway imaginations, or even as downright frauds.

PREHISTORIC AND PRIMITIVE ROOTS

In his most recent book, *Eternal Life?*, the controversial contemporary Christian theologian Hans Küng concludes that "belief in immortality has always existed."[1] Because we are limited in what we can infer of the practices and beliefs of prehistoric human beings, we need to turn our attention to preliterate primitive cultures. They are thought to share many of the characteristics of prehistoric cultures, as well as providing, in their own right, valuable insights into other possibilities of being human besides what so many of us prejudicially define as "civilized."

Such prehistoric or primitive practices and beliefs include the acceptance of a nonphysically based spirit or soul as the essence of people, as well as of animals, plants, and supposedly inanimate things like mountains and stars; survival of physical death by such a human essence; communication with these discarnate beings, as in ancestor worship; belief in, and communication with, various forces of nature, and with gods that personify aspects of Nature and human nature; the reception of information that leads to healing; and altered-state activity accompanying paranormal and mystical states and phenomena, resulting in enhanced understanding. Insofar as all of these things are believed to involve sources that lie beyond physical reality and the embodied human mind, they bear examination in our exploration of channeling.

In primitive cultural groups, usually one person is known as the shaman, healer, counselor, or wise one. This person is the official intermediary between his or her peers and the invisible spirit realm. In order to reach the altered or trance state needed for channeling activity, the shaman engages in chanting, singing, dancing, sleep deprivation, fasting, smoking herbs, hyperventilating, or ingesting psychoactive plants. Anthropologist and religious studies author Mircea Eliade, in his book *Shamanism: Archaic Techniques of Ecstasy,* cites the practice of trance communication with human and nature spirits in cultures as diverse as Siberian and South American, Tibetan and Finnish, West Indian and Korean.[2]

Exemplifying the striking similarities found across the world's preliterate peoples, here is a typical scene described by a field anthropologist in Africa, in which evil spirits are being expelled and good spirits invited in to heal a nervous disorder:

> The arifa [ceremony leader] dragged a half-paralyzed woman into the courtyard . . . The music suddenly gave a leap into a space out of this world . . . as if under the influence of an invisible helper . . . The possessing spirit shook her fragile frame like a gale in a winter tree, twisting and bending her until a spark of life and vitality rushed through her paralyzed limbs.[3]

In Bali, the shaman, known as "pedanta Siva," does breathing and chanting exercises, along with bell ringing, flower throwing, and ballet-like movements.

The bell was rung loudly for the last time and then suddenly stopped. The summoned deity had arrived and had entered the pedanta's body. The pedanta's movements now became strangely tense, as if directed by a being outside himself. Slowly he touched his forehead, throat and shoulders with sandalwood powder . . . then, raising his hands in a superbly hieratic pose he guided his soul from his lower body to his head; trembling violently, his eyes rolling in ecstasy, he began to recite in a deep, changing voice the prayers for the world. This is a trance state in which the subject does not completely lose consciousness and in which he brings himself back to his normal condition without external aid. For this he sprinkled water toward him "to bring his soul back to his stomach" and slowly removed his divine attributes.[4]

Consider next the case of the Akawaio Indians of Guyana, South America. The shaman is taught by his uladoi, or partner, who, according to tradition, may be either incarnate or a ghost teacher. The shaman's job is to attract sympathetic spirits and ghosts, to talk with them and engage them in matters at hand. He is thought to be able to contain a number of discarnate entities at one time. One native informant, Basil of the Kamarang River, speaks about the abilities of some local shaman: "Even if Joe's spirit, Joe akwalu, is in his body, other spirits can still come down and be inside him. With a real piai'chang, an eneogei (clairvoyant), the spirits stay down and all go back at the end of the seance, one after another."[5]

In the following description a contemporary African, who had been diagnosed by a local hospital as having a cancer that would require amputation of his leg, visits a witch doctor:

When he entered the kraal, she [the witch doctor] was already deep in trance whining and mewing like a lioncub. She had the skin of a lioness over her head, symbolizing the totem (lion) and that the medium was a woman . . . In trance the medium began to speak in an old man's husky voice, definitely not the voice of the woman . . . The presenting spirit identified himself as a chief under Mzilikazi the great Matabele king and said that he had died after the Europeans took Matabeleland . . . [A researcher] checked all this out and found it to be correct . . . In trance this witchdoctor who knew nothing about the African with cancer confirmed everything that the hospital had told him.[6]

There are thousands of such documented incidences of channeling phenomena among primitive peoples of all continents and all races. The similarities throughout are strong.

ANCIENT EGYPT, CHINA, JAPAN, AND INDIA

Contemporary clinical and research psychologist Robert Masters, who with his wife, philosopher and psychologist Jean Houston, directs The Foundation for Mind Research in Pomona, New York, is a leading authority on the mystical and paranormal in classic Egyptian culture. "Egypt," he reports, "is where, as far as we know, the use of trance in achieving mystical states and talking to the gods really began." He cites the use of "essential statues" as "kinds of teaching machines used by the priests and priestesses to put them into trance where they could see and communicate with the gods."

Under hypnosis, a number of the clients Masters has seen as a therapist have appeared to channel the Egyptian god Sekhmet. The correlation he has found among their reports, and comparisons of these reports to historical documents, have led Masters to believe that the same god or archetype that was channeled thousands of years ago may still be channeled today.[7]

The Egyptian culture in its prime stretched from 5000 B.C. for almost five thousand years. Its *Book of the Dead* establishes that the Egyptians shared a central preoccupation with death and postdeath phenomena.[8] In the middle of the second millenium, the pharaoh Amenhotep IV, later Akhnaton, experienced a transcendental vision in what could be speculated to be a channeling-type manner, and dedicated himself to bringing about a movement toward belief in "one ever-living God." However, because of the long-entrenched Egyptian predisposition toward polytheism, much of Akhnaton's teaching was forced underground. A succession of mystery schools arose around it with assorted esoteric activities and secret rites accessible only to a few.

The early Egyptians saw *du,* or breath, as the vital principle, which at death could separate from the body and become *ba,* or spirit. *Du* was the embodied soul; *ba* was the disembodied spirit. They also believed in a third, weaker aspect, the *ka,* a kind of etheric subtle-energy version of the physical body.

Since channeling is predicated on the assumption that living intelligence capable of communicating with us on earth can exist in dimensions—like the fabled afterlife—that are not physical as we know it, communications with deceased human beings compose the largest category of channeled sources thoughout history.

The Egyptians regarded the afterlife as similar to life on earth, with the *ba* spirit retaining the status and qualities that had been attributed to the embodied *du.* A member of the priestly caste, for example, would be expected to stay priestly in spirit, while the dead peasant would become a disembodied peasant. This theme—that one retains aspects of the earthly personality after death—is echoed by the majority of channeled reports to follow.

In many early cultures, *incubation* meant seeking information by way of dreams thought to contain dream-channeled material. The "Instructions from Merikare," traced to 2100 B.C. Egypt, for example, tell us that dreams are sent by the gods so that we may know what is true and what is to come.[9] Later, we will consider in more detail dream channeling, in which it is supposed that the sources transmit to the channel while he or she is dreaming. This channeled material is incorporated into the dream, and the channel must recognize it as such and decipher it upon awakening.

In a papyrus record dating from nearer to the time of Christ, a Greek in Egypt recalls his mother's experience when she was tending him through a serious illness. "A divine and terrifying vision came to her. There was someone whose height was more than human, clothed in shining raiment and carrying in his left hand a book." This was said to be the god Imhotep-Asclepius.[10] Such clairvoyant channeling involves visual rather than verbal information reception. It will be explored more fully in chapter 6.

The ancient Chinese called the soul *kuei,* meaning "to return." They also referred to the soul as *ch'i* (breath) and *ming* (light). In addition, their word *p'o* was similar in meaning to the Egyptian *du* (breath). One record notes: "The corporeal *(p'o)* goes downward, and the conscious *(ch'i)* is on high.

The Chinese believed that the soul continues to live after bodily death, but they were not sure where it went or what its awareness might be. During sleep, they believed, the soul left the body and wandered through dream realms. Early historical Chinese reports contain descriptions of channeling-like communication from such souls.

The earliest known instance of use of a planchette-type device (see chapter 6) occurred in China about four thousand years ago. It consisted of a branched bough held by two persons. The spirits were beseeched to "descend into the chi." The *chi,* a wooden affair much like the later divining rod, would begin to move about, spelling out the spirit message on paper or in thinly spread sand. This was an early case of what came to be known as automatism, in which the unconscious muscular impulses of those holding the device are reputed to be guided by discarnates.

Wu was the name given to full- and light-trance channels in China. They were seen as shamanlike individuals who could consort with the spirit world. In the first century A.D., Wang Ch'ung wrote:

Among men the dead speak through living persons whom they throw into a trance; and the wu, thrumming their black chords, call down the souls of the dead, which then speak through the mouths of the wu.

In the Han dynasty, Emperor Wu was known to consult a female *wu* whose source was a princess no longer in the physical world. Her message was written down and thereafter became the law. In 825, the ruler Li-Hsiang was told by a female *wu:* "I am a spectre-seer who can summon spirits by calling them hither . . . [some] have a vital spirit which is so vigorous and healthy it enables them to speak with men from time to time . . . [others are] so exhausted that they are obliged to employ me as their mouthpiece."[11]

The first written records of trance possession in Japan appear in the eighth century A.D. in chronicles describing life when the gods were said to dwell in Japan. On the grounds of the great national shrine of Ise, one of the temples is dedicated to "Rough August Soul," the spirit of the Sun Goddess in the form she assumes when she enters and mediates information and guidance through people. A number of early empresses were reported to become divinely possessed, delivering oracular messages. There were two kinds of shaman/channels: the *kan-nagi,* attached to the imperial court, and the *kuchiyose,* in local villages.

Also in the eighth century, the esoteric Shingon sect of Shintoism was founded, known for its oracular, mediumistic, and divinational practices. The shaman used a *gohei* wand, shaped like a zigzag of lightning, to call the god's body to descend into the medium. The *nakaza,* or trance voice of the god, followed.

The early Indians also worshiped the spirits of the dead. In one ancient text, it is written that "they [spirits] come flying like a winged bird," summoned by those still on earth. The Indian realm of demigods presented a strange brood: assorted supernatural spirits, demons, evil spirits, and sprites. Early Indian history contains a number of descriptions of the channeling of such entities. It was thought that channeling these characters could invite possession.

To this day, Indians believe that with death the human soul moves into a variety of human or animal bodies for additional lifetimes, according to the degree of evolution of that individual spirit. H. P. Blavatsky and Alice A. Bailey are just two of many recent teachers who reported having channeled information that echoes this Indian view of afterlife and reincarnation.

Once more, the importance of afterlife and reincarnation for us lies in this: at the center of the story much channeling has to tell us is the odyssey of the human spirit as a slowly evolving, death-surviving, multi-lived being operating within and transmitting from more than just the physical realm. And with this picture comes the belief that other, non-human, beings also exist within other dimensions and are capable of communicating to us.

THE GREEKS

Among the ancient Greeks, *keres,* spirits of the dead, were supposed to have escaped from the *pithos,* the jars used to house corpses. The spirits' habit of hanging around earthly dwelling places gave rise to a variety of rituals and incantations to get rid of them. Plato wrote, "There are many fair things in the life of mortals, but in most of them there are as it were adherent keres which pollute and disfigure them."[12] Sticky tar was even painted on doorways to catch the spirits' invisible flutterings.

By the time of the Thracian Dionysian cults of the sixth century B.C., which used possession-like entranced shamans as channels, there was a well-established pantheon of discarnate gods. These Dionysian channels have often been characterized as choosing the intoxicated right brain, rather than the Apollonian reasoning left brain, to connect with paranormal information and energy sources. Besides wine and other plant-based drugs, they used physical and mental practices to alter consciousness.

The Greeks saw the human spirit as having its origin in the divine heavens, unencumbered by the constraints of a physical body. As they told it, a kind of fall had led human beings to their earthly predicament. They pictured "wheels of generation" and "circles of necessity," not unlike the Indian world view. They practiced various Orphic, Dionysian, and Eleusian mystery rites in an ongoing attempt to seek communication, redemption, and return to that heavenly home. Philosophers Plato, Pythagoras, Heraclitus, and Plotinus held this doctrine.

In Hellenistic Greece, we find images of the nonphysical realms taking shape and terminology becoming more specific. *Angelos,* for example, came to mean messenger, either human or supernatural; *daimon* (later daemon or demon) meant divine being; *theos* was god. In the writing of Philostratus, we find Apollonius telling a young boy, "It is not you who behaves in an insulting manner, but the daemon who drives you to do this, and you don't know it."[13] Plato quotes Socrates as confiding, "By the favour of the Gods, I have since my childhood been attended by a semi-divine being whose voice from time to time dissuades me from some undertaking, but never directs me what I am to do."[14] Thus, 2000 years ago we seem to find the same cast of channeled characters—spirit guides, guardian angels, and assorted higher (and lower) nonphysical intelligences—as is the case today.

The Greeks also related channeling to prophecy, or *manteia*.[15] While Plato wrote in *Republic* and *Laws* that "prophecy is the noblest of the arts," he speaks against necromancy, the art of predicting the future by communicating with the dead.[16] Socrates remarked, "the special gift of heaven . . . prophecy is a madness, and the prophetess at Delphi and the priestess of Dodona, when out of their senses have conferred great benefits on Hellas . . . but when in their senses, few or none."[17] Prophecy is an aspect of channeling to the extent to which there is either an identified paranormal source or a nonidentified general source for the prophetic material. The Greek *manteia,* for example, were known to involve both kinds.

A form of sleep or dream channeling, in which the soul in sleep is freed to leave the body and communicate with higher beings, dates back to the Orphic school. The body sleeps, but the soul is wide awake and possesses what today we would call extrasensory perception (more on sleep and dream channeling in chapter 6). From this Orphic school arose the most visible and famous of the Greek channels: the oracles.

The oracles were individuals who would go into a trance or a milder altered state of consciousness in order to access telepathic, clairvoyant, or clairaudient powers. It is recorded that some could allow their systems to fall under the influence of a particular discarnate spirit, which would then speak through them. Their best-known paranormal power was prophecy, or the demonstration of precognitive abilities. Sometimes oracles ingested herbs, teas, potions, wine, or vapors to facilitate the transition into a channeling mode. Oracles were often situated in caves where communication was supposed to occur with spirits of the underworld through cracks in the rock:

> The pythia [female medium] at Delphi received her inspiration in historic times from Apollo . . . [She] became ecstatic by inhaling a vapor that rose through a fissure in the earth . . . the god penetrated her body and forced her to yield to his guidance . . . the divine afflatus . . . she succumbed and uttered words that were not her own but those of the god who controlled her.[18]

In another instance of the trance oracle, we find the classic description of full-trance channeling:

> A female automatist will suddenly begin to speak in a deep male voice; her bearing, her gesture, her facial expression are abruptly transformed; she speaks of matters quite outside her normal range of interests, and sometimes in a strange language or in a manner

quite foreign to her character; and when her normal speech is restored, she frequently has no memory of what she said.[19]

There is ample evidence that some versions of the Ouija board were in operation in early Greek times. As early as 540 B.C., Pythagoras was holding seances in his sect in which "a mystic table, moving on wheels, glided toward signs, which the philosopher and his pupil Philolaus, interpreted to the audience as being revelations supposedly from the unseen world."[20]

The concept of the muse (or muses) is central to channeling. In Greek mythology, the muses were goddesses who inspired human creativity. In many classical views, the muse gives the poet his song, for example, and may even sing through his lips. More generally, the muse has long been considered the personification of a guiding genius or principal source of inspiration. To the extent to which this guidance or source is seen as falling outside of the individual's own self or physical reality, it fits the description of channeling. As James Fadiman points out, "Remember, as the Greeks differentiated worthwhile dreams from useless dreams, they also said that the muses are a way of understanding that there are external forces that support certain activities if you are in tune with them. So, in a way, the muses are early channels."[21]

OTHER EARLY CULTURES

Throughout the British Isles, the Celtic bards had a time-honored reputation for channeling. Animals and plants were said to act as vehicles for messages from the nonphysical realm. Macculuch, noted scholar of the religion of the ancient Celts, describes a medium going into full trance at least three thousand years ago.[22]

Among the early Babylonian and Assyrian peoples, the gods were thought to communicate by signs, either spontaneously or provoked. Spirits of the dead, as well as the gods, could be consulted. Revelations were said to come through divinely inspired men, priestesses, and dreams (incubation).

In the Arab world, somewhere during the tenth to sixth centuries B.C., depending on which historian you go by, the fabled prophet Zoroaster put together the *Avesta* text—various apparently channeled explanations and guidelines pertaining to the spirit world and to earthly existence. It became the basis of a religion that still exists.

The Islamic tradition began in the early seventh century A.D. when the prophet Muhammad received a rich assortment of visionary material from the divine presence Allah, whom he called the Lord. According to his own and others' accounts of Muhammad's experiences, he would satisfy our description of being a channel. He received his teachings by dream, by waking vision, and by voice. At one point, "an angel in human form," some say the angel Gabriel, called Muhammad's name. Through the angel, so the story goes, Allah showed him writing that he was able to read and later recall, although until that time he had been totally illiterate. Much of the books of the Koran, the bible of Islam, stemmed directly from Muhammad's channeled material.

The Arabs designed a system to account for the operations of the *nafs,* the breath of the undying spirit of each individual. In sleep or in an altered state, when the soul of the one unconscious is no longer in charge, the body could be entered and manipulated by another spirit. When this possession occurred, the spirit was known as *jinn,* from which our words *genie* and *genius* derive.

The early Semite Hebrews thought that the spirits of the dead possessed greater awareness and knowledge than those still on earth. While the nonphysical domain was clearly supernatural for the Hebrews, they believed quite a mix of spirits inhabited it. For example, although the word *elohim* was later capitalized to become a name for God, it was first used variously to denote powers, ghosts, gods, the human dead, and angel-like beings.

THE RISE OF MONOTHEISM

Around 1000 B.C., monotheism moves to the center of spiritual life, with its belief in a single transcendental spirit called Yahweh (or Yaweh), later known as Jehovah, or The Lord God, to whom the people of Israel were bound. The Mosaic doctrine arose from the prophet Moses, who might be seen as a channel for Yahweh. Because of the message "Thou shalt have no other gods before me," the concept of one God gained the unqualified respect and allegiance of an increasing number of people. In this period, the various traditions typically did not deny the existence of discarnate spirits or other nonphysical, nonhuman entities. Rather, they simply forbade the worship of any but the one God.

Prophets of the new monotheism believed they had a guarantee for their source, the singular transcendental Being, and that its truth would come only through those people who had been selected by Yahweh, such as Moses and the prophets to follow. False prophets, then, came to mean channels who falsely claimed to mediate the voice of the one God. Perhaps some of them were genuine channels whose sources were beings other than the authorized one God.

Thus we find hundreds of instances in the Old Testament of Yahweh channeling to his chosen in order to spread his word to the people of Israel. For example, dozens of passages in Leviticus and Numbers begin, "And the Lord spake unto Moses, saying . . . " Also, there are many self-identifying statements of the following kind: "I am the Lord your God."[23]

Moses could be considered the first channel to become a prophet of Yahweh, with his voices and visions, burning bushes, and tablets. David followed around 1000 B.C., then Solomon, Samuel, Daniel, Elijah, Elisha, Ezekiel, Jeremiah, Isaiah, John the Baptist, and a number of lesser lights throughout the millennium before Christ. Over and over, these individuals reported that "the word of the Lord came also unto me, saying . . . " They either heard words clairaudiently or saw visions clairvoyantly that they believed came directly from the Lord. Undisputably, each experienced and then taught "under inspiration." In Jeremiah, for example, we watch the unfolding of a new kind of channel vehicle:

> Then the word of the Lord came unto me, saying, Before I formed thee in the belly, I knew thee . . . and I ordained thee a prophet unto the nations . . . and whatsoever I command thee thou shalt speak. Be not afraid of their faces: for I am with thee to deliver thee, saith the Lord. Then the Lord put forth his hand, and touched my mouth. And the Lord saith unto me, Behold, I have put my words in thy mouth.[24]

Anything other than the word of the one God became suspect under the new system. A recurring theme arose of tension between many individuals capable of channeling and the chosen few who claimed that they alone spoke the word of the Lord. The assortment of local gods, spirit guides, higher Selves, and discarnate humans that served the channels who were not prophets were called familiar spirits; the channels were deemed wizards, witches, and worse. The Bible contains many warnings like these:

> Thou shalt not suffer a witch to live . . . There shall not be found among you any . . . that useth divination, or an observer of times, or an enchanter, or a witch, or a charmer, or consulter with familiar spirits, or a wizard, or a necromancer. For all that do these things are an abomination unto the Lord . . . Regard not them that have familiar spirits, neither seek after wizards, to be defiled by them: I am the Lord your God . . . And when they say unto you, Seek unto them that have familiar spirits, and unto wizards that peep, and that mutter: should not a people seek unto their God?[25]

In the Witch of Endor case (1 Sam. 28), Saul, unable to get information he needs from Yahweh, and having previously outlawed mediums, secretly seeks out the dead Samuel by way of "a woman who hath a familiar spirit."

> And the woman said unto Saul, I saw gods ascending out of the earth. And he said unto her, What form is he of? And she said, An old man cometh up; and he is covered with a mantle. And Saul perceived that it was Samuel . . . And Samuel said to Saul, Why hast thou disquieted me, to bring me up?

As spirit worship and cults of the dead gave way to the monotheism of Yahweh, or Jehovah, channeled sources came to be seen as manifestations either of the Lord and his own, or of Satan and his own. But belief in the separate existence of spirits never died out completely. Alleged discarnate humans and familiar spirits continued to be channeled. As late as the third century A.D., the historian Tertullian remarked that "the world was still crowded with oracles."[26]

Today a large percentage of the world's population calls itself Christian, and the Church's views have changed little with regard to the channeling phenomenon: if a reported occurrence is not a certifiable contact from God or his chosen ones, then it is seen as most likely a contact with lower spirits, whose trustworthiness is contested.

Throughout history the major religions have tried to monopolize the channeling of "the one truth." More broadly, there has always been a parallel struggle over who will decide what to make of the phenomenon in general, whether it be a priest calling it the word of God or a scientist calling it hallucinations or wish fulfillment. Those who channel say they experience for themselves profound evidence of their source material. Such firsthand experience appears to be a matter of personal revelation for them. But those who take on the role of authority try to decide for others what is really going on with channels. We should weigh carefully the criteria used for deciding whether someone is communicating with a nonphysical being or with God, if only because of the presence of competing schools of interpretation and judgment.

JESUS CHRIST

One of the chief assumptions of this book is that channeling includes most major recorded spiritual communication between physical and nonphysical beings. The earlier prophets and later saints of the world's religious traditions may have been channels of extraordinary spiritual import.

Few Christians, however, would be willing to grant that Jesus was merely a channel. The contention or faith remains that he was not just the Son of God but that he was God in human form. His would not be a case of trance mediumship in which the human body was taken over and used by God. For, according to doctrine, in Jesus' case nothing came through an intermediary; the channel and the source were one. Yet to read Jesus' words sometimes gives the eerie feeling that he was sent to earth to channel guidance from "home" or from a "parent" spirit.

The picture that emerges from Christ's words in the Bible is strikingly similar to the channeled material of the last 150 years: Jesus was spirit incarnated for a particular lifetime. He took his identity and guidance from his parent source and asked that we identify with him and with his relationship to his (and our) Father. At the same time, an occult hierarchy of various levels and densities of spirit, full of revelation, voices, and visions, can be traced. For example, in Matthew, Christ says, "For it shall be given you in that same hour what ye shall speak. For it is not ye that speak, but the Spirit of your Father which speaketh in you." On another occasion, as Jesus spoke, "behold a bright cloud overshadowed them: and behold a voice out of the cloud, which said, This is my beloved Son, in whom I am well pleased."[27] In Luke we read: "My mother and my brethren are those which hear the word of God and do it."[28] And in John we find the richest assortment of material:

> Hereafter ye shall see the heaven open, and the angels of God
> ascending and descending upon the Son of man . . . The words
> that I speak unto you, they are spirit . . . Ye are from beneath; I
> am from above: ye are of this world: I am not of this world . . . I
> do nothing of myself; but as my Father hath taught me, I speak
> these things. And he that sent me is with me . . . He that is of God
> heareth God's words . . . The Father is in me, and I in him. . .
> Whatsoever I speak therefore, even as the Father said unto me, so I
> speak . . . In my Father's house are many mansions . . . The words
> that I speak unto you I speak not of myself: but the Father that
> dwelleth in me, he doeth the works . . . For I have given unto them
> the word which [the Father] gavest me.[29]

In the famous experience of Saul on the road to Damascus, in Acts 9:3−7, it appears that Saul is channeling like the earlier prophets, only now the source is the discarnate Jesus:

> And suddenly there shined round about him a light from heaven:
> And he fell to the earth, and heard a voice saying unto him, Saul,
> Saul, why persecutest thou me? And he said, Who are you, Lord?

And the Lord said, I am Jesus whom thou persecutest . . . Arise, and go into the city, and it shall be told to thee what thou must do. And the men journeying with him stood speechless, hearing a voice, but seeing no man.

Saint John the Divine, in the book of Revelation, written about A.D. 68, also seems to have channeled Jesus, among an assortment of other characters, constituting the richest biblical case of channeling:

I was in the Spirit on the Lord's day, and heard behind me a great voice, as of a trumpet, saying, I am Alpha and Omega, the first and the last: and, What thou seest, write in a book . . . And I turned to see the voice that spake with me. And being turned, I saw seven golden candlesticks; And in the midst of the seven candlesticks one like unto the Son of man . . . And he laid his right hand upon me, saying unto me, Fear not . . . I am he that liveth, and was dead; and, behold, I am alive for evermore . . . Write the things which thou hast seen . . . and the things which shall be hereafter.[30]

In 1 John 4:1–3, the disciple John returns to emphasize the use of discernment in receiving channeled-type information: "Beloved, believe not every spirit, but try the spirits whether they are of God: because many false prophets are gone out into the world." What John prescribes is to this day held by many to be the best means for observers to discriminate and interpret channeled material, and to protect themselves against the encroachment of "lower" spirits.

Part of the Christian legacy is the Holy Spirit, sometimes called the Holy Ghost, which is said to appear as a nonphysical spiritual presence that is also part of the one God and capable of being channeled.

In the cases of Peter and Paul in the New Testament, the nonphysical realm has become "heaven," discarnate beings "angels," and almost any channeled spirit is "The Holy Spirit" or "The Holy Ghost."

And suddenly there came a sound from heaven as of a rushing mighty wind, and it filled the house . . . And they were filled with the Holy Ghost, and began to speak with other tongues, as the Spirit gave them utterance . . . While Peter thought on the vision, the Spirit said unto him, Behold, three men seek thee . . . [and] the Holy Ghost fell on all them which heard the word.[31]

Such speaking in tongues, or glossolalia, is still practiced in many fundamentalist churches to this day.

Finally, Paul, in 1 Corinthians, provides organized Christian religion's definitive exposition of the individual's relationship to the Spirit, or to the nonphysical realm in general:

> But God hath revealed them [words of wisdom] unto us by his Spirit . . . Now we have received, not the spirit of the world, but the spirit which is of God . . . Now concerning spiritual gifts, brethren . . . there are diversities of gifts, but the same Spirit . . . And there are differences of operations, but it is the same God which worketh all in all. But the manifestation of the Spirit is given to every man . . .
>
> What? came the word of God out from you? or came it unto you only? If any man think himself to be a prophet, or spiritual, let him acknowledge that the things that I write unto you are the commandments of the Lord . . . Wherefore, brethren, covet to prophesy, and forbid not to speak with tongues.[32]

THE DARK AGES TO THE MID-NINETEENTH CENTURY

During the Dark Ages, countless cases of obsession and possession were reported, usually involving "unclean" or evil spirits. Possession and obsession appear to be forms of spontaneous, or unintentional, channeling, in which unevolved entities are said to infiltrate an embodied person against his or her will. Many works of art depicted macabre possessing spirits known as incubi and succubi. Those who practiced divination of various kinds, like scrying (see chapter 6), and those who worked with evil spirits were referred to as the Specularii. The Christian Church considered them punishable heretics. Outside of the orthodox religious systems, local seers, witches, wizards, and other mediumistic types held sway. While the organized Christian Church did its best to keep control with its magnificent cathedrals, crusading armies, and brutal inquisitions, this was mostly a time of spiritual anarchy, superstition, and fear.

Even in those harsh and undistinguished times, monasteries of Christian monks and nuns showed signs of channeling, spiritual or otherwise. Saint Odile in seventh-century France supposedly received detailed material that seemed to point toward events that later came to pass, including air power and the rise of Hitler:

> The time is come when Germany shall be called the most bellicose upon the earth. The epoch is arrived when from her bosom shall arise the terrible man who will make war on the world . . . The

conqueror will start from the banks of the Danube . . . His arms shall be flaming and the helmets of his soldiers covered with spikes which will throw off sparks, while their hands brandish flaming torches . . . He will win victories on land, by sea, and even in the air. For his warriors will be seen, winged, in unimaginable career riding up into the firmament to catch the stars in order to hurl them down on cities from one end of the universe to the other, igniting great fires.[33]

In the twelfth-century, Merlin, the half-legendary Welsh-British bard and seer connected to King Arthur's court, was reputed to be capable of many feats of mental and physical channeling. Elsewhere in Britain, Scottish channels such as Thomas the Rhymer were known for their second sight.[34]

Also in the twelfth-century, Saint Hildegarde of Bingen reported that an inner voice commanded her to write down what it told her. On being presented with this material, Pope Eugene II pronounced it the voice of God. Hildegarde also was known to have fallen into possessed spells during which she produced glossolalia, or speaking in tongues.

In the fourteenth century, Richard Rolle of Hampole channeled enough material to become known as the father of English mysticism. In his book *The Fire of Love,* he includes descriptions of a special kind of clairaudient channeling later called nad, or transcendental music, by D. Scott Rogo. "When I was sitting in the same chapel," Rolle recounts, "I heard above me the noise of harpers, or rather of singers . . . I perceived within me, I know not how, a melody and a most delightful harmony from heaven."[35]

The early fifteenth century saw the celebrated case of Joan of Arc. The thirteen-year-old girl heard her name called three times by a disembodied voice as she stood in a blaze of light: "Joan, go to France where there is a great pity."[36]

The clairvoyant and precognitive material of the later fifteenth-century semi-mythical English medium Mother Shipton also appears to have come true. Like a number of other prophetic mediums before and after her, she chose to record what she received in poetic form:

Carriages without horses shall go,
And accidents fill the world with woe.
Around the earth thoughts shall fly
In the twinkling of an eye . . .
In the air men shall be seen
In white, in black, in green;
Iron in the water shall float
As easily as a wooden boat.[37]

Joseph Karo, a late-fifteenth-century Spanish Talmudic scholar of the Kabbalist mystery school, was one of a number of Jewish mystic channels reported throughout history. His source was called "maggid," a term given to an agent of celestial speech and the spirit of *Mishnah,* a Jewish holy book. As one historian put it, "Karo would lose his ordinary frame of mind and speak in a changed voice."[38]

Perhaps the best known channel of things to come is Michel de Nostradamus. Born in 1503 with "certain astral aspects which predisposed him to this work," he was reported to sit nightly looking into a bowl filled to the brim with water, listening at the same time to what he thought was his familiar spirit. The apparent accuracy of what he channeled made him a resource for kings and various other leaders throughout Europe. Here, in 1555, he counsels his son about channeling:

> Some persons may arrive to whom God almighty may be released to reveal by imaginative impression some secrets of the future . . . When a certain power and volitional faculty came upon them, as a flame of fire appears, they grew inspired, and were able to judge of all inspiration, human and divine alike . . . But the perfect knowledge of causes cannot be acquired without divine inspiration; since all prophetic inspiration derives its first motive principle from God the creator . . . For the human understanding, being intellectually created, cannot penetrate occult causes.[39]

At the same time in Spain, two of the greatest Christian mystics, Saint Teresa of Avila and Saint John of the Cross, felt themselves opening to transcendental influence. "While I was beseeching our Lord today that he would speak through me," Saint Teresa begins her *Interior Castle,* "I began to think of the soul as if it were a castle made of a single diamond or of very clear crystal . . . I commend myself to the Holy Spirit, and by Him from this point onward to speak for me."[40]

In *Ascent of Mount Carmel* and *Dark Night of the Soul,* Saint John articulates the accepted church doctrine regarding channeling, but also attempts to describe how difficult it can be to stay true to one's source:

> Although it is the spirit itself that works as an instrument, the Holy Spirit oftentimes aids it to produce and form those true reasonings, words and conceptions. And thus it utters them to itself as though to a third person . . . When the understanding communicates in this way with the Divine Spirit by means of this truth, it begins to form within itself, successively, those other truths which are connected with that whereon it is thinking, the door being opened to

it and illumination being given to it continually by the Holy Spirit Who teaches it . . . nevertheless, deception may, and does, frequently occur . . . for inasmuch as this illumination which it receives is at times very subtle and spiritual, so the understanding cannot attain to a clear apprehension of it.[41]

George Fox, born in 1642 in Leicestershire, England, is a good example of a visionary channel who paved the way for a new religious movement—the Friends, or Quakers, as they would later come to be known. Fox's oft-repeated words, "The Lord opened unto me," echo those of Ezekiel, "And the hand of the Lord was upon me":

As I was walking in a field on a first-day morning, the Lord opened unto me that being bred at Oxford or Cambridge was not enough to fit and qualify men to be ministers of Christ and I wondered at it, because it was the common belief of people. But I saw it clearly as the Lord opened it unto me, and I was satisfied and admired the goodness of the Lord, who had opened this thing unto me that morning.[42]

Cagliostro and Cazotte, two eighteenth-century French prophet-seers, had an impact on the courts and decision making of their day. They provided, for example, detailed and lucidly channeled information of the impending French Revolution.

One of the most curious eighteenth-century European channels was Comte de Saint Germain, also known as Prince Rakoczy of Hungary. Several modern channels claim they are vehicles for his "ascended master" spirit. His ongoing connection to channeling is more complex and far-reaching than that of most other historical individuals.

One of the true giants of channeling literature appeared in the eighteenth century: the Swedish scientist turned mystic Emanuel Swedenborg. A middle-aged, well-respected scientist with nearly one hundred publications to his credit, Swedenborg seemed in every way a well-adjusted professional. He wrote, at age fifty-six, that he began to have extremely vivid and prolonged visions, voices, sojourns, and visitations. By his own prolific accounts, he probably spent more hours channeling than anyone before him. Time and again, he reported, angels visited him and took him in his spiritual body into the nonphysical realm, including the classic heaven and hell, giving him guided tours. In the remaining years of his life, he wrote (with all the analytical care and descriptive prowess of his earlier technical works) at least sixteen major books on these experiences, including *Heaven and Hell, Divine Love and Wisdom,* and *Arcana Coelestia.* In his preface to *Heaven and Hell,* he stated simply the facts as he saw them: "Today's churchman knows almost nothing about heaven, hell, or his own life after death."[43]

The following excerpts shed some light on channeling:

I am well aware that many will say that no one can possibly speak with spirits and angels so long as he lives in the body . . . [but] I have seen, I have heard, I have felt . . . When spirits begin to speak with man, he must beware lest he believe in anything; for they say almost anything; things are fabricated of them, and they lie . . . And as I desired to know in what manner these men [biblical prophets] were actuated by spirits, I was shown by means of a living experience. To this end I was for a whole night possessed by spirits who took possession of my body . . . A thousand times I have seen them [disembodied human spirits], heard them, and talked with them—even about the fact that people in the world do not believe that spirits are what they are . . . The spirits were heartsick at the persistence of this ignorance on earth, especially within the church.[44]

During the same period, Joseph Smith in the United States claimed to have channeled material from an angel named Moroni. This experience led him to seek out revelatory tablets buried in upstate New York and then to lead his people west to the "promised land." The contents of these tablets and his interpretations of them became *The Book of Mormon* and the foundation of the Mormon church, or the Church of Jesus Christ of the Latter-day Saints.

On the other side of the world, in the final quarter of the nineteenth century, a twenty-eight-year-old Japanese peasant girl was reported to have received divine revelation in a trance state lasting three days. Afterward, Miki Nakayama was honored by those Japanese who followed the Tenrikyo sect as a god-possessed saint, "a living shrine of the God Tenri." Her sect was an extension of the ancient channeling-oriented Shingon sect, which in turn had branched off from Shintoism. The following is a sample of what Nakayama channeled from "Tenri-O-no-Mikoto," or "God the Parent":

I am the Creator, the true and real God. I have the Preordination for this Residence. At this time I have appeared in this world in person to save all mankind. I ask to let Me have your Miki as My living Temple . . . What I think now is spoken through Her mouth. Human is the mouth that speaks, but Divine is the mind that thinks within. Listen attentively to Me! It is because I have borrowed Her mouth, while I have lent My mind to Her.[45]

THE SPIRITUALIST ERA

Except for the present, there has never been as rich a period of channeling activity and interest in it as occurred during the mid-nineteenth century under the name *Spiritualism* (usually termed *Spiritism* in Europe). What we now call channeling was called mediumship during the Spiritualist era, and channels were called mediums. The sources being contacted, almost without exception, were considered to be the spirits of deceased human beings. Some authorities still make a distinction between the terms *channeling* and *mediumship,* with the latter reserved for communication only from deceased human beings, while *channeling* covers communication with all other kinds of intelligences not associated with embodied minds or with physical reality. Throughout this exploration I have chosen to include mediumship within my definition of channeling.

The Spiritualist period represented a powerful resurgence of activity and interest in channeling. What accounted for this worldwide movement? Did particular cultural factors soften the ground? By the mid-nineteenth century—the start of the Spiritualist era—there was a loosening of and a turning against the results of the materialistic and rationalistic world view that had been dominant since the seventeenth-century Enlightenment, leading to a disposition toward transcendental or nonmaterial realities.

Then, too, the charisma of the mediums themselves was to some degree responsible for the near-cultlike movement that grew up around them. In addition, the printed media was reaching the height of its power and was able to spread the newest fads and scientific discoveries farther, wider, and faster than ever before. Further, just as the banning of a book may only lead more people to seek it out, so the vehement opposition to mediumship by traditional organized religion, and by the majority of the press, academia, and scientists of the day, meant that many others were led toward, not turned away from, the phenomenon. Finally, the human story is punctuated with both local and global periodic cycles of movement toward the physical realm as the primary reality, or toward inner, or spiritual, superordinate realities and truths. Spiritualism and our present wave of channeling activity would appear to be two of the most wide-scale moves in the latter direction.

Several cases set the stage for the Spiritualist era. The documented work of Frau Frederica Hauffe, the German Seeress of Prevorst, foreshadowed the great influx of channeling activity that was to sweep the world in the 1850s.[46] Until her death in 1824, Frau Hauffe heard spirits and went into trance voice on their behalf. Her form of physical mediumship (chapter 6), consisting of seemingly intelligent raps and knockings, as well as the subject matter of her channeled material, were typical of what was to follow.

Near pastor Edward Irving's Church of Scotland in England, a study group known as the Albury Prophets was sharing spirited readings and interpretations of the Bible. In July 1830, almost everyone in the group began to speak in tongues and demonstrate other channeling and possession behavior. Soon this activity had spread to Irving's congregation. Argument and competition followed: Who was channeling what? Whom to listen to? Whose source was real? Which interpretation to trust?[47]

In the United States, the religious group of gentle and unassuming folk called the Shakers had been formed. In 1837 a strange and colorful phenomenon spread through these usually somber, straitlaced people. Spirits claiming to be discarnate American Indians sought to use Shaker community members periodically to reestablish contact with earthly life. These alleged spirits asked permission first and did not enter the Shakers' bodies without being invited. It was reported that an entire tribe at a time would take over, whooping, singing, dancing, eating, and conversing with one another in their native language.[48]

The man who would come to be called the first prophet of Spiritualism, Andrew Jackson Davis, was born in New York in 1826. Like Joan of Arc and George Fox before him, he claimed to receive his first channeling while out walking in a field. During these early experiences, he thought he was in communication with the spirits of Galen, the ancient Greek healer, and Swedenborg, who had died fifty years earlier.

Davis's multivolume published work was given the name *The Harmonial Philosophy*. It is an odd mix of perennial wisdom and original detail in an uneven, archaic style, with grammatical and factual errors reflecting the channel's own limited education.

Giving grounds for prophet status, Davis wrote, "a truth that spirits commune with one another while one is in the body and the other in the higher spheres . . . will ere long present itself." And a year later, the very night before the Fox sisters bade in the Spiritualist era, we find: "About daylight this morning a warm breathing passed over my face and I heard a voice, tender and strong, saying, 'Brother, the good work has begun—Behold, a living demonstration is born.' "[49]

All of the channeled material of this period, including Davis's, describes the basically spiritual rather than physical nature of human beings and of the universe at large. It is rich with descriptions of the afterlife dimension provided by the disembodied human beings said to inhabit it. The sources offer suggestions for leading a more aligned, healthy, and fulfilling life in accordance with the truths of this larger spiritual reality as they see it. Guidance is offered for daily problems and possibilities. The majority of the Spiritualist material purports to be detailed private communications from deceased loved ones and relatives, directed at—and of interest only to—those seeking them out by way of the services of mediums.

The modern renaissance of mediumship that has been labeled the Spiritualist movement was launched in 1848 in a modest Hydesville, New York, farmhouse belonging to John Fox. In March, his wife and two young daughters noticed strange sounds in the house. Before long, the entire household witnessed rappings, knockings, and moving furniture. One evening, after the family had gone to bed, the wind picked up and the house was loud with a variety of inexplicable sounds. John Fox went downstairs to secure the window sashes, which were flapping. Because of all the commotion, the rest of the family accompanied him. The younger daughter noticed that each time her father shook the sash, there was an apparently connected knocking within the wall. Mrs. Fox described what followed:

> My youngest child Cathie [Kate] said, "Mr. Splitfoot, do as I do," clapping her hands. The sound instantly followed her with the same number of raps. When she stopped the sound ceased for a short time. Then Margaret said in sport, "No, do just as I do. Count one, two, three, four," striking one hand against the other at the same time; and the raps came as before . . . I then thought I could put a test that no one in the place could answer. I asked the noise to rap my different children's ages, successively. Instantly each one of my children's ages was given correctly. I then asked: "Is this a human being that answers my questions so correctly? There was no rap. I asked: "Is it a spirit? If it is, make two raps." Sounds were given . . . I then said: "If it is injured spirits make two raps"; which was instantly made, causing the house to tremble . . . I ascertained by the same simple method that it was a man, aged 31 years, that he had been murdered in this house and his remains buried in the cellar.[50]

As the night wore on, the Foxes excitedly summoned neighbors to bear witness. As the days passed, the rappings and knockings continued, and people came from farther away as word of mouth spread through the countryside. A neighbor, after watching the minimal code used thus far, suggested that a more precise language be established by saying the alphabet quickly and asking the spirit to strike at the appropriate letter, then repeating the alphabet for the next letter, and so on through each word and sentence.

Now the alleged entity was able to spell out more of his story. His name, he said, was Charles B. Rosma, and he was an itinerant peddler who had been murdered on the premises and buried under the house. When digging was undertaken, human bones were found. Fifty-six years later, another excavation unearthed the peddler's tin box and other bones and belongings. Today the Fox house, along with Rosma's remains, are displayed in nearby Lily Dale, New York, headquarters for the Spiritualist movement.

To escape the pandemonium at the Hydesville house, the sisters moved to different locations, but the knockings and rappings simply reappeared wherever they moved. Two things were clear: the phenomenon worked best at night, and the presence of one or more of the Fox sisters—now including a third, Leah—was required. It was reported by the family that at times these occurrences "sounded like the frequent discharges of heavy artillery." And as fresh groups of curious onlookers arrived and a sense of performance grew, "tables rocked, objects moved, guitars were played and psychic touches were experienced." There were reports of strange lights and of partial manifestations.

The peddler Rosma was reported to have been replaced by a variety of communicating entities, many displaying considerable wisdom and insight to share with those assembled. At Leah Fox's house one evening, the following was rapped out: "Dear friends, you must proclaim this truth to the world. This is the dawning of a new era; you must not try to conceal it any longer. When you do your duty God will protect you and good spirits will watch over you."

The press reported the upstate New York occurrences throughout the country and abroad. In November 1849, the first meeting of "Spiritualists" was held in Rochester, New York. Meanwhile, dozens of others claimed to be capable of facilitating coded information by way of physical mediumship, as the Fox sisters did. Clairaudient and clairvoyant channeling, trance voice, and automatic handwriting (see chapter 6) were added to the list of feats performed by various Spiritualists.

Well-known people were drawn to the phenomenon, such as authors James Fenimore Cooper and William Cullen Bryant, a host of notable academics, judges, politicians, physicians, and ministers. New York Supreme Court Justice John Worth Edmunds became convinced that something was happening when he found that he could put unspoken mental questions to Margaret Fox while she was in trance and get strikingly accurate responses. Later, his daughter Laura would "go under" to speak in tongues. Governor Tallmadge of Wisconsin claimed to have received spirit writing from the late South Carolina Senator John C. Calhoun.

New York newspaper editor Horace Greeley also visited the Fox sisters. After a number of experiences, he was moved to write in his New York *Tribune*:

It would be the barest cowardice not to say that we were convinced beyond doubt of their [the sisters'] integrity and good faith in the premises. Whatever may be the origin or cause of the "rappings," the ladies in whose presence they occur do not make them. We tested this thoroughly and to our entire satisfaction.[51]

Not all the excitement was positive, however. On more than one occasion it looked as if an angry mob was out to lynch the girls as latter-day Salem witches.

Determined skeptics of a less violent kind were also moving in. Six scientists from the University of Buffalo solemnly agreed that the knocking-type channeling was done by a "snapping of the joints," despite the fact that on more than one occasion the girls were stripped naked, weeping, tied hand and foot, and left standing on pillows, while the rappings carried on. One doctor was quoted as saying that if sounds as loud as he had heard were made by people cracking their joints, it would kill them.

The years passed and Spiritualist incidents and their investigators numbered in the thousands, including a committee of noted Harvard scientists who engaged in considerable observation and questioning but disagreed on their findings and refused to publish.

The sisters' reputation began to sink, and it was not the outside investigators who did the most damage; it was the sisters themselves. The pressure to produce convincing demonstrations on cue was apparently exhausting. Being treated like test-tube specimens took its toll. At one point, Margaret allegedly broke down and confessed to a friend that the sisters had arranged with a Dutch servant girl to hide in the basement and do their rapping for them. Although this could not have accounted for the majority of cases, it gave skeptics grounds for dismissing the entire phenomenon.

Sibling jealousy and blame also exacted a price. All three Fox sisters married, some more than once; all, to varying degrees, sought refuge in alcohol. Margaret became an alcoholic. Thirty years after it had all begun, their relationships with each other had badly deteriorated. Leah had turned Catholic and was trying to take custody of Kate's two children. Margaret, who had sided with Kate, published a letter in the New York *Tribune* in which she severed her ties with Spiritualism and claimed the whole thing had been a fraud. To get back at Leah, Kate joined Margaret in this confesssion. A year later, Margaret completely reversed herself, saying that the initial fraud exposé was done for money, under the influence of anti-Spiritualists. But the damage had been done, and it was ample ammunition for the press and disbelievers. Shortly thereafter, within three years of one another, all three sisters died.

But Spiritualism did not die with them. By this time, those who had become convinced of the authenticity of the channeling, based on personal investigation, had grown to constitute a small army of dedicated Spiritualists on both sides of the Atlantic. Representing this group, Sir Arthur Conan Doyle, creator of Sherlock Holmes, wrote:

> The peddler seemed to have been used as a pioneer, and now he had found the opening and the method, a myriad of Intelligences were swarming at his back. Isaac Post had instituted the method of spelling raps, and messages were pouring through. According to these the whole system had been devised by the contrivance of a band of thinkers and inventors upon the spirit plane, foremost among whom was Benjamin Franklin . . . that they still lived and still loved was the constant message from beyond.[52]

What did this surge of psychical, interdimensional activity mean? The sources themselves sometimes supplied the answers. When Governor Tallmadge asked two channels what the purpose of the movement was, he received the same answer through both: "It is to draw mankind together in harmony, and to convince skeptics of the immortality of the soul."[53]

The Spiritualist movement peaked shortly after World War I. Sociologist Geoffrey K. Nelson attributes the decline to fraud and deception, attacks by the traditional churches, who branded it as demonic, a hostile press, and insufficient organization, doctrine, and ritual.[54]

Harrison D. Barrett, first president of The National Spiritualist Association, in a bold address at the end of the nineteenth century, stated:

> At a communication from Spiritland, Alexander, Czar of Russia in 1861, was impressed to liberate 60,000,000 serfs and make them free men. This is a historical fact and can be proven. About the same time, Abraham Lincoln received a message from Spiritland that caused him to decide to strike away the shackles from the limbs of 6,000,000 slaves. This is another fact that cannot be disputed. If it has done this much for rulers of the world, what will it not do for common humanity?[55]

Consider the case of Lincoln just cited. Nettie Colburn was reported to be a trance medium advised by spirit guides to contact President Lincoln. This precipitated an interaction between the two that lasted from 1861 to 1863, with numerous witnesses to each meeting. Among other things, her alleged guides counseled Lincoln not to put off acting on the Emancipation Proclamation. Through her guides, Colburn convinced Lincoln that the best thing he could do for his Union soldiers' flagging morale during the Civil War was go to the front lines at Fredericksburg. He did so, with apparently remarkable results for his troops and their effort.[56]

In her journal, Colburn describes the initial encounter:

> Mrs. Lincoln informed me that she . . . desired to see a trance medium . . . Some new and powerful organisms obtained possession of my organism and addressed Mrs. Lincoln, it seemed, with great clearness and force upon matters of State . . . [Mrs. Lincoln said] "This young lady must not leave Washington. I feel she must stay here and Mr. Lincoln must hear what we have heard . . . [later with the President] "So this is our little Nettie" . . . He began asking me questions in a kindly way about my mediumship . . . "Well, how do you do it?" . . . While he was yet speaking, I lost control. For more than an hour I was made to talk to him . . . I shall never forget the scene around me when I regained consciousness. I was standing in front of Mr. Lincoln, and he was sitting back in his chair, with his arms folded upon his breast, looking intently at me . . . "My child, you possess a very singular gift; but that it is of God, I have no doubt. I think it more important than perhaps anyone present can understand."[57]

Meanwhile, across the Atlantic, Allan Kardec was doing paranormal research and writing in France as early as 1850. His books included *The Spirits' Book* (1861), *The Mediums' Book,* and *The Gospel as Explained by Spirits* (1864). He coined the term *Spiritism,* which became the European counterpart of *Spiritualism.* Millions throughout Europe were influenced by the material he produced by way of automatic writing and the use of the planchette (chapter 6), both of which he considered more trustworthy than trance voice (because of loss of consciousness), hearing voices, or seeing visions (because of complications with interpretation).

In *The Spirits' Book,* a compendium of spirit responses to a wide range of his questions, Kardec asked his supposed spirit source, "What definition can be given of spirits?" The automatic writing responded, "Spirits may be defined as the intelligent beings of the creation. They constitute the population of the universe, in contradistinction to the forms of the material world."[58]

One of the international stars of the Spiritual period was Daniel D. Home, a Scottish immigrant to the United States, considered by many to be the most effective channel of the last 150 years. In 1855 he began a much-publicized tour of England and Europe, where he conducted seances in the homes of politicians, nobles, and cultural leaders in a dozen countries. Among those who experienced his work were Napoleon III, Czar Alexander II, and the writers Leo Tolstoy, Alexandre Dumas, and Anthony Trollope. In England, he attracted the attention of poet Elizabeth Barrett Browning, which drove her husband, poet Robert Browning, to write and publish a harshly satirical poem entitled "Mr. Sludge, the Medium."

Home never accepted payment. He was never caught perpetrating a fraud. And no investigator was able to discern what caused the phenomena associated with him. These, besides full-trance voice channeling and clairaudient and clairvoyant light-trance reception, included a rich variety of physical mediumship acts such as materialization and levitation (kinds of channeling are discussed in chapter 6). Unlike many other channels, he worked in broad daylight, in dozens of different locations unfamiliar to him, and before the most reputable witnesses.

In one situation, after Home (or the entity using him) had held live coals in his hands, unharmed, he said:

> All these phenomena only show our superior acquaintance with natural laws, and our power over material substances. Mankind ought to have the same power over the material world in which he lives; you little know the power that is in you; had you faith, you could do things you little dream of . . . Dan [Home] is going to awake now; do not tell him what has occurred, but let him wash his hands.[59]

The growing controversy surrounding Spiritualist-era mediumship seemed to crest with the case of Florence Cook. According to Sir Arthur Conan Doyle, she was one of the most accomplished mediums who ever lived; but according to biographer Trevor Hall in *The Medium and the Scientist,* she was a dramatic fraud.

Cook would be seated within a screened cabinet or other enclosure. This kind of contraption, along with subdued lighting, was supposed to help coax forth and "condense" spirits. Unfortunately, it also provided the appearance of concealment, ideal for the chicanery many suspected.

In the spring of 1873, while Cook was tied and entranced, numerous witnesses reported that a full-length female figure emerged from the cabinet, faintly luminous and veiled in a gauzy fabric. It spoke, claiming to be Annie Owen de Morgan, daughter of the famous pirate Sir Henry Owen de Morgan, later governor of Jamaica. This figure, who came to be known as "Katie King," made many appearances during the next few years. The game for the doubters seemed to be to find out if Cook was in the cabinet while King was outside.

Cook went to the best-known, most reputable investigator of channeling at that time, Sir William Crookes. She hoped he would attest to the authenticity of "Katie King." Crookes agreed to an extended period of research. According to Crookes's notes and letters, it was not long before he became convinced of the authenticity of the phenomenon.

In spite of her many inexplicable demonstrations, Cook, like the Fox sisters, was supposed to have confessed on more than one occasion to fraud. Hall, her biographer, agreed: "The weight of evidence appears to show that Florence Cook's mediumship was shamelessly fraudulent. Once this is accepted, then the conclusion that William Crookes became her accomplice seems inescapable."[60] Hall believed that Crookes, a world-famous scientist and president of the Royal Society, had compromised himself in an infatuation or love affair with Cook.

Other channels of the period, such as William Eglinton, Henry Slade, and the Davenport brothers, were accused of indulging in fakery as well by some researchers and declared genuine by others. The British Eglinton was accused of using various phosphorescent fabrics and thin telescoping rods to tease and twitch the "materializations" about. For others, this was just an example of the kind of remedies channels kept on hand in case their real gifts did not work.

The international scientific community moved into high gear to get to the bottom of this strange near-epidemic strangeness. During the last two decades of the century, a simple—some thought crude—Italian peasant woman, Eusapia Palladino, was subjected to some of the most extensive investigations of any channel before or since by the leading researchers in England, Europe, and the United States.[61]

Virtually every one of her investigators concluded that Palladino showed an ability to display authentic channeling, primarily physical mediumship. Interestingly, she earned their scientific respect in spite of the fact that she also was known by these very same scientists to be the most notorious cheat of all the channels examined! Perhaps because she was such a simple, uneducated, childlike peasant and her attempts were so obvious and unsophisticated, she was forgiven.

Rev. William Stainton Moses, whose abilities first surfaced in 1872, was one of the giants of channeling at the close of the century. His two books, *Spirit Teachings* and *Higher Aspects of Spiritualism,* rich in religious and philosophical wisdom, came to him through automatic writing from his alleged controls, "Imperator," "Rector," "Doctor," and "Mentor."[62] (See the glossary and chapter 5 for explanation and description of "controls.")

In 1882 in New York City, a 900-page book was published entitled *OAHSPE,* the partial subtitle of which was "A New Bible in the Words of Jehovih and his Angel Ambassadors; A Sacred History of the Dominions of the Higher and Lower Heavens on the Earth for the Past Twenty-Four Thousand Years . . . " It is still in print and is considered the Kosman Bible of the Essenes of Kosman.

John Ballou Newbrough, an Ohio-born dentist living in New York City, was the automatic-writing channel for this vast work. He recalls that the project began one night in 1870 "when I felt a hand on my shoulder. A voice said: 'Wake up, doctor.' " He arose to find that "the room was lit up with pillars of a soft light so pleasing to the eyes that it was indescribable. I saw great numbers of beautiful spirits or angels. They did not have wings." He heard that he must purify himself for the next ten years in preparation for the work he was asked to do.

After ten years of living according to their criteria, Newbrough was revisited:

> The same voice spoke: "You have done well. You have passed our test . . . Now we want you to buy a typewriter and place it on this table. We will thereafter awaken you one hour before dawn each morning, and you will sit in this chair before the typewriter and put your hands on the keys . . . We will control your hands and arms and perform the task for you, so don't worry. You must not look at what is written until it is finished."[63]

The work was writen in the literary style of the Old Testament, but its content is radically different in many respects.

In 1886, in sight of California's Mount Shasta, twenty-year-old Frederick S. Oliver completed the clairaudient writing of *A Dweller on Two Planets*. Oliver served as scribe for a nonphysical entity calling himself "Phylos the Thibetan." Concerning the origins of the book, Oliver wrote, "An adept of the arcane and occult in the universe . . . is the Author . . . For a year my occult preceptor educated me by means of 'mental talks' . . . I would be awakened at night by my mentor and write by lamplight, or sometimes with no light, in darkness . . . I was always conscious of every surrounding, quite similar, in fact, to any stenographer."[64]

In his preface (through Oliver), "Phylos" identifies himself: "I, Theochristian student and Occult Adept, am one of a class of men who do know and can explain these mysteries. I, with other Christian Adepts, influence the inspirational writers and speakers."[65]

The book is rich with detailed descriptions of life on ancient Atlantis (where "Phylos" had lived). Dozens of specific technological marvels are described that had no counterpart in Oliver's day but have since been invented—the monorail, blimp, airplane, rocket, talking typewriter, voice-recognition computer, video, laser, and more.

Lenore Piper, born in New Hampshire in 1859, was reported to be a consistently effective channel who was able to withstand the tightest scrutiny. She specialized in trance voice and later in automatic writing. Her first control spirit was an Indian girl named "Chlorine," then a French doctor, "Phinuit," and "George Pelham," who had been a member of the American Society for Psychical Research before his death in 1882. Later, "Imperator" and other entities who had earlier used Rev. William Stainton Moses claimed to work through Piper, saying she needed to be associated with a purer and higher source.

In 1885, the prestigious Harvard psychologist-philosopher William James launched an investigation of Piper. Here is what he wrote following his first sitting (the channel, as usual, was unaware of the identity of her sitters, James and his wife).

My impression after the first visit was that Mrs. P. was either possessed of supernormal powers, or knew the members of my wife's family by sight and had by some lucky coincidence become acquainted with such a multitude of their domestic circumstances as to produce the startling impression which she did. My later knowledge of her sittings and personal acquaintance with her has led me absolutely to reject the latter explanation, and to believe that she had supernormal powers.[66]

Madame H. P. Blavatsky, who founded the Theosophical Society, was a controversial figure. Her chief work is contained in *Isis Unveiled* and *The Secret Doctrine* (1888). She believed she was a channel under direct inspiration from "The Tibetan" and other Eastern "Masters" or "Mahatmas." She wrote, "There are passages entirely dictated by them and verbatim, but in most cases they only inspire the ideas and leave the literary form to the writers."[67]

Blavatsky saw thinkers and writers such as herself as the recipients of thought transference in channeling inspiration from "more evolved spirits," both embodied and disembodied. She saw this as a matter of two sympathetically related minds being "tuned to respond magnetically and electrically."

Although she wrote of human masters and beings on other levels of reality, she claimed that *her* guides, responsible for the essential content of her published work, were incarnate spirits, though there were other materials suggesting that they could move in and out of embodiment at will and were as much at home on nonphysical as physical levels of reality. Still, Blavatsky believed it was not appropriate to apply the life-after-death Spiritualist controversy to her work.

In 1889, referring to herself in the third person, Blavatsky wrote:

Great are the desecrations to which the names of two of the Masters have been subjected. There is hardly a medium who has not claimed to have seen them. Every bogus swindling society, for commercial purposes, now claims to be guided and directed by "Masters," often supposed to be far higher than ours! . . . Only fourteen years ago, before the Theosophical Society was founded, all the talk was of "Spirits." They were everywhere, in everyone's mouth; and no one by any chance even dreamt of talking about living "Adepts," "Mahatmas," or "Masters."[68]

One of the stranger documents of the period was written by a pioneer in multiple-personality research, French physiologist Theodore Flournoy. In his book *From India to the Planet Mars: A Study of a Case of Somnambulism with Glossolalia,* published in 1900,[69] the subject was a young, attractive Hungarian woman in her early thirties, whom he dubbed Helene Smith.

She would speak as "Simandini," daughter of an Arab sheikh, and as "Marie Antoinette," both supposedly past-life incarnation personalities of hers. The strangest, however, was her "Martian Romance," a good part of which consisted of glossolalia expressions of the supposed Martian language, along with drawings and paintings depicting Helene's visions of an alleged Martian life.

Robert James Lees was responsible for another classic channeled work, *The Life Elysian.* His case seems similar to Newbrough's experience leading up to *OAHSPE.* Both sought to be of service through their contact with nonphysical beings.

The Life Elysian's narrator, "Aphraar," said to be a recently deceased Englishman, tells stories of life on the nonphysical plane and the interdimensional linkage with earth. In the following excerpt, "Aphraar" is trying for the first time from his new spirit realm to establish contact with his own still-living father through a channel much more experienced than he with the process:

It was now my turn to take control of that most marvelous of all telephones [the channel] and try to make my voice heard for the first time across the supposed unbroken silence of death . . . "Can you hear me?" I asked, but . . . the sound of my own voice startled, almost terrified me . . . My Recorder [the channel] though he could not see me, evidently grasped the situation, and also appreciated my discomfiture. "Did my voice startle you?" he asked.[70]

F. W. H. Myers has come to be considered one of the most outstanding investigators and chroniclers of channeling. His life spanned almost the entire channeling renaissance of the nineteenth century. He was born in Cumberland, England, in 1843 (five years before the advent of the Fox sisters) and died in 1901. His monumental two-volume work, *Human Personality and Its Survival of Bodily Death,* has been a model for evenhanded, thorough research.

At every turn, he provided the best observational data and thought available. With the channel Rev. William Stainton Moses, Myers co-founded the London Society for Psychical Research. Myers became convinced of the authenticity of channeling and the survival of physical death only when contact was established through a medium with his early love, Annie Marshall, a few years after her untimely death.

Although the field of psychology came to be dominated by the thought of Freud and others, many today think that Myers's concept of the subliminal mind—used to help understand the channeling process—will still find its place among the chief paradigms of psychological thought.

> I propose to extend the meaning of the term [subliminal], so as to make it cover all that takes place beneath the ordinary threshold, or outside the ordinary margin of consciousness . . . And I conceive also that no Self of which we can here have cognizance is in reality more than a fragment of a larger Self. We find that the subliminal uprushes—the impulses or communications which reach our emergent from our submerged selves—are often characteristically different in quality from any element known to our ordinary supraliminal life . . . We can affect each other at a distance, telepathically; and if our incarnate spirits can act thus in at least apparent independence of the fleshly body, the presumption is strong that other spirits may exist independently of the body, and may affect us in similar manner.[71]

Regarding his lifelong research into channeling, Myers concluded that the evidence proves there is survival of physical death, communication "between the spiritual and material worlds," and "the surviving spirit retains, at least in some measure, the memories and loves of earth." Finally, he places channeling within a grander context:

> They [the discarnate humans being channeled] commune with us, like Persephone, willing and eager, but "dazed and dumb with passing through at once from state to state." They cannot satisfy themselves with their trammeled utterance . . . This is their willing contribution to that universal scheme by which the higher helps the lower, and the stronger the weaker . . . In this complex

of interpenetrating spirits our own effort is no individual, no transitory thing . . . Our struggle is the struggle of the Universe itself;
and the very Godhead finds fulfillment through our upward-
striving souls.[72]

ENTERING THE TWENTIETH CENTURY

Starting in 1894 and continuing for the next thirty years, physician Carl
A. Wickland, with his wife as trance-voice channel, conducted hundreds
of dialogues with supposedly disembodied spirits who were channeling
through his clients. In his book *Thirty Years Among the Dead,* first published in 1924, he wrote:

On one occasion I conversed with twenty-one different spirits,
who spoke through my wife; the majority giving me satisfactory
evidence of being certain friends and relatives known to me while
they were incarnated. In all, they spoke six different languages,
while my wife only Swedish and English. From one patient, Mrs.
A., who was brought to us from Chicago, 13 different spirits were
dislodged and allowed to control Mrs. Wickland, and of these,
seven were recognized by the patient's mother, Mrs. H. W., as relatives or friends well known to her during their earth lives.

Here is an excerpt from a 1918 interchange with a spirit apparently
possessing a patient, Mrs. L. W., and apparently unaware that she was
indeed a spirit:

Doctor: Do you realize that you have passed out of your body?
Spirit: I don't want my hands held. I am a lady of means [an
expression often used by the patient] and want to be shown the
courtesy and respect due a lady.
Doctor: Wouldn't you like to go to the spirit side of life?
Spirit: I do not like to hear such things. I am no spirit.
Doctor: Look at your hands; do they belong to you?

Spirit: For a time I have been myself and I have been in a dark
place. Before I was in prison we could talk one at a time [control
the patient] but now I am all alone. You have no right to put those
burning things on me.
Doctor: That kind of electrical [shock] treatment is very good
for earth-bound spirits—ignorant ones.
Spirit: Ignorant! How dare you talk like that to me? How dare
you?

> *Doctor:* Don't you know that you have passed out of your mortal body? You have lost your physical body.
> *Spirit:* How do you know I have?[73]

Ohio-born Levi H. Dowling—known simply as Levi—channeled the popular *The Aquarian Gospel of Jesus the Christ,* first published in 1907 and still in print. He claimed to have channeled directly from the akashic records, the alleged celestial memory bank containing a record of all that has ever occurred. His wife, Eva S. Dowling, "scribe to the messenger [Levi]," writes:

> When but a boy he was impressed with the sensitiveness of the finer ethers and believed that in some manner they were sensitized plates on which sounds, even thoughts were recorded . . . Forty years he spent in study and silent meditation, and then he . . . learned that the imaginings of his boyhood days were founded on veritable facts, and that every living thing is there recorded.[74]

James E. Padgett was a conscientious, analytical Vermont lawyer for thirty-five years before reluctantly claiming to receive messages from spirits for the last eight years of his life (he died in 1923). For a long time, Padgett wrote, he refused to believe the sources were who they claimed to be, especially Jesus. But eventually he reached the point where he could say, "I believe in the truth of these communications with as little doubt as I ever believed in the truth of a fact established by the most positive evidence in court." The work became documented in the multivolumed *True Gospel Revealed Anew by Jesus.*[75]

Frederick Bligh Bond, a British archaeologist and architect, spent many years excavating the ancient Glastonbury Abbey in England. In 1907, while awaiting the appointment to begin work and wondering where to dig, Bond and his colleague Capt. John Allen Bartlett, an amateur historian with a passing interest in automatic writing, decided to playfully experiment with Bartlett's abilities. While asking about the abbey, they seemed to tap a control who was trying to help them, for the written response was: "All knowledge is eternal and is available to mental sympathy. I was not in sympathy with monks—I cannot find a monk yet."

Volumes were to follow from automatic writing. The main purported spirit control identified himself as "Johannes Bryant," 1497–1533, a monk from "the company of Avalon." He was part of a group that called itself "the Watchers."

Decades later, in the fourth edition of *The Gate of Remembrance,* Bond wrote:

As long as Johannes remained as a communicator voicing his thought and memory through one channel . . . there was still legitimate room for doubt as to whether he might not be a subconscious dramatization of the dream-life of the medium J. A. [Bartlett] . . . The day for such doubts is definitely past for me . . . Johannes Bryant has returned and spoken to me through no less than five independent mediums . . . And the last manifestation of his presence has all the marks of that same vivid and most human personality which was so evident in the script of J. A. received a quarter of a century earlier.[76]

Another highlight of this period was "Patience Worth," who identified herself as the spirit of a Massachusetts woman who had been killed by American Indians in 1675. Her channel, Pearl Curran, was a housewife with an eighth-grade education who had never traveled far from her St. Louis home. The communications began with the recently invented Ouija board and moved to more rapid automatic writing and trance voice. "Patience," who had her share of witty dialogues with Curran and her sitters, settled into the more serious work she said she wished to pursue with her channel: producing a body of creative literature. She was recorded to have gone on to channel a great deal of published poetry, as well as six novels, including *The Sorry Tale*, a powerful description of the life of Christ. The works in near-flawless seventeenth-century English, were widely praised by literary critics. The noted psychic researcher Walter Franklin Prince made an exhaustive study of Curran/"Worth" in *The Case of Patience Worth*, published by the Boston Society for Psychic Research.

World War I acted like a door to the "other side," making possible a constant river of two-way communications. Tens of thousands of young people were being killed every month, while increasing numbers of people were seeking communication with the dead. Some of the best-known cases of this period were recorded in the books *Private Dowding, Raymond, Letters of a Living Dead Man, Letters of the Dead,* and *War Letters from the Dead.*

Private Dowding, recorded in automatic writing, was published in 1918 by the channel W. T. Poole. It is the record of the communications of Thomas Dowding, a young British teacher who was killed by shrapnel on the French battlefield:

How necessary that some of us should speak back across the border! The barriers must be broken down. This is one of the ways of doing it. Listen therefore to what I have to say: Physical death is nothing. There is really no cause for fear. Some of my pals grieved for me . . . I fell, and as I did so, without passing through any apparent interval of unconsciousness, I found myself outside myself! . . . I do not find it easy to express myself. If the ideas are not clear, that is not your fault. You are setting down just what I impress upon you. How do I know this? I cannot see your pen, but I see my ideas as they are caught up and whirled into form within your mind. By "form" perhaps I mean words . . . You are kind to me. You loan me a power I do not possess any longer—the power to convey information to my fellow human beings on earth.[77]

One of the most intricately woven channeling cases is that of Raymond Lodge, youngest son of famous English physicist Sir Oliver Lodge. Raymond was fighting in Flanders in 1915. At that time, the spirit of Richard Hodgson, a well-known psychic investigator who had died in 1905, was reported to have come in automatic handwriting through the famous channel Lenore Piper to present a message, relayed by Hodgson from his fellow discarnate, F. W. H. Myers, that contained a quotation from a passage of the classic poet Horace. Sir Oliver Lodge interpreted Horace's text as portending some blow to himself that Myers wanted to soften. Shortly thereafter, on September 15, 1915, the Lodges received notice that their son had been killed.

Meanwhile, another parent had established automatic-writing contact with her son Paul, who had also been killed. A week after Raymond's death, she claimed to hear from her son: "I have seen that boy, Sir Oliver Lodge's son; he's better and has had a splendid rest, tell his people." Lady Lodge, along with a friend who had recently lost two sons in the war, asked for a sitting with the noted channel Gladys Osborne Leonard. "Raymond," through Leonard, spelled out via table-tilting code: "Tell father I have met some friends of his . . . Yes, Myers."[78] Later, by trance voice, Leonard's control "Feda," the spirit of a somewhat immature young Indian girl, was able to relay from Raymond detailed afterlife descriptions that closely resembled channeled material from other sources.

Sir Oliver put this material together, with his own narrative, in *Raymond, or Life and Death,*[79] and it soon became a best-seller. Many could identify with the death of a loved one in the war and, through Raymond, could vicariously partake of this supposed victory over death.

Gladys Osborne Leonard, who helped with the "Raymond" material, went on to become one of the major channels of the twentieth century. A steady flow of research involving Leonard and "Feda" was published in the proceedings of both the British and American Societies for Psychical Research.[80]

THE PERSONALITIES

The following excerpts, involving "Feda" and another discarnate human spirit, "John," give an idea of the difficulties "Feda" could have in struggling to interpret the messages she would relay from fellow discarnates:

[*John:*]When I am unable to make my meaning reach her [Feda] in the form of words, . . . if I then project a thought of some concrete object, Feda may remark "I see so-and-so," but . . . it is really my thought of it which has reached her.

[*Feda:*] Feda cannot hear all he says all the time. Isn't it a nuisance? Have to catch parts, like when many things are thrown at you and you catch what you can . . . When speaking fails, they show something, or try to make Feda feel.[81]

During her channeling career (1925–1941), another major early twentieth-century figure, Canadian-born Mina Stinson Crandon, was known as Margery and her channeling as the Margery Mediumship.[82] The Boston Society for Psychical Research was shaken up by a series of apparent exposés of Margery and of psychic investigators reportedly in collaboration with her.

Crandon's control was her friend and brother Walter, who had shown psychic ability. He had been crushed by a train at age twenty-eight. The alleged spirit of "Walter" appeared to retain his salty, sparring character. This made him one of the most thoroughly studied controls.

"Walter" suggested a long series of fingerprint and handprint experiments in which, with a boost of energy from Crandon, "Walter" was to impress his own partially materialized fingers into malleable dentist's wax. It was discovered, however, that many of the prints were of Crandon's dentist, very much alive, from whom the wax had been procured. Believers wrote this off as an honest mistake by the person keeping and recording the casts; however, it was proof of fraud for many others.

To test Margery and others, *Scientific American* magazine in 1922 offered $2500 to anyone who could prove to an illustrious Harvard University committee that he or she was a genuine channel. No one was awarded the prize.

Between 1924 and 1931, Geraldine Cummins, an Irish professor's daughter without formal education, found herself employing automatic writing to channel the supposed spirit of F. W. H. Myers, who had died more than two decades earlier.

The Road to Immortality: Being a Description of the After-life Purporting to be Communicated by the Late F. W. H. Myers was published in 1932. Here are some excerpts from "Myers" about his new perspective on channeling:

> There is a continual interpenetration of thought between the visible and invisible worlds and that is what makes communication with you all the more difficult. If we could separate and classify the vast accumulation of floating thought from the living and the dead, it would be far more easy then, with the way clear, to send you one easy flow of thought from one individual discarnate mind. It is possible to get lost in the vast forest of men's fancies, more particularly when you go as a discarnate explorer.[83]

In her later years, Cummins became the channel for an exceptionally detailed work called the Cummins-Willet scripts, published as *Swan on a Black Sea*,[84] considered by many to be one of the most-respected volumes in channeling literature.

FOUR NOTABLE TWENTIETH-CENTURY CHANNELS

Edgar Cayce

Edgar Cayce, one of the biggest stars in this unusual firmament, is probably the most widely known American channel. By the time of his death in 1945, he had become known to millions as the unassuming, rather colorless gentleman who could lie down, "go to sleep," and "see" into the distant bodies of strangers seeking his diagnosis and advice about their health.

Dozens of Cayce books are still in print; biographies alone include *There Is a River* by Thomas Sugrue, *Many Mansions* by Gina Cerminara, *You Will Survive After Death* by Sherwood Eddy, and *The Sleeping Prophet* by Jess Stearn.

Born in Hopkinsville, Kentucky, in 1877, Cayce began his unusual work around the turn of the century. After he mysteriously lost his voice, a doctor suggested that Cayce learn to hypnotize himself to deal with the symptoms. Between then and his death, some 30,000 case records accumulated of what Cayce said during self-induced trance states. These have been cataloged and made available by the Association for Research and Enlightenment (A.R.E.) in Virginia Beach, Virginia, an organization set up to continue the study and dissemination of Cayce's work.

There has been some debate about what kind of channel Cayce was. Hugh Lynn Cayce wrote of his father:

> In the usual sense Edgar Cayce was not a medium. His voice was always his own. No guides or controls came forward to identify themselves and take over his physical body. In communicating with the minds of people either living or dead, the flow of information seemed to come through his own unconscious. Even when in a few instances specific entities were mentioned as the source of the data, there seemed to be an attunement of Edgar Cayce's unconscious mind with theirs. His voice and body were not affected. The physical body may be only a small part of the real self, the total "entity" or soul. It seems that in certain degrees of unconsciousness there are areas which may be doorways to co-existent dimensions of mental activity. When movement in consciousness, sometimes called loss of physical consciousness, takes place, the more extended self is able to "see," "feel," "hear"—know—beyond what we now sense of time space. Certainly Edgar Cayce's experiences describe this type of movement of consciousness and perception in other dimensions. Mediumship may, it seems to me, be extended between co-existing states of mental activity in time-space, as well as those between the so-called dead and the living.[85]

Some of Edgar Cayce's trance expressions appear to contain references to channeling. The discourse is in a ponderous, outdated style. Some claim this indicates that the source communicating through Cayce (or the unknown part of Cayce communicating) can be identified with an earlier, perhaps biblical, period in history.

Questioned about the sources of anomalous communication like telepathy and channeling, the entranced Cayce once replied, "To be sure, the experience is a portion of the Mind; but Mind, as we have given, is both material and spiritual . . . To make it simple—yet more complex: 'Know: the Lord thy God is ONE!' Know the Lord thy God is One!." Following this basic premise, the voice grows specific:

> It is not presumed, supposed, or proposed, to be a calling upon, a depending upon, a seeking for, that which is without—or that outside of self; but rather the attuning of self to the divine within, which is [the divine] a universal or the universal consciousness . . . Also there are those who have attuned themselves to a consciousness not wholly within themselves, but prompted by those who would become prompters—as in any attunement that is ever attempted in material consciousness, it is subject to same.[86]

On another occasion, Cayce was asked, "What is the source of the automatic writing I have received? Should I develop this?" The answer:

Ever let that which thou would gain through thy writing be inspired by the best in self as magnified through the Christ, than any ENTITY or spirit or soul! While these seek for expression ever, they be seekers as thyself. And as He gave, if the blind lead the blind both shall fall into the ditch. Be then led rather by that which comes from thine own soul, which thou meetest in the temple of thy body, thy God in thee . . . For as the prophet of old has said, if even an angel of light proclaims other than that which thy Savior has given, have none of it! In thy meditations, then, much hast thou grown in thy closeness to Him . . .

Write, yea . . . but let it be prompted by the spirit of the Christ with thine own spirit.[87]

The following exchange was recorded on another occasion after Cayce, still in trance, had concluded his usual schedule of diagnosis and prescription readings of absent clients. Here he seemed to fill the more traditional role of the channel mediating between two worlds. Referring to the discarnate spirits, he says, "These sought . . . to communicate that there might be known only their continued existence in a world of matter, but of finer matter." Notice the way he seems to be alternating between passive clairaudient and active trance-voice functions.

Cayce: There are some here [in spirit] that would speak with those that are present [physically], if they desire to so communicate with them.

Mrs. Cayce: We desire to have at this time that which would be given.

Cayce: [after a long pause] Don't all speak at once. [pause] Yes, I knew you would be waiting . . . Yes? Haven't found him before? All together now, huh? Uncle Porter, too? He was able to ease it right away, huh? Who? Dr. House. No. Oh, no—no, she is all right. Yes, lots better. Isn't giving any trouble now . . . Haven't seen her? Why, where have you been? Oh. She is in another change? How long will they stay there? Oh, they don't count time like that . . .

Mrs. Cayce: I don't hear. Will you repeat the message for me?

Cayce: Mamma and Dr. House and Uncle Porter and the baby . . . we are all here. Grandpa has built the home here, and it's NICE! And we are all waiting until you come, and we will all be here ready . . . we are getting along FINE, doing well, yes! . . . We are on that plane where you have heard it said that the body and the mind are with those things we have built [from prior earthly experience].[88]

In an interesting twist, after Cayce's death writer Jess Stearn reports hearing from him through a medium, Madame Bathsheba. Stearn was told that "he's very pleased you're going to do this book about him. Anytime you're in difficulty, he'll be right over your shoulder and it will go amazingly quickly." At that point, according to Stearn, he had told no one of his plans. The book was written in a matter of weeks. Stearns claimed that even the title *The Sleeping Prophet* was provided by Cayce. To date, millions of copies have been sold.[89]

Eileen Garrett

Like other young "sensitives," Eileen Garrett had a childhood in Ireland and England at the beginning of this century that was filled with invisible companions. With a relatively unhappy early life that included the suicides of both parents, she also fits the classic profile of those driven into introverted fantasy lives by early trauma.

Garrett was invited to the United States in 1931 by the American Society for Psychical Research to begin an exceptionally rich period of channeling demonstrations that would occupy her until her death in France in 1970. Garrett was not only one of the major channels of the twentieth century—there were no incidents of fraud or charges of deception of any kind in her career—she was also one of the leaders in research into the psychic realm. She pioneered the publishing of her own work and others through a variety of publishing houses.[90] In 1951, she became the founding director of the Parapsychological Foundation, which remains one of the most respected organizations investigating the paranormal.

Garrett's main control was "Uvani" or "Ouvani" (spellings vary), "the keeper of the door." Others included "Abdul Latif" (the psychic healer), "Tahoteh" (the giver of the word), and "Ramah" (the giver of life). One of her most famous sessions was a 1930 sitting in which an attempt was made to contact Sir Arthur Conan Doyle, who had recently died. But something unforeseen happened. Having supposedly contacted Doyle, "Uvani" reported:

I see for the moment I-R-V-I-N-G or I-R-W-I-N. He says he must do something about it. He is not coming to you—does not belong to anyone—apologizes for coming, for interfering. Seems to be anxious to speak to a lady in the body. Speaks of Dora, Dorothy,

Gladys. He says, "Never mind about me, but do, for heaven's sake, give this to them. The whole bulk of the dirigible was entirely and absolutely too much for her engine capacity."[91]

Then, with a deepening of Garrett's voice, the one referred to by the control "Uvani" allegedly took over. He identified himself as "Flight Lieutenant Irwin," captain of a blimp that had crashed in France before information of the crash could have reached the sitters or the channel. When the transcripts of the session were later studied by authorities, the detailed technical information provided was found to be completely accurate. In addition, there was consensus that Lieutenant Irwin was the only one who could have provided the in-flight accident details heard from Garrett.

In the following interview shortly before her death, Garrett discussed her ideas on channeling with characteristic detachment:

> *Garrett:* The information obtained through my psychic abilities, so many facts concerning so many people, must be contained in the cosmos . . .
> *Question:* What is your opinion about the dimensions you have been able to tap in your unconscious?
> *Garrett:* In my sittings, I believe that I am able through the aid of the controls—who may be split-offs of my own personality, how do I know?—to gain helpful information . . .
> *Question:* Is this what most analysts you have seen have concluded about your mediumship?
> *Garrett:* I think in general, yes, that I somehow have another channel to the subconscious or to other people's subconsciouses, but without any adverse effect on my own psyche . . . I had also gone to see Carl Jung, the great Swiss psychologist . . . He felt that I somehow had access to the far reaches of my own subconscious as well as the collective unconscious, a term which he used to describe that vast, unexplained link between mind, nature, and the universe.[92]

Alice A. Bailey

Alice la Trobe-Bateman (later Bailey) was born into a privileged family in Manchester, England, in 1880. Her protected childhood was nevertheless an unhappy one. In her autobiography, she wrote of an ongoing battle between her soul and her personality that started early in life and never really ended. At fifteen, Bailey had her first meeting with the spiritual teacher who would later match her up with the mysterious being who would choose her to channel volumes of arcane work. This powerful material, often called the Alice Bailey work, would be published in decades to come by the Lucis Trust.

In 1919, a breakthrough in communication occurred that set the scene for the remainder of Bailey's life as a channel, for it was then that her chief source, "The Tibetan," entered the picture. She described her first meeting with "The Tibetan":

> I had sent the children off to school and I thought that I would snatch a few minutes to myself . . . I sat down and began thinking and then suddenly I sat startled and attentive. I heard what I thought was a clear note of music which sounded from the sky, through the hill and in me. Then I heard a voice which said, "There are some books which it is desired should be written for the public. You can write them. Will you do so?"

Although initially against it, she soon decided in favor of working with the source. She describes her brand of channeling:

> I would like to make it quite clear that the work I do is in no way related to automatic writing . . . I assume an attitude of intense, positive attention. I remain in full control of all my senses of perception and there is nothing automatic in what I do. I simply listen and take down the words that I hear and register the thoughts which are dropped one by one into my brain . . . I have never changed anything that the Tibetan has ever given me. If I once did so He would never dictate to me again . . . I do not always understand what is given. I do not always agree. But I record it all honestly.[93]

As with the Blavatsky/Theosophical material, and more recent contemporary channeled material from other sources, we find in the Bailey work the same occult cosmological hierarchy: physical, etheric, astral, mental, causal, and higher inhabited levels of existence.

Arthur Ford

Born in Florida in 1896, Arthur Ford first became aware of his abilities at an Army training camp during World War I when he found himself dreaming the casualty lists from France before they were published days later in the newspapers. After the war, he became an ordained minister and began practicing in Kentucky. He soon found that his extraordinary gifts were unavoidably leading him into a different kind of life. "My mediumship, by this time, had taken over more and more of my life," he wrote. "In 1924 I went to New York, where I found myself much in demand for platform appearances as a lecturer and demonstrator of psychic phenomena."[94]

In answering his own question, "What actually happens in a seance?" Ford wrote:

The control takes over the bodily mechanism hospitably vacated for the occasion by the sleeping medium. The hypnotic sleep, incidentally, is very deep; pins have been stuck into my flesh during trance without my waking. From this new position the control accepts messages from waiting discarnates and relays them through the medium's physical body to the sitters. Messages between discarnates are transmitted not only by words but sometimes as thought-symbols: "Big ben . . . a watch . . . a clock . . . oh yes, he's saying it's just a matter of time" . . . In trance, another personality of about the same energy-pattern—the control—moves in, as it were, to keep store. Thus Fletcher [Ford's control] is, in a limited way, "alive" for the time being, while I have the experience of being "dead"—free to roam, for a while, in the unobstructed universe.[95]

Ford's career was best known for two particular incidents. In the first, Ford was the channel who relayed information allegedly sent by the spirit of the deceased magician Harry Houdini (see details in chapter 4). The other was a much-publicized incident involving Bishop James A. Pike and his twenty-one-year-old son, James Pike, Jr., who committed suicide with a pistol in 1966. Shortly after his son's death, Bishop Pike began to experience strange poltergeist knockings and movements, found books left open at certain passages, and observed other anomalous phenomena in his apartment at Cambridge University. It was suggested to him that this might be his son trying to establish contact and that he should work with a channel to reach him.

Pike chose Ena Twigg, perhaps the best-known medium in England at the time. Her life, rich with hundreds of convincing trance sittings, is represented in her autobiography, *Ena Twigg: Medium*. Although she claimed not to know Pike or anything about his son, she gave the bishop much detailed information regarding the son's regret over his suicide and information about drugs as well.

A year later, Ford and Allen Spraggett, religious editor of the *Toronto Star*, were invited to appear on a television talk show at the Canadian

Broadcasting Corporation's Toronto station. On the way into the studio, Pike asked Ford if he might have a sitting regarding his son. Ford replied, "Why not right now?" Pike and the television audience found themselves listening to the control "Fletcher," through Ford's entranced body, describing material supposedly relayed by James Pike, Jr., and others. Ford recalls some details of that session:

> An abundance of fresh material came through Fletcher, not only from Pike's son, but from other discarnates who had known the Bishop. The younger Pike identified the drug he had previously mentioned [through Twigg] as LSD . . . The suicide had been the result of a "bad trip."[96]

THE BEGINNING OF THE MODERN ERA

Stuart Edward White

A set of books written by Stuart Edward White has the reputation of being among the most lucid and thoughtful in channeled literature. White, the author of more than fifty books, is best known for those that deal with the channeling of his wife Elizabeth (Betty) and their friend Joan (a pseudonym). For the last twenty years of their thirty-five-year marriage, Betty grew increasingly psychic, reportedly able to leave her body during trance. In what the sources called her higher vibratory beta body, she was said to visit various nonphysical realms, including the afterlife realm of physically deceased humans. She became ever-more adept at channeling information from individuals claiming to be from these other realms and referring to themselves as the "Invisibles."

This material from Betty provided the heart of four books written by her husband. *The Betty Book: Excursions into the World of Other-Consciousness*[97] has been issued in a number of paperback editions in recent years and has been widely read.

White tried to bring as open and skeptical a mind to the phenomenon as he could, confiding that "there must always remain in my mind some slight question as to detail: How much is Betty? How much is the subconscious of the psychic?"[98]

The story took a novel turn with a remarkable role reversal: Betty, once the channel but no longer physically alive, became one of the "Invisibles" allegedly channeled by her old friend Joan, whose earlier experiences as a channel were documented in the book *Our Unseen Guest*, written by Joan and her husband Darby (also a pseudonym).[99] In her first attempt as a source, "Betty" provided an assortment of detailed information as evidence of her survival and identity to her husband's satisfaction. Then she attempted to describe her new role:

> You see our last book [*Across the Unknown*] tells about how I went "out," how I came into contact while I was still living on your side, how anyone can teach himself to come in contact, to some extent at least, with this side. Now I must evolve a method for telling how we *come back,* how I do it, so that you can receive more easily. You have learned how to project your consciousness into my present state of existence and draw sustenance from it; but you do not know how to permit us, on this side, to project ourselves back to you. I did the one thing there; now I must do this here . . . If Joan and I can only work together until I can rub out the wrinkles in her brain—it's all here to be told. It requires a keyedupness from the spiritual side; a calmness from the physical.[100]

The experiences of White and Darby conversing with the "Invisibles" through Joan are chronicled in *The Unobstructed Universe* and *With Folded Wings*.[101]

What is the message of these various books spanning thirty years? There is one universe, we are told, within which all is consciousness— the only reality—in various stages of evolution. Depending on one's level of consciousness and stage of evolution, the part of the universe that one experiences is basically either an obstructed one (the earth plane) or unobstructed (the world of "Betty" and the "Invisibles"). We are told that the concepts of matter, space, and linear distance obstruct us, while the unobstructed state is open to essences, to all possibilities, to the universal flow of consciousness from which all things come. "All created things are constantly in contact with spiritual forces of some kind," one of the "Invisibles" tells us; and we are asked to meditate on "the sensation of being in this spiritual blood stream pouring on earth conditions."[102]

The Urantia Book

The most gigantic single volume of channeled material ever to see print is the 2100-page *The Urantia Book,* published by the Urantia Foundation in Chicago. Urantia is the name for planet earth used by the sources of this work. Received during the 1930s through automatic writing by individuals who chose to remain anonymous, the material purports to present the history and structure of the universe, as well as the life of Christ and the history of our planet.

Of this material, one of the supposed sources declares: "The Urantia papers . . . constitute the most recent presentation of truth to the mortals of Urantia. These papers differ from all previous revelations, for they are not the work of a single universe personality but a composite presentation by many beings."[103]

The papers present a bewildering hierarchical array of evolving beings and their spiritual domains. A sample passage:

> Your world, Urantia, is one of many similar inhabited planets which comprise the local universe of Nebadon. This universe, together with similar creations, makes up the superuniverse of Orvonton, from whose capital, Uversa, our commission hails. Orvonton is one of the seven evolutionary superuniverses of time and space which circle the never-beginning, never-ending creation of divine perfection—the central universe of Havona. At the heart of this eternal and central universe is the stationary Isle of Paradise, the geographic center of infinity and the dwelling place of the eternal God.[104]

The preceding quotation is said to have been expressed by an "Orvonton Divine Counselor, Chief of the Corps of Superuniverse Personalities assigned to portray on Urantia the truth concerning the Paradise Deities and the universe of universes."[105] Other alleged channeled sources for the various papers include "Universal Censor," "Chief of Archangels," "Melchizedek," "Brilliant Evening Star," "Life Carrier," "Chief of Seraphim," and the "Midwayer Commission."

We are told that, for our part in this vast, minutely detailed scheme of things, we each possess

> the God-knowing mortal mind and its indwelling divine spirit, the Thought Adjuster . . . God has descended as the Adjuster to become man's experiential partner in the achievement of the supermaterial destiny which has been thus ordained. The fragment of God which indwells the mind of man is the absolute and unqualified assurance that man can find the Universal Father in association with this divine Adjuster.[106]

Four British Cases

These cases are at the heart of the legacy of twentieth-century British channeling.

A number of books have been published from the reputed source "Silver Birch," who was said to be the spirit guide for a British group that began in the 1930s and was called Hannen Swaffer's Home Circle, centered around medium Maurice Barbanell.

In his book *This Is Spiritualism,* Barbanell wrote, "Because of the constant, growing materialism in which man lives, he more or less automatically cuts himself off from the spiritual world, which is as much a part of his natural habitat as is the physical world."[107] Compare that with words reported from "Silver Birch": "We [the communicating spirits] have a gigantic system of misrepresentation to oppose. We have to undo the work of centuries. We have to destroy the superstructure of falsity that has been built up upon the foundations of creeds."[108]

Let us briefly return to British channel Ena Twigg, who was one of those through whom Bishop James A. Pike's son was supposed to have communicated after his suicide in 1966.

Three years after his son's death, Bishop Pike was lost and later died in the Israeli desert. The following exchange was recorded between Pike's friend Canon John D. Pearce-Higgins and the alleged spirit of Bishop Pike, supposedly after his death, speaking through Twigg:

> *Twigg/Pike:* Help me . . . Oh God, help me . . . Help me, please help me . . .
> *Pearce-Higgins:* Where are you? . . . God bless you . . .
> *Pike:* I'm lost . . . I'm lost . . . Help me—I'm lost . . . God help me . . .
> *Pearce-Higgins:* On earth—or somewhere else?
> *Pike:* I'm in a nowhere, John.
>
> *Pearce-Higgins:* Are you dead?
> *Pike:* Dead . . . Yes, I'm nowhere . . .
> *Pearce-Higgins:* Your body is dead . . . Your body is dead . . .
> *Pike:* And I don't belong anywhere, do I?
> *Pearce-Higgins:* Oh yes you do . . . my dear boy . . .
> *Pike:* Where, where, where is this?
> *Pearce-Higgins:* You belong to the upper regions. You're just in the mists right now that we often go into for a time when we pass over, so I understand . . . You have your faith in God.
>
> *Pike:* But this mist . . .
> *Pearce-Higgins:* This is what they call the River of Death . . . It's a sort of temporary condition that we go through, I believe . . .
> *Pike:* [Angrily] They shouldn't do that to me!
> *Pearce-Higgins:* I think everyone has it . . . Have you seen anyone you know, or are you alone still?
> *Pike:* No, not alone.

> *Pearce-Higgins:* Your friends . . .
> *Pike:* Many people here, but I can't see anyone.[109]

The White Eagle Lodge is among the most influential spiritual groups in England today, publishing many books by Grace Cooke, who channeled an entity known as "White Eagle." Her work spanned thirty years until her death in 1979. Cooke's books included *The New Mediumship.*[110]

"White Eagle," thought by Cooke to have been a North American, perhaps Mayan Indian, supposedly spoke about how he operated through her, reminiscent of earlier Spiritualist-era descriptions:

The human instrument I use was related to me in past incarnations. She has been trained through many lives to become my mouthpiece. There is complete harmony and at-one-ment between us [the operator and the instrument]. When a communication is to be made we draw close to her and speak into a golden disc of light we can see at the back of the head. It can be likened to an etheric microphone built of substance extracted from the human soul and the physical nervous system. It is a finer form of matter of higher frequency than physical matter, therefore unseen by earthly people . . . [We] concentrate our thoughts on this golden disc, and transform our thoughts into words which are spoken through the voice of the human instrument.[111]

Recently, channel Jill Cook, who counts the same "White Eagle" as one of her controls, was retained as a psychic consultant on the set in the making of the American film *Poltergeist II.* According to the director, it was often more "White Eagle's" expertise than Cook's that was sought.

The English author who used the pen name Dion Fortune, best known for her book *Psychic Self-Defense,* was one of England's leading authorities on psychic matters in this century. *The Cosmic Doctrine,* supposedly channeled by Fortune, remains one of the most elegant attempts to describe the workings of the universe. We are told that *The Cosmic Doctrine*

was received from the Inner Planes [by Fortune] during 1923 and 1924. The one who gave it is a human being evolved to a very high level. The Personality of his last incarnation is known but not revealed, but it may be said that it was of a world-famous philosopher and teacher. In the terminology which is used in esotericism, this individual is one of the "Greater Masters."

Fortune's entity speaks:

> What are the Masters? Human beings like yourselves but older. They are not Gods, nor Angels, nor Elementals but are those individuals who have achieved and completed the same task as you have set yourselves. What you are now, they were once. What they are now, you can be . . . If there is nothing higher than yourselves, what hope have ye?[112]

Recent American Channels

Ruth Montgomery Ruth Montgomery became one of the best-known and most widely read American channels of the 1950s. Her books, which have sold millions, include *Born to Heal, A World Beyond, Here and Hereafter, Companions Along the Way, The World Before, A Search for the Truth,* and *Strangers Among Us.* Unlike the old stereotype of channel as a reclusive, unstable oddball, Montgomery has for decades worked in the public spotlight in Washington, D.C., a writer respected by a variety of politicians. This highly visible and reputable aspect of her life is recorded in *Hail to the Chiefs: My Life and Times with Six Presidents.*

A typical channeling session for Montgomery often begins with a voice within saying, "This is Lily and the group." She describes "Lily," her chief control, as "moralistic, high-minded Lily . . . sometimes an irritant, impatiently pushing me toward the goal of perfection that I am too earthbound to achieve."[113] She calls those she channels her "Guides."

According to Montgomery, her old friend and fellow medium Arthur Ford joined "Lily" as a key source of channeled material after his death in 1971. Ford's spirit is supposed to have been responsible for much of Montgomery's book *The World Before,* which purports to contain descriptions of the earth's origins, the reality of fabled Lemuria and Atlantis, and other prehistoric and biblical material.

Montgomery was one of the first channels to use a typewriter for automatic writing. She recalls, "Late in that heavy-hearted January day after the telephone call [telling her that Arthur Ford had died], I suddenly felt an impelling urge to go to my typewriter and try automatic writing. No sooner had I murmured my usual prayer for protection and placed my fingertips in touch-typing position than the writing began."

She then watched passively as the following seemed to type itself:

> Ruth, this is Lily and the group. Arthur Ford is here and wants you to know that he is as young as the merry month of May. He feels

great and does not want you to grieve. He is so glad to be here, more delighted than you will ever know, for he has secretly yearned to make this trip of exploration and finds it much more beautiful than he had imagined or glimpsed while in trance. A ball of fire! He's so glad to be rid of the worn-out body which caused him such pain.[114]

Ruth Montgomery's "Guides" add their voices to the growing chorus of consensus that we live in a basically spiritual universe:

The soul is . . . that which reincarnates again and again until eventually it will hopefully reunite with the Creator as a part of the Divinity. The spirit is the essence of the Creator which is ever present and uplifting. We draw from various places this essence called Spirit . . . Thus we may be linked with other souls through this same substance of spirit upon which we draw throughout our earthly habitation.[115]

In *Strangers Among Us,* Montgomery's "Guides" provide descriptions of coming changes in our world, a theme heard repeatedly in channeling in the last thirty years.

The New Age has begun, but will not be fully recognized as such until the shift of the [earth's magnetic] axis has eradicated some of the evils of the present age. The earth will be swept clean of the beastliness and cupidity [lust] that now surrounds us, and will see the flowering of civilization in which the best of man's instincts are given full range. Those times will see communication by mental rather than vocal or pictorial processes.[116]

Jeane Dixon   Often associated with Ruth Montgomery, Jeane Dixon is another Washington, D.C.—based writer who has remained in the public eye for decades. She is probably the best-known "prophet" in the United States. Since we are interested in prophecy only insofar as the precognitive material seems to come through channeling, it is interesting to consider her description of the process of prayer and communication with God, who she claims is her source:

At such times [of prayer] I develop a degree of concentration that shuts out all distractions of the surrounding world and makes way for Divine Presence. I empty my mind in order that I may be filled with the Spirit of God. Finally, during my meditations, when my spirit is calm and He is ready, God talks to me.

I know then, beyond all doubt, that the channel is coming directly to me from the Divine, the Lord our God, because I feel it and sense it. I know it is not the channel of Satan, because his channel I have felt and sensed too; and I definitely know the difference. So according to my wisdom I follow the Lord's channel, because that is my Lord's will.[117]

Ruth Norman and the "Unarius" Books Unarius Publishers of El Cajon, California, is responsible for at least sixty volumes of channeled material spanning the last thirty years. In 1954, Ernest L. Norman first claimed to be in contact with extraterrestrial beings, such as "Nor El," who identified his home as the "spiritual worlds," specifically the higher-dimensional counterpart of the planet Mars. Before long there were seven books in the Pulse of Creation Series. Norman was joined in this endeavor by his wife, Ruth, who also claimed to be able to channel these beings. The two worked together until his death in 1971, when he, too, supposedly became one of the channeled sources.

Ruth Norman enlisted Vaughn Spaegel and Thomas Miller to be what she calls "subchannels," aiding her in receiving, transcribing, and publishing dozens of volumes. Spaegel and Miller are supposedly channels in their own right, but are especially able to "piggyback" on the energy beam that she claims to establish between herself and her sources.

Ruth Norman's thirteen-volume set, *Tesla Speaks,* is named for her discarnate colleague, the late pioneer of electrical research Nikola Tesla. The material is a virtual Who's Who of nonphysical human spirits, including many noted scientists presenting a variety of technical information. These so-called sources include Plato, Socrates, Heraclitus, Baruch Spinoza, Blaise Pascal, Martin Heidegger, Sigmund Freud, William James, Karen Horney, Nicolaus Copernicus, Johannes Kepler, Isaac Newton, Alessandro Volta, Hermann von Helmholtz, Gregor Mendel, Alexander Fleming, Joseph Priestly, James Maxwell, Alexander Graham Bell, Albert Einstein, Max Born, and J. Robert Oppenheimer. Most of these sources claim to be working on joint research projects, some of which involve beaming energy and information into our level of reality.

At the heart of the technical information provided by this channeling is what Norman calls the Interdimensional Science of Unarius. In the words of one of the sources, this deals with "the energy transferences . . . the regeneration of energy constituents from one dimension to the next. This transference of energy creates harmonic wave forms. With the regeneration of compatible inphase wave forms, the energy [or information] can be built up and sustained."[118]

What distinguishes the Normans from most other channels is that they single themselves out as exalted players in cosmic mythology that is supported by their sources. As their higher-Self identities, they claim to be archangels. They seem to possess a kind of innocent audacity despite their unqualified, exorbitant claims. Needless to say, for many in the channeling field, the Normans constitute somewhat of an embarrassment. They are presented here, however, not only because of the large amount of work they have put forth, but because of the genuinely intriguing nature of much of it.

The past two chapters have presented a rich assortment of examples of channeling, covering 5000 years. As we have seen, the messages of channeling have remained both timeless and timely in their themes throughout the centuries and across diverse cultures.

3
WHO DOES IT?

On the basis of the rich assortment of examples we have explored in the first two chapters, certain questions inevitably arise. The nature of these questions provides the beginnings of a sort of classification system that will help guide our further exploration of channeling: Who does it (what kinds of channels are there)? What do they say (what kinds of information get channeled)? Who are they channeling (what kinds of sources, or entities, get channeled)? And how do they do it (what kinds of channeling are there)?

In this chapter we'll look at the people who do channeling. What kind of people are they? Can any generalizations be made about their backgrounds, personalities, and belief systems? What are their attitudes regarding their channeling experience? How little, or how much, like the rest of us are they?

Both historically and at present, those claiming to channel seem to be average people. A pattern emerges of typical relationships, family settings, money worries, usual life problems and challenges being met. Channels have included Ph.D.s and high school dropouts; all kinds of personality types and traits, introverts and extroverts; clerks, truck drivers, business executives, writers, teachers, scientists, scholars, suburban housewives, graphic artists, and salesmen. Myriad backgrounds are represented: religious, agnostic, and atheist; different ethnic groups, nationalities, cultures, and creeds. You probably wouldn't be able to pick out someone who is a channel at the neighborhood barbecue or in line at the supermarket. With very few exceptions, they function completely normally. They just appear to be able to tune into, or provide a conduit for, information currently unavailable to others. Whereas some of us might have unusually fine singing voices, or lucid-dream every night, or have extraordinary imaginations, some of us channel.

There have been more women channels than men, especially over the last 130 years. Some observers speculate that women have more of what the Chinese call the *yin* quality, which includes a more receptive orientation and an attunement to the life within; while men possess more of the *yang* quality, which is oriented toward survival and manipulation in the material world. In addition, there is some clinical evidence to show that women tend to dissociate more than men, leading to fragmented aspects of personality that grow out of touch with one another. Psychiatrist Jan Ehrenwald, for example, points to research that he thinks shows that women are more heavily weighted in favor of right-brain-hemisphere function, which he believes is both the "cradle of genius" and the seat of dissociated activity.[1]

In attempting to determine personality attributes shared by those who seem to have a high degree of success in receiving paranormal information, noted parapsychologist Gertrude Schmeidler found that relaxation, extroversion, spontaneity, and good rapport appeared consistently in her most successful subjects. Other prevalent characteristics included: a generally open attitude and a people-oriented disposition; a tendency to perceive in a global rather than a fragmented manner; a particularly rich imagination; strong curiosity and creativity; and an openness to what Schmeidler termed self-transcendence.[2] Others have noted similar traits.

CORRELATION WITH UNHAPPY CHILDHOOD

There is a certain inability to "put away childish things" on the part of some channels who are driven into a Peter Pan syndrome by unhappy childhoods and who as a result refuse to or are unable to ever fully join the adult world. The acclaimed channel and psychic Eileen Garrett was a textbook case. Following her birth, her mother committed suicide; her father did the same shortly thereafter. Raised by a foster mother who lacked any sensitivity to the paranormal, Eileen grew up lonely and withdrawn. She had behavior problems in school. At eighteen she married a much older man, and sexual problems arose for her.[3] No wonder she escaped into a fantasy life of imaginary characters and other dimensions, one might conclude.

Some clinical psychologists tell us that there does seem to be a correlation between unhappy childhoods and channel-like behavior in at least some individuals deemed to be channels. Others who have studied channels, however—such as Gordon Melton, director of the Institute for the Study of American Religions and professor of religious studies at the University of California, Santa Barbara—can claim, "There doesn't seem to be anything pathological about mediums. They are in all respects fairly normal people who happen to go into trance."[4]

One of the first attempts to look carefully at the personality profile of the contemporary channel has been made by Los Angeles psychologist Margo Chandley, whose recently completed doctoral dissertation is based on extended interviews with thirteen vocal trance mediums. She has researched dozens of others as well. Her findings may help us to balance our picture.

Besides her own work studying channels, Chandley says that much of the basis for her view of the channeling personality is drawn from the experience and writings of fellow California psychologist Hal Stone. Stone is co-author with his wife, Sidra Winkelman (also a psychologist), of *Embracing Our Selves.*[5] Among his clients and students are multiple personalities and channels, as well as people who are simply "working on themselves," as the self-help-revived "human potential" movement puts it.

"One out of four people in this country have been abused or neglected," Margo Chandley points out, and therefore channels fitting that profile may not be so surprising. Some of the channels she studied readily shared such a background in recounting their lives; for others the truth of this kind of a past came out only through Chandley's auxiliary role as a counselor as well as a researcher. "I was a catalyst for them to unblock this place where they really did go into their intuition to start to channel through the imagination because of their childhoods," Chandley says.[6]

Chandley and Stone see each of us working to integrate the actual and potential aspects of who we are. When we sit down to experience someone channeling, "we forget that there's a part of each of us that hasn't been taken care of yet," Stone says. Since, according to them, we are, by the nature of our own nonphysical consciousness, coextensive with all other nonphysical multidimensional reality, then the process of supplementing current actual self with potential self can get complex as well as creative. Drawing the old line between *self* and *other* requires a whole new way of thinking and talking.

What kind of people channel, then? Some experts contend it is a retreat from a painful reality that is at the heart of the textbook channeling case; others, in sharp contrast, suggest it is an outgoing and accepting nature. Are channels people who can't cope with their own lives, shutting down to outer life in favor of inner fantasy? Or, on the contrary, are they people who have found a way to cope even better with life, to open themselves to even larger, useful possibilities of consciousness? There is evidence from many quarters supporting both views. How can we resolve this dichotomy?

According to Chandley and Stone, channels comprise that small but growing percentage of us who are experimenting (many unconsciously) with the nonphysical realms of their being. Channels are those who are going through a natural growing and learning process: co-creating their own nonphysical energy possibilities, first experiencing them as separate from their creative involvement with them, but eventually integrating them into an expanded sense of self. They believe this is the direction in which we are all headed. *Channel* is just the name currently being given to the kind of person who happens to be doing it first. In Chandley's words:

> Until we have really looked at the balance of who we are, we can't say we are God unless we also say we are the devil. We're both. If we let entities out there in the world attach to us, we don't take responsibility for our own physical process. And I think it's our responsibility. We *are* the universe. We are our own universe, and we are the Creation. And to put it outside ourselves doesn't seem to benefit . . . We must be the individuals that we are and live in the world as aware individuals acting and demonstrating that accep- tance. And that's what I really feel the channels are doing, bridging the mind-field into an integrative personality. I think we *are* going to become integrated. I really feel we're going to take this [chan- neled] energy and integrate with it. Right now I think we have to separate it to see how separate we are. And I believe that the channels have done that for us; they've separated out to the point of, "how much can you separate?"

SEVEN STAGES IN CHANNELING DEVELOPMENT

Through her dissertation research, Chandley has developed a seven-step personality development model that shows the stages most channels go through in their attempt to integrate this energy. In the first phase, *conceptualization,* each of the channels has had some kind of an experi- ence of a nonphysical reality beyond themselves. In the second, or *prepa- ration,* phase, definite contact with nonphysical reality occurs, causing physiological as well as psychological repercussions in the channel. In the third, *gestation,* phase, Chandley says, "the mediumistic personality seems to be consciously developing within the emotional system a sense of the physical and nonphysical relationship of energies." In the next, or *recognition,* phase, the channel begins to define and accept the nonphysi- cal energy system within his or her own physical system and usually gives it a name. The fifth, or *activation,* phase involves making a con- scious choice to become a trance channel and making final adjustments between the energies involved. In the sixth, *integration,* phase comes a final balancing of the energy systems, physical and nonphysical, allowing the channeling of the discrete source with "comfort and serenity" based on a "trust between the nonphysical energy and the medium." In the final phase, *maturation,* the question is addressed: "Is there a separate mediumistic personality, or do the six [earlier] phases lead to a final self-actualized personality?" For Chandley, maturation would mean such integration and actualization. Not all channels she has studied have reached this state.[7]

In Chandley's and Stone's view, being a channel involves co-creating with what we might call pre-entity energies, which exist in a nonphysical realm beyond the channel's self and which contribute to what is experienced by the channel and others as entities and their information.

In light of this picture, consider the following kind of channel, the one who willfully surrenders himself to the role of intentional channel. One of the most eloquent tales of this is told in *The Impersonal Life* by automatic handwriter Joseph S. Benner. By 1916 Benner said he felt he could no longer resist the growing inclination to give himself over as a vehicle to a larger presence, to let his mind be subsumed by (or co-creatively interact with) a larger Mind or Being. Here Benner writes a letter of intent to his eventual source, "God":

Dear Father,
Thou hast placed in my heart a great desire to give forth unto the world the message of the "impersonal life." I know that this is thy desire and that thou hast chosen me as the medium through which thou wilt bring into manifestation. I now ask thee to remove from me everything that hinders the outward manifestation of this desire, and that thou now supply me with all the means necessary to give perfect expression of "the impersonal life," both in my own life and to the millions of my fellows in the manner to which thou hast shown me.[8]

Most intentional channels today make themselves available to others for private sessions, demonstrations, workshops, and teaching. An increasing number accept money for their channeling work. And many have worked hard to integrate into daily life what they have learned through channeling. Many feel that their sources chose them to be channels; others admit they are (or are accused by others of) seeking out the role for a variety of reasons, conscious and unconscious.

Many channels maintain a certain doubt and open-mindedness about what they are experiencing. As Berkeley, California, channel Richard Lavin puts it:

I would ask myself, what is this? What am I doing here? Am I really contacting dead people or nonphysical entities or ghosts or extraterrestrials or whatever, or am I just so intensely creative and so intensely self-deceptive that I can do just about anything? I still don't know the answer to that question . . . The fact that I'm not the only one doing it gives me some indication that there is *something* going on. Unless we are *all* going crazy.[9]

THE CHANNEL'S LOT

Some channels are more interested in whether the results are beneficial for them (or others) than in knowing if the messages actually originate with otherworldly entities. Los Angeles channel Alan Vaughan tells how his life has changed since he began to channel his source "Li-Sung":

I find things opening up almost miraculously now. Call it grace or whatever . . . It was as if as I began to embrace him to allow him to assist me, that he opened up a whole new series of doors for me . . . And so life is not only more interesting, it's a lot more easy in a lot of ways.[10]

Many channels have become firm believers in, even followers of, their sources, working to make the channeled material available for sale by book or tape. From Madame H. P. Blavatsky and Alice A. Bailey to contemporaries such as Meredith Lady Young, channels have established publishing vehicles, foundations, and corporations to feature themselves and distribute their material, serving as a bridge between worlds. Some see their channeling as a mission they have been called to do, perhaps because of past lives in which they have karmically earned the ability. Channeling, then, is the central focus of their contribution and their chief learning task in the continued evolution of the spirit. Others go along with the role of acting as a vehicle in a simpler and more humble manner, placing no special significance on the situation or on themselves. Most channels today do not like being singled out as strange, for they believe that the rest of us can do what they do if we only open ourselves to it.

So, if channels are connected to higher, more privileged information sources than the rest of us, why aren't they more "healthy, wealthy and wise"? One conjecture is that there is personal, unconscious, and unresolved material within them, just as in the rest of us, so that they may find themselves in difficulty because of complex, novel experiences due to channeling. Whatever its origins, channeling may provide an opportunity for the channels to have their egos tested, evolved, even transcended. They have their hands full. We all have our moments of self-doubt, shaken self-esteem, and questioned competency; imagine wondering who you really are, what you are doing in this world, and what life is really all about when you are hearing voices, seeing visions, or going into trance.

If the channel is lucky, he or she may be part of a subculture that supports the channel, psychologically and financially; to the degree to which many channels lack this, they may suffer. We all have to function within a consensus reality, and to draw public attention to oneself as a channel can court suspicion, ridicule, or fear in others, as well as lead to conflicted feelings and uncertain self-image in oneself. The delicate balance between external and internal validation can be thrown off simply by being different, both in one's own and in others' eyes.

This survey of the nature of those who channel will conclude with five brief case studies, chosen because the stories are typical of the more established channels working today. Their stories may help us better understand what goes into making the successful channel. (All quotes are taken from my private interviews with the channels.)

PORTRAITS OF FIVE CHANNELS

Tam Mossman

Tam Mossman first became involved with channeling while working as a trade book editor at Prentice-Hall Publishing Company in Englewood Cliffs, New Jersey. In 1968, he started editing the "Seth" material that came through Jane Roberts, and for over fourteen years he served as editor for all of the Roberts "Seth" books while she was alive. In 1975 he began to channel his own entity, "James." His first of many public demonstrations was held at the University of Virginia at Charlottesville. More and more people began to value "James's" messages, and increasing numbers sent Mossman their own channeled material for evaluation. Eventually this led him to leave the publishing world to edit his quarterly channeling journal, _Metapsychology_ (subtitled _The Journal of Discarnate Intelligence_), from his home in Philadelphia. It is now the premier journal of its kind in the world. In it he features "James" and material from dozens of other channels, especially those whose work is not yet well known. Recently, Mossman moved with his wife and children from Philadelphia to Charlottesville to devote full time to his channeling work.

Referring to the variety of channeling activity at present, and to the ultimate importance of our own respective selves, "James" uses an analogy: "In an art museum you will find people painting in all different styles, but they're all expressing the one visual experience. Each channel is a view, not only of our reality, but theirs. _You_ are the ultimate reality."

Mossman describes his particular kind of light-trance channeling. When he normally thinks and expresses himself, he says, it is "like a hose with air in it," with ideas coming sporadically. "But when 'James' comes through, it's an even flow. The rhythm is different." He reports remaining conscious during the channeling experience; but when it is over it becomes "like a dream: if you wake up, it fades and you need to be reminded of it by another, or by reading the material later." He says that he *feels* the words or the sense of the message that needs to be encoded into words. "Sometimes he ['James'] will pick out an exact word; other times he lets me shop around and pick the words." During the process, Mossman says, "My mind is blank. So when I receive 'James,' that's how I know it's him and not myself."

Mossman remains undecided about the ultimate nature of who or what he is tapping into. Using an analogy of hearing music, he wonders, "When you channel, are you getting Leonard Bernstein conducting the symphony orchestra live, or are you getting the *recording* of it?"

One thing he *is* sure of is the process: "Let go of your personal ego. If you're open, you'll be free of ego. Let the source have *carte blanche;* don't keep it on a short leash. The material is the goal—to bring through good material."

He provides three rules for channeling. "First, be patient. In fact, channeling may *not* be your thing! Second, once you get into your own channeling material, use your own judgment. Like an editor, ask: Is this the best?" He also thinks that an entity should be able to explain itself, showing development beyond the human, beyond what would be the channel's own response. And you can ask for a more evolved source if you wish. "Channeling is not a blind date for eternity."

He warns, "A lot of channeling is done for self-aggrandizement in today's society, where publicity and hype are a big item." (He adds that he tries to watch out for this temptation in himself.) Also, since in his opinion the "subconscious has a grid through which the entity must express itself," one must be as clear on as many levels as possible and be prepared to consider that a certain amount of what comes through is only the unresolved parts of oneself.

Pat Rodegast

As a child, Pat Rodegast recalls, she was more religious than psychic. "I was always seeking to tell everybody in my family that they shouldn't argue, that they shouldn't swear. I was deeply religious, which is strange because I came from an atheist family, except for my grandmother. I always knew that there was a greater law and that the law was love."

By 1972, Rodegast, who had not pursued her education beyond high school, had become a successful executive secretary living in Connecticut, married with children. Then she started meditating. Morning and night, she'd practice getting comfortable and quieting her mind. She became involved in meditation groups. She started "seeing things," but didn't know what they meant. Soon "Emmanuel" began to communicate through her.

She describes the effect that becoming a channel has had on her life:

> It's been wonderful for my life, because it's really caused me to just do a lot of housecleaning . . . It forces me to be much clearer than I assume in my laziness I would have been. It has released me ultimately, but not by my conscious design, from a tiresome career as an executive secretary. It all evolved very organically. I've never advertised, never pushed this, and that feels good. It helps me trust it . . . It has required that I trust; that I make changes in my life that from my mind's point of view I should have been scared silly to do, but I wasn't and haven't been . . . I just find that it's had a most beneficial effect.

Continuing the theme of "housecleaning," she believes that "when anybody begins to channel, there's a very real responsibility for you as a human being to take absolutely seriously what is happening, to take absolute responsibility for it, and to be as clear as possible, and by that I mean to work on your 'stuff' for the rest of your life." As she puts it, "the fact that you have to surrender in front of three hundred people, or even one, is awesome if there's ego there. I mean it can be impossible. And ego's only there if you're afraid."

Each time she wonders if "maybe it's all just me," she says, her source "comes along with an answer I have no idea where it came from, or with a concept I couldn't *possibly* have conceived of." When asked how she knows "Emmanuel" isn't herself, she replies, "Oh, I would love it if it was me; but it's not my human personality, and I know that." Today "Emmanuel" is drawing ever-larger audiences, and *Emmanuel's Book,* complete with glowing preface by psychologist guru Ram Dass, is selling well nationwide. In addition, she and her source find themselves working with psychotherapists in developing new approaches to counseling. "It's wonderful what an incredible interface there is between the gods of our time who are the therapists and the world of spirit. It seems like such a natural blending."

And how does Rodegast channel?

What I find necessary is to remove my active mind from its dominant role . . . The more I am removed from my intellect, and the
more I am clearly in the moment of Now surrounding what happens, the less I know before it's said. It's a willingness to simply say,
I trust, I trust, I trust . . . I walk in a state of absolute unprepared-
ness wherever I go now. I just have to let my mouth say it. It's my
mouth saying it but not my mind . . . The more I can simply
surrender, which is my task, the more I can simply say the first
words . . . And I am hearing him just like everybody else is
hearing him, because I don't know what he's going to say until
it's said . . . When I lift to channel and I touch that loving, there
is no one in the room that I don't absolutely know and love."

What does Rodegast think the recent proliferation of channeling
means? "That the changes that are predicted in dire tones by some are
really the changes in consciousness; that humanity, 'Emmanuel' says,
has followed fear to the point that fear is terrified of itself." Nuclear
armament and the threat of world destruction are a great teacher, she
believes. "The world is waking up, saying, 'this can't happen.' And when
people begin to wake up, my sense is that the world of spirit, the world
of greater truth, is *there*." She pauses and then says "Emmanuel" has
just told her to tell me that "The only enemy is fear, and in learning to
perceive the nature of fear, you are then free to perceive the nature of
loving, which is your task."

Jose Stevens

For many who think that all clinical psychologists see channeling as
simply games of the personal unconscious, it is sobering to find one who
considers himself an "out of the closet" channel and believes his source
does not originate within himself. Jose Stevens, a clinical psychologist in
his late thirties married and a father, living in Berkeley, California, first
began channeling in the mid-1970s. He recalls the relationship between
his childhood and his current experience:

I was a Catholic, with guardian angels and all that sort of thing. I
remember the nuns would always say, "You'll just have to accept it
on faith." And now here I am much later and I realize I'm about to
say the same thing. Channeling is very much like that for me, like
having guardian angels . . . I was very aware of this as a child. I
used to sit in church and be bored to death with the service, yet
while sitting there I used to be totally aware that there were other

dimensions beyond this one. It was really a magical time for me. So, I just knew it. And today it's the same. I can't prove it or describe it without sounding silly. It's just a knowingness.

During the last ten years, Stevens reports, "I've experienced growth at an *extremely* accelerated rate. It's a shock to me at times. I'm changing so fast I can hardly keep up with it." Having channeling as part of his life, he says, is "like doing a good thing, like I'm gardening; something that's wholesome." Part of the goodness-of-it involves his profession. "Being a psychologist, in a way I have a vehicle already to move channeling into my life, so that I don't have to interrupt it. It's not that working with people is something new. It's just that now I get to work with people in a kind of expanded way." This includes a private practice, individual and group channeling sessions, workshops and courses for developing channels, and writing about and publishing the material of his chief source, the same group entity "Michael" that was detailed in chapter 1.

Still, "I'm pretty careful," Stevens admits. "I've gone out of my way to be 'cool' in the American view of credentials," implying that he realizes that having such credentials makes both his claims for channeling more credible and his own mind and character less open to derision. While he knows that being a channel can disrupt the lives of some, he feels that it has only benefited his:

> For me it hasn't been particularly difficult in my life. It's only been a major contribution to develop my channeling ability . . . I suffered greatly in the first part of my life. I was depressed a lot. I was anxious. I basically was confused and didn't have a true sense of meaning. I struggled for a long time. I find that the more I channel, the happier I am, my life works better, my relationships work better. I'm just really pleased with the results. I don't find any problems whatsoever. However, I have been careful about how I put it out there . . . and I make sure I live in the right place [Berkeley]. I know I'd be crucified in certain communities. I would be considered crazy right off the bat.

Stevens was initially trained as a social worker and spent a number of years on the staff of the state mental hospital in Napa, California. He then returned to school to obtain a Ph.D. in counseling psychology. While in private practice, he became interested in how intuitive and psychic skills are developed. This led, starting in 1976, to three years of study at the Berkeley Psychic Institute, during which time he learned to become a "psychic reader." This involved developing a light trance with

eyes closed, in control, conscious and receptive, followed by an experience of seeing pictures in his mind's eye, which he would describe or
interpret for whomever he was "reading."

After this initial stage of his development, while an instructor at
nearby John F. Kennedy University, he found himself having episodes of
a kind of open channeling sometimes called inspirational speaking:

> I would move from a regular teaching mode . . . and I'd suddenly
> feel this shift and I'd feel this bolt of energy inside. And suddenly I
> would start talking faster, and I'd push my notes aside . . . It was
> sort of like me looking at myself and saying, "Where is this coming
> from? What am I saying?" . . . It wasn't looking at pictures any-
> more, it was just directly talking . . . Sometimes I'd be amazed at
> the material; I'd marvel at the connections . . . I would learn a ton
> from what I'd said . . . Some of the stuff I hadn't previously felt
> that I knew; I hadn't studied it . . . But I thought, maybe this had
> come from my subconscious.

During this time, Stevens began reading some of the early transcripts of the original local group claiming to channel the entity named
"Michael." "'Michael' described what a channel was and how it worked,"
Stevens remembers, "and I realized then that what was starting to happen was that I was moving into a channeling mode." He became more
familiar with it. "It can only happen when I'm sufficiently relaxed, or
distracted by something like teaching, so that I don't worry about it or
be bothered that I'm not intellectually in control anymore."

He describes how hard it has been to consciously allow the channeling process to take place. "According to the 'Michael' system, I'm intellectually centered." This means being less able to get out of the way, to
let go of the intellect's desire to stay conscious, in control and analytical.
Emotionally centered personality types, Stevens points out—such as his
wife, Lena, who is also a channel—find it much easier to loosen conscious control and to enter an altered state in order to channel.

"I know that there are full-trance channels," he says, "and they
don't know *what* happens. I'm not that way. I don't let go of my body so
completely. I like to be around, and that's part of the scholar-type trait."
But losing some control is necessary. "It is definitely a process of surrender," he reflects. "You have to say, 'I want to let go, I want to
surrender.'"

Stevens's experience is similar to that of a growing number of channels today. "I remain semi-cognizant of what I'm saying. At the moment
I'm saying it, I'm kind of watching it being said. I have a grasp of the
topic and I hear sentences coming out. But later if someone asks me, 'Do

you remember talking about X?,' it's vague . . . it comes back kind of like a dream." He aims for a "meditative kind of state: very relaxed, but energized . . . it's that place in between . . . and then it's just a matter of somebody asking me a question and it begins." He sometimes feels fatigued afterward and may have a glass of beer or wine to "ground" himself.

Stevens draws upon his messages from "Michael" to help interpret the current resurgence of channeling throughout the world. (See chapter 1 for a description of the "Michael" world view):

> The majority of the population on the planet right now is in the very late "young soul" stage. That accounts for a young soul's style in the world: a lot of competition, power, materialism, struggles over goods. We're at a cusp time where a majority of the population of the earth is ready to shift over to the beginning of the "mature soul" stage . . . It's a major transition. We try not to let people who are going through adolescence do it without any guidance. They need lots of support, teachers, models, guides, mentors. We need that on a global scale and we're getting it. As people become mature in their views, they are also much more open to considering other possibilities. With that expansion of consciousness comes much more available help, which comes forth in the form of channeling . . . It's a very exciting time to be alive, and it's very scary. Yet I believe we will make the transition before we destroy the planet.

Sanaya Roman and Duane Packer

Besides being channels, Sanaya Roman and Duane Packer are among the most experienced teachers of channeling working today, and their experiences have involved hundreds of fellow, fledgling channel personalities. (The following material was originally drawn from their unpublished manuscript *Opening to Channel.*)

Roman was a former marketing consultant to small businesses in Northern California before channeling became her full-time profession. At eighteen, she was told by a psychic that she would become a channel within ten years. After college, she started into business, loving her work. She read the Jane Roberts "Seth" books that were being published throughout the 1970s. She and several friends began to work with the Ouija board, and her chief control, "Orin," began spelling out messages in 1977.

After a car accident, she experienced a change in her perception:

Doorways seemed to open onto other dimensions. It was as if I could see the future and know I would be right. When I ended somewhat dazed and right side up [after the accident], I knew a shift had taken place inside me. I put away the Ouija board that night and began channeling directly through my voice . . . I closed my eyes and listened in the same way I had "listened" to the messages as they came through on the Ouija board. At first the messages I received sounded like a tape recorder going too fast. Ideas would zoom across my awareness before I could speak them.

Gradually, she says, she was able to align herself to receive the impulses more clearly by learning how to "step down" the control's higher energy. " 'Orin' explained that my body was like an electric wire that could only handle twenty volts, and he was more like fifty volts." In her own analogy, "It was like finding a station on TV that I could bring in as long as I held the thought of it steady and unwaveringly in my mind."

Meanwhile, geophysicist Duane Packer, who had been a consultant on the geologic safety of dams built in earthquake regions and had founded and managed a successful petroleum exploration company, was facing a crisis in his own life. Something was missing. In 1982, a friend gave him a present of a channeled reading by Sanaya Roman's "Orin," who told him that his life would soon change. A natural healer who had been exploring body healing techniques for more than seven years, Packer helped Roman with a back problem after the reading. They soon became friends. Shortly, his own guide "DaBen" began coming though.

Packer remembers the psychic experiences that led to his channeling: "The trees no longer looked like trees but like vibrational patterns, and I could see right through them. I was really concerned about my sanity." He would drive alongside a woman and look over to see "a cocoon of light and energy lines all around her body." During this time, he was experiencing a deep split between the analytical, material orientation of his scientific and business background, on one hand, and these unusual experiences that he was unable to deny, on the other.

One day while driving, the name "DaBen" came to him. Later, Roman's source "Orin" brought up the same name. He recalls the next step:

As "Orin" had me say the name "DaBen" and invite the presence closer, I began to get hot and cold. I started seeing Sanaya in colors and layers, as if I could see right through her. The entity seemed to come closer and become more real. The physical sensations were very strong, my lower diaphragm was vibrating uncontrollably and

I was gasping for breath . . . I realize in retrospect that if it hadn't been a startling experience I wouldn't have believed it was real.

Packer's life began changing rapidly. He left his job. "I knew that for my sanity I would have to find some logical, scientific explanations for channeling." Packer, the scientist, soon came to realize:

It wasn't any one thing that convinced me of the reality of channeling, but a series of events that began to add up. There was a consistency to what "DaBen" said. Even if he talked months later about a topic, it would take up exactly where he had left off before. He would tell me things were going to happen and they did.

By 1984, Roman and Packer (and their sources) had joined forces. "We started channeling together and it seemed like our guides, 'Orin' and 'DaBen,' knew each other. They often wanted to talk about the same topics, one taking up where the other left off." The sources refer to themselves as "beings of light. We are able to navigate the fourth dimension as well as the fifth and higher dimensions. We have evolved beyond the causal plane and come from what you call your multidimensional reality."

Their sources suggested that, as they became more experienced, Roman and Packer teach channeling. Today, only two years after undertaking this work, they claim to have taught more than 200 people how to channel. Based upon this experience, they have written *Opening to Channel* to help others learn how to channel.

Because of the hundreds they have worked with as well as their own experience, Roman and Packer may be especially well qualified to explain what kind of people become channels. Of their successful students, they write:

They have ranged in age from 18 to 70 . . . often very curious and open-minded. They are aware, sensitive and in touch with their feelings. They are people who enjoy learning and opening to new skills and knowledge . . . People involved in creative fields of all kinds are natural channels—writers, healers, therapists, poets, musicians, artists, planners, designers, and so on. People who channel come from all walks of life, from many professions. The qualities most highly valued by the guides are dedication, enthusiasm, and willingness to be a channel . . . [They are] usually very kind to other people . . . sincere, hard-working . . . They have vivid imaginations and like to daydream or fantasize. They tend to be emotional and spontaneous, forgiving and loving. They seem to be able to anticipate other people's needs.

Packer describes his own particular kind of channeling experience:

Questions relating to what is life or how reality is formed will lead to trying to decipher images of wave patterns. The patterns challenge me to pick a word from my vocabulary to describe waves . . . I experience an energy being directed out to those listening . . . I experience "DaBen" as a very radiant energy, loving, exacting, who has a great caring. I experience his knowledge as being very detailed and extensive. Some of the information is so complex that he has been assisting me in developing words and a language to transmit them.

In comparison, Roman describes her experience of channeling "Orin":

I experience "Orin" as a very loving, wise, gentle being with a distinct presence. He has attitudes, beliefs, and perspectives, as well as a breadth of knowledge that goes beyond anything I consciously know. There is a richness of impressions that goes beyond any of the words that he is saying. While I am conscious I am not able to affect the words as they come through. I can stop them, but I can't add my own words or change the message. Sometimes I feel whole hunks of information floating around . . . I go into a very deep trance when channeling information for books and relaying information of universal concern. When I am channeling for other people, my trance is lighter.

What do Roman and Packer think of the present resurgence of channeling activity? They agree with Jose Stevens and others that "because this is a very important transition time for the earth," many "high guides" are present and want to assist us. They say they are being told by their guides that mankind's spiritual self is awakening, resulting in an "accelerated desire for evolution and spiritual growth." People will need guidance. Therefore, they say, large numbers of people will be opening to channel in the next five to ten years.

TWO
THE MATERIAL

4
WHAT DO THEY SAY?

What do the channeled messages teach? Is it knowledge that is available from any other source? Can the subject matter itself help us to determine whether channeling is what it purports to be: communication from those on another level of reality? Are the messages threatening or peaceful? How useful are they for our daily lives?

While some are satisfied that many of the messages could come only from the purported sources, others dismiss them all as fraud, or as having been manufactured by the channels' own unconscious, or as having been received paranormally from the minds of other people. As far as the tone of the material in general, it is positive, stressing the reality of a larger, spiritual universe and our own creative self-determination in this lifetime. Many people find these messages to be relatively useless: vague and facile psychobabble, permutations and paraphrasings of stereotypical material already in the public domain. Many others, however, report that their day-to-day lives are definitely enhanced by channeled information and guidance.

TWO APPROACHES TO JUDGING CHANNELED MATERIAL

In general, there appear to be two basic schools of thought today about the content of channeled material. On one hand, there are those who say the material must stand on its own merits, irrespective of where it is supposed to come from. We must weigh it for ourselves, using our reason and intuition. More specifically, content analysis—an inductive research approach that attempts to derive patterns and generalizations from textual data—may be employed (an example will follow). In addition, field-testing the material through personal experience can help establish its value.

On the other hand, there are those who choose to investigate the channeling phenomenon by exploring the nature of the supposed other-dimensional sources by means of their messages. Here the approach is to narrow down the material to that which could *not* be coming from the unconscious of the channel or from the minds of others to the channel by way of what parapsychologists call general extrasensory perception, or GESP. While serious research in this area was done between the 1860s and 1930s,[1] virtually none has been conducted since. Perhaps the recent tremendous resurgence of channeling may inspire new research.

As the spirit of "Helen" reports via the automatic writing of one contemporary channel, "When people receive messages from here, you are helpless to determine who the senders are, so it is only by the character of the contents of each message that you can have any feeling of security that the person whose name is attached is giving the message."[2]

A good example of inductive, content analysis and verificational/corroborate approaches to studying channeled material involves research being proposed by a team (including myself) from the Foundation for Mind/Being Research in Mountain View, California. Transcripts are beginning to be analyzed of material coming through two different channels allegedly from all seven deceased Challenger astronauts. After reading the material gathered thus far, the researchers have agreed that the material can be sorted into four basic categories. They comprise two basic domains: personal material that could be checked with the astronauts' surviving families, friends, and co-workers for authenticity, and technical references that could be checked with NASA. The researchers now are seeking grant support in order to go back through the material, highlighting passages according to which category they fit. Where consensus is found among readers, the results are typed into a computer for later checking by astronaut and category. At the same time, team members will be searching published interviews with the crew to rule out the possibility that any of the material could have been known by the channels beforehand. Finally, passages from this material will be compared to other channeled material from other sources, in order to seek commonalities of description—for example, of the nonphysical domain the sources now claim to inhabit.

In this book, I have in general left to you the task of evaluating the content of the channeled material presented. Other than in the section to follow, called "Proof" from Discarnate Human Spirits, I have not pursued the kind of rigorous analysis of the second approach, because of limited space.

One of the ways, however, in which I do try to offer some argument on behalf of the sources being who they are purported to be, is in pointing out on occasion the commonalities of information across different kinds of channels and sources throughout history. Of course, some will claim that such consensus may only represent a tapping into a shared wish-fulfillment fantasy or into Jung's collective unconscious. But then, it is the very commonality of what we *incarnate* minds have to say that leads us to presume the objective truth of *our* shared reality here on earth.

California trance channel Richard Lavin is one of many who sees confirmation of validity in the strong similarity between the material from his source, "Ecton," and that from other channels. "It really feels like all this is the same stuff: the nature of our own creativity; the nature of our own knowledge that's available to us; the nature of how big we are beyond the illusion we've led ourselves to believe we are; and the power that's available."[3]

Judith Skutch, publisher of *A Course in Miracles,* also stresses a unity across purported sources.

I find that careful examination of the materials available in what I call high quality information often leads to finding the same perennial philosophy or ancient wisdom expressed through "different voices." Thus one can check it out in content, tone, and scope, measuring the statements against what you know as the loftiest thoughts of the ages.

For Skutch, this is an exciting thought, because it means that the information is accessible to everyone, and "it doesn't matter what name one gives to the source."[4]

Psychologist James Fadiman is another who believes that the burden of proving the message's value must lie with *it,* not with the reputed identity of its source:

The quality of the information is independent of the source. I've heard the president of the most powerful country in the world behave like a total fool again and again. So merely because he comes from a reputable source—being the president—doesn't make his information of any value. So if someone says their name is Ramtha and they're a nasty, aggressive, hostile being in a former life and now they're really very nice, that doesn't make their information good or bad . . . I have read a certain number of things that are obviously very high quality information, and I've also read a lot of junk. If I read the notebooks of Leonardo da Vinci and he said that he didn't do them, that makes a lot of sense to me, because they're beyond the science of the day . . . What interests me is the quality of the information.[5]

Psychologist Charles Tart has a similar view, although he is interested in using the messages to better understand the nature of the sources as well:

I don't count the content per se as evidence of independent existence. In this sense, you take something like *A Course in Miracles*. I find that content very inspiring and stimulating, but almost totally irrelevant to the question: Did this come from an independently existing disembodied entity? The face that the content is inspiring and useful has almost nothing to do with the ontological status of the entity.[6]

Throughout history, material alleged to be channeled tends to fall into the following categories: what long has been called Ageless Wisdom; guidance for daily living and other personal messages; various "proof" from the sources; descriptions of the realities experienced by the sources; information about the past and future; subject matter for artistic and creative expression; and scientific, technological, and medical/healing information. We will briefly examine each in turn.

AGELESS WISDOM

Virtually all of the sources above the lower astral levels tell us that from their vantage points they know the entire universe to be a living spiritual Being of which each is a living part. According to Universal Law, we are evolving through a series of embodied and disembodied lives toward an eventual reunion with the one God, which is the underlying identity of All That Is. In the meantime, we maintain an ongoing condition of identity with this God, though we are unaware of it. It is by virtue of the higher Self that we are connected to this deeper truth.

Some call this view of deeper reality the Ageless Wisdom. Scholars, when they cease looking for differences among the world religions, see in their commonalities such wisdom. The various occult, esoteric, and mystery school teachings repeat the theme. British author Aldous Huxley coined the term *perennial philosophy,* which he described as:

The metaphysics that recognizes a divine Reality substantial to the world of things and lives and minds; the psychology that finds in the soul something similar to, or even identical with, divine Reality; the ethic that places men's final end in the knowledge of the immanent and transcendent Ground of all being—the thing is immemorial and universal.[7]

Part of this wisdom, contained in a consensus across most of the channeled material of all ages, is that the universe is a multidimensional, living Being, which some call God, and that it is inhabited by aspects of itself—sentient beings of consciousness—on many or all of its other dimensions besides the physical as we currently experience it. And so we keep hearing messages about, and from, the etheric, astral, mental, causal, and other dimensions of this expanded Nature. Furthermore, according to this channeled wisdom, wherever a being, personality, or entity may be within this cosmological hierarchy, he, she, or it is always in a process of learning for the purpose of evolving into ever-more unity with the one Being that is the source and destiny of all separate beings. Finally, we are told that love reigns over wisdom, light, and pure force or energetic power, as the supreme reality of all creation. We in our "classroom" on earth are pictured as slowly learning to be loving beings that reflect the nature of our Creator. Most versions speak of us as essentially of the same quality or nature as our Creator and thus undying—having many opportunities and contexts for this learning and evolution to take place. Hence the recurrent theme of reincarnation, or multiple projections of the experience-gathering vehicle of consciousness.

In their recent book *Higher Creativity,* Willis Harman and Howard Rheingold outline the main themes of the perennial wisdom as they see them: "The most essential part of the Self is the supraconscious," which goes by many names, and which is "not ordinarily accessible to conscious awareness." It may be accessed by various means. Meanwhile, the everyday ego self is locked in a survivalist struggle with this higher Self, with which it must eventually align and into which it must then be integrated. Also, "All persons are hypnotized from infancy by the culture in which they grow up." In our case it is the current materialistic consensus reality. Enlightenment involves realizing this illusory state of our daily entranced experience, and awakening to the more real reality lying behind it: "At higher states of consciousness there is awareness of participation in a transpersonal Mind, of the oneness of all." The enlightened person learns to give all questions and problems to the higher Self, or "supraconscious mind which is identical to the One Mind."[8]

Some channeled material, like the recent *A Course in Miracles,* spiritually counsels us with a suggested "curriculum." If we follow it, we are told, it can align us with the deeper, truer, and more loving ways of the one Universal Being. That is, many of the lessons for learning the truth of the perennial wisdom are spelled out in the form of tasks and activities by those in the role of our teachers, both in and out of the flesh.

GUIDANCE AND PERSONAL MESSAGES

Often the sources claim to have detailed knowledge of the channel's private life or the lives of other individuals present during a channeling session. They say this information is available to them within certain limits according to their stage of growth and the purpose to which it is to be used. As a result, the sources are said to be able to provide individually tailored advice. This guidance may be about personal decisions, personal problems with relationships, family, work, finance, career, health, and sex. Sources may teach people how to end old patterns and start new ones, or how to face hardships, illness, and death. Well-known channel Edgar Cayce was responsible for health-related channelings to thousands of individuals, with a reported accuracy rate of 90 percent regarding the medical information.

In problem-solving sessions, the interchange between source and recipient often sounds identical to a counseling session. When the source is allegedly the spirit of a loved one, the counseling can be intimate and highly individualized. In such cases, we get a glimpse of loving counsel about the little daily things that the source is able to continue to observe even after death.

For example, through *In Silence They Return,* Minnesota housewife Judy Boss shares her automatic-writing communications from her husband, Mac, following his death in an automobile accident. Trying to remain a part of the family, he provides investment tips to his wife, inspires a neighbor to get one of his sons ski boots, and keeps his hand in parenting the children. Judy Boss recalls a typical incident:

> One night, I went over to the University of Minnesota to hear a speaker. I was home by 11:00 o'clock. As I started to [automatic] write, I received a scolding from Mac. WHY DON'T YOU STAY HOME MORE OFTEN? . . . YOU'RE TIRED AND THE CHILDREN MISSED YOU AND WANTED YOU HOME . . . "O.K. Mac," I said. "What happened while I was gone?" MARY WOULDN'T GO TO BED AND JIMMY MISSED YOU. I called to Kevin. "Kevin, what happened while I was not at home?" "Well, Mary would not go to bed," he said, "and Jimmy wanted to sleep in your bed. I guess he was lonesome for you."[9]

Here is a brief excerpt from *Always, Karen.* "Karen" died of cancer in 1970 in Southern California while in her early twenties. She helped her mother, Jeanne, take down her messages via automatic writing. An example: "Mom . . . I am really here. My world really exists. Mine is the real world; yours the reflection. You will one day enter my world, and I urge you to be ready. Don't permit yourself spiritual laziness on the earth plane."[10]

Sometimes, the alleged spirit of a notable personality attempts to convey some kind of personal message, either to loved ones or to the world at large that he or she has left. In the following example, former President John F. Kennedy is said to be brought through by the prolific Orange, Massachusetts, trance channel Elwood Babbitt (who has reportedly spoken as more than 150 distinct personalities in the last twenty years).

Let me say in all truth that I was not deserving of that high position. It was a position that was bought and not earned, and in finding myself incapable for this great task I knew and had intuitive thought that I would not have it long. I did not know how it [the assassination] was going to happen, but now [that] I do I can understand, for there was a greater force outside of myself and outside of your world that relieved me of that position.[11]

"PROOF" FROM DISCARNATE HUMAN SPIRITS

One of the most important aims of channeling is to provide proof of the survival of human personality beyond physical death. For many people, this is the *sine qua non* for accepting channeling as a whole. As proof of their identity, entities typically provide clues such as a pet name used by a spouse, the location of lost personal items, or descriptions of incidents meaningful only to the surviving significant other.

In one example from South Africa, published in *From My World to Yours,* young "Mike Swain," killed in an automobile accident, speaks to his mother through trance voice channel Nina Merrington:

The other morning, just after sunrise, you left the bedroom and went down to the garden in your dressing gown, and you picked a single, perfect white rose. I was with you then . . . Mum, if you *do* get depressed again, go into the garden and pick another flower. I shall be there with you again . . . The only real bust-ups you and I got into were when you made me study half the night for those exams! I appreciate why you did it; but if we'd only known what was going to happen, there'd have been no need for you to take such a bloomin' great broomstick to me![12]

The leading parapsychological explanation to account for the accuracy of channeled messages is that the channel picks up the relevant information via unconscious telepathy or GESP from the unconscious minds of other living humans, usually the "sitter" who is seeking contact with the deceased. Yet there are many cases in which one is hard pressed to maintain this view. For example:

My uncle was run over by a truck in 1928 . . . and then died, as we all thought he would finally, of a concussion in the back of his head. During a seance in England in 1934, my father was put in touch with someone said to be his dead brother. He told of his death, and stated that he did not die of his skull injury but that "it came from the bones" . . . It struck me in 1956 that I could check the facts through the hospital records . . . During the post-mortem the cause of death was found to be not the skull fracture but a brain embolism caused by a lower bone thrombosis [a clot from the bone, which causes a blood stoppage in the brain].[13]

There are other forms of proof, including the use of codes, book tests, cross-correspondences, and word-association tests.

Before he died, magician Harry Houdini and his wife agreed on a secret code that he thought would prove the continuation of human existence beyond death. In February 1928, after Houdini (and his mother) had died, the following message was transmitted through the full-trance channel Arthur Ford by his control "Fletcher." Here "Fletcher" relays a message from Houdini's mother:

Mine is the word "FORGIVE," capitalize that and put it in quotation marks. His wife knew the word and no one else in all the world knew it . . . Now that he is here with me I am able to get through. Tonight I give it to you, and Beatrice Houdini [Houdini's wife] will declare it to be true.

Houdini's wife did indeed confirm this. In a later session, "Fletcher" continued:

A man who says he is Harry Houdini, but whose real name was Ehrich Weiss, is here and wishes to send his wife, Beatrice Houdini, the ten-word code which he agreed to do if it were possible for him to communicate. He says you are to take this message to her upon acceptance of it, he wishes her to follow out the plan they agreed upon before his passing. This is the code: "ROSABELLE** ANSWER** TELL** PRAY** ANSWER** ANSWER** TELL** ANSWER** ANSWER** TELL" . . . He says the code is known only to him and to his wife, and that no one on earth but those two know it.

Ford then went to see Beatrice Houdini and quickly reentered the trance state so that "Fletcher," and Houdini through "Fletcher," might communicate with her. "Fletcher" said:

This man is coming now, the same one who came the other night. He tells me to say, "Hello, Bess, sweetheart" . . . He says the code is one you used to use in one of your secret mindreading acts. [Beatrice confirms that they are the words.] He smiles and says, "Thank you, now I can go on." He tells you to take off your wedding ring and tell them what ROSABELLE means.

Houdini's wife removed the ring and sang a little song. "Fletcher" continued: "He says, I thank you, darling. The first time I heard you sing that song was in our first show together years ago." Mrs. Houdini nodded her head in assent. Then Houdini proceeded to relate through "Fletcher" the intricacies of their code that involved certain letters in the earlier ten-word passage. "Fletcher" then asked, "Is this right?" "Yes," replied Mrs. Houdini with great feeling. "Fletcher" concluded the session:

He says, "Tell the whole world that Harry Houdini still lives and will prove it a thousand times and more." He is pretty excited. He says, "I was perfectly honest and sincere in trying to disprove survival, though I resorted to tricks to prove my point for the simple reason that I did not believe communication was true, but I did no more than seemed justifiable. I am now sincere in sending this through in my desire to undo. Tell all those who lost faith because of my mistake to lay hold again of hope, and to live with the knowledge that life is continuous. This is my message to the world, through my wife and through this instrument.[14]

F. W. H. Myers, the noted nineteenth-century researcher of channeling and related phenomena, is credited with having invented the cross-correspondence method of proving survival. This approach was used by a number of purported discarnates to strengthen claims that

THE MATERIAL

channeling does in fact connect people with the dead. As British researcher Raynor C. Johnson points out in *The Imprisoned Splendour,* critics could claim that the channeled material was really being drawn from "the medium's own subliminal mind or derived by her telepathically from the minds of other living persons who knew" the supposedly channeled person; but the cross-correspondence approach might prove convincing. Using Myers as the example, Johnson writes:

> Suppose that Myers (whom we will postulate as surviving) divided his message into phrases and fragments, sending some of these through the script of one automatist and some through the script of a second and of a third. These fragments, which to the automatist would seem meaningless and incoherent, if placed together skillfully by an independent person would show purpose and planning by a mind independent of the automatists.[15]

Perhaps the most comprehensive set of cross-correspondence ever recorded centered around the British Society for Psychical Research group in Cambridge. Myers, who had died in 1901, along with a few of his deceased friends, were said to communicate to channels throughout the world during a forty-year period. The channels included writer Rudyard Kipling's sister in India and Mrs. Coombe Tennant (known as Mrs. Willet), Dame Edith Lyttelton (known as Mrs. King), and Helen Verrall in England. Other channels in Europe and the United States also reported related communications from the same sources. The sitters included Sir Oliver Lodge and the second Earl of Balfour. Intricate webs of information from the same sources to the different channels provide powerful argument on behalf of channeling and survival of death.

Carl Jung reported a general kind of book test in the following spontaneous, clairvoyant channeling episode:

> One night I lay awake thinking of the sudden death of a friend whose funeral had taken place the day before . . . Suddenly I felt that he was in the room. It seemed to me that he stood at the foot of my bed and was asking me to go with him . . . I follow[ed] him in my imagination. He led me out of the house, into the garden out to the road, and finally to his house . . . He climbed on a stool and showed me the second of five books with red bindings which stood on the second shelf from the top. This experience seemed to me so curious that next morning I went to his widow and asked whether I could look up something in my friend's library. Sure enough, there

was a stool standing under the bookcase I had seen in my vision, and even before I came closer, I could see the five books with red bindings . . . The title of the second volume read: *The Legacy of the Dead.*[16]

The typical case involves specific content within a given book. In a good book test, it should be possible to rule out telepathy or GESP by the channel. Laura Archera Huxley reports to have received, by way of the clairvoyant medium Keith Milton Rinehart, such a detailed, convincing book test from the spirit of her husband, writer Aldous Huxley, following his death.[17]

In her book *The Mediumship of Mrs. Leonard*, Susy Smith provides a good example of a book test. A young Englishman, Edward Wyndham Tennant, had recently died in World War I. The chief interest of his father, Lord Glenconner, had been forestry, and on family walks the father would often remark on how the young trees were being ruined by "the beetle." According to Smith, "Young Bim [Edward] had been known to whisper to his mother at the start of a family walk, 'See if we can get through the wood without hearing about the beetle!' "

A year after his death, Edward sent to his father, through Gladys Osborne Leonard and her control "Feda," a message to go to "the ninth book on the third shelf counting from the left to the right in the bookcase on the right of the door in the drawing room. Take the title, and go through it to page 37." The book was *Trees*. At the bottom of page 36 and at the top of 37 was: "Sometimes you will see curious marks in the wood; these are caused by a tunneling beetle, very injurious to trees."

Word-association tests were the subject matter of channeling research earlier in this century. They, too, attempted to provide evidence that the entities were who they said they were. W. Whately Carington, early twentieth-century psychic researcher, sought to utilize the psychological word-association test designed by Carl Jung. Jung's idea was to draw into conscious awareness certain forgotten material in response to selected cue words. Tested in this manner, the subject would provide latent material unique to him or her. Carington hoped that, by posing this test to supposedly discarnate human spirits through their channels, the personalities of sources could be identified. Carington reported:

We may be willing to grant any amount of play-acting ability on the part of the subconscious mind of the medium. But the association words we received seemed quite characteristic and typical of the personalities involved in life, as subsequently verified by friends and relatives known to them when living.[18]

Some critics argue that no matter how convincing channeled evidence seems to be for the survival of physical death, the channel still may be unknowingly drawing data from the collective unconscious, Universal Mind, or akashic records, none of which necessarily requires that we survive physical death as individuals. Once more, we are left to decide for ourselves.

DESCRIPTIONS OF LIFE
IN NONPHYSICAL REALMS

Dr. Jesse Herman Holmes, a leading Quaker and head of the Department of Religion and Philosophy at Swarthmore College in Pennsylvania for twenty-five years, was reported to be channeled some years after his death in 1942. In the book of his material, *As We See It from Here,* "Holmes" describes the inevitable mix of descriptions of other dimensions that we are liable to get because of the variety of levels of evolvement from which he and his fellow discarnates operate:

> Information concerning the worlds of spirit has been given through many years. This information is diversified and relates to experiences of various entities who have found themselves, or elected to be, in any one of the various wavelengths of the spiritual energy, in one of the worlds of Spirit. Therefore the information from such persons will not be consistent in all points. It is merely an expression of signposts along the way.[19]

Most channeled material does concur, however, that life in the realms beyond our physical dimension involves a much closer relationship between the mind and the seeming matter of the environment being experienced. Often phrases like "the living light that constitutes all things" are used.

A good example of the detail possible with this kind of material is *Life in the World Unseen,* by channel Anthony Borgia speaking for Monsignor Robert Hugh Benson after Benson's death in 1914. Here is a description of Benson going sailing in the "spirit world":

> Ships are meant to float and move upon the waters; they are animated by the living force that animates all things here, and if we wish to move them over the water we have but to focus our thoughts in that direction . . . Our host handles his craft skillfully, and increasing and diminishing its speed he could create, by the

different degree of movement of the water, the most striking alter-
nations of colour and musical sound, the brilliant scintillations of
the sea showing how alive it was. It responded to the boat's every
movement as though they were in complete unison—as indeed
they were.[20]

Another example, containing myriad correlations with hundreds of
other cases like it, involves a man in England receiving highly detailed
descriptions from his father, who has recently died of a stroke:

Looking at my surroundings, I became aware that I was in a large
building of multi-colored stones, each vibrating a tune like a great
orchestra, and as they vibrated they gave off the most enchant-
ing music . . . Later on I found out that specially trained souls are
trained in the use of thought forms to allow the soul to settle down
in suitable and familiar surroundings. Whatever you wish is supplied to you, whether it is a farm, factory, halls of music, science
laboratory, college of arts.
 I walked out into the golden sunlight and saw how much
quicker my perception and vision were . . . I queried whether
there is a different sun for each plane of spirit, and I was told that
there is. Each sun is the replica of the master sun and working on a
different colour vibration.[21]

Many channeled messages provide information about the kind of
reality experienced by newly deceased humans. In *Testimony of Light,* the
deceased Sister Frances Mary (Banks) of the Community of the Resur-
rection in South Africa, was reported to have contacted her friend,
British channel Helen Greaves. Echoing many other reports, the Sister
finds herself recovering in a kind of hospice on a new level of reality:

I am in a kind of rest home now. It is run by the Sisters of the
community to which I belonged when in incarnation. They are so
kind and gentle with me. I am now lying in a bed, high up on a
terrace, that looks out over a vast sunlit plain. It is a beautiful
scene, and so restful . . . I am recuperating from the illness which
brought disintegration to my physical body. I feel content and calm
and at peace.

Repeating the theme found throughout descriptions of such other-
worldliness, the Sister states that the essence of whatever is experienced
on her new level of reality seems to be a function of living mind:

This is indeed a world of thought. You live, of course, also in a thought world, only with you, thought has been crystallised very deeply into matter and much of the illusion of that existence has become "solidified" in the earth mind. Mind has often closed away reality from itself. Here we are what we appear . . . Light here is literally the substance and matter of our thought life. Thus, as our thoughts become attuned to the vibration of Creative Divinity, so the substance of our bodies changes, becoming less dense and reflecting more Light.[22]

In light of the previous description, consider the following account, supposedly provided by the spirit of the late psychologist and philosopher William James, as channeled by Jane Roberts:

Nowhere have I encountered the furnishings of a conventional heaven, or glimpsed the face of God. On the other hand, certainly I dwell in a psychological heaven by earth's standards, for everywhere I sense a presence, or atmosphere, or atmospheric presence that is well-intentioned, gentle yet powerful, and all-knowing . . . At the risk of understating, this presence seems more like a loving condition that permeates existence [here], and from which all existence springs . . . While I am tempted to say that it moves in waves because of its mobile nature, this is not true. Instead it appears out of itself, at each and every point in the universe . . . This same omnipresent light seems to attract the smallest of my psychological seeds . . . I believe that comprehension of this atmospheric presence is automatically meted out according to the needs and conditions and nature of the perceiver.[23]

THE FUTURE AND THE PAST

Some channeling cases are thought to provide prophetic information that gives a glimpse of what is to come. Other sources purport to share with us information about individual past lives or the planet's history.

One generalization that can be made from studying the prophetic channeled literature is this: To a startling degree the sources agree that a tremendous change will come to the world as we know it, before the end of this century. Sources such as Saint John in the biblical book of Revelation, Nostradamus in the sixteenth century, Swedenborg, Edgar Cayce, and recently Maurice B. Cooke's "Hilarion" all go into considerable detail about how the current reality will give way, through painful upheaval, to a more harmonious and loving spiritual age. Much of the channeling from "space brothers" also deals with impending destruction, which they say must precede the coming of the new millennium. Yet we are told that this purported change need not be seen as negative. As author Marilyn Ferguson points out: "There is a lot of channeling coming in that has to do with the idea that the apocalyptic thing is a transition in consciousness. It's nothing to be afraid of."[24]

Although the channeled material speaks of probabilities more than inevitabilities, the sources say, the former quickly become the latter. The exercise of free will *can* affect the future of the individual and the species. However, the inertia of millions, even billions, of people with entrenched belief systems, or thoughtforms, keeps thinking and behavior relatively the same within an individual lifetime and even from one lifetime to the next. We are counseled that, sooner or later, some things *are* inevitable. Basic lessons, challenges, opportunities, and relationships are unavoidably laid out for us, even laid out *by* us, beforehand. We then proceed to live through and to learn from them.

The following describes the higher physical or nonphysical pollution supposedly left in our psychic environment from past beliefs, feelings, and behaviors, which now continues to affect our existence. However, although our past helps to create the inertia of our current condition and our probable future, "the present release of greater understanding is vouchsafed to mankind today because of the Christ and every avatar whom God has so lovingly sent to the earth," according to "The Great Divine Director," through channel Elizabeth Clare Prophet:

> There do exist, then, in the atmosphere throughout the entire planet, floating forcefields or grids containing scapegoat energy of mankind's wrong thought and feeling . . . And the conflicting harmonic rate of vibration of these fields is such as to bring about great discomfort to elemental life as well as to mankind . . . making for innumerable clashes referred to by beloved Morya as "human dissonance" which are actually impediments to the full harmonic orchestration of the brotherhood of man . . . [Yet] shall perceptive men halt the release of destructive energy to the world. Thus shall new bolts of the blue lightning of divine love strike the earth with liberating fervor.[25]

With regard to the past, the sources speaking through Edgar Cayce, Ruth Montgomery, and many others describe the mythical civilizations of Lemuria and Atlantis, as well as details about the biblical Garden of Eden and the Flood. Other material involves the purported truth behind the mythic gods and beasts of early cultures. Sources claiming to have been present in those times describe the seeding of life on this planet and the relationship of our species long ago with other beings not of this earth. Some material, such as *OAHSPE* and *The Urantia Book,* even describes the origins of the earth, the solar system, and the entire physical universe as we know it.

An excellent example of this kind of past-history channeled information is the following, presented by "Hilarion" through Canadian Maurice B. Cooke. It closely parallels similar material from sources channeled by, for example, Ruth Montgomery and Edgar Cayce.

One of the most advanced times upon the earth took place just before the sinking of the great Continent of Lemuria in the Pacific Ocean some 26,000 years ago. This was a period during which there was a great deal of contact between the human race and other galactic groups of greater advancement, both technically and spiritually. There were scattered colonies of the galactic visitors on the earth in that epoch, and one of the most marvelous was that at what is now called Tiahuanaco [in the South American Amazon].[26]

SUBJECT MATTER FOR ARTISTIC/CREATIVE EXPRESSION

Deceased poets, playwrights, painters, dancers, actors, and composers are also said to use their natural talents for creative self-expression in the new realm. They say through channels that occasionally they try to impress their creative energies on their colleagues on earth, who then experience inspiration, creative ideas, or new directions. In rarer full-trance cases, the discarnate creative spirits simply use a cooperating channel's body to directly manifest material on the physical plane.

Perhaps the best-known channel of musical material from supposed spirit sources was London housewife Rosemary Brown, who had no musical education. Brown's autobiographical book *Unfinished Symphonies*[27] chronicles her lifelong association with the supposed spirits of such great composers as Liszt, Beethoven, Debussy, Chopin, Schubert, and Bach. More than four hundred new compositions are reported to have come through her in this manner. She claimed that the spirit of the nineteenth-century Liszt visited her in a clairvoyant vision when she was seven and promised that he would work with her as she got older.

In *The Music of Rosemary Brown,*[28] Ian Parrot relates painstaking attempts by critics to prove Brown's playing to be only imitation, conscious or unconscious. But her ability to reflect the creative quirks and nuances of the different composers convinced many in the musical world that something beyond mere imitation was occurring.

A computer study was even done to match Brown's new music with known pieces by the composers. Conductor Leonard Bernstein, after playing a piece that Brown said was transcribed from the spirit of Rachmaninoff, declared it to be "the real Rachmaninoff."[29]

The alleged spirit of Liszt apparently got around. The noted contemporary American composer Virgil Fox, seated before the organ at Saint Stephens cathedral in Vienna, wondered how to interpret an old score by Liszt, which he had found in the choir loft. Researcher Frank C. Tribbe describes what happened next:

> Glancing (by chance) past the side of the organ keyboard, Fox saw a tall, thin man, dressed as a nineteenth century maestro, who was watching him intently. Almost immediately, he recognized the figure of Liszt, because of the close resemblance to many paintings and prints of Liszt he had seen. And at that moment he began to receive telepathic instructions from Liszt as to how the piece was to be played.[30]

The literature also contains many examples of automatic painting. In some of these cases, visual artists report material directly given through them by discarnate spirits of certain well-known artists; in other cases, they experience a more open channeling kind of experience, yet one that definitely feels self-transcending as to source.

The late James W. Hyslop, when he was president of the American Society for Psychical Research, reported studying a man named Frederick Thompson, who, at the turn of the century, was suddenly seized with the desire to do a great deal of drawing and painting with no prior art background. Thompson claimed that he was inspired, perhaps even possessed, by the spirit of some deceased artist. Shaken by the whole affair, Thompson sought out Hyslop. A number of channels employed by Hyslop corroborated messages from "the spirit" of Robert S. Gifford, an American painter who died just before Thompson had begun painting. In addition, Hyslop compared the drawings made by Thompson with the last ones done by Gifford and found them to be the same style and content. According to Hyslop's research, Thompson had never seen Gifford's work.[31]

Perhaps the most publicized channel of this kind working today is Luis Gasparetto, a respected South American physician. Numerous studies of his work describe a typical session: He is tied to a straight-back chair and carefully blindfolded. His shoes and socks are removed. Brushes, paints, and blank canvases are placed on the floor within reach of his feet. He then enters full trance and claims that the spirits of assorted discarnate artists, such as Rembrandt and Picasso, use his feet as well as hands to paint pictures. Some art experts have pronounced them to be in the manner of the discarnate artists.

SCIENTIFIC/TECHNOLOGICAL MATERIAL, HEALTH, AND HEALING

In this category, I present material especially for those of you who are scientifically inclined and thus far may not have found much substance in channeled material. Here you can begin to see the rich possibilities for both theoretical and applied research in this area.

While some purported sources of technical information, such as the "space brothers," do not seem to be of human origin, most identify themselves as disembodied human spirits who were once scientists, inventors, engineers, doctors, healers, and researchers on earth. They tell us that they are able to continue their work once they have left the physical plane and that they now have more knowledge and resources at their disposal without the economic survival constraints of earthly life. Many communicate that they can tune into a wealth of scientific ideas existing in the akashic records and in "timeless nonphysical realms of possibility."

In chapter 1, we were introduced to Canadian channel Maurice B. Cooke's source "Hilarion," who dictated information about a new healing technology using inert gases under strong pressure and magnetic fields. Cooke claims to have constructed a model that works. Now consider "Hilarion's" reassertion of the concept of an *ether* (or *aether*, as Cooke spells it), discarded by mainstream physicists earlier in this century. This material also ties such an ether to a multidimensional universe within which forces operate transdimensionally. Recent interdimensional "wormhole" theories of physics would tend to support such a view.

The substance which defines the space of the real world is a tenuous material with properties of elasticity. Its basic nature allows it to stretch, to contract, to flow as a current of water does, and to carry vibrational wave disturbances. This substance permeates all of the three-dimensional matrix . . . in the physical universe.

The error which scientists have made in regard to the electron is to assume that the electron is *something* . . . Surrounding the condensed packet of aether [that is the proton] are concentric rings of high transverse vibration, and it is in these concentric rings that the various electrons take form . . . The aether is in such an agitated state that small openings or breaches in its texture spontaneously arise. Each "hole" in the aether becomes a spinning vortex through which the aetheric substance spins out into the fourth dimension. The aether which passes outwardly through the spinning hole arcs back into the aetheric matrix *at* the proton itself. The constant flow of aether into the proton from the fourth dimension provides sufficient material for the proton to remain in its contracted or condensed state, because the impingement of light against the proton tends to promote the re-expansion of the proton back to the more rarified condition which the rest of the aether maintains.[32]

As in the Cooke material, we find in the channeled books of the late Waynesboro, Virginia, artist and scientist Walter Russell messages (from "God") that conveyed to him, he claimed, direct knowledge of how the basic universal forces of electromagnetism, gravity, and atomic energy really operate. In the following excerpts, first published in 1947, we can see foreshadowings of certain aspects of later astronomical and sub-atomic theories about Nature. There is also a suggestion of an understanding of what would become the light-based technology of lasers and holography:

In My universe there is but one form from which all forms appear. That one form is the pulsing cube-sphere, two halves of the heart-beat of My dual thinking. All forms pulse, therefore, all forms are two, one form for the inbreathing pulse, which generates, and one for the outbreathing, radiating one. The cube is the sphere expanded by the outward breath to black rest in cold space, and the sphere is the cube compressed to the incandescence of white-hot suns by the inward breath.

For, to thee I again say, all things are Light; and Light separates not; nor has it bounds; nor is it here and not there. Man may weave the patterns of his Self in Light of Me and of his image in divided lights of Me, e'en as the sun sets up its bow of many hues from divided Light of Me, but man cannot be apart from Me, as the spectrum cannot be apart from the Light of Me . . . Verily, I say, every wave encompasseth every other wave unto the One; and the many are within the One, e'en down to the least of waves of Me.[33]

Continuing these themes, in *The Book of Knowledge: The Keys of Enoch,* James J. Hurtak (discussed in chapter 1) claims to have received technical information from two nonphysical beings. "Enoch" and

"Metatron." To get some idea of how dense and complex this material is, consider the following two samples:

> The valency of transfiguration takes place when the biogravitational energies which control the positive centropy of the DNA coding of intelligence are centered within a new spectrum of star energy controlling molecular-magnetohydrodynamic fields.
> Every electron has a mathematical counterpart of Light threshold which survives the body. By measuring the wave form of this Light threshold, the Higher Evolution can recode the consciousness of a human being . . . by energizing magnetogravitational fields around your body, your molecular structure can be changed and your body reconstituted on another wavelength of light.[34]

Since 1957, Texas psychic researcher Ray Stanford has been trance-channeling entities who call themselves the "Brothers" and who have provided technical information that Stanford and others have occasionally tried to research:

> They told us how to build a complicated research device . . . [that] would isolate a person from outside electromagnetic fields while enclosing him in a very high-energy electrostatic field. The Brothers say that the effect achieved would be very much like that which happened to Moses on top of Mt. Sinai . . . Physically, the only thing that could have caused it was [that] the major electrolyte of the body, ATP, was energized. This is one of the things we hope to do with this device—energize the ATP and enhance the process of consciousness.[35]

The assorted Ruth Norman *Unarius Science* books (mentioned in chapter 2) are filled with detailed descriptions—attributed to well-known deceased scientists—of how to build devices that operate on vortical wave energy downstepped from higher dimensions into ours. But to date, no one seems interested in researching this rather intriguing material.

Finally, there is a wealth of channeled material that falls into the category of medical guidance and healing. The majority of the Edgar Cayce messages was of this kind. The Association for Research and Enlightenment (A.R.E.), which grew up around Cayce's work, claims that his alleged sources were at least 85 percent accurate in their diagnosis and in the success of the remedies and curative procedures that they prescribed. Similarly, contemporary channel Kevin Ryerson, based on feedback from his clients, claims at least a 75 percent rate of accuracy and success with the work of his sources in this area. Some holistic physicians have made informal studies of the Cayce and other channeled prescriptive information and have found that much of its jibes with the traditional folk medicine of preliterate cultures. Other investigators have found that some of the concepts and techniques in the channeled material can be understood only through the theories of the most recent "new science." Given the increasing quantity of channeled material of a medical/healing nature, research in this area seems crucial.

Four of the most substantial centers of research on the scientific aspects of channeled material are A.R.E. in Virginia Beach, Virginia; William Kautz's Center for Applied Intuition in San Francisco (mentioned in chapter 1); George W. Meek's Metascience Corporation in Franklin, North Carolina; and Andrija Puharich's Elf Cocoon Corporation in Dobson, North Carolina. Yet, in general, there have been few if any serious attempts in recent years to study what, above all other kinds of channeled material, seems especially susceptible to testing and verification. This may be because, in the still-prevailing atmosphere of scientific conservatism, most credentialed scientists choose to "stay in the closet" with regard to such controversial activity.

5

WHO ARE THEY CHANNELING?

Questions such as "Do ancient beings in far-away galaxies really speak through American housewives?" are bound to arise in any examination of channeling. The assortment of supposed sources challenges the imagination and strains credibility. The sources presented here are described in the same terms used by the channels to identify them or by the reputed sources to identify themselves. In each case, you the reader must evaluate the specific content of the channeled material in order to decide for yourself whether it is authentic.

A majority of the thousands of cases comprising the channeling literature involve sources described as individual, separate beings, in the sense of *entities* as defined in the glossary. As was mentioned in the Introduction, some people don't like the concept of entities as sources in the channeling process; they reject the implication that the information source is a being or personality completely separate from the channel. Such people prefer to use less limiting concepts in trying to understand channeling. I have tried in this chapter to include *all* of the reported kinds of channeled sources, not just the kinds that could be construed as entities. In fact the kinds of sources are organized in this chapter to begin with those that are perhaps least clearly distinguishable from the channel's self.

We will thus begin with the channel's higher Self, then gods and God, the Universal Mind and the collective unconscious, and group beings. The sources are presented in this sequence so that certain interconnections can be highlighted. The remaining sources have in common the feature that they are all said to possess a greater quality of individuality, a self-awareness, and an intentionality, choosing to communicate to us from a nonphysical realm. This group includes Jesus Christ and other "ascended masters"; nonhumans from angelic and other realms; a particular kind of nonhuman called "space brothers"; and, finally, discarnate human spirits—the largest class of all.

THE CHANNEL'S HIGHER SELF

> There is in all of us a higher man . . . a man more entirely of the celestial rank, almost a god, reproducing God. When the soul begins again to mount, it comes not to something alien, but its very self. The self thus lifted, we are in the likeness of the Supreme.
>
> —Plotinus[1]

> The man identifies his real being with the germinal higher part of himself . . . He becomes conscious that this higher part [shares the same boundaries] with a *more* of the same quality, which is operative in the universe outside of him and which he can keep in working touch with . . . Is such a "more" merely our own notion, or does it really exist? If so, in what form should we conceive of that "union" with it of which religious geniuses are so convinced? . . . The higher faculties of our own hidden mind . . . are controlling the sense of union with the power beyond us.
>
> —William James[2]

James Fadiman, one of the founders of transpersonal psychology, believes "there's no doubt that there's a higher organization of self which is less greedy and less opportunistic and less run by the kind of Freudian value system."[3] Many of us, he feels, are haunted by the presence, occasionally experienced, of such a higher Self.

Any psychologist will tell us that we are each composed of a body, senses, emotions, memory, will, ego, conscious intellect, imagination, and unconscious processes. Most of us would identify our selves as our waking, self-aware consciousness. But consider an analogy: as the conscious ego is supposed to be served by the rest of the system, so the entire system itself (including the ego) is the learning vehicle for the evolution of the higher Self, or simply the Self. This higher Self has been known throughout history and across all cultures by many names. Ralph Waldo Emerson and other nineteenth-century New England Transcendentalists coined the term *oversoul*. Moderns refer to the *superconscious*.

The chief contention is that the lower-self package, which is composed of the day-to-day self, its body, focal consciousness, and personal unconscious, is only a projection of the higher Self for experiencing the earth plane. Through these experiences, both the earthly component and the higher, non-earthbound Self can waken, unfold, and increase in awareness. In the larger picture and in the longer run, this growth is of a spiritual (not material or intellectual) nature.

The channeled literature claims that this higher Self channels downward through an umbilical connection (occult name: *antahkarana* or *antakarana*) between two levels of being, the higher Self and lower self. This process moves from the subtler, higher-frequency realm to the denser, earthside realm of our everyday reality. There is a constant communication between these levels, but because of a kind of amnesia and dissociation, the earthly part is not usually conscious of its own higher aspect and what it is providing. The argument is that if the local ego were constantly aware of this larger context, then certain learning experiences for which a localized, earthly existence is necessary might be disrupted.

From this perspective, channeling one's higher Self is not so much a case of self-transcendence as of expanded self-awareness. The greater Self, which is separately conscious of that lesser self as part of it, seems to lend some of its own consciousness to the consciousness of its less-aware component. Furthermore, the awareness of the higher Self is said to be more connected to and in communication with other levels of reality and with ultimate truth than is the lower self.

British channel Stuart Wilde speaks of "The higher Self within you that is training on the inner plane. By getting in touch with it inside you," Wilde believes, "you get in touch with all that there is." Just "quiet the ego to allow the infinite energy of the higher Self to take a greater part of your consciousness. All channeling in my view is . . . aligning to that higher Self.[4]

Ken Wilber, formulator of Spectrum Psychology and a leading figure in transpersonal psychology and consciousness research, reports:

> I *do* think there is a higher Self, and ultimately there is nothing but that higher Self and everything that's manifest is a manifestation of that Self. I think when people start growing toward that Self, they get intimations and inspirations from it . . . When people start getting a glimpse of the higher Self, it's a direct, immediate obvious thing. It does not come couched in pseudoscientific language. It's simply realizing your own mind . . . you just wake up, and that doesn't have any of the machinations of long-distance calls from "the nine guys running Alpha Centauri."[5]

Author-lecturer and publisher of *A Course in Miracles* Judith Skutch echoes this theme:

> For me at this point in my own acceptance/understanding of [channeling] . . . I believe it's all within, and that the higher part of our knowing is allowed to be given to us in a form that we will most accept . . . To me channeling is the receptivity of the particular person to suspend judgment and willingly allow the Self that

knows more, that is one with the eternal and limitless knowledge, to give its message in whatever form is applicable.[6]

Morro Bay, California, psychiatrist Ralph B. Allison, one of the leading authorities on multiple-personality disorder, is a firm believer in and practitioner of the higher Self. Distinguishing it from normal ego consciousness, Allison equates the high Self with the concept of the Transpersonal Self formulated by fellow psychiatrist and Psychosynthesis founder Roberto Assagioli. As Allison describes it:

We each have access to it. We don't have to go to somebody who's on a stage [the channel]. We can do it privately, quietly. I can do it sitting in the car; when I'm on the stand at court; when I'm in the office with a patient. You do it when you *need* it, and it's available to you then, and you don't need these people on the stage.

Allison sometimes refers to his own higher Self, or an aspect of it, as "Mike," reserving final judgment on who or what "Mike" might ultimately be (including part of himself). Below he gives an example of his experience. It is fascinating to conjecture on the contrast represented here: the doctor and authority benefiting from his awareness of possessing more than one level of self, while the patient he is treating suffers from a confusion of multiple identities. Patients, according to Allison, don't listen to higher helpers, so they suffer. Therapy involves teaching them to listen.

I remember when I used to drive to the hospital at night on an emergency call to see one of these patients. I didn't know what I was going to do when I got there, but I had a nurse in a panic. I would just switch up to that higher level and let things go. And when I got to the hospital, the whole treatment plan was laid out in my head, and I'd do whatever that higher level told me to do and, what do you know, things worked out . . . All of us have it available.[7]

GODS AND GOD

Prayer is then no longer words or thoughts; prayer is no longer asking God to do something. It is a state of silence in which you can be receptive to the word of God. The mind is still.
—Joel S. Goldsmith[8]

Midway through the 1980s, a Gallup Poll provided the following figures: 94 percent of adult Americans questioned believed in God or some universal spirit; 84 percent believed that "God is a heavenly father who watches over us and can be reached by our prayers"; 69 percent said God led or guided them in making decisions; 36 percent said God had spoken directly to them "through some direct means"; and 11 percent said God "speaks out loud though a direct verbal message." These findings generally concur with similar surveys taken over the past fifty years.[9]

Naturalist Alfred Russel Wallace believed in a hierarchical model of communication that ranged from the human to the godlike to God. He conceived of the concept of evolution by natural selection at about the same time as Charles Darwin. But Wallace thought that the presence of higher human faculties implied a spiritual nature. "It seems only logical" he wrote, "to assume that the vast, the infinite chasm between ourselves and the Deity is to some extent occupied by an almost infinite series of grades of being, each successive grade having higher and higher powers in regard to the organization, development, and control of the universe." According to Wallace, the higher grades of the "infinite God" could influence the lower by means of telepathy, as if all were taking place within a single mind.[10]

Philosopher Huston Smith, author of numerous books on religion, notes that prior to the rise of the modern West every society we know anything about has taken for granted that superhuman beings exist and that under exceptional circumstances we can communicate with them. In a private interview he drew a distinction between God and lesser intermediate beings from which information might derive.

> I do believe that beings greater than ourselves exist. I likewise believe that some of these may be in touch with us in ways we are not normally aware of. Regarding information that derives from them, I distinguish what has come to be called channeling from Revelation. Revelation proceeds directly from God, as to Moses on Mount Sinai. Even when Revelation includes an intermediary, as in the case of the angel Gabriel who transmitted the Koran from Allah to Muhammad, the intermediary neither adds nor detracts, so for all practical purposes the message still proceeds from God directly. In channeling as I would use the word, the source of the message is not God but a lesser spirit of some sort—a demigod, an angel, a departed soul, whatever.[11]

As one opens to the higher Self and has experiences not identified with the usual self or environment, confusion can arise in trying to identify the source of these experiences. Because of our loss of memory of the true relationship between self and higher Self, the lower self often experiences and interprets its own higher aspect as being godlike or God, external and independent of the experiencing self. The higher Self has at times been termed the transcendent self. But a distinction should be made between the transcendent and godlike on one hand, and what most world religions deem to be God, or the one Supreme Divine Being, on the other. There is the difference between the personal (Jesus)and impersonal (Absolute) God, for example. Many people accept the ideas that God communicated to various mystics, saints, and prophets throughout history. However, they may draw the line when it comes to accepting that the same God could be channeled today through some of their otherwise ordinary neighbors.

Like the channeled entity "Lazaris," who uses the term God/Goddess/All That Is, most of the channeled material on this subject stresses that God is all that is, is all in all, the unity that contains all disparate parts. If so, perhaps the higher Self channeling through to the lower self is simply a shift in awareness; that is, nothing changes but our attention.

Or, on the other hand, perhaps *everything* changes but our attention. But what does it mean to say that God is all that is? When the channel senses that an angel or other divine representative has gained his or her inner ear, does this mean that a more aware aspect of the one Being—God—is communicating from "on high" to a less-aware mortal station, the channel? Such a pantheistic view of God-as-all-things seems fraught with unresolvable problems when it comes to dealing with interacting individual identities. Even the proverbial "still small voice within" could be seen as a particular individuation of the one universal intelligence. According to the channeled literature, the higher one ascends on the spiritual evolutionary ladder, the more unity one feels with God *and* with creation.

Sometimes a source will claim to be God but then will thwart our expectation of what messages should originate from such a source. A recent example comes through Sante Fe, New Mexico, channel Ceanne DeRohan in *Original Cause: The Unseen Role of Denial*.[12] Her source purports to be God telling us Its story: how, as an evolving being Itself, It had to learn to integrate aspects of Itself that It hadn't initially recognized as Itself—Heart, The Will, Mother, and The Son. The book reads like a terribly sophisticated, almost universal display of classic split personality. Some interpreters consider it to be the honest searchings of a genuine, though certainly less than ultimate, nonphysical entity as a separate focus of consciousness, which is trying to come to terms with understanding itself and is being channeled by DeRohan. Others see it similarly but make the entity out to be simply an alter personality of the channel. For all we know, perhaps *each* center of consciousness, whether located by us inside or outside of a "self," *is* God, or part of God, learning to come to terms with, express, and integrate all the parts of itself.

If, according to this speculation, we are all individuations of the one God, then it would appear that some of us are further evolved in consciousness than others. We are all playing out the different identities of who we are, or, perhaps, who we think we are or who we would like to be. Thus the Ouija board often yields the likes of "Marie Antoinette," "Jesus Christ," or "the Archangel Michael." It is then up to each channel's delicate mechanisms of discernment to interpret the true identity of the source.

Those of us who read channeled material must discriminate as well. We must often open up to a level of larger wisdom to best distinguish the truth of a matter, channeled or otherwise. Thus we may need to intuitively contact our higher Self in order to decide the source and credibility of allegedly channeled material. This could lead to the rather circular notion that one needs to use the Self to detect the Self, or to use the God within in order to know God.

As John White, editor of *The Highest States of Consciousness,* among other books, has pointed out, this is close to the traditional warning that sacred traditions make: true spiritual growth means seeking to know God above all, recognizing that pursuit of intermediate-level knowledge or faculties, such as those acquired through channeling, is ultimately unsatisfying and detrimental to God-realization.[13]

THE UNIVERSAL MIND AND THE COLLECTIVE UNCONSCIOUS

Opening your channel to the higher realms . . . This greater collective consciousness has been called God, All-That-Is, the Universal Mind. This higher creative intelligence is the source of all life . . . Through your channeling you will find a closer connection to this source energy . . . you will make contact with a guide or your own source self (often called your higher self) which will act as a bridge to the higher collective consciousness.
—Sanaya Roman, channel[14]

In current psychological thinking, the normal ego has a dissociated yet intuitive relationship with the unconscious aspect of the larger psychological system of which it is a part. Similarly, in our enlarged model here, each of our psychological systems is like an ego embedded within the greater collective Universal Mind. Part of this Universal Mind (or collective consciousness), of which we are normally unconscious, may be channeled by us. This interpretation may be applied to cases in which the source of the channeled material cannot be identified as possessing individuality as we know it.

Many today share this growing pantheistic and mentalist view of all-as-one-mind. Philosopher Jean Houston:

> Freud in his last work said if we are part of the unity, then we can have access to all the solutions at some level, and that's what we are learning to do in our time, hopefully. And what the whole channeling phenomenon is about is people having separate and collective breakthroughs in ways of releasing . . . what Huxley called the "cerebral reducing valve" . . . [There's] a movement of attention from conscious states to depth states in which an enormous amount of information is stored . . . I'm willing to say that the psyche is much larger than we think it is and is engaged at many levels with an ecology of consciousness that is broader than its own local base.[15]

Physiological researcher and former UCLA professor Valerie Hunt adds her concept of a mind-field:

> The source of everything is the mind-field . . . memory of past lives is carried in the mind-field . . . the most powerful force in the world today is the mind. The mind is a field that can contact anything . . . The major thoughts that have ever been thought are in the field. We tap into a thought form and it is available to us, and that mind of ours can just plain go get anything it wants.[16]

Or, as Tuella, the New Mexico channel of "Ashtar" and other "space brothers," puts it:

> Since all is mind, man has but to tune in to any particular mind to *become* that mind with which he shall identify himself . . . As we tune in to the God-Mind through our God-head, all things which we seek can be revealed as needed and divinely permitted.[17]

Carl Jung also spoke in terms of a collective unconscious whose contents are composed of various archetypes, or racial memories of the most often repeated human beliefs and behaviors. As we contact the archetypes—by dream, myth, art, or religious and meditative states—our psyches are energized by them, and we translate them into our own individual experiences. The "wise old sage" archetype, for example, may be an expression of what we have been calling the higher Self, spirit guide," Master, or God within. (In chapter 7 we will look in greater depth at Jung's concept as it relates to channeling.)

GROUP BEINGS

We are the spark of consciousness that exists and is aware of its existence, that creates thought that creates reality just as you are. We do it with a greater level of awareness and we do it without form. That is the difference. We have a multileveled consciousness . . . that is why we refer to ourselves as "we" . . . We are aware of our existence on multiple levels of awareness. If we were ever to be physical, we would have to be a number of people because we couldn't all fit into one bodily form.

—The entity "Lazaris" describing itself[18]

Group entities occasionally appear as sources. A group entity or group mind is described as a coherent bundle of still-individual or once-individual beings. As the individuals spiritually evolved, they claim, they reached a point where further growth meant pooling themselves into a larger Self.

Group beings mentioned in chapter 1 include "Seth Two," "Michael," "Lazaris," and "Ra." Here "Ra—an humble messenger of the Law of One"—is channeled: "I am Ra . . . We are those who are of the Law of One. In our vibration the polarities are harmonized; the complexities are simplified; the paradoxes have a solution. We are one . . . We as a group are what you would call a social memory complex, [who first] made contact with a race of your planetary kind which you call Egyptians."[19]

Some take the perspective that, rather than channeling a separate group being, the channel (and indeed each of us) is by nature part of such a group being. The individual then channels a hitherto unknown alter personality of his or her larger subsuming self. The various "Seth" books present the concept of the oversoul—that each of the personalities on earth is in fact part of a larger entity that evolves by gaining experiences and learning by means of its numerous simultaneously incarnating components. Thus there are times when a person can channel the entity to which he or she belongs. This may be the basis for those who claim to channel their own past-life reincarnational selves.

JESUS CHRIST AND OTHER ASCENDED MASTERS

Much channeled material purports to be from Jesus Christ and other highly evolved spiritual beings: the "masters" "Hilarion" and "Saint Germain"; "K. H." ("Koot Hoomi") and "D. K." ("Djwal Kul"), who were said to channel through Alice A. Bailey and Madame H. P. Blavatsky, respectively; various "archangels," "Mother Mary," "Chohans" of the various "rays," "Masters of Wisdom," "El Morya," "Lord Gautama," "Maitreya," "Vishnu"; and "guardians of the planet," those of the "White Brotherhood," the "White Lodge," and the "Spiritual Hierarchy," to name a few.

Most of these claim to have experienced incarnations as humans on earth or similar planets. Or, if not, they claim to have some caretaking and teaching role with regard to this planet. They say they are "ascended," meaning that they no longer have the need to incarnate into physical bodies for further spiritual growth. They could manifest in physical form if they chose to, they say, but would do so only if it served the spiritual advancement of all human beings.

These ascended masters are said to be fully and consciously operating as their own higher Selves. We are also told that they are related to *our own* higher Selves. Some observers believe that these spiritual masters may be a vehicle to enable us to experience our own larger nature. The fact that the Christ is said to be channeling through some of us, for example, may simply be our way of experiencing our own potential Christ consciousness.

Of the dozens of contemporary examples, one exceptionally beautiful and compelling case of Christ as purported source is *New Teachings for an Awakening Humanity,* channeled by Virginia Essene and published in 1986 by Spiritual Education Endeavors of Santa Clara, California.

NONHUMANS: THE ANGELIC REALM, DEVAS, ELEMENTALS, PLANTS, AND ANIMALS

This group of sources appears truly alien to most of us. If it is true that "all is one in God and God is in all things," then there should be nothing in the universe, in any kind of manifestation or on any level of being, that is not intimately related to us. This is, in fact, what the "highest" channeling sources tell us.

As we saw in chapter 1, in the Findhorn community of northern Scotland in the early 1970s, Dorothy Maclean and David Spangler claimed to have channeled angels and the other-dimensional voices of entire plant species. Others at Findhorn claim to have channeled fairies, sprites, elves, and Pan himself.

Amid the trauma of war-torn Budapest in 1943–1944, a group of Hungarian artists claimed to converse with angels. Their experience was set forth in the book *Talking with Angels*.[20] Examples of supposed angelic channeling by West German Gabriele Wittek were mentioned in chapter 1. For more on the angelic realm, consider one of the most recent studies, H. C. Moolenburgh's *A Handbook of Angels*, published in England in 1984.

Barbara Rollinson-Huss in Broomfield, Colorado,[21] and Joan Ocean in Laguna Beach, California,[22] are just two of dozens of contemporary channels who claim to be in communication with nonhumans such as dolphins.

EXTRATERRESTRIALS

As mentioned in chapter 1, during the last thirty years there have been many reports of channeling from beings whose home is other than planet earth. They are called "space brothers," "off-planet beings," or simply "extraterrestrials" by those who have channeled them. The "space brothers" have told us through a hundred different channels that some of them reside on planets in the same frequency domain as ourselves, the one we call physical. In the majority of cases, however, the aliens claim to come from vibratory domains finer than ours, usually from the etheric level between the physical and the supposed astral plane of deceased human spirits. They say they have the technology to transform their vibratory rate in order to enter our perceptual range, giving us occasional "close encounters" with UFOs. But, when channeling, they claim to be communicating to earthly channels from their own native vibrational level.

DISCARNATE HUMAN SPIRITS

More sources of this kind have been channeled than any other, and because it is the largest category, it is subdivided here. The nineteenth-century Spiritualist movement discussed in chapter 2 was involved almost exclusively with channeling deceased or disembodied human spirits. Spiritualist mediums to this day say their principal work is to give comfort to the bereaved and to expand the world view and inspire the spirituality of others by providing evidence of the continuation of human life after death. Therefore, many in the field of paranormal communication, such as researcher D. Scott Rogo, prefer to make a distinction between this kind of communication, which they call mediumship, and communication from other sources, which they call channeling.

In the Introduction, polls were cited indicating that a great many people today who would hardly think of themselves as channels nevertheless believe in survival of physical death and even claim to have experienced communication with the deceased. A growing number of researchers echo Rogo's conclusion: "I am favorably impressed by the evidence for survival, and I think that the survival explanation *does* account for some cases of mediumship and post-mortem communication better than any other theory."[23]

One of the central views expressed through channeling is that when our bodies die, the intact higher frequency of nonphysical being moves consciously to a new realm. This new realm is the environment most appropriate for learning for that particular spirit's mental-emotional "higher vehicle."

The channeled material tells us that when individuals move to "the other side," they maintain their level of spiritual development, their basic level of awareness and understanding, and even their essential personality traits. Discarnate human spirits therefore are likely to be as much a "mixed bag" as people on earth. Therefore, in listening to channeled reports, discrimination on our part is called for. As parapsychologist and consciousness researcher Charles Tart puts it, "dying does not necessarily raise your IQ."[24]

In the case of *disoriented spirits,* the literature gives many versions of a curious theme: some people, after death, are not aware that they have physically died. They simply do not understand their new situation, perhaps because of a discrepancy between their belief systems while alive and the supposed reality after death. Others express bewilderment and fear, caught within what they take to be a confusing dream from which they are unable to awaken. Starting in the latter part of the nineteenth century, Spiritualist groups initiated "rescue circles," centered around a medium, to ease the transition of distraught, recently departed human spirits who were not yet acclimatized to their new realm and thus remained "earthbound."

The Tibetan Buddhist *Book of the Dead* presents the procedure for undergoing the transition period between physical death and reincarnation back on earth or on some subtler level of reality like the "god realm." In his view, Ken Wilber sees this as

a period when the soul is basically waking up and doesn't believe it's dead. The texts usually say it's very confused, frightened . . .

The question is, what does it mean if there's an entity that stays around four or five years? That would mean in this cartography that it's basically incarnated as a "hungry ghost," or one of the god realm.[25]

Sometimes the spirits are of those to whom the channel (or someone employing the channel) had been close while alive. Channels report that some people, after death, miss their loved ones on earth, grieving for them even in their new life. In some cases, a medium might act like an "interdimensional telephone" to open lines of communication. We are told that prior shared experience and common beliefs keep these ties alive, with love the strongest bond of all. The most typical message is one of consolation and reassurance of life after death.

The channeled literature also issues a warning to those spirits eager to remain in contact with earth: too much communication can be hazardous to your spiritual health. All of the writings agree that spirits bound to earth are slowed down in their evolutionary process. On the other hand, people on earth who spend too much time preoccupied with the "other side" may be ignoring the learning experiences necessary for *their* spiritual growth. A letting-go on both sides is strongly recommended by the more highly evolved sources.

Some channeled sources were (or still are) high achievers, claiming that they were formerly scientists, inventors, statesmen, writers, painters, or composers. They say that their gifts remain with them and that they wish to transmit information or creative work for the betterment of society. While, they tell us, they are still able to pursue their talents on the nonphysical realm, they choose to communicate to us as well.

Most channels report that when they first explore the potentials of their linkage with the nonphysical realm, they usually find themselves in contact with one particular entity more than others. This control spirit plays a special role: it explains phenomena, facilitates communication, and mediates between other spirits desiring to use the channel. Controls, once having come through, usually stay with a channel for his or her lifetime. We have seen many examples of such controls in chapters 1 and 2; Gladys Osborne Leonard's "Feda" and Arthur Ford's "Fletcher" are prime examples.

Some souls, alleged to be more highly evolved than most on earth, seek to assist others in their evolution. Their goal is to raise humanity to a new state of consciousness where love and harmony reign. They are referred to, or refer to themselves, as teachers, guides, guardian spirits, or guardian angels (though they are really discarnate human spirits).

In *Companions in Spirit,* channel Laeh Maggie Garfield lists a variety of kinds of guides: lifetime guides (which she also calls guardian angels), other personal guides, guides for the day, guides for single attributes, guides for traumatic moments, mythological guides, totem animals, and guides for entire families.[26]

Some of these guides and teachers tell us via their channeling that they will return to earth for further development. Others say they no longer need earthly lives. We are told that the more evolved they become, the more they find their path is one of teaching and service to those less evolved; hence the need to communicate to us on earth. In their terminology, they have moved from the level of *chela* (student on the spiritual path) to *initiate, adept,* or *master.*

One of the most articulate channeled teachers, who called himself "The Tibetan," worked through the mediumship of Theosophist Alice A. Bailey:

> Suffice to say that I am Tibetan disciple of a certain degree, and this tells you but little, for all are disciples from the humblest aspirant up to, and beyond, the Christ Himself . . . I am a brother of yours, who has travelled a little longer upon the Path than the average student, and has therefore incurred greater responsibilities. I am one who has wrestled and fought his way into a greater measure of light than has the aspirant who will read this article, and I must therefore act as a transmitter of the light, no matter what the cost . . . My work is to teach and spread the knowledge of the Ageless Wisdom wherever I can find a response . . . It is for you to ascertain [its] truth by right practice and by the exercise of the intuition.[27]

At the other end of the reported spectrum of human spirits is the category popularly known as lower astrals. Recall how the channeled teachers (through channels such as Blavatsky and Bailey) tell of a universal, hierarchical organization within which the earth plane occupies the lowest, or most dense, sphere. There follow, in ascending order of subtlety or refinement, the etheric, astral, mental, and so on. Each plane is reputedly subdivided in turn. Higher planes supposedly involve an ever-growing closeness to God, or the source of all.

Most deceased humans allegedly go to the middle and upper subplanes of the astral domain (sometimes called "Summerland"). We are told that, of all disembodied spirits, the lower astrals are most attracted to the physical realm and are most problematic because they are least spiritually evolved. After death, they frequently report believing that they are still living on the physical level, and as a result they are frustrated or belligerent with regard to their circumstances. In addition, following the channeled maxim "kind attracts kind," these lowest astral types are drawn to those human beings who are of a similar level of maturation, such as criminals, addicts, and generally, the most crassly materialistic and self-absorbed. Still, it is said via channeling, *all* spirits are immortal and inevitably must evolve spiritually.

Finally, as part of this lower aspect, comes the rather unpleasant phenomenon of possession, in which lower astral spirits are said to infiltrate the physical/emotional/mental system of a human being. Their aim is to gain control of a human nervous system so that they can resume some form of physical existence.

The channeled material tells us that we leave ourselves open to possession, or milder cases of obsession, by neglecting or abusing our minds and bodies. For example, we are told that drug and alcohol addiction wear down the nervous system, rendering it vulnerable to unwanted influence or takeover by another. Such unnaturally altered states may create a "leak" through which an alien consciousness may enter.

When an entity attempts possession, it is definitely a case of unwanted, spontaneous channeling. The entity wishes to *control* more than to *communicate*. The higher sources claim that an attempt to influence or take control of a human being against his or her will goes against Universal Law.

Psychiatrist Ralph B. Allison, who has done extensive work with multiple-personality patients, says, "I have come to believe in the possibility of spirit possession." He has developed a spectrum to cover what he calls the possession syndrome. At one end of the spectrum is the clinically typical picture where part of the person's own mind splits off and then seems to turn around and possess him or her; "then we get into being possessed or controlled by a spirit that does not have a body at the time"; and then there is "possession by demonic spirits from satanic realms, and that's an area I don't care to discuss or be part of— it's a theoretical possibility." One contemporary psychologist who *does* care to be part of this is Edith Fiore, whose clinical experiences are reflected in her just-published book, *The Unquiet Dead: A Psychologist Treats Possession.*[28]

But who is to say what these spirits really are? Parapsychologist Stanley Krippner, in his study of multiple-personality disorder and mediumship in Brazil, points to the culture-specific way in which possession must be seen, claiming that "such terms as 'possession' lack culture-free, objective definitions."[29] Even the definition of possesssion held by Western clinical psychology—that it is a case of multiple personality—could be seen to be a product of a particular culture (Western psychology), with no more ultimate proof for the exclusive truth of its point of view than other cultures have for theirs.

Channeled material also speaks of even more dangerous sources (alluded to by Allison): nonhuman demons, evil spirits, forces of Satan or Lucifer, and the "Dark Brotherhood." These entities await every opportunity to tempt and control human spirits. Historically, the negative presence of lower astral human spirits has been attributed to these demonic entities.

The operations of the "Dark Brotherhood" have been described in detail by the source "Master Hilarion," through the mediumship of Canadian businessman Maurice B. Cooke. These beings are portrayed by "Hilarion" as "the loyal opposition" to the "White Brotherhood," the spiritual hierarchy of higher guides, guardians, and Masters. The latter group is said to be responsible for helping less-developed spirits on the spiritual path. The "Dark Brotherhood," on the other hand, "act as testing agents for the human race of man, as forces whose task it is to weed out from the human flock the souls . . . [who] are not developed enough to allow them to move forward into the higher ground of spiritual achievement." "Hilarion" adds, however, that "they can only influence those who *allow* them the necessary access, and they would not waste their energy on souls who remain firm in the truth."[30]

Half of the 1919 Danish work *Toward the Light: A Message to Mankind from the Transcendental World* is reputed to have been channeled from "Ardor," the "youngest of the eldest" of God's sons, historically known as Satan.[31]

Perhaps these archetypal dark influences offer us some kind of allegory about our nature. According to the channeled material, this whole process takes place so that we can better understand the nature of temptation, the pitfalls of power, and the need to remain responsible to the highest spiritual good.

Time after time, through different kinds of channels and channeling, similar messages are given. Evidently, the message is as important as the medium, and as various. Yet it is very important not to leave a wrong impression by the note on which this chapter happens to end. Rather, the vast majority of human (as well as other kinds of) spirits reported to be channeled throughout history, and especially in the present, come across as benign, loving, and helpful. On the whole, the majority of recorded sources appear to be a good deal more spiritually evolved and oriented than most of us, their fellow spirits embodied now on the earth plane.

Given this fact, it is interesting to note some recent observations made by sociologist Earl Babbie in a recent interview with me regarding the nature of discerning good from bad channeled beings. He and his wife Sheila have been conducting interviews with entities through their channels.

Assuming it's real, how do you tell a good from a bad entity? The way we've been approaching it is, ask the entities that. And we're starting to see some consensus emerging . . . it has to do with *empowerment:* If the entity is trying to get you to follow it or is trying to get you to give up your power to it, then you should really watch out . . . Many of the entities say they are intending to put themselves out of business. They want to just empower people to get in touch with their own intuition or higher Self or whatever . . . [so] that in the future everyone will be kind of channeling something.

6

HOW DO THEY DO IT?

Imagine experiencing something like an alcohol blackout: you lose consciousness and awaken to be told that you were doing and saying things you don't normally do and say. You cannot remember anything. And the strange thing is, you had not been drinking.

Or imagine having the malady known as narcolepsy, in which you involuntarily fall asleep during the day. Or imagine you hear a voice that you would swear is not your own, speaking to you inside your head.

If these things were to happen to you, would you feel you were losing your mind or your self-control? Or might you welcome such experiences with curiousity, even invite their return? For centuries our culture has placed a premium on knowing clearly *who we are,* on being able to identify *that which is other than ourselves,* and on knowing what is supposed to be causing what. Because *identity* and *control* have been central to our world view and to our sense of what (and who) is real, we need to consider channeling within the context of both concepts. Indeed, channeling may be characterized primarily in terms of an *identity* (the source), apparently foreign to that of the channel, exercising *control* over the perceptual, motor, cognitive, or self-reflective capacities of that person once he or she has relinquished or altered control or sense of self-identity.

There appear to be two basic kinds of channeling: *intentional* and *spontaneous.* In intentional channeling, the person who is channeling controls the phenomenon and can usually produce it at will, or is at least a willing participant. In spontaneous channeling, on the other hand, the individual is not able to control the activity and is at the mercy of its comings and goings. Spontaneous channeling has an unbidden, intrusive quality; those who prize personal autonomy and control see it as a violation of the individual's integrity by uncontrollable forces. In some cases, however, the spontaneous channel does want the contact but is unable to control its form or timing. One example of spontaneous channeling is J. Z. Knight's first encounter with "Ramtha" (described in chapter 1). Most of those who later become intentional channels begin spontaneously. Another example is the book test message presented to Carl Jung in a dream (see chapter 4).

There is also a distinction to be made between mental and physical channeling. *Mental* channeling involves mediating information—thoughts, words, images, and feelings. In *physical* channeling, on the other hand, the channel (or the source) affects the physical environment in some way. This may involve healing of the physical body, materialization, or the bending or movement of an object. Cases of this kind are far more rare than the mental kind, although in the heyday of the Spiritualist era they were often more prevalent than mental channeling. Still, parapsychologist Stanley Krippner claims that "it is difficult to talk about mediumship without dealing with physical mediumship."[1] This book is primarily about mental channeling, but this chapter will conclude with a brief description of the kinds of physical channeling that seem directly involved in mental channeling.

Third, there is a basic distinction between what might be termed *classic* channeling (usually called simply *channeling* throughout this book) and *open* channeling. The former involves anomalous but identifiable sources, such as the entity "Lazaris" through Jach Pursel or "Emmanuel" through Pat Rodegast. Open channeling involves tapping information from other than individual identifiable sources (first described in the Introduction). The distinction is a matter of whether the channel (or witnesses) can identify the source or whether the source identifies itself. This has both experiential and relativistic aspects. For example, those believing that they are open channeling might unknowingly be classically channeling material from sources that choose to remain anonymous. Examples of open channeling might include someone sensing a strong, anonymous warning of an impending accident that he was then able to avoid, or a writer receiving the idea for a new book through a lucid inspiration. (We will look in depth at open channeling in chapter 9.)

Channeling occurs in a spectrum of varieties, from highly esoteric and rare unconscious trance mediumship on one end, to the more commonplace open channeling on the other. In 1953, Harry Stack Sullivan, a pioneer in the development of psychiatry, distinguished three kinds of waking experience.[2] *Prototaxic* experiences occur prior to or without symbols mediating personal awareness; examples are the experiences of human infants, and of entranced mystic intuitives with their supposed direct knowing. *Parataxic* experiences involve symbols but in a very private, relatively unsharable way, as with the inner workings of the imaginative, daydream, and artistic processes. *Syntaxic* experiences involve symbols with awareness, thus enabling them to be communicated to others. All our waking experiences fall within these three categories.

Twenty years later, psychologist John Curtis Gowan, who built on Sullivan's system, suggested in his book *Trance, Art and Creativity* that *prototaxic* experience involves loss of ego control and awareness, usually with no memory afterward (trance). *Parataxic* experience includes images with self-awareness, but the meaning is not always clear or easily controlled by the ego or capable of being shared with others (art). *Syntaxic* experience involves conscious awareness, is ego-controlled and understood by symbolic means that permit its communication to others, thus opening such private experience to consensus (creativity).[3]

Gowan places the phenomena of schizophrenia, trance, hypnotism, drug-induced states, automatic writing, and the experience of the numinous, or spiritual, dimension in the *prototaxic* category; archetypes, dreams, ritual, myth, and art in the *parataxic* category; and conscious, manipulative creativity, meditation, and "peak experiences" in the *syntaxic* category. This seems to follow Sullivan's system.

We can place all of the major categories of channeling discussed in this chapter alongside the three divisions depicted by Sullivan and Gowan. Classification is made according to how little or how much self-awareness the channel appears to possess during the channeling experience. Full (unconscious) trance, sleep, dream, and most historical physical channeling fall within the *prototaxic* category. Under the *parataxic,* we have (semiconscious) trance, or mildly altered-state, channeling, together with most clairaudient and clairvoyant channeling. In addition, some of the more altered-state activity of open channeling among artists, musicians, writers, and public speakers would fall under the parataxic. Finally, automatic writing, the Ouija board, and most fully conscious open channeling would be of the *syntaxic* kind. To the extent to which categorization could be according to the degree of *conscious control* being exercised by the channel over his or her own *motor behavior,* we would need to place automatic writing and the Ouija board under prototaxic. In such cases, all conscious control is absent with regard to the movements of the body, although the mind appears to be in its normal self-aware state.

FULL TRANCE

While John David set up the tape recorder, Steve leaned back in his chair and tried to relax. After some five minutes of quiet, it was obvious he was having trouble, and John David, thinking perhaps it might help calm him, asked Steve to look into his eyes and told him to relax. Steve closed his eyes again, breathed easily for a moment or two, and then began to speak in a voice which was of the same tenor as his normal voice, but strikingly more intense. The first thing he said in a state of trance was, "You haven't permitted me to be in touch with you for a while . . . I have come to you to explain the systematization of the universe . . . I am called Sepotempuat."

In the middle of the session, Steve fell out of trance. It was as if someone has shaken him out of a sound sleep, and momentarily, he didn't realize where he was. "I don't know what happened," Steve said to John David . . . "You asked me to look into your eyes. Up to a certain point, I could do that, then all of a sudden I found myself veering off, and after a moment, I don't know any more what happened."[4]

Perhaps the most perplexing kind of channeling, and yet the kind most popularized by the media, is what is called full-trance mediumship. The medium or channel appears to go unconscious or into trance, and someone or something else appears to occupy the brain and body and use it for speaking, writing, or moving about. Usually, when a trance channeling session is over and the individual regains normal consciousness, he or she cannot remember anything that occurred during the session. Occasionally, however, a channel remembers an out-of-body experience of floating near the ceiling and watching his or her body being used by another.

Some trance channels claim they simply quiet themselves briefly, close their eyes, and "step aside" or "vacate the seat of consciousness." In a moment or two, they say, they are replaced by a new speaking source. The return to consciousness appears to be equally swift and subtle. Other channels describe undergoing more prolonged and dramatic transitions into and out of unconscious states. This may require the help of other (physically embodied) persons, sometimes called directors or coordinators. The medium may shudder, slump, and moan, in the kind of behavior known to accompany the loss and recovery of consciousness in situations like fainting or awakening with a start.

During the trance sessions, the controlling entity usually has a tone of voice distinctly different from the channel's normal voice; at other times, the voice sounds flat or monotonous, like an automaton. Most of the major channels of the last hundred years have been of the trance voice kind. Those capable of this extreme kind of channeling are usually capable of more conscious channeling as well.

In some cases the body of the channel is used in other ways. While the entity "Seth" was channeled via Jane Roberts's body, for example, he would ask for a glass of beer or wine now and then. He claimed to enjoy the material realm through Jane's senses. Moving back and forth in the Robertses' old rocking chair, he'd boom out his dictations to Jane's husband, Rob, in a decidedly male tone. Similarly, 35,000-year-old warrior king "Ramtha" uses the body of channel J. Z. Knight, an attractive Washington state housewife, to stride among his audience, challenging, interacting, stroking and embracing individuals as he answers questions and provides counsel.

Trance-channeled expression may involve handwriting as well as speech, and the material is often not in the channel's normal handwriting. Full-trance mediumship also may involve singing, dancing, or painting—virtually anything we can normally do with our bodies. Deceased artists and musicians allegedly have continued their creative expression through trance channels (We looked at some of this material in chapter 4.)

Still, to say that a trance state exists may not tell us much, for the related phenomena of trance and automatic behavior are not very well understood.

SLEEP CHANNELING

In the following example, purported "space brothers" from another dimension describe how one aspect of their advanced technology is used to contact us:

> The operation to which we refer is called the Somnivision Project. With it ideas are imprinted into selected people during sleep . . . We can cause anything from merely a vague memory of the "dream" to a verbatim recording in the brain. This can be compared to a radio feeding a tape recorder . . . The reason we do this during sleeping hours is that in a conscious state, the active mind tends to distort the information.[5]

During the natural sleep cycle or during a nap, an individual may receive channeled information that is not part of a dream. Upon awakening, he knows something that he did not know previously but is unable to recall how he received it. He may have only the feeling that while he was asleep, some kind of communication occurred and certain knowledge or skills were imparted. He may suddenly find himself proficient in a new language, or have a strong desire to visit a particular place or begin a certain project. He may have the sense, on awakening, that he has had an experience rich with words, like reading or attending a lecture. These unconscious experiences may perplex him, yet they are meaningful events in the context of his waking life.

Some researchers explain this as a kind of sleep learning by way of unknown teachers. Indeed, some entities, while being channeled in other ways, have claimed that they often provide information to the unconscious mind of their sleeping channels.

DREAM CHANNELING

I dreamt . . . that I was seated at a desk, engaged in a business conversation with an unknown gentleman . . . Towards me, in front, advanced Robert MacKenzie . . . I addressed him with some asperity, asking him if he did not see that I was engaged. He retired a short distance with exceeding reluctance, turned again to approach me . . . "What is all this, Robert?" I asked somewhat angrily. "Did you not see I was engaged?" "Yes, sir," he replied; "but I must speak to you at once . . . I wish to tell you, sir . . . that I am accused of doing a thing I did not do, and that I want *you* to know it, and to tell you so, and that you are to forgive me for what I am blamed for, because I am innocent." Then, "I did not do the thing they said I did."

On that I awoke . . . when my wife burst into my bedroom, much excited . . . "Oh James, here's a terrible end to the workman's ball—Robert MacKenzie has committed suicide!" With the full conviction of the meaning of the vision, I at once quietly and firmly said, "No, he has not committed suicide." "How can you possibly know that?" "Because he has just been here to tell me." [MacKenzie, it turned out, had drunk a poisonous wood stain, mistaking it for whisky.][6]

A channel entering trance is similar in some ways to an ordinary person entering the dream state and different in others. Dreaming involves initiation of the rapid eye movement (REM) period characteristic of the dream phase of sleep. It also involves paralysis of all voluntary muscles except those controlling eye movement. Neither of these is true of trance states. All of us sleep and dream, but very few go into trance. On the other hand, the normal dream state, like the trance state, can be a source of unusual material. As in full trance, the dreaming self seems more receptive to anomalous communication than the waking self, either because waking consciousness is absent or because some other kind of mind is present instead.

In dream channeling, the source may appear in the dream in some straightforward way, as a speaking figure like Robert MacKenzie in the example above. On waking, the dreamer may immediately realize that some kind of unusual personal communication has taken place and may even know with whom it occurred. Or, later on, the individual may realize that something from beyond his or her own dreaming self was responsible. Or the source may appear in symbolic form. For example, suppose the figure of Superman appears to you in a dream, telling you not to take your usual commuter train. On awakening and remembering this, you decide to drive to work. Later you learn that the train crashed; you might have been killed if you'd been on it as usual. While a few diehard fans might claim that the source was in fact Superman, it might in fact have been a source coming from beyond your individual mind and using a symbolic disguise. Or the Superman form might have been the way your own unconscious mind made sense of the brain impulses, whether those impulses had their origin inside or outside your system. We saw in chapter 2 how the interpretation of such dream material, then called incubation, goes back as far as ancient Egypt and Greece.

Some say the communicator or source chooses the dream period because the dreaming channel is then operating on the same level of reality as the source. For example, in the last century, D. D. Home first became aware of his channeling abilities as a boy when his best friend appeared in a dream to tell him he had just died. The next day, Home was informed that his friend had died the night before 300 miles away.

In cases of lucid dreaming, the dreamer becomes aware he is dreaming. Aware yet remaining within the dream, the lucid dreamer is often moved to try to invoke people and situations in the dream to interact with at will. On such occasions, some have tried to establish communication with people in the afterlife domain.

Gregory Scott Sparrow conducted lucid-dream research with Edgar Cayce's Association for Research and Enlightenment (A.R.E.). While lucid dreaming, Sparrow tried to make contact with higher spiritual sources. He later reported having had a series of encounters with a ball of "living light" that felt to him to be a connection to higher truth. Yet every time he moved toward the light in an attempt to possess it, he said, it receded or disappeared, only to return later for another round. Finally, he said, the light source telepathically told him that the way to his heart's desire was not in selfishly desiring it, but in learning to curb his possessive appetites.

One rather strange case of dream channeling is chronicled in *Through the Curtain* by neuropsychiatrist Shafica Karagulla and Viola Pettit Neal,[7] collaborators and lifelong friends. For years Neal claimed to enter a natural sleep state at night, during which she experienced lucid-dream installments of an ongoing classroom situation attended by herself and others who were out of their physical bodies. This case seems to possess the related characteristics of lucid dreaming, dream channeling, and out-of-body experience.

LIGHT TRANCE

I felt this tremendous rush of energy come over my head, over the front, and my own consciousness began to recede to the back of my head, and Li-Sung [the source] began to channel through me . . . [there was] a wonderful feeling of merging of consciousness.

—Alan Vaughan[8]

In light-trance channeling, the individual has partial or full awareness of what is going on in the surrounding environment, as well as within him or her, at the time of the channeling. The entity transmitting to or through the channel—operating the vocal cords or writing hand— is said to be a co-dwelling personality, working alongside the channel. However, if the telephone were to ring, for example, the channel would hear it, be able to interrupt the session to answer it, and then resume channeling with no undue disruption of the process. This is said to involve some kind of temporary cohabitation of the seat of consciousness. It involves only a partial "stepping aside," as opposed to what is required for a full trance.

CLAIRAUDIENT CHANNELING

One vicious winter morning in Pennsylvania . . . there was an almost but not quite audible command, "Watch your driving, son! Something is going to happen!" Someone had so obviously spoken to me that I looked at the seat beside me. It was empty . . . Suddenly that silent voice, that thought from inside me, shouted, "Slow! Slow quick!" I stamped on the brakes. A boy leaped out from the sidewalk between two parked cars [and was avoided]. This signal was from quite outside myself, almost like the buzz of an alarm clock on a bedside table . . . "You are—who?" I asked the emptiness . . . The invisible prophet promptly answered. His words came into my mind in customary silence, as if I were thinking words to write on a typewriter. This was the message: "Don't talk. Think your talk. I am dead . . . You mortals and we immortals have been struggling to reach across the divide between life and life-forever, with every method from the cold Ouija board to the genius of Christ. But so slowly, so pitifully!"

—Ralph Knight[9]

During this widespread type of channeling, the medium is either fully conscious or in a mildly altered state. He gains the attention of the "mind's ear" by quieting himself and listening within, even though he can hear ongoing outer sounds at the same time. He is then able to hear a voice or sense some kind of language transmission seeming to come to him from within. His job as a channel is to repeat what he hears to others present who can record it, or to record it himself—or perhaps, as in the above example—just to step on the brakes.

When the voice is strong, channels say, it seems to come from the center of the head. When it is weak and indistinct, it seems like "thoughtforms," preverbal "feeling forms," or a direct knowing experienced as somehow connected to language. The channel then expresses this material in words. "Ashtar," one of the sources of the contemporary New Mexico channel Tuella, speaks of "the telepathic thread of experiencing soundless words within the mind," and "the flow of frequency within your being when that familiar voice is heard . . . [with] a vibrational form of recognition."[10] A great many contemporary channels operate in this manner.

There is considerable debate over how much the channel might color such material with his own words, beliefs, and expectations. Most observers agree that the source and its message are limited by the vocabulary and semantic capabilities of the channel, yet there are cases where the transmitted material clearly seems to exceed the limits of the channel, and does so in a striking manner.

In channeling of this kind, there may be little difference experienced between material originating within oneself and material originating from beyond oneself. It may be that some forms of channeling are extensions of ordinary abilities. For example, we all experience something similar when we are about to say or write something and it eludes us—it's just "on the tip of the tongue." Many published writers and seasoned speakers confide that some of their ideas seem to come from out of the blue. They say that passages sometimes seem given to them; they hear and merely repeat them.

CLAIRVOYANT CHANNELING

On the night of October 10 or 11, 1906, I lay in bed thinking, and was not even drowsy. Suddenly I became conscious that I was not alone. I saw a lovely woman enter my room, robed in white glittering garments, something like spangled muslin . . . She bent over me and said, "I want you to describe me to a gentleman at the Hall on Sunday . . . Take a good look at me, so that you will remember all the details.

I said to myself: "Look here, Turvey, you have got Spiritualism on the brain, and it is making you imaginative, and subject to delusions."

The "Spirit" said, "Oh no, I am no a delusion; do describe me. See! I change to earth clothes to make it easier." Then she seemed to go "out," like an electric lamp, and "on" again in an instant; but now she was in a sealskin jacket, a green skirt, patent leather boots, a toque with a feather and buckle. [All of this was immediately recognized by the man on Sunday.]

—Vincent N. Turvey[11]

The clairvoyant channel reports receiving information in the form of imagery seen with the mind's eye. The channel believes, however, that the imagery in question is not normal mental imagery but is generated from outside her. These images can be like two-dimensional photographs, or three-dimensional holograms, or moving sequences. Such imagery can be of concrete objects, abstract light patterns, or patterns of energy. The mental "cloud chamber" may be phosphorescent with dreamy wisps of surreal scenes suddenly shifting into a crisp image spelled out in detail.

Consider this excerpt from Ann Rogers's book *Soul Partners*:

As I sat down on the edge of the bed, I heard a voice say: "Look up high on the wall; we are going to show you something." The first thing I saw was a moving network of live lines all intertwined like a fish net. It broke apart and there upon the white wall was a large picture being projected from somewhere. I watched it change from one life scene to another.[12]

Like the clairaudient channel, the clairvoyant can supposedly distinguish between material coming from her own mind and material from outside it. This discriminative capacity is complex and idiosyncratic, involving subtle nuances of feeling and intuition. A channel must sense within what is of the self and what is not.

Sometimes channels must complete a picture of unclear phenomena. And even when presented with specific imagery, they may go beyond describing its face value and presume to ascribe a particular meaning to it, using their own intuition. For example, a channel may be sitting with someone who is seeking guidance and whose father happened to have died recently, although the channel doesn't know this. She may then see in her mind's eye an image of a man with a pained expression, and say: "I see a man. I sense a father energy."

Channel Francine Steiger, wife of Brad Steiger, best-selling author on the paranormal, reports interpreting images during channeling sessions for clients. She might see a rose, for example, and wonder if it symbolizes an impending birth. She says that when she queries such ambiguous images, she usually sees in her mind's eye "a big yellow N or Y," for no or yes.[13]

Often, when images of people are involved, the clairvoyant interprets information from nuances of expression or body language; but channels also report receiving verbal messages with the imagery. For example, the image of a peaceful farm flashes in the mind's eye of a channel. It's accompanied by a subliminal message from an unseen spirit guide indicating that the person who asked for the session will soon be at peace about a current domestic disturbance. If that telepathic dose of meaning had not been superimposed on the image, the channel might have groped for possible connections: "Did you ever live on a farm?" "Are you thinking of moving or buying property?" The fact that most channels are reputed to be highly intuitive helps them in this task of interpretation.

Two Special Cases: The Akashic Records and Scrying

A special kind of clairvoyant channeling is known as reading the akashic records. (Recall Levi H. Dowling and his *Aquarian Gospel,* mentioned in chapter 2.) The *akashic records* are purported by various esoteric teachings to be the universal memory bank, the cosmic record of all that has happened thus far in the cosmos. Data are supposedly recorded on the "inner planes" in a frequency domain set aside for this purpose. It can be likened to a vast holographic video disk capable of storing unlimited data.

Most channels who claim to read the akashic records go into full trance, though some have remained conscious. They report seeing specific scenes highlighted or unfolding—sometimes bewildering panoramas of detail like those reported by people who have been near death and claim to have seen their entire lives flash before their eyes.

Scrying is a form of divination reminiscent of the stereotyped gypsy fortune-teller gazing dreamily into a crystal ball. Scrying means gazing into crystal or into any other clear medium, like water or a cloudless sky. With a relaxed yet intentional focus, the seer observes various images coming into focus out of the clear background.[14] Nostradamus wrote that he looked into a clear bowl of water each day to obtain his visions.

AUTOMATISMS

Automatic Writing

> I remember the first day, standing at the piano, pen in hand, arm free so that it could be moved easily, waiting expectantly. I didn't have to wait more than a moment before the fingers that held the pen began to tingle . . . The pen moved, first in circles, then in interlocking ovals along the paper, like those we used to form as children in penmanship class . . . I had to develop the inner freedom to let the pen move freely, not to hold back out of fear or timidity, but rather go with it in spirit and let the communication happen through me . . . At first the pen moved slowly but firmly, and then, little by little, the pace picked up and I found my hand writing sentences. At this time the words and sentences were all run together. The free, rounded movement seemed to be the essential element. I never knew what had been written until after the pen stopped moving and I was able to read it, separating each word with a short vertical line.[15]

Although this kind of channeling was mentioned in both full-trance and light-trance channeling, it merits its own category because of the dissociated quality unique to it. The channel is usually awake and aware but completely separated from any sense of controlling the writing activity. There are hundreds of published instances of this kind of channeling. Whether fully or partially unconscious or fully awake, the automatic writer appears to have his arm and hand controlled by another.

Some use the term *amanuensis*—meaning one who takes dictation from another—for a channel of this type.

The chief characteristic of this phenomenon is that it is an *automatism*—that is, the motor activity involved with the writing occurs automatically and unconsciously, with no intentional control exercised by the channel. (In chapter 7 we will look at the clinical condition known as depersonalization, in which the subject considers part of the body and its behavior as separate from his or her person.) Although the automatic writer is unconscious with regard to the activity of part of the body, the mind is otherwise clear and alert. Therefore, this kind of channeling is considered less prototaxic, in Gowan's sense, than a full trance with its global loss of consciousness and control.

The Ouija Board, Planchette, and Pendulum

Our landlady found a board in the attic and we borrowed it . . .
The third time we tried it, the little pointer finally began to move
beneath our fingertips. It spelled out messages supposedly coming
from a Frank Withers [an aspect of "Seth"] who had lived in
Elmira and died during the 1940s . . . We were surprised that the
board worked for us. I thought it was a riot, two adults watching
the pointer go scurrying across the board . . . Then on December
8, 1963, we sat at the board again, wondering whether or not it
would work . . . Then suddenly the pointer began to move so
quickly that we could hardly keep up with it.

Rob asked the questions, then we paused while he wrote the
answers the pointer spelled out. Frank Withers had given simple
one- or two-word responses in previous sessions. Now the answers
become longer, and their character seemed to change . . . "Do you
have a message for us?" Rob asked. "CONSCIOUSNESS IS LIKE
A FLOWER WITH MANY PETALS," replied the pointer . . .
This was the first time the pointer spelled complete sentences. "Is
this Jane's subconscious talking?" Rob asked. "SUBCONSCIOUS-
NESS IS A CORRIDOR. WHAT DIFFERENCE DOES IT
MAKE WHICH DOOR YOU TRAVEL THROUGH?"[16]

Most people have heard of the Ouija board. Thousands of homes
have one stuck away somewhere along with rainy-day playing cards,
dominoes, and Monopoly games. The Ouija board was invented by
Elijah J. Bond and William Fuld in Baltimore around 1892. In 1966,
Parker Brothers, Inc., purchased all rights to the Ouija board, and since
then millions have been sold. Each set consists of a flat board on which
are printed in a semicircle all the letters of the alphabet, along with the
numbers 0 through 9, "Yes," "No," and sometimes "Maybe" and
"Goodbye," depending on the model. The only other component is a
small two- or three-inch-wide platform built on three inch-long legs,
whose tips are smooth to allow for easy sliding over the board's slick,
varnished surface. The little platform, sometimes called a planchette,
has a pointer to designate the letters over which it stops to spell out
messages.

Even though the participants lightly maintain fingertip contact with
the platform as it moves, this too is considered a case of automatism or
automatic physical activity that is beyond the conscious control of the
individual.

In a 1983 national survey, more than 30 percent of those who had
used the Ouija board said they did so to try to communicate with the
dead; almost as many had tried to contact living persons; the rest either

tried to reach nonhuman intelligences like spirits, angels, and pets, or to develop psychic abilities.[17]

The device has a reputation for attracting the lowest class of channeled entities. It is reported that one can contact a hodgepodge of imposters and tricksters "coming through." In the most comprehensive study to date, *Ouija: The Most Dangerous Game,* Stoker Hunt writes, "Because of the intimate nature of the information revealed, the Ouija board is incredibly seductive. The more suggestible a 'player,' the more dangerous the Ouija game."[18] Hunt presents a sobering gallery of cases in which individuals reportedly relinquished personal judgment, lost control, even killed loved ones, under the direction of invisible guides of the Ouija board. "In early stages of obsession or possession the victim becomes increasingly reliant on the Ouija board. He craves more and more revelations."

Psychic authority Susy Smith agrees. "Warn people away from Ouija and automatic writing until you have learned to be fully protected."[19] Still, the outstanding "Seth" material had its origins with the Ouija.[20]

A high-tech version of the Ouija board, called the Psi-Writer, was invented by Kenneth Wilcoxon in order to facilitate the work of a so-called spirit named "Addison." This entity claimed to be frustrated with using the cumbersome Ouija board to channel his novel *The Jupiter Experiment* through two California Quaker sisters, Margaret and Maurine Moon, in the early 1970s. A sixteen-inch-square board, printed with letters, punctuation marks, and numbers, was covered with a transparent acrylic sheet to facilitate the movement of the Ouija-type platform. The platform was fixed with a small magnet, and every time it passed over a letter it closed a small electric switch positioned underneath that letter. These switches, in turn, were connected to an electric typewriter, which could type out the chosen letters faster than the Ouija board could operate.[21]

The planchette is essentially a cross between automatic writing and the Ouija board. It is a movable platform supported on two casters, with the third balancing leg holding a pencil aimed downward. Paper is placed on a surface underneath. As with the Ouija, one or more persons lightly touch the planchette with no conscious attempt to move it. Soon the thing begins to move seemingly by itself; but in this case it slides around intricately so that the pencil can write the message in script. Descriptions of the use of this kind of device date back thousands of years to Chinese and other cultures.

In the case of the pendulum, a small weight is fastened to the end of a string or chain. The user grips the string, ascertaining which motions signify yes and no. After establishing contact with the source, the user proceeds to interrogate it, noting the yes/no responses of the pendulum's motion. Sometimes pendulums are poised over letters of the alphabet, maps, or other material.

Other divinational procedures akin to pendulums include witching, or dowsing, for water or hidden items; and psychometry, said to be the ability to tap paranormal information stored in physical objects. To fit my definition of channeling, however, the use of pendulums or other related approaches would have to involve amplification or mediation of subtle-energy information of sources from levels of reality other than our own.

OPEN CHANNELING

I received an inspiration which was not of this world. In ten months I wrote about eight hundred poems . . . I would come home to an empty house after the work day was over, sit down at my writing table and burst into tears, and then the spirit of inspiration would descend upon me. I wrote and wrote with a swiftness I could not comprehend. I was not in a trance but I didn't know what I was writing until I set about making a clean copy . . . it couldn't be a question of some sort of automatism. But I conceived these poems as if they were not written by myself.[22]

Open channeling simply means the ability to channel thoughts, images, feelings, and information from what appears to be other than the normal self, and other than from fellow embodied minds or from physical reality. This occurs in an apparently ordinary way, with none of the uncontrolled, alien sensations attributed to other channeling situations. There is no identifiable source for the message received, which is what distinguishes open channeling from other categories of classical channeling. The term open channeling encompasses much that falls within the traditional concepts of intuition, insight, inspiration, and imagination. What "comes to mind" seems to come from a larger realm than one's self or experience. Some kind of self-transcendence appears to be taking place, some kind of reaching beyond the usual possibilities.

The importance of open channeling is that, by definition, it allows anyone to participate in the experience of channeling. The difference is only the degree to which individual minds naturally draw from some larger mind. Perhaps it is our own larger mind or higher Self we are contacting. Perhaps, as various groups claim, it's some more inclusive mind, collective unconscious, holographic Universal Mind, or the omniscience of God that is tapped. (We will consider open channeling in more detail in chapter 9.)

Instances of open channeling may be found among creative writers, thinkers, scientists, inventors, and artists. For example, in *inspirational writing,* the writer has the experience of anonymously being fed material.

Many describe the related experience of *inspirational speaking.* Marilyn Ferguson, author of *The Aquarian Conspiracy,* is one of these:

> There is a point in your evolution as a public speaker where you have learned essentially to be a vehicle and to put yourself in the right state of mind . . . When this happens, you'll find yourself saying things that you don't even know why you are saying them. And then somebody will come up to you afterward and tell you that was exactly what he needed to hear. Channeling is a two-way street. It's feedback and feedforward. It isn't just the mind of God through you to whomever. It's the needs of whomever through you to the source of the information and back around again.[23]

PHYSICAL CHANNELING

> Mr. Slade [the medium] sat at the end of the table . . . We sat still about ten minutes, when I observed something like a misty cloud between myself and the wall. When my attention was first drawn toward the phenomenon, it was about the size and color of a gentleman's high-crowned, whitish-grey felt hat. This cloud-like appearance rapidly grew and became transformed, when we saw before us a woman—a lady . . . The materialized spirit glided and walked about, causing the table to shake, vibrate, jerk and tilt considerably . . . The spirit form, within two feet of our unmoved hands . . . then dissolved, and gradually faded from our vision.[24]

Physical or objective, as opposed to mental or subjective, channeling is defined as the human ability to channel unknown energies that affect the physical environment in ways that can be directly experienced by persons other than the channel. There have been reports of this phenomenon occurring through history. It's peak, however, seemed to be during the late nineteenth century. Examples include materialization and dematerialization, levitation, teleportation (the moving of an object or person without physical contact), table tiltings, knockings, rappings, poltergeist activity, and the imprinting of clay, wax, magnetic tape, or photographic film. Beyond these is the realm of psychic or paranormal healing, representing still more forms of physical channeling.

In the mid-nineteenth century, hundreds of people experienced message by means of knockings, rappings, and table tiltings, heralding the onset of the Spiritualist movement. In concert with people acting as physical mediums, disembodied spirits were alleged to be able to affect the environment in crude ways, communicating messages in code. This process is similar to others we have considered, except that here the medium need not be in direct contact with the matter affected. Some have speculated that physical channeling is a kind of relayed psycho-kinesis, or mind-over-matter process, while mental channeling is a kind of telepathy between our level of reality and another.

In *manifestation* or *materialization,* the alleged entity appears partially or fully to those present, often speaking at the same time. Both voice and visage are witnessed with the ordinary senses, in a nonaltered state of consciousness.

Direct voice involves hearing an unknown voice alone. People suppose that this process involves condensing or lowering the vibration of the entity's subtle energies, while at the same time borrowing paranormal energy from the physical channel, in order to manifest a presence in the physical realm. This enables the vibration of physical air waves that strike eardrums so that those present report experiencing the same external, objective voice giving the same message. Sometimes a metal trumpet is used in order to condense and focus energy. It is usually never touched but is reported to often float about the darkened room with the voice emanating from it.

All of these different kinds of channeling seem to involve a source—someone or something—communicating from another level of reality to or through the channel. Given that the sources are not from our level of reality (or from the channel's own mind), what kinds of sources could they be? The next two chapters will attempt to answer this. In the process, some multidimensional views of the universe will be presented to provide a hypothetical home for the supposed beings that present themselves through human channels.

THREE

POSSIBLE
EXPLANATIONS

7
PSYCHOLOGICAL EXPLANATIONS

I don't think we even know how we see the tree outside our own window. What hope, then, that we can understand modes of communication that proceed from intelligences quite unlike ourselves?

—HUSTON SMITH[1]

Humankind cannot bear very much reality.
—T. S. ELIOT

How can we best explain channeling? Which schools of thought, and what analytical tools, can we use to explore its mechanisms? And how would each support its respective explanation?

Explanation, by definition, must go beyond the simple acts of observation and description to include *interpretation.* Looks deceive, the saying goes. If appearance is in the eye of the beholder, *understanding* is deeply embedded in the idiosyncrasies of the human mind entertaining it. In previous chapters, we have looked at many descriptions of what appears to be happening in cases of channeling; however, these reports may fall short of satisfying our hunger to understand the true nature of what is going on. That hunger may be different for each of us. The fundamentalist Christian may explain channeling in terms of demons, while the computer programmer may explain it in terms of interchangeable mental programs, each with visual and verbal inputs and outputs. Each of these people could, no doubt, find others who saw things as he did. But what if he couldn't?

In his recent book, *Deviant Science: The Case of Parapsychology,* University of Pennsylvania professor James McClenon speaks of the problems in our culture of being considered *deviant* for pursuing anomalies (such as channeling) that have what he calls "low ontological status." This means that such phenomena are seen as having relatively low reality compared to our usual experience of what is real. "Deviance," he writes, "can be defined as 'those acts, attributes, and beliefs which, when performed or made known . . . elicit an evaluative social sanction.' " That is, by their beliefs and actions, the deviant court is being put back in line with the larger social structure and belief system. The scientist who stays open to the possible reality of channeling runs into this problem by holding what McClenon calls "beliefs . . . that violate some of the [current] metaphysical foundations of science."

Earl Babbie is an example of someone speaking from the vantage point of a traditionally trained social science researcher trying to come to terms with the difficult subject of channeling. He confides, "It gets very muddy about what a human being is; what the individual is."[2] He wonders: "How do you study something like this which contradicts a lot of the foundations of conventional science?" His answer:

> The easiest answer is to say that they [the channels] are "nuts," and we know how to study "nuts." We can study pathologies and delusions. Or, as an alternative, we can go over the hill and say science is all phony in some way—all linear and superficial, too positivistic . . . What I propose for myself is this: to find a way of looking at this subject that lets me maintain my scientific integrity and also to respect the integrity of what I'm studying. To approach it with an open mind that is supposed to characterize science, but doesn't always . . . I'm clear that if I can really study channeling the way I'm supposed to, I'll come out with a more robust understanding of science in general.

In investigating channeling, Stanford neuroscientist Karl F. Pribram warns, "Don't mix up understanding, explaining, describing, and speculating." To take an accurate description of something that is real to the person describing it, and refer to a hypothetical explanation, for example, may invalidate the truth of the description. At the same time, "don't elevate description to being explanation if it's just description." Pribram's suggestion in channeling research is to "stick with description, because that's the truth of it; it can't be denied. It says: 'Look, this is really something being experienced and described, which now needs explanation. We don't understand it yet; it's something asking to be understood.' "[3]

Marcello Truzzi emphasizes the undeniable authority exercised by what is called phenomenology, or first-hand personal experience. He uses himself—a noted skeptic—as an example:

> Let's say I believe I saw and heard my deceased father. I could later come up with a number of alternative explanations. But if I feel convinced at the same time that it was my father, well, then I can

sympathize with someone who has had such an experience. It's like the saying: "If it looks like a duck and it walks like a duck, the response is that it must *be* a duck."[4]

Accepting something as real because most people experience it the same way is different from accepting it based on one's personal experience. The former might be termed explanation and interpretation by *consensual validation;* the latter, by *subjective validation.*

At this time in our culture, our most respected systems of explanation, which come from science, operate by consensual objective validation rather than by private subjective validation. The empirical evidence to support various theories making up our dominant explanations lies overwhelmingly in the physical world, not within us. Although *empirical* means being guided by observation and experience, hearing an inner voice is not sufficient grounds in our culture to argue that the voice is real.

Yet consensuality does not necessarily guarantee objective truth. As Truzzi puts it, "a lot of this channeling is the sociology that creates it. And now we have a channeling subculture; people are hearing each others' stories. There's a kind of collective error, rather than a zeroing in on a collective truth."

Reality is, of course, explained differently by different academic disciplines, such as geology, internal medicine, astrophysics, or applied mathematics. And students of the history of science know that few disciplines have remained the same over the centuries—even over recent decades. Many modern scientists would consider the explanations given by preindustrial cultures to be merely myths. But a myth may also be a valid way to explain the world, a kind of story made up by the human mind to describe certain phenomena with which it is confronted. Channels appear to live in their own mythic worlds of disembodied voices, extraterrestrials, and gods, while technologically oriented people live in a world of printed circuits and glowing screens of data. If history continues as it has, one hundred years from now many of our currently unimpeachable explanations may be seen as outdated and limited, perhaps even mythological.

Given this relativity of truth within the larger unfolding crazy quilt of history, the wisest scientists in all ages have tended to be open, curious, and humble about the finality of their knowledge. We will keep this in mind, tempering the following explanations of channeling with a balance between openness and humility on the one hand, and precision and rigor on the other.

The four major disciplines used in this book to try to explain channeling are psychology (including experimental, cognitive, and clinical); parapsychology and consciousness research; psychophysiology (including neuroscience and medicine); and physics and paraphysics. We will cover the first two in this chapter and the other pair in the following chapter.

Psychology is arguably in the best position to provide a relevant and reasonable contemporary explanation for channeling. It is the chief discipline through which the scientific, analytical mind can attempt to come to terms with subjective, idiosyncratic material.

To examine channeling within the context of psychology triggers questions such as: What is the nature of the individual? Where do we draw the line between self and not-self? Once we draw it, what kinds of interaction can take place across it? How open or closed is the individual system in this interaction? And what is the unconscious mind?

As noted parapsychologist Stanley Krippner puts it:

> I think that for me channeling is an interesting topic because it really calls into question the concept that Westerners have of self and the dogma by which they approach that concept not realizing that other cultures have a quite different view of the self. And I think that whatever the final verdict is on the process of channeling, we will have learned something in terms of the capacities of the human psyche.[5]

EARLY TWENTIETH-CENTURY VIEWS

At the beginning of this century, a number of explanations of the human psyche contended for supremacy. Those views that had been born out of Spiritualism and related psychical research lost out to a new breed of experimentally based behavioral science.

One casualty was F.W.H. Myers's notion of the *subliminal self* (1903), first mentioned in chapter 2—the part of the mind beneath the threshold of consciousness that was seen as "a more comprehensive, profounder faculty" than the conscious or *supraliminal self,* which we habitually identify as ourselves. By way of this subliminal self, Myers said, we can each be open to the mysteries of larger mind, to a wider universe of energy and possibility. This subliminal self might help account for channeling, but this concept has won only limited acceptance in mainstream psychological literature.

Theodore Troward, a contemporary of Myers, went beyond subliminal self in his 1909 interpretation of *subjective mind:* "The subjective mind in ourselves is the *same* subjective mind at work in the universe giving rise to the infinitude of natural forms with which we are surrounded, and in like manner giving rise to ourselves also."[6] But Troward's thinking, too, failed to be incorporated into the mainstream.

Similarly, the contribution of naturalist Alfred Russel Wallace has been virtually forgotten compared to the man with whom he shared the theory of evolution and natural selection, Charles Darwin. For Wallace, the existence of higher faculties implied a spiritual nature and a spiritual hierarchy in creation:

There must be an unseen world of spirit, which causes changes to take place in the world of matter; and evolution on this planet must be directed and aided from outside by superior and invisible intelligences, to which man, as a spiritual being, was susceptible. Moreover these intelligences very probably exist in a gradated series above us.[7]

Furthermore, Wallace claimed that those spiritual beings could communicate with us by telepathy since we shared their spiritual nature. Needless to say, his view has not been adopted by twentieth-century science either.

William James of Harvard, who dominated turn-of-the-century psychology, tried to do his part to import a larger view of the self and its relations with the universe into the thinking of his colleagues, but with limited success. In *The Varieties of Religious Experience,* James wrote: "In the religious life the control (from outside) is felt as higher, but since on our hypothesis it is primarily the higher faculties of our own hidden mind which are controlling, the sense of union with the power beyond us is in a sense of something, not merely apparently, but literally true."[8]

At about the same time (1893), Thomson Jay Hudson, in *The Law of Psychic Phenomena,*[9] distinguished an objective mind that deals with everyday experience, and a subjective mind that is turned inward, controlling our inner being and coextensive with those inner planes involved in channeling and other psychic experience. Hudson made even less of an inroad into the development of psychology than did Myers. Unfortunately for them, and for so many others then and now, their terms referred to realities that could not be objectively investigated as physical phenomena were. It is curious that some of Freud's and Jung's ideas (which we will discuss later) were accepted into the mainstream of psychological thinking even though they are no easier to investigate by such rigorous criteria.

Two other turn-of-the-century contemporaries who failed to have their ideas integrated into the dominant body of psychological thought were Richard Bucke and Ralph Waldo Trine. Bucke's 1901 study *Cosmic Consciousness*[10] distinguished between a lower or simple consciousness and a higher cosmic consciousness. He proceeded to survey cases of those individuals whom he thought displayed the latter, looking for similarities, much the way James had in his *Varieties of Religious Experi-*

ence. Ralph Waldo Trine, in his book *In Tune with the Infinite* (1897), depicted what we are calling open channeling as something natural to all of us. "In just the degree that we come into a conscious realization of our oneness with the infinite life, and open ourselves to the Divine to flow," he believed, "do we actualize in ourselves the qualities and powers of the infinite life, and do we make ourselves channels through which the infinite Intelligence and Power can work."[11]

None of the prevailing explanatory models in behavioral or experimental psychology seems hospitable to the kinds of phenomena we include within channeling. In contrast to the theories of Myers, Troward, Wallace, Hudson, Bucke, and Trine, these accepted views portray the unconscious as predominantly a closed system. They have no room for the idea of a personal trapdoor through the unconscious or subliminal mind that leads out in a larger mental or spiritual universe.

Since contemporary psychology has yet to fathom the nature of the unconscious mind, however, a way may yet be open for considering the unconscious in light of some of these older models of the mind. In the most recent book-length study of the nature of the unconscious, *Americans and the Unconscious,* Bradley University religious studies professor Robert C. Fuller points out that "modern culture's fascination with science has given the concept of the unconscious its salience as a symbol of humanity's higher nature." This notion of the unconscious has "served to deflect facile attempts to reduce explanations of human behavior to the scientific categories of material (physiological) and efficient (environmental condition) causes." Fuller continues:

> Insofar as the individual can be seen as unconsciously linked to a nondetermined motivational force . . . the unconscious has made it possible to recognize the role of final or ultimate causes—those that lie beyond the psychological dimension proper—in guiding human behavior. In so doing, the unconscious had enabled psychology to perform a variety of religious and cultural functions for which it would otherwise be ill equipped.[12]

M. Scott Peck, author of *The Road Less Traveled,* is an example of a contemporary psychiatrist who thinks this way. "Since the unconscious is God all along," he writes, "we may further define the goal of spiritual growth to be the attainment of godhead by the conscious self."[13]

According to fellow psychiatrist Stanislav Grof, research should focus on two important issues. One is "the question of the triggering mechanisms that make it possible for various unconscious contents to emerge into consciousness." The other is "the question of the individual's attitude toward the content of these experiences."[14]

Faced with the still-unresolved nature of both the unconscious mind and of channeling, some researchers today might find themselves agreeing with the conclusions of psychologist Walter Franklin Prince almost a century ago, after his prolonged study of channel Pearl Curran and her source "Patience Worth":

> Either our concept of what we call the subconscious mind must be radically altered so as to include potencies of which we hitherto have had no knowledge, or else some cause operating through, but not in, the subconscious of Mrs. Curran must be acknowledged.[15]

CLOSED MODELS OF THE PSYCHE

The current mainstream psychological explanations agree that we each have a conscious part and an unconscious part. The conscious part is limited to working with normal perceptions, personal memory, and the mental representations fashioned from them. The unconscious part is seen as a repository of perceptions, memories, and representations not readily available to conscious awareness. It too is capable of certain internal flexibility of combinatory play among its components. This play accounts for our dreams, imagination, creativity, and other subjective activity. And it would certainly account for anything falling under the auspices of channeling. All of these explanations need nothing external to the unconscious mind to account for channeling.

Much of this closed model of the psyche derives from experiments in subliminal perception in which the subject can perceive a stimulus without conscious awareness of it. Current understanding of the psychological system also stems from research in perception, mental representation, memory, and internal symbolic transformation and retrieval. One example is recent research in what is called state-specific learning and memory.

According to Dr. Justine Owens of Stanford University,

> the organism's state acts as a cue or prime that promotes access to material learned in a similar state. The encoding of the to-be-remembered information is associated with the mood, drug, or hypnotic state, and this association facilitates retrieval of the information when the person reenters that state. Thus, you get a *significant difference* in the amount recalled between similar [learn and test] states and dissimilar ones.[16]

POSSIBLE EXPLANATIONS

This state-specific nature of mind, then, gives rise to various kinds of relatively isolated complexes that are, to varying degrees, unavailable to each other or to the conscious awareness of the subject. All such state-specific aspects would be thought of as part of the closed system of the individual, and channeling would be explained as the rising of such states into the spotlight of consciousness, to take control of motor mechanisms for voice or hand, or to activate the language centers and sensory apparatus deep within the central nervous system. However, by this view, states of consciousness are partial, transitory states and could not under any circumstance exist as a complete identity separate from the individual's parent system. Also, the model as currently accepted would rule out the possibility of the existence of a psychological or conscious self that lives on after death. Nor could these partial selves enter into another individual to operate within the spotlight of his or her consciousness.

Current experimental models also have been built on research in conditioned learning. From Pavlov's dogs to Skinner's pigeons to today's cybernetic models of human beings, psychologists view learned behaviors as resting largely upon networks of unconscious associations constructed in the mind from environmental stimuli and various internal representations. Behaviorists believe us to be ignorant of the bases of much of our own behavior, operating predictably in the world based on conditioning made outside of conscious awareness.

Recall some of the main kinds of channeling behavior: an individual hears a voice that seems to come neither from himself nor from the known environment; or she experiences someone other than herself using her hand to write or her vocal cords to speak. These situations, according to the model of conditioning, can be explained as functions of certain patterns of association formed unconsciously by memories, mental representations, and the combinatory play of creativity. Ideational planning and motor execution programs are also involved, along with more subtle programs for making meaning. There is no need for the behavioral scientist to bring in the mythic notion of a nonphysical yet conscious being to account for the behaviors attributed to channeling.

A good deal of the prevailing model of the autonomous person in restricted interaction with the environment has been drawn from medical research involving brain-damaged subjects. Throughout, one theme prevails: human beings are essentially closed systems with a certain range of causation, association, and response; they alone can operate the bodies they inhabit. There is no room in these explanations for the brain, writing hand, or speaking voice of one person to be activated by another intentional agent.

Later we will consider some recent research that may force an update of this model. This research seems to show that certain frequencies of electromagnetic energy can be transmitted in a "wireless" manner to the individual human brain, evoking predictable sensations, perceptions, or other subjective experiences. If this can be so, then our existing psychological explanations will have to expand to include new possibilities of who or what might be "pulling the strings" of the brain and body in a given situation. For now, however, experimental and behavioral psychology continue to hold to the view that the only real behaviors and experiences are those generated by the environment and perceived by the five senses, or those generated from within by the human brain.

A FREUDIAN VIEW OF CHANNELING

Sigmund Freud, the father of psychoanalysis, begrudgingly addressed channeling-type phenomena on occasion during his career: "The Uncanny" (1919), "Psychology of Occult Phenomena" (1921), "Psychoanalysis and Telepathy" (1921), "Dreams and Telepathy" (1922), and "A Neurosis of Demoniacal Possession in the Seventeenth Century" (1923). Yet he remained deeply skeptical throughout his life. Despite Freud's extreme caution regarding the paranormal, he did write that "an alliance of, and collaboration between, psychoanalysts and occultists would seem to be both plausible and promising."[17]

Regarding the resurgence of interest in what he called occult phenomena, Freud wrote:

> The study of so called occult facts . . . the real existence of psychic forces . . . is but one manifestation of the devaluation which, ever since the world catastrophe [World War I], has affected everything established; it is part of the attempt to probe the great upheaval toward which we are drifting and whose scope we are unable to fathom as yet. It is surely an attempt at compensation, which seeks to regain by other—supernatural—means the lost appeal of life on this earth.[18]

Yet Freud stayed open to the possibility that "if still other phenomena, as, for example, those maintained by the Spiritualists, should be proven, we should then consider the modification of our 'laws' as demanded by the new experience."

Freud explained channeling-like phenomena in terms of wish fulfillment and the reemergence of material repressed into the unconscious. In his 1923 article on seventeenth-century demoniacal possession, he wrote that "what in those days were thought to be evil spirits to us are base and evil wishes, the derivatives of impulses which have been rejected and repressed."[19]

In all cases of repression and transformation, Freud said, the analyst would need to learn to read, by way of the cryptic text of behavior, the underlying meaning or intent that was seeking a symbolic means of expressing itself. Ironically, it would often be so indecipherable that even the well-trained analyst could not readily decode it. According to the Freudian view, our dreams are made of such repressed and transmuted personal stuff. So are our creative expressions as a culture, and our healthy and not-so-healthy expressions as individuals.

A follower of Freud, therefore, might interpret the voices, visions, and expressions of channeling as repressed material unavailable to the conscious mind that seeks ways to get by the gate-guarding mechanism. One way it can get by is in the garb of fantasy that evades the limits and demands of external reality. Repressed material might present itself as a different self. Such a persona, resurrected from the unconscious depths, can permit the acting out of forces and motives thought by the conscious to be forbidden. For example, if one has buried pain based on a long-repressed traumatic experience, a wailing alter personality may be able to express it; and if a childish playfulness that would embarrass the adult is deeply buried, then a playful persona may come forth to discharge the spontaneity of that pent-up energy.

Many cases, however, do not fit this view easily, because the content channeled cannot be explained as part of the individual's repressed psychic material in any of the ways acceptable to the psychoanalytical view. If such personal unconscious material can only consist of fantasy productions, innate instinctual drives, or perceptions and memories derived from interaction with external reality, then much channeled material cannot be explained. One would have to say either that those unconscious forces have true universal and transpersonal qualities to them; or that the ego's interface with external reality somehow includes extrasensory or nonphysical means. In either case, we have tampered with the basic closed-system assumption held by Freud. As we shall see, Carl Jung was able to go beyond his colleague's thinking by developing a more open model of the psyche. Before turning to Jung, however, let us speculate about the nature of channeling by drawing on Freud's concept of Eros.

Eros, according to Freud, is the deep unconscious life instinct itself—extending beyond the sexual libido and desirous of connecting and uniting, generative, embracing, and self-perpetuating. It dwells in all of us. We might speculate from this point of view, then, that all mystical and transpersonal experiences could be traced to a biological homing instinct for the prenatal womb condition, and to the all-consuming pleasure-seeking drive of the selfish infant for uninterrupted connection to the mothering source. The desire would remain within us to reconnect with the source, to feel deeply and truly connected and at one.

The channeled material speaks in chorus of a remarkably similar theme: We are one. We need to recognize, reclaim, and reunite with our God-source, our underlying deeper identity. We have blocked and repressed the love continually welling up from within—our true Eros nature—and we have blocked its flow to us from all living creation: the Eros of God. Eros has been transformed through evolution, the speculation concludes, and is foreshadowed in the experiences and teachings of the channels, psychics, mystics, visionaries, and selfless lovers.

One critique of this speculation is based on Ken Wilber's *pre/trans* fallacy. This contends that it may be erroneous to impute transcendental wisdom or spiritual reality to regressive infantile or in utero states; and, on the other hand, it may be equally inaccurate to think that various mystical and transcendental states are simply a mindless, infantile reuniting with the womb. The former are *prepersonal;* the latter are *transpersonal.*

Consider another possibility with regard to Eros: the hypothesis that those who exercise generosity and caring for others—attributes of Eros—appear to derive positive effects from it. A study by Boston University psychology professor David Mclelland discovered that indifferent student subjects showed stepped-up immune systems after watching a film of Mother Teresa lovingly tending to the poor and sick. He conjectured that perhaps conventions emphasizing these virtues have been developed in most societies because of their health and survivalist benefits. "The results," he concluded, "mean that she [Mother Teresa] was contacting the consciously disapproving people in a part of their brains that they were unaware of and that was still responding to the strength of her tender loving care."[20] Virtually every book of contemporary channeled material includes exhortations to love, help, and serve.

JUNG AND THE COLLECTIVE UNCONSCIOUS

Swiss physician/psychoanalyst Carl Gustav Jung did not concur with Freud's model of the human being predicated on selfish infantile sexuality. He broke away from Freud's thinking, in order to expand the notion of unconscious pleasure-seeking and instinctual motivation to include nonsexual cognitive and spiritual aspects.

Jung wrote that "the psyche is not an indivisible unity but a divisible and more or less divided whole" composed of various complexes of psychic material. Within this divided whole, "the ego-complex forms the center characteristic of our psyche. But it is only one among several complexes."[21] Jung further thought that the appearance of communication from nonphysical spirits could be accounted for by these complexes, which become repressed and separated from normal waking consciousness. These complexes might project themselves in a form, he said, which is experienced by the individual as separate from himself.

In 1902, when the international Spiritualist movement was in full swing, Jung completed his M.D. thesis, "The Psychology and Pathology of a So-Called Occult Phenomenon." In it he studied a young girl whose experiences involved "double consciousness," somnambulism, and what we would call channeled contact with discarnate entities. He concluded that "spirits, therefore, viewed from the psychological angle, are unconscious autonomous complexes which appear as projections because they have no direct contact with the ego."

Jung also examined the biblical account of the blindness and channeling-like experience of the Apostle Paul (born Saul) in terms of a complex:

> The vision of Christ on the road to Damascus marks the moment when the unconscious Christ-complex associated itself with Paul's ego. The fact that Christ appeared to him objectively, in the form of a vision, is explained by the circumstance that Saul's Christianity was an unconscious complex which appeared to him in projection, as if it did not belong to him. He could not see himself as a Christian; therefore, from sheer resistance to Christ, he became blind and could only be healed again by a Christian.[22]

Besides the complex, Jung believed that the "shadow" side of each person—the least evolved and understood part—could on occasion present itself in ways that might appear to be something or someone other than the normal self.

Jung provided another possible explanation based on what he called the impersonal or collective unconscious:

> Its contents are not personal but collective; that is, they do not belong to one individual alone but to a whole group of individuals, and generally to a whole nation, or even the whole of mankind. These contents are not acquired during the individual's lifetime but are products of innate forms and instincts . . . the primordial images which have always been the basis of man's thinking—the whole treasure-house of mythological motifs.[23]

Channeling, by this view, might be the individual tapping into the material of this racial memory. With regard to the chief contents of the collective unconscious—what Jung called *archetypes*—psychologist Robert Masters says: "I subscribe to Jung's definition of an archetype as an essentially irrepresentable energy constellation which can nonetheless be represented."[24] While this concept of the collective unconscious and the archetypes may open the door for a more self-transcending view of communication, it is still consistent with a basically closed model of the human psyche.

Jung, however, did report a number of personal experiences that resemble channeling. Late in his life, writing in *Memories, Dreams, Reflections*,[25] he recounts a number of visionary (or hallucinatory) experiences. Perhaps most interesting is the mysterious circumstance surrounding the writing of an early 1916 piece he called *Septem Sermones ad Mortuos*, or *Seven Sermons to the Dead*. He later considered this to be part of his "juvenile" period and hoped serious readers of his work would ignore it. These sermons are a continuation of earlier conversations with "inner figures" that had been published in his *Red Book*. They are written in a rather bibilical style, similar to much channeled literature, and they reflect a personality ("Philemon") and a perspective quite different from Jung's earlier and later work.

Today Jung is associated with a fairly open view of human nature, embracing psychospiritual and metaphysical realities. On one occasion, while trying to come to terms with the identities of supposedly channeled spirits, he confided:

> I once discussed the proof of identity for a long time with a friend of William James, Professor Hyslop, in New York. He admitted that, all things considered, all these metapsychic phenomena could be explained better by the hypothesis of spirits than by the qualities and peculiarities of the unconscious. And here, on the basis of my own experience, I am bound to concede he is right. In each individual case I must of necessity be skeptical, but in the long run I have to admit that the spirit hypothesis yields better results in practice than any other.[26]

One contemporary philosopher and psychologist who continues the lineage of Jung today is Jean Houston. "These [channeled] 'entities' as we call them—Seth or Saul or Paul or Jonathan—are essentially 'goddings' of the depths of the psyche," she says. "They are personae of the self that take on acceptable form so that we can have relationship to them and thus dialogue." Today she believes that "the traditional archetypes do not have for many people the power they once held. People are in a kind of free-form archetypal search. And so you get the Seths and the Salems and the myriads of very personal guides that are filling the psyche." These entities are, for Houston, the "projections and creations of the immensity that is the personal and collective unconscious."[27]

SILBERER'S AUTOSYMBOLISM AND PROGOFF'S DYNATYPES

Psychologist Herbert Silberer coined the term *autosymbolism* to refer to a process in which feelings and ideas tend to be spontaneously represented in symbolic form. In this way, the individual experiences unconscious symbolic material without understanding its source or meaning. This process bears a resemblance to Freud's idea that wishes, feelings, and experiences relegated to the unconscious mind by repression are expressed in camouflaged or symbolic ways. Silberer, however, claims that the creative flow of unknown material into symbolic manifestation is a natural, not a problematic, process. He does not share Freud's emphasis on repression of material intolerable to the conscious that must be changed before it can be expressed and experienced. Silberer's view does involve the concept of dissociation, however, since the individual is not consciously aware that the symbolically expressed material has its origins in himself.[28]

A kind of transpersonal version of Silberer's autosymbolism is presented by Jungian psychologist Ira Progoff. His 1957 study of the well-known channel Eileen Garrett was published in 1964 as *The Image of an Oracle*.[29] Since Garrett had no conscious knowledge of the identity of her sources, Progoff believed he had to "approach the trance personalities not as spirit entities but as symbolic forms of dramatization."

The individual human psyche for Progoff is a "reflection of larger, transpersonal principles." This leaves the psychological contents of one's experiences as "symbolic expressions and elusive intimations of what this other dimension of life may be." The psyche of the channel, therefore, is "a vehicle of something much larger than the individual whose name it bears."[30]

Progoff coins the term *dynatypes* for the Jungian archetype-like "specific potentialities for life expression that are present in the seed of the personality." By viewing the individual as inherently creative and expressive, Progoff has chosen to make a number of "ventilating holes" in the traditional closed model of the self without committing himself to the ultimate source of channeling.

Silberer and Progoff both give credence to channeling as the creative dramatic expression of natural, perhaps transpersonal, forces of those aspects of the psyche of which we are normally unconscious. Jess

Stearn, author of *The Sleeping Prophet,* remembers a conversation with his friend, channel Arthur Ford, which may shed further light on this theme. "You know I sometimes question myself," Ford confided to Stearn. "I question Fletcher, the guide I believed in so implicitly. I wonder if I wasn't dramatizing my own subconscious." Stearn replied, "It really doesn't make much difference, because if you're dramatizing your own subconscious, you don't know where that's coming from anyway . . . It could have come out of Universal Intelligence and you could have just tuned into it." The only thing that really matters, he concluded, "is the truth of what comes through."[31]

HYPNOSIS, TRANCE, AND COGNITIVE PSYCHOLOGY

Channeling has been likened to hypnosis, to the altered state of consciousness known as trance, and to the various involuntary, dissociated states connected with them.

E. Mansell Pattison, Joel Kahan, and Gary Hurd of the Department of Psychiatry, Medical College of Georgia, see trance as a functional mode of consciousness, not as an illness or aberration. Trance, they say, has been "institutionalized in such a way that the form, practice, and experience are culturally learned patterns of behavior." They define *possession trance* as "an interpersonal event, in which there is *possession* by, or entranced impersonation of another being, in the context of communal activity and witness to the behavior."[32] This would certainly seem to describe that majority of trance channeling cases from antiquity to the present in which the channel is not alone during the experience. It could even be argued that trance channeling during the last hundred years *is* a learned pattern of behavior, complete with (sub)cultural expectations on the part of the channel and others in attendance.

"The usual definition of hypnosis, which is only one kind of trance," points out Robert Masters, "is that it's an agreement between two people that one will provide suggestions and one will accept them."[33] For psychiatrist Jan Ehrenwald, author of *New Dimensions of Deep Analysis,* hypnosis and autohypnosis are "as a result of what I described as 'doctrinal compliance' by a suggestible subject with the hypnotist's subliminal suggestions or 'demand characteristics.' "[34]

Perhaps the sitters or audience in the channeling experience become "compliant" so as to be hypnotized by the "demands" of the channel and by their own expectations and desire to believe. Carl Raschke, professor of religion at the University of Denver, is one current researcher of channeling who shares this view. He speaks of J. Z. Knight, who channels "Ramtha": "Knight puts herself in a self-induced hypnotic state that mesmerizes an audience already predisposed to accept that 'God is everywhere.' " He concludes that "the New Age movement, with its emphasis on human potential psychology, has given these people [channels] a certain credibility . . . It's a form of mass hypnosis that is leading to mass acceptance of the irrational."[35]

Hypnosis researcher T. R. Sarbin points to evidence that the hypnotized or self-hypnotized person will often behave as he thinks a hypnotized person is expected to behave. Perhaps in so-called trance channeling, the individual is behaving as he thinks a trance channel is supposed to, in a way he has learned from the channeling subculture, in an elaborate piece of role-playing of which he is not consciously aware.

There are even those who claim that we *all* operate under a form of mass hypnosis all the time in our everyday material reality, since we share the same unconscious presuppositions and "hypnotic suggestions" about what is real and what is not, which then leads us to the experiences we have. By this view, channels have simply hypnotized themselves, or those who experience them, in a different way than the rest of us.

Throughout the later nineteenth and early twentieth centuries, there was an interesting overlap of research into hypnosis, channeling, and various sorts of "hysterical" or "dissociative" states. Keeping in mind some of the reported characteristics of channeling with which we have become familiar, consider the eminent nineteenth-century psychologist Pierre Janet on hypnosis (and perhaps channeling) as a dissociative condition: "In this process, a system of ideas, emotions, and behaviors could split off from the personality and exist with a certain degree of autonomy in the unconscious. This dissociated material could be brought into consciousness through the use of hypnosis [or self-hypnosis]."[36]

In William James's turn-of-the-century study of channel Lenore Piper for the Boston Society for Psychical Research, he concluded that hypnosis makes psychic phenomena more likely to occur than in normal waking consciousness. He also discovered what he termed "a will to impersonate" and a freedom exercised by the alleged channel or psychic to explore "the dramatic possibilities" of consciousness. Theodore X. Barber, a leading present-day hypnosis researcher, chooses to use the phrase "fantasy prone personality," pointing up the correlation between such and susceptibility to hypnosis.

Stanford psychologist and professor emeritus Ernest Hilgard, a leading contemporary authority on hypnosis, describes a case reported by George Estabrooks, a psychologist who had hypnotized a friend in order to elicit automatic handwriting:

Estabrooks (1957) reported an experiment with a friend who was reading *Oil for the Lamps of China* while his right hand, screened from view by passing it through a cloth curtain, was engaged in automatic writing. The hand was not in awareness because of hypnotic procedures; it was also anaesthetic. However, when Estabrooks pricked the hand with a needle, it wrote a stream of profanity "that would have made a top sergeant blush with shame." This went on for five minutes and included an attack on the hypnotist for having pricked him. The subject continued his reading calmly, "without the slightest idea that his good right arm was fighting a private war."[37]

Although there is no agreed-upon definition of hypnosis, most experts would concur with Hilgard that it involves relaxation of muscles, drowsiness, increased suggestibility, enhanced imagination and availability of past visual memories, a lack of desire to carry out usual plans, and reduction of reality testing.

There has long been debate about the degree of awareness in the hypnotized person. Has he somehow "gone to sleep"? The familiar depiction of Edgar Cayce as "the sleeping prophet" reflects the idea of trance channeling as similar to sleep. But hypnosis is *not* a form of sleep as measured by any psychological or physiological criteria. On the contrary, most authorities would concur with Herbert and David Spiegel that hypnosis is "a state of attentive, receptive, intense focal concentration with diminished peripheral awareness."[38]

Psychologists William Kroger and William Fezler provide a theory of how hypnosis works, likening the brain to a computer (the parentheses are theirs):

The greater receptivity in a receptor (the subject) enables messages (sensory inputs or precepts) to be received clearly from a transmitter (the operator) with a minimal degree of interference (noise) either in the external environmental communication pathways (channel), or in the internal receptor of the subject. This enhances the transmission of reception of signals.[39]

Applying this theory to channeling, we could say that people who appear to channel are in a hypnotic altered state that allows them access to messages from transmitters or operators to which they would not have access under normal mental conditions due to internal and external noise.

To apply another hypnosis theory to channeling, the purported channeling sources may create, by their unusual presence to consciousness, a version of what one of the giants of hypnosis, Milton Erickson, practiced as the "confusion technique" of hypnotic induction. In Erickson's approach, there is an initial dimming of outer reality for subjects and the introduction of some form of confusing or disorienting material into their experience. The initial confusion can be due to shock, stress, or uncertainty. This detaches them for their habitual mental sets and conscious biases (like thinking that there cannot be voices in one's head, or that there is no such thing as consciousnesses existing in a dimension other than the physical). Then, in the face of the uncertainty, a restructuring is needed and sought. It is at this point that receptivity is at its greatest. Hypersuggestibility is then the automatic acceptance of any input that will help them restructure their belief systems and end the intolerable confusion. Thus, the impingement of paranormal material (such as genuine channeling upon one's belief systems,) or the disorienting experiences provided by a fake channel, could break someone loose from his usual mental dispositions. Thus he would be made even more receptive to the very material that set the process in motion.

Recently interviewed for a San Francisco area television program on channeling, Stanford University professor and hypnosis authority David Spiegel described his belief that channeling is the result of self-hypnosis:

> They put themselves in a trance and they very vividly act out what it would be like. So it's a fantasy acted out in a very intense way . . . I think what it proves basically is that dramatic elements of a trance channeler . . . the sudden physical change, the change in tone of voice, the change in dialect, the change in preoccupation from everyday things to sort of global, cosmic activity—is something that can happen [through self-hypnosis]. But you don't have to invoke spirits.[40]

Hypnotically induced hallucinations can include experiencing the presence of something that cannot be seen or heard by others, or experiencing the absence of something that *is* there to others. For example, the hypnotized subject can carry on a two-way conversation with a fictional being that no one else can experience. Again, this could account for many of the voices and visions reported in channeling. There is a possibility, then, that a channel is a self-hypnotized person communicating with sources that he, she, or others have suggested and that are unavailable to anyone else.

As research psychologist Charles Tart reports:

From my studies with hypnosis, I know that I can set up an apparently independent existent entity whose characteristics are constructed to my specification. And the person hypnotized will experience that as if it's something outside of his own consciousness talking. So there's no doubt that some cases of channeling can be explained in a conventional kind of way. There's nothing psychic involved.[41]

There is a remarkable similarity between the self-inductive processes of hypnosis, meditation, communion, and prayer and the preparatory actions of channels, shamans, oracles, or visionaries. They involve relaxation and concentration, turning inward, focusing on certain sounds, words, or images, and intending to change one's state of consciousness. This may point to a similarity of the states reached, given the similarity of the ways of reaching them. One might speculate, for example, that supposedly transcendental states are reached by self-hypnosis; or that self-hypnosis may involve self-transcendence and contact with other levels of reality.

Many hypnotherapists help the client contact an "inner advisor" for gaining access to information that the normal waking self does not have. Even people who may not accept channeling may see this as an acceptable procedure. It is a permission-giving device that allows deeper access to one's inner resources. On the other hand, this is no proof that the inner advisor contacted through hypnotic induction is not something or someone—spirit guide or guardian angel—separate from one's psychic system. Such inner advice is often reported to be wise and useful beyond the norm.

Hypnotic Age Regression and Reincarnation

One of the most unusual applications of hypnosis is regression to a younger age. There are many documented cases of subjects having been hypnotically regressed back to birth—and, some claim, to periods before birth, even before conception. Do such prebirth experiences reflect the close relationship among hypnosis, personal imagination, and dreams? Does hypnosis merely free the individual to enter bizarre flights of fancy? Most psychiatrists, psychologists, and professional hypnotherapists believe that age regression works, at least in cases involving a return to periods early in one's life. The detail and accuracy of age-appropriate material retrieved by subjects is well documented. For example, John and Helen Watkins report that if hypnotic regression returns an adult to age six, "the six-year-old ego state should contain the various thoughts, motivations, attitudes, feelings and behaviors that determined the individual at that age."[42] (This recalls the earlier notion of state-specific learning.)

In the extreme case of *past life* hypnotic regression, hypnotists report taking their clients back before birth into prior lives. In these cases, the hypnotized person appears to speak with another personality and from another vantage point. Subjects sometimes describe an earlier existence in enough detail for researchers to find corroborative evidence. Ian Stevenson, professor of psychiatry at the University of Virginia Medical School, has done some of the most meticulous and convincing work in this area. There is even a professional organization called the Association for Past-Life Research and Therapy, composed of counselors, psychiatrists, and psychologists who work in this field.

Yet, since it is virtually impossible to separate fact from fiction with regard to such hypnotically induced experiences, one hypothesis that cannot be overlooked is that an altered state of consciousness permits the creative imagination to embellish assorted unconscious material. More ambitious speculators might go so far as to say that the imagination may be playing with material gathered by means of unconscious ESP from the minds of other living people, or from the collective unconscious.

There is a striking similarity between the transcripts from past-life subjects and the channeled literature. The age-regressed subject operates like a channel, in that normal consciousness has apparently stepped aside, allowing another personality to come through. For example, psychologist Morey Bernstein, while hypnotizing housewife Virginia Tighe in 1952, found a person speaking through the entranced Mrs. Tighe who identified herself as "Bridey Murphy," who had lived centuries earlier.[43]

With such cases, researchers disagree as to whether the entity is the actual historical past-life persona of the hypnotized subject; or a channeled being separate from the subject and her past lives; or a subpersonality of the subject's dissociated unconscious mind. Careful content analysis of the information communicated in these situations is often the only way to begin to resolve the matter. To date, the method leaves much open to interpretation.

In their 1970 book *Psychic Discoveries Behind the Iron Curtain,* Sheila Ostrander and Lynn Schroeder reported on the research of Vladimir L. Raikov in Moscow. Placing his art students in deep hypnotic trance, he suggested to them that they were the reincarnation of various famous Russian painters from the past. This evoked in the students the ability to demonstrate extraordinarily enhanced artistic creativity that they were otherwise unable to exhibit. This is another example of something like

Myers's notion of the *genius* in each of us (chapter 9) that can be called forth through altered-state and programming techniques. Perhaps a process of unconscious self-hypnosis, together with the unconscious suggestion that some deceased human being, or one's own higher Self, is going to speak to or through oneself, lies beyond some or all channeling in cases where the individual genuinely believes he or she is not imagining or faking the situation.

Spiritual Hypnosis

Clearly, hypnosis has some kind of evolutionary adaptive value in all cultures. It's found in practically every culture in history in the practice of religion, for getting in contact with the gods and getting into different ecstatic and mystical states . . . Religious and spiritual trances have a different quality to them as people describe it. When a person seems to go into an authentic spiritual dimension, the whole feeling of it is different. The body is differently experienced. There is a numinous quality of light. All the sensory components of this are likely to be different than in ordinary trance.
—Robert Masters[44]

Czechoslovakian-born psychologist Peter Daniel Francuch survived political imprisonment in Soviet concentration camps and emigrated to the United States, where he worked in mental hospitals and in private practice. In his book *Principles of Spiritual Hypnosis,* Francuch provides a possible way of bridging traditional notions of hypnosis with the experience of channeling. First he describes hypnosis as

a vital link between the different spheres of the human mind and of the human personality through which the higher mode of awareness of these spheres is possible, attainable, and approachable within and without temporal-spatial categories of the so-called objective reality.[45]

Based on his experience of hundreds of subjects, Francuch adds the special case of *spiritual hypnosis:*

Spiritual hypnosis deals with that part of hypnosis that enables man to perceive, to realize, and to experience events and happenings out of a spatial-temporal context and in different dimensions than that of matter and the natural world. In a narrower sense, spiritual hypnosis is a process through which rebirth, renewal, restructuring, changes of conditions and states take place, based on the laws of the human mind and the uniqueness of personality make-up through which self-actualization and communication with God and the spiritual world is not only possible, attainable, but desirable, and it is in order.[46]

Perhaps, in Francuch's terms, channels induced themselves into a kind of spiritual hypnosis.

Ernest Hilgard: Hypnosis and Cognitive Psychology

Stanford professor emeritus Ernest Hilgard has speculated on the nature of voluntary action and thought as they relate to hypnotism. He also has made the experimental discovery of what he calls the hidden observer. And he has attempted a "neodissociation interpretation of divided consciousness." All of this may shed light on the channeling processes.

Hilgard reminds us of the common experience of withdrawal of alertness from behaviors that have become habits. He writes of two separate human functions: the executive function, which involves planning and goal-directed behavior; and monitoring function, which maintains a "pulse-taking" role and provides a feedback loop to keep track of action and perception. The two functional systems must be combined for harmouious operation, Hilgard says. The phenomena associated with hypnosis and dissociation result from an imbalance or separation between the two systems. This can result, for example, in a suspension of the monitoring function while certain behaviors arising from the executive function operate outside of conscious awareness. This would be experienced as a loss of consciousness with regard to those behaviors. A variety of channeling behaviors could be explained by this imbalance or separation of functions.

Hilgard also points out that a close relationship has been shown to exist between voluntary action and conscious control. We may find that channeling-like behavior occurs when normally voluntary actions, like speaking and writing, are turned over to unconscious control, which acts like conscious control except without awareness. According to Hilgard, a distinction can be made between an activity carried out with no awareness and an activity carried out with awareness but without conscious control.[47] Both phenomena can be found in hypnosis and perhaps in channeling, leading to the hypothesis that channeling is the expression of a consciously or unconsciously self-induced hypnotic state within which involuntary behavior takes place.

In the view of cognitive psychology, thinking about an action can lead to it. Thoughts of action carry within them the seeds for carrying out the action; they need only to be "plugged in" for actualization. Short of this psychomotor fulfillment, one would experience the unfolding of the action pattern only in imagination, memory, or dream. In hypnosis, the hypnotist's suggestions replace normal "self-talk" or self-suggestion used to initiate daily activities. Conversely, the channel's self-talk, probably on an unconscious level, could become the suggestion leading to a dissociated state. This state, in turn, could create subjective experience, such as telepathic-type information reception; or physical behavior, such as automatic writing.

The *hidden observer,* according to Hilgard's theory, is that aspect of the subject that appears to know everything taking place but is not part of normal waking consciousness or part of the hypnotized self. Hilgard writes:

We found in some demonstrations and experiments within our laboratory that two kinds of information processing may go on at once within hypnosis; some aspects as ordinarily studied; other aspects are available only when special techniques have elicited the concealed information. When these techniques are used, the additional information is reported as though it had been observed in the usual manner. Because the observing part was hitherto not in awareness, we have come to use the metaphor of a "hidden observer" to characterize this cognitive system.

We had found that material not in the subject's awareness could be recovered through the writing of the hand of which the subject was unaware. It seemed worth testing this highly hypnotizable subject, whether, by analogy, "automatic talking" might yield results similar to automatic writing . . . It should be noted that the "hidden observer" is a metaphor for something occurring at an intellectual level but not available to the consciousness of the hypnotized person. It does not mean that there is a secondary personality with a life of its own—a kind of homunculus lurking in the shadows of the conscious person. The "hidden observer" is merely a convenient label for the information source tapped through experiments with automatic writing and talking.[48]

One can infer that Hilgard does not wish others to take too many liberties with his discovery, such as imputing to it an autonomy bordering on the transpersonal, yet the concept of the hidden observer could be applied to our speculation on the nature of sources in channeling. There is an undeniable similarity, for instance, between the channeling literature's concept of a higher Self and Hilgard's concept. One difference might be that material said to be channeled from the higher Self often cannot be accounted for in terms of the limited resources of the hidden observer operating within Hilgard's closed model.

He writes: "The hidden part doesn't deal with pain. It looks at what is, and doesn't judge it. It is not a hypnotized part of the self. It knows all parts . . . The hidden observer is watching, mature, logical, has more information." (Quite a contrast with the problematic repressions in Freud's concept of the unconscious.)

Hilgard concludes that multiple subsystems run under a central control. This concept of central control replaces the older concept of will. He also calls this the *executive ego*. Hypnotic suggestion can activate the subsystems and manipulate the hierarchies involved. "What characterizes [the state] as hypnotic," he concludes, "is the change in voluntariness from the point of view of the subject. The less it is felt to be under the subject's control, the more it has been dissociated from the normal executive functions, regardless of how it is represented in consciousness . . . The modifications of controls can be described as dissociative if the usual controls are inoperative and are replaced with new ones."[49]

Some may choose to explain channeling phenomena in this manner; that is, the sources channeled are the expression of one's own dissociated subsystems. Others, however, may believe that simply to provide new terms like *executive function, control mechanism,* and *subsystem* does not help us understand what is really going on. Hilgard shares Freud's underlying assumption that we are closed psychological systems. The metaphor of the individual as a steam engine has simply been replaced by that of the individual as a computer.

Such explanations may go a long way toward helping us understand how everything is supposed to work *within* a person; they serve less well in helping us understand how the energies, information, or will of *other* conscious beings might affect such systems. We have used psychology thus far to examine some ways in which we generate experience and behavior *from within.* Later we will turn to some physics models that attempt to describe how we might receive material from beyond ourselves.

CLINICAL PSYCHOLOGY AND PSYCHIATRY: NORMAL VERSUS ABNORMAL

The following two stories will set the context for our clinical consideration of the nature of the channeling experience. The first is from clinician Armand DiMele, founder of The DiMele Center for Psychotherapy and Counseling in New York City; the second is from philosopher Jean Houston.

A few years ago, I was doing past-life work on myself for two years. A large black horse kept reappearing in my images. I believed this horse to embody my higher Self. Although the image was very vivid, I was suspicious. Only we humans need to put form to things. At the highest level of consciousness there is no form. I was very quick to embrace the form of the black horse. One of my few early childhood peaceful memories is of my mother reading me *Black Beauty.* My mother died the year I began my past-life work. By fixating on the image of the black horse, I had maintained dependency on her and was not letting her go. By facing that need in me, the black horse dissolved, and the next experiences I had of my higher Self, or of whatever spirit forms might come through me, were formless. What I learned in most of my personal spiritual work is that if it takes a physical form that I want to identify, then it's a neurotic need on my part. If it stays formless and has the endless potential of going anywhere, then I am more apt to believe it.[50]

The story I like to tell is when my father was writing the *Edgar Bergen and Charlie McCarthy Show.* One time my father and I came into Edgar's room. He didn't know we were watching him. Edgar was talking to Charlie and we thought he was rehearsing, but he was not rehearsing. He was asking Charlie questions: "Charlie, what is the nature of life? Charlie, what is the nature of love?" And this wooden dummy was answering quite unlike the being I knew on the radio. A regular wooden Socrates, he was. It was the same voice but it was a very different content altogether. And Bergen would get fascinated and say, "Well, Charlie, what is the nature of true virtue?" and the dummy would just pour out this stuff: beauty, elegance, brilliant. And then we got embarrassed and coughed. Bergen looked around and turned beet red and said, "Oh, hello, you caught us." And my father said, "What were you doing?" And he said, "Oh, I was talking with Charlie. He's the wisest person I know." And my father said, "But that's your mind; that's *your* voice coming through that wooden creature." And Ed said, "Well, I guess ultimately it is, but I ask Charlie these questions and he answers, and I haven't the faintest idea of what he's going to say and I'm astounded by his brilliance— so much more than I know." To me that was a classical channeling instance where the dummy was used as amanuensis of depth structures of Bergen's mind.[51]

Are channels pathological? Would they be diagnosed by a professional psychologist as mentally ill? Most of us would agree that people who channel are abnormal, since abnormality merely implies falling outside the mainstream. Channels seem to be deviant in the statistical sense, but except for the fact that they may pose a threat to the belief systems of others, there is little evidence that they are pathological or dangerous to themselves or others.

Psychiatrist Stanislav Grof, in his *Beyond the Brain: Birth, Death and Transcendence in Psychotherapy,* points out that "the medical model of mental illness has considerably weakened by overwhelming evidence from history and anthropology, indicating the relativity and culture-bound nature of the criteria for mental health and normalcy."[52]

Professionals mostly use two criteria to establish the existence of mental disorder: a painful symptom (distress) or impairment in functioning (disability). By this definition, it would be difficult to describe channels as suffering from a mental disorder, for they do not typically report suffering, nor are they witnessed as suffering, such distress or disability.

Of course, in cases of trance channeling or even milder forms of clairaudience, clairvoyance, and automatic writing, the normal personality of the channel *is* disabled with regard to interacting with external reality. In this sense, the channel suffers from a recurring disability every time channeling takes place, a disability no less incapacitating than, say, an epileptic seizure—to which, by the way, it sometimes bears a strong resemblance. And yet only rarely have cases been recorded in which channeling led to self-inflicted pain or hurting someone else. In fact, there have been numerous cases in which someone without formal training allegedly performs delicate surgery while under the influence of a discarnate doctor;[53] and others in which someone who had no artistic training paints a lovely picture or plays the piano while channeling a deceased artist. During this time the channel is unable to relate to the outside world in any other way. In these respects, channeling appears at worst as a trade-off for another kind of enabling control.

Given the statistically abnormal nature of the experience, it is curious that relatively few channels report discomfort; although some researchers, such as Margo Chandley, have found evidence that perhaps more channels suffer discomfort than readily admit. Many channels report initial disbelief, disorientation, and guardedness; even fear that they are losing their minds. But firsthand accounts indicate that something about the direct experience of the phenomenon and the meaning derived from it brings many of them a feeling of comfort, even gratitude, after the initial shake-up of life as usual. Reported cases of obsession or possession are the exception and have been known to lead to, or to be the result of, mental illness.

It is unusual, though, for someone who channels to suffer real impairment. Rather, the ability to channel could be seen as a gift, or as just some kind of problem one has with reality or with one's mind (although problematic it has been known to be). An argument could be made for the *enabling* rather than the *disabling* nature of the phenomenon. Yet, since the acclimatization to becoming a channel can take time, there can be periods of early disability that are compensated by later enabling ones. Time and again, we find instances of those who provide useful information and insight to themselves and to others by means of channeling.

Using the *DSM III*

The bible for clinical psychologists and psychiatrists is the *Diagnostic and Statistical Manual of Mental Disorders,* or *DSM III,* published by the American Psychiatric Association and now in its third edition.[54] The acknowledged state of the art regarding the categorization of mental disorders, this manual is used by professionals to make diagnoses of patients and is considered authoritative in courts of law. Some of its key categories and definitions may help us better understand the mainstream perspective on channeling.

Delusions and Hallucinations   *Delusion* is defined by *DSM III* as "false belief based on incorrect inference about external reality and firmly sustained in spite of what everyone else believes and in spite of what constitutes incontrovertible proof to the contrary."

One particular kind of delusion relevant to channeling is defined in *DMS III* as the "*delusion of being controlled* in which feelings, impulses, thoughts or actions are experienced as being not one's own, as being imposed by some external force. This does not include the mere conviction that one is acting as an agent of God." Certainly the first part of this description fits virtually all cases of channeling. It is interesting to note the exception in the case of acting as an agent of God. One wonders why the psychiatric profession thinks it is acceptable to consider oneself as being used by God, but pathological to consider oneself as being used by a discarnate human spirit. The answer to this must be that acceptance of the existence of God is more a part of consensual reality than acceptance of the existence of discarnate spirits. Curiously enough, it appears that psychiatrists and psychologists are willing to step beyond the religious establishment in their apparent acceptance of people other than saints who think and act as agents of God.

But are channels actually receiving information from God or other transcendental beings? Without recourse to objective proof that God or Godlike beings are actually at work through human channels, the burden of proof must rest on the content of the channeled material itself. Many have chosen to make their own decisions regarding the validity of channeled sources by testing the channeled material's value in their life experience.

Grandiose delusions are those "whose content involves an exaggerated sense of one's importance, power, knowledge, or identity." This would seem like a good label to pin on those who claim to be channels for Jesus, Buddha, Krishna, Archangel Michael, and the like. To some, this seems to be the ultimate case of name-dropping, of gaining importance because some spiritual notable has chosen you as a vehicle for his high-flown verities. What about the person who claims that a voice from a higher mental plane is conveying to him the true unified field theory that will revolutionize science? Undoubtedly an attention getter, for better or for worse. Yet many channels, to the contrary, say they feel bewildered or embarrassed by the responsibility placed on them. Most do not believe they chose their channeling gifts; rather they feel they were chosen by their sources.

Hallucination is "a sensory perception without external stimulation of the relevant organ. A hallucination has the immediate sense of reality of a true perception, although in some instances the source may be perceived as within the body (e.g., an auditory hallucination may be experienced as coming from within the head rather than through the ears)." This seems to fit the experience that most clairaudient and clairvoyant channels have described. The sense that the communication comes from "within the head rather than through the ears" is especially prominent. Psychiatrists assume that the source of hallucinations is neurological activity within the individual. Many cases of channeled communication, however, could not be explained as hallucination because the specific content of the material appears to surpass what might have been the result of self-generated impulses.

Identity Disorder *Identity* in *DSM III* is defined as "the sense of self, providing a unity of personality over time." Various pathologies include problems with identity, and we will need to weigh whether certain manifestations of channeling could be construed in such pathological terms with regard to identity. Indeed, alterations, splittings, and mergings of identity comprise the single most pronounced trait of the phenomenon, according to descriptions by witnesses and by channels themselves.

In the category of *identity disorder,* an individual is reported to have difficulty answering the question "Who am I?" On the surface, this might be one way to describe some characteristics of those who channel; however, in most cases, channels are quite clear about their personal identities. What they may not be clear about is who or what their alleged entities are. Sometimes the internal distinction between self and not-self is subtle indeed, leaving the channel as much in the dark as the observer.

Later in a section on multiple personality, we will look more closely at the issue of identity disorder.

Psychosis and Reality Testing   *Psychotic* indicates "gross impairment in reality testing." Do the behaviors and beliefs of the channel lead to such impairment?

Normal means being able to adequately carry out *reality testing*—that is, the ongoing process of matching one's inner world with consensus reality, in order to keep the inner world in line with the outer, public one. This definition reveals a hidden bias: the belief that external reality is somehow more real, more believable, than subjective reality and therefore can be used as a measuring rod. As long as the official definition of reality testing is matching private inner reality with outer reality, we will be at a loss to make a case for a competing kind of reality testing—an alignment of outer reality with inner reality.

Most of us probably would agree that almost every day we test out certain ideas or people in the physical, public world. And we test what we make of *their* reality against what we sense to be our *own* inner reality, whether we call this our heart, soul, conscience, or higher Self.

The status of the proposed alternative kind of reality testing—outer against inner reality—would hinge on our collective ability to experience in common and describe a greater inner reality. Much of the current channeled literature claims that we are moving in that direction. Could someone reported to be a channel properly be called psychotic in the context of the research lab, the mental hospital, or the court of law? Figuratively speaking, do abiding members of the current consensus reality have the right to make a citizen's arrest of someone who claims to hear Moses, aliens, or a dead grandmother?

We don't seem to have a problem with Christians who claim to know Jesus Christ and converse with him on a daily basis. But what happens when someone hears about a neighbor who has begun to channel something like "Futon, the Galactic Oversoul" by candlelight? Is the reaction "Fine, as long as he keeps passing his reality testing and stays a good neighbor"? Or are beliefs and practices that are just too different now too close for comfort?

The phenomenon of channeling, burgeoning as never before throughout the world, may be paving the way for a creative evolutionary shift in the concept of reality—and in how we live our lives. Or it may be offering early warnings of an impending break into a mass psychotic episode, a latter-day Dark Ages with little redeeming value. In either case, an honest, open attempt to come to terms with channeling triggers a critical reconsideration of some of our most basic psychological and existential assumptions about reality.

Schizophrenia Some of the characteristics listed in the *DSM III* under the well-known, broadly used category of schizophrenia might well apply to channeling: "bizarre delusions; somatic, grandiose, religious, or other delusions; auditory hallucinations; disturbances in perception; thought disorder; or disturbance in sense of self."

Particularly interesting are the disturbances in content of thought: "One's thoughts, as they occur, are broadcast from one's head to the external world so that others can hear (thought broadcasting); thoughts that are not one's own are inserted into one's mind (thought insertion); thoughts have been removed from one's head (thought withdrawal); or one's feelings, impulses, thoughts or actions are not one's own but are imposed by some external force (delusions of being controlled)." These certainly seem to parallel various channels' experiences with telepathy, voices in the head, automatic writing, and the informing presence of invisible "others" in general.

Furthermore, "the sense of self that gives the normal person a feeling of individuality, uniqueness and self-direction is frequently disturbed [in schizophrenia]. This is sometimes referred to as a loss of ego boundaries and is frequently manifested by extreme perplexity about one's own identity and the meaning of existence, or by some of the specific delusions described above, particularly involving control by an outside force." Channeling is probably not attributable to schizophrenia in the majority of cases in which the sense of self seems to be enhanced, expanded, and helped and in which the information obtained is said to add to, rather than detract from, the private and public quality of life for the individual and for others.

Marcello Truzzi points to the all-too-human nature of what others might consider thought disorder: "Belief in extraterrestrial life, for example, has been shown to often be related to the need for affiliation; so it may be related to loneliness, as well as a desire for attention-getting. Most people want to be special."[55] Gerald Larue, chairman of the Committee for the Scientific Examination of Religion, focuses on the delusional nature of channeling for channels and those who comprise the channeling subculture: "Channels give simplistic answers, and they give you that touch of magic and the esoteric." He sees this as "a typical religious experience. It's uplifting, but it's not real. You have to come back for another fix, like drug addiction."[56] If channeling springs from the unreal, as Larue says, one wonders whether the billions on the planet who hold transcendental-type religious beliefs are equally addicted to something "not real." If so, what would that say about the mental state of the prevailing consensus reality?

Factitious and Malingering Behavior Two interesting related *DSM III* categories of mental disturbance are *factitious disorder* and *malingering*. In a factitious disorder, "psychotic symptoms are under the individual's voluntary control and are likely to be present only when the individual thinks he or she is being observed; behavior under voluntary control is used to pursue goals that are involuntarily adapted. Such an individual may claim memory loss, hallucinations (auditory and visual), and dissociative and conversion symptoms."

Malingering is "the voluntary production and presentation of false or grossly exaggerated physical or psychological symptoms. The symptoms are produced in pursuit of a goal that is obviously recognizable with an understanding of the individual's circumstances."

That is to say, the patient with factitious disorder does not know she has simply made up her story of hearing the voice of Jesus (for example) in order to compensate for some childhood sense of inferiority that she has long repressed; however, the malingering patient intentionally lies, telling people (for example) that he has been in telepathic communication with the Virgin Mary and admonishing them for their spiritual inadequacies. The former is an unconscious falsity, the latter a conscious play for attention.

In our earlier consideration of the Spiritualist movement, we came across numerous attempts to uncover cases of fraud. These may well have involved both factitious and malingering behavior, for there were cases of intentional trickery as well as cases of people genuinely not knowing they were inauthentic. Such factitious and malingering behaviors are undoubtedly true today with some of those professing to be channels. Though we still lack sound methods for discerning which is the case, there are those channels—like D. D. Home, Lenore Piper, and Eileen Garrett—whose veracity appears to be beyond doubt.

Amnesia Amnesia may hold clues to channeling. Trance channels typically claim they do not recall what occurred while they were "out."

Automatic writers also frequently say they have no awareness during the process and no idea about the source or content of the writing until they read it afterward. The concept of *psychogenic amnesia* as defined in DSM III may be applicable here: "The essential feature is a sudden inability to recall important personal information, an ability not due to an organic mental disorder. The extent of the disturbance is too great to be explained by ordinary forgetfulness."

One bizarre kind of amnesia is called *psychogenic fugue*—"the sudden, unexpected travel away from home or work and the assumption of a new identity and an inability to recall one's previous identity." This would seem to describe some rare cases of prolonged, spontaneous full-trance channeling or possession (some use the term *walk-ins* as well). But for the clinician, the new personality or entity involved in fugue is only the projection of the patient's unconscious mind; the possibility of independent nonphysical identities, capable of putting on or taking off the "glove" of their own or others' bodies, is out of the question.

Depersonalization and Dissociation   *Depersonalization* is one way of explaining automatic writing or other channeling automatisms in which the individual is a passive spectator of the involuntary movements of part of his body as if it were not his own. In depersonalization, there is "an alteration in the perception or experience of the self so that the usual sense of one's own reality is temporarily lost or changed. This is manifested by a sensation of self-estrangement or unreality." Self-estrangement implies that a part of the self becomes alienated from the rest of the parent self so that the latter feels the former as separate. This occurs when the estranged part uses the body to communicate in automatic writing. The clinician would argue that the communicating aspect, which is experienced as not-self, is in fact always the self—part of the one complex self of the channel.

A *dissociative disorder* "is a sudden, temporary alteration in the normally integrative functions of consciousness, identity, or motor behavior. If the alteration occurs in consciousness, important personal events cannot be recalled. If it occurs in identity, either the individual's customary identity is temporarily forgotten and a new identity is assumed, or the customary feeling of one's reality is lost and replaced by a feeling of unreality." Therefore, psychologists might say that the dysfunctional disintegration of the self gives rise to channeling. In this case, information comes from within, not through, the individual. One aspect of the split or dissociated personality reemerges, seemingly with a life of its own. As F. W. H. Myers put it in 1903, "Our psychical unity is federative and unstable; it has arisen from irregular accretions in the remote past; it consists even now only in the limited collaboration of limited groups."[57] While both the clinician and Myers would agree to the unstable and complex nature of the psyche, the clinician would impute *all* channeled sources to such dissociated aspects of the individual's psyche, while Myers would not.

Multiple Personality Several popular books, such as *The Three Faces of Eve, Sybil*, and *The Minds of Billy Mulligan*, and the 1987 publication of *When Rabbit Howls*,[58] a study of a woman with as many as ninety-two personalities operating within her, all have placed the phenomenon of multiple personality more in the public eye than any other mental disorder except schizophrenia. Multiple-personality disorder, or MPD, is perhaps the most intriguing kind of dissociation. As defined in *DSM III*, "the essential feature is the existence within the individual of two or more distinct personalities, each of which is dominant at a particular time. Each personality is a fully integrated and complex unit with unique memories, behavior patterns and social relationships that determine the nature of the individual's acts when that personality is dominant." This appears not only to describe channeling but also to address the strikingly autonomous nature of the channeled sources, which seem to have their own histories, memories, beliefs, and personalities.

Most of the MPD literature is, nevertheless, based on the prevailing closed model of a human being, in which alter personalities arise from within the psyche; channeling implies a personality entering from *outside* the psyche of the channel. There are, however, a growing number of clinicians and researchers who are beginning to believe that at least some of the alter personalities are actually impinging from outside the multiple's psyche, as in the case of unwanted possession. One of the leading proponents of this view is Ralph B. Allison, in his book *Minds in Many Pieces*.[59] We'll look at Allison's ideas later in this chapter.

There appears to be a relationship between cases of MPD and cases of channeling. Researchers point out that some 97 percent of all known MPD cases have a history of childhood trauma, usually a combination of emotional, physical, and sexual abuse.[60] Many channels, according to Margo Chandley's study, also appear to have a background of neglect or abuse (she may perhaps define this more broadly than some others do). Yet there are differences between MPD and channeling. Seventy-five percent of MPD subjects report having personalities who are under twelve years old, while virtually no reported channeled sources are children. Also, most multiples have more than one alter personality, while a majority of contemporary channels appear to have only one source.

In a recent article entitled "Multiple Personality and Spirit Possession" in *Psychiatry*,[61] anthropologist Michael G. Kenny reminds us of the culture-specific flavor of explanations for possession: "The spirit-possessed person acts out the role of a specific deity and recalls nothing about having done so; in the same way, the various phases of multiple personality identify themselves through different names." Other cultures treat possession in a very matter-of-fact way. Kenny concludes that we can only be certain that the presences *are* alien for the person who is experiencing them. By refusing to recognize the internal realm of nonphysical spirit and spirits, in Kenny's terms, he says Western scientists remain at a loss to explain these potentially related phenomena.

Stanley Krippner echoes this culture-specific way in which a person or a people treats the reality of MPD or channeling. But in the face of his own MPD research, Krippner does admit to the seeming universality of the fact that "the human being is extremely malleable. People can create personalities as required to defend themselves against trauma, to conform to cultural pressures, or to meet the expectations of a psychologist, medium, or exorcist. This malleability has both adaptive and maladaptive aspects."[62]

William James, one of the pioneers of Western psychology, was moved to remark in 1909:

> The refusal of modern "enlightenment" to treat "possession" as a hypothesis to be spoken of as even possible, in spite of the massive human tradition based on concrete human experience in its favor, has always seemed to me a curious example of the power of fashion in things "scientific." That the demon-theory . . . will have its innings again is to my mind absolutely certain. One has to be "scientific" indeed to be blind and ignorant enough to suspect no such possibility.[63]

New York City clinician Armand DiMele is one of the many professionals today who believe that most alter personalities are not channeled, though the door is left open that some cases may be genuine.

> In dealing with multiples you need to call on the highest possible powers the person has, and you actually invite that thing in through a hypnotic state. But when it comes in it comes in so clearly, so beautifully, and filled with information one couldn't have had any idea about. I have spoken to "spirit voices" who have come through multiples that have told me things about my childhood. Specifics, like things that hung in the house. There's some undeniable evidence that something happens, something we don't understand and can't measure. Yet I believe that most channeling being done is through the pathological need of the person doing

the channeling. I don't think that most of the people who claim to be channels are channels.[64]

DiMele's ambiguity is shared by transpersonal psychologist Ken Wilber. "I think that anyone familiar with depth psychology," he points out, "knows the extraordinary transformation that can occur to somebody in a dissociative state is stunning." Wilber believes that by hypnosis and other procedures "we can generate amazing phenomena in a state without the necessity to postulate something like ghosties running around whispering in their ear." Nonetheless, he adds, "I *do* think there are some ghosties running around whispering in peoples' ears." Wilber continues:

At its worst, "channeling" is a dissociative phenomenon, basically of the hysterical variety. I find a lot of it to be narcissistic—"I am channeling what God says"—a very primitive state, in my opinion. And I think analysis bears that out. That's the extreme, and I think 90 percent of what I've seen falls into that category. Some of the sources may be slightly inspired by transcendental subjects or materials, but the line through which it comes is pathological, particularly narcissistic and borderline pathological. But at the other extreme, there definitely is a transcendental domain. One of the ways that people get in touch with it is through a "crack in the cosmic egg." It opens up a bit, and basically what's allowed in is an influx of transcendental or perennial truth.[65]

Co-consciousness Another psychologist with a more open view of dissociative phenomena is John Beahrs. In his article "Co-consciousness: A Common Denominator in Hypnosis, Multiple Personality, and Normalcy," Beahrs reintroduces the concept first articulated by psychic researcher Walter Franklin Prince more than half a century earlier. Co-consciousness is described by Beahrs as "the existence within a single human organism of more than one consciously experiencing psychological entity, each with its own identity and self-hood, relatively separate and distinct from other similar entities." What is interesting about Beahr's view is that he believes that this co-conscious condition is natural for all of us. Only rarely does it become problematic.

With co-consciousness now the norm, the Multiple Personality Syndrome can no longer be seen as a freak of nature, but rather as a paradigm of how a process common to each and all of us can go wrong. Furthest from scientific understanding is the nature of the executive function or organizing force which gives us our sense of

cohesive selfhood, and it is just this function which is most im-
paired in the multiple personality.[66]

While channels almost always claim to possess a normal sense of
their own identity, they also experience themselves mediating expressions from other identities, or having their own identity replaced by
another, temporarily and usually intentionally. Such sources, for Beahrs,
would be the "consciously experiencing psychological entities" of this
natural co-conscious state. The co-conscious state becomes abnormal or
pathological only when it goes wrong, which presumably occurs only
when the individual reports distress or dysfunction; for example, being
unable to reclaim control of what Hilgard called the executive function
or executive ego self from unwanted, spontaneously appearing alter
personalities.

In his book *MultiMind: A New Way of Looking at Human Behavior,*
Robert Ornstein refers not to a single executive function, but to a semi-
organized mental operating system. He writes:

> Instead of a single, intellectual entity that can judge many different
> complex kinds of events equally, the mind is diverse and complex.
> It contains a changeable conglomeration of different kinds of
> "small minds"—fixed reactions, talents, flexible thinking—and
> these different entities are temporarily employed—"wheeled into
> consciousness"—and then usually discarded, returned to their
> place after use . . . In part, the "me" who is responsible and whom
> society recognizes as responsible resides in the ability to control
> the diverse systems within. Something has to command the wheel-
> ing in and out of one or more of the small minds.[67]

Could channels, then, by Ornstein's view, be literally small-minded?
Returning to the concept of an executive function, used by Hilgard and
most other cognitive psychologists, it is the responsible "something" of
Ornstein's that is said to be in control, to organize and control the
various subsystems, complexes, alter personalities, or psychological entities of which we are composed. Some of the alleged channeled sources
identify themselves, rather than the waking ego, as the voice of this
executive function or higher Self; or they claim, like some kind of hidden observer, to have a better vantage point than egos regarding the
basis of personality cohesion. Our tendency to identify ego consciousness as that controlling and cohering function, many channeled sources
tell us, is an illusion we have grown used to because of the value we
place on physical reality and our own bodies, with which the ego is
particularly designed to identify and interact. In truth, the sources con-

tinue, we each have a deeper identity that is more inclusive and more knowing than the ego. It would appear that this identity proclaimed by many channeled sources runs deeper than the controlling mechanism of Beahrs, Hilgard, Ornstein, and others.

James Fadiman is another contemporary psychologist who has adapted a type of co-consciousness model:

> I've had some experiences of a voice coming into, not through me, and at one point I said, "Why do you have this scurrilous vocabulary?" He said, "Well, I have your mind to work with." It made total sense. It occurred at a time in my life when it didn't feel like me. But that's what dissociation feels like. The old dissociation theories prior to the Freudian [such as Janet] I'm more and more seeing as making better sense than the Freudian position which has taken over. The idea that we are not unified simply fits the evidence better and allows channeling a lot more space.

As the leading cognitive scientist and MIT professor Marvin Minsky writes in his recent book *The Society of Mind,* "One part of me wants this, another part wants that. I must get control of myself . . . If there is no single, central, ruling self inside the mind, what makes us feel so sure that one exists?"[68]

The psychologist Paul Federn had perhaps the most detailed model for looking at dissociation, multiple personality, and co-consciousness. An associate of Freud, Federn shared with Jung the view that there was a psychic energy other than sexual energy. According to Federn, *subject or ego cathexis* is the process of an individual investing psychic energy into any physical or psychical object so that he experiences that object as "I" or "my," such as "that is my arm." On the other hand, *object cathexis* is the process of investing psychic energy into an object so that it is experienced as "it" or "not-me." For Federn, an ego state is an organization or pattern of mental elements that are ego-cathected with self-energy, making it a kind of subself bound together by some common principle in response to a long-term need and with discrete consciousness separate from the rest of the self. Depending upon the permeability of the membrane between the ego state and the rest of the self, there may be some "cross-talk," or there may be none at all, leaving the experience of two (or more) separate, autonomous systems.[69]

Contemporary research psychologists John and Helen Watkins have adapted Federn's system to channeling-type phenomena:

> For example, if an idea such as "I am thinking about my dead mother" becomes conscious, but its activating energy is *object*

cathexis, then it is experienced as a perception, as if it were an object. The thought becomes a hallucination. The individual reports "seeing" his mother, not thinking about her, and we diagnose him as psychotic. If the idea of the dead mother then has its object cathexis removed and replaced with ego cathexis the individual tells us simply that he is "thinking" about his mother—and we no longer regard him as psychotic. Changes in subject (ego) and object (it) energies determine what is experienced as a part of one's self and what is not.[70]

According to the Watkins, some ego states are highly energized, have rigid boundaries, and emerge spontaneously. They possess well-defined motivations, feelings, and attitudes and sometimes give themselves names. They may cooperate with one another or with the executive (chief) ego state of the self. One must bear in mind, of course, that all such models would attempt to explain the sources in channeling as the dissociated energy of the channel's self.

Contributions from Clinicians

Automatic writing is typical of dissociated behavior in the eyes of the clinician. In the 1920s, research psychiatrist Anita Muhl of St. Elizabeth's Hospital in Washington, D.C., found that inducing automatic writing and drawing in her mentally disturbed patients helped to bring to the surface problematic repressed material. In her book *Automatic Writing: An Approach to the Unconscious,*[71] she concluded that because it was relatively easy to induce the behavior in so many of her patients, the potential to do it might be available to "normal" people as well. Yet, for Muhl, what the patients displayed in the name of automatic writing was classic dissociated, automatistic behavior emanating from personal, repressed material, not from outside the individual. Muhl also warned that automatic writing, done by very troubled people while alone, might lead to breakdown of the personality. What her research contributes to our understanding of channeling is a view of the relative ease and universality of the dissociated automatic-writing process, irrespective of what the ultimate nature of the source of the material might turn out to be.

German psychiatrist Hans Bender, in "Psychic Automatisms" (his M.D. thesis), proposed the existence of "mediumistic psychosis" in many of the patients with whom he worked. He studied patients diagnosed as schizophrenics who, before their illness, had practiced some form of automatism that opened what Bender called communication with their Other. The automatisms included motor-control kinds, such as coded table rapping, trance voice, writing, Ouija board, and pendulum; and sensory kinds, such as hallucinations involving voices, visions, thoughts, and the sensation of being controlled by another. Some of the cases he reported would seem to us to be genuine channeling. Some of the incidents involving malignant-type entities led to (unsuccessful) suicide and murder attempts.[72]

By using automatisms, Bender said, splits of mediumistic psychosis led to disruption of normal personality that was different from schizophrenia. It does "not shatter the psyche into pieces," he wrote, "rather it creates functional units which act more or less independently of each other. It is not a splitting off, but a functional liberation of partial systems."[73] Both Muhl and Bender stressed the usefulness of such channeling-like activity.

Psychiatrist Jan Ehrenwald, in his recent book *Anatomy of Genius: Split Brains and Global Minds* (1986), presents his research on a variety of pathological and "optimum performance" individuals. Of the famous medium Eileen Garrett, he writes, "She walked a tightrope between the extremes of madness and genius." His conclusion about channeling:

Mental dissociation, culminating in hysterical trance states, has from time immemorial formed a veritable breeding ground for secondary personalities. Such trance states have served as a mouthpiece for the medium's own unconscious wishes, hopes, and expectations, but also for diverse ecstatic, visionary or prophetic utterances . . . In rare cases they may be possessed of a veridical quality and contain elements suggestive of extrasensory perception.[74]

Wilson Van Dusen spent fifteen years as a clinical psychologist on the staff of Mendocino State Hospital in Ukiah, California, where he had the opportunity to examine thousands of mental patients. He was also deeply immersed in the writings of the eighteenth-century channel Emanuel Swedenborg, whose many volumes describing nonphysical domains and their inhabitants stand as an internally consistent vision in channeling literature. In Van Dusen's book *The Presence of Other Worlds,* he writes, "An accidental discovery in 1964 permitted me to get a much more detailed and accurate picture of psychotic hallucinations than had previously been possible. I gradually noticed similarities between patients' reports and Swedenborg's description of the relationships of man to spirits. I found that Swedenborg's system not only is an almost perfect fit with patients' experiences but, even more impressively, it accounts for otherwise quite puzzling aspects of hallucinations."[75]

Van Dusen gained the confidence of patients and had long "dialogues" with their hallucinations—which, he said, became entities who often appeared frightened and disoriented. "They felt that a psychologist might want to kill them, which was, in a sense, true. The reader may notice that I treat the hallucinations as realities—that is what they are to the patient."

He reported that patients consistently felt they had contact with another world or order of beings. "Most thought these other persons were living. All objected to the term 'hallucination.' Each coined his own term, such as the Other Side, the Eavesdroppers, air phone, etc."

Swedenborg had gone to great lengths to describe the inhabitants of Hell and Heaven with whom he believed he was communicating. Similarly, Van Dusen writes of his patients:

> I learned of two orders of experience, borrowing from the voices themselves, called the higher and the lower order. Lower-order voices are similar to drunken bums at a bar who like to tease and torment for the fun of it . . . The higher order is much more likely to be symbolic, religious, supportive, genuinely instructive. It can communicate directly with the inner feelings of the patient. It is similar to Jung's archetypes, whereas the lower order is like Freud's id.

Van Dusen concludes:

> It is in itself remarkable that Swedenborg and persons separated by different cultures, different assumptions of the world, different experiences, and two centuries of time could so describe inner experiences alike. One implication is that this inner world may be stable and consistent over centuries of time, certainly more consistent than the outer natural world.[76]

Van Dusen's view of the consistency of this inner world seems similar to Carl Jung's concept of archetypes and the collective unconscious. Van Dusen didn't think Swedenborg was mad. But while he does point to the similarity between Swedenborg's and his patients' descriptions, it is not clear whether Van Dusen believes in the objective external reality of what they experienced. In this regard, Van Dusen's view of the objective nature (and location) of channeled sources remains elusive, as does the view of Jungian-type psychologists we have heard from, such as Ira Progoff and Jean Houston.

Emphasizing that his extensive experience with multiple-personality and related types of clients has been as a clinician, not a formal researcher, psychiatrist Ralph B. Allison has come to believe that *disembodied* minds can exist, and that *embodied* minds are capable of being and doing much more than was once thought. In a recent interview, he told me:

> The mind and the brain are not the same. The brain is a structure. The mind is the energy that inhabits that structure. But obviously it can be elsewhere, and that can be demonstrated with out-of-body experiences, [as when] the brain is in one place on the operating table and the mind is up on the ceiling looking down on the surgeon who's in a panic, and the person's dying.
>
> When I talk to the alleged spirits [of his clients], they say "Don't worry about where we come from or what's our address, or where we've lived before" . . . Some of these entities say very clearly: "I am a part of her or him [the client], and I broke off when he or she got raped," or something like that. And that's part of the human package. Others [entities] say: "I had my last lifetime as a Sioux Indian in the Dakotas and I was a multiple then, and now I've been sent by God here to help her [the client] with her troubles—I'm an expert at it." Who am I to argue? I don't know who they are. So I'm just telling you what they tell me. They don't come with ID cards. You just have to say, "Do you operate like what I think a spirit is like or do you operate like something else?"

Allison explains, "I'm in the business of helping people, and I could care less where the information comes from. Does it work?" His conclusion from decades of experience with clients: "The human mind can do anything. It can create the whole kit and kaboodle. Don't knock it."

Finally, psychologists Hal Stone and Sidra Winkelman have developed what they call a voice dialogue process, whereby they work to draw out and converse with what they call the subpersonalities of disturbed as well as perfectly normal people. In an interview with me, Stone describes what he and Winkelman mean by subpersonality, as well as Jungian-type archetypes:

> Subpersonalities represent those people inside of us, those parts of us that are conditioned by family and society. They live inside of us, but they're literally conditioned behaviors. And then the archetypes are essentially internal energy patterns, behavior patterns, but they come from a deeper level of the psyche . . . basic predispositions toward certain thought and behavior patterns, feel-

ings, that are innate but are also subject to conditioning in the course of life.

According to Stone, these inside energies are in all of us as subpersonalities and may on occasion manifest themselves in either useful or problematic ways. They can also be responsible for what many people believe are channeled sources. Besides these inner "little people" (not unlike Ornstein's "small minds"), Stone and Winkelman have also found ample evidence for the existence of what they call outside energies that can also manifest as (perhaps even *be*) discrete personalities, for good or ill. And, like Van Dusen and Allison, they've learned to dialogue with both kinds.

There is the awareness of this fact in modern times that there *are* energies outside and certain people seem to be able to get connected to them and to have them come through . . . In our work at different times, different voices will come in from strange places . . . sounding like a voice from a past life. Occasionally an entity will jump in. And we talk to these voices and deal with them exactly as we would an internal [subpersonality] voice system.

The goal of their therapy and teaching, Stone emphasizes, is to help each person become what they call an integrated, accepting, and discerning aware ego. Until this occurs, problems can arise in therapy, in life, and in the special case of channeling:

When there isn't an aware ego, the tendency of people is to bond to the entity, exactly as in the transference of client and therapist. What happens is that usually the son or daughter side of a person bonds to the entity, and the entity becomes the knower, and the person becomes the receiver of the knowledge, really the disciple to the entity. That's okay for a period of time, if it's a stage in the development of a person. However, there is a large number of people who literally lock into the transference to the entity. And because the entity is disembodied, the tendency is to value it more than it should be. The aware ego recognizes that there are energies out there just as there are energies inside of us, and it learns to evaluate those energies and to take advantage of them and use them and learn from them . . . When you don't have an aware ego—and this is an enormous problem today—the tendency is to make the entity too much into an all-knowing god energy and to literally lock into the transference process. We stress learning to honor all energy without being identified with it . . . and this includes the entities that come through the channeling process.

Based upon the experiences of seasoned clinicians such as Van Dusen, Allison, and Stone, we may not be able to arrive at a simple either/or decision about the origins of channeled material. Some channels may be featuring their own subpersonalities or alter personalities, while others may be connecting with energies from the nonphysical "ethers" with which the nature of consciousness itself is inextricably intermixed.

PARAPSYCHOLOGY AND CONSCIOUSNESS RESEARCH

Parapsychology

Some of the most eminent scientists of the late nineteenth and early twentieth centuries chose to investigate channeling and related phenomena under the name of "psychic" research. By the 1920s, Duke University research psychologist J. B. Rhine and others decided to distance themselves from "psychic" research—associated with the stageshow hoopla of mediums and the suspect seance chambers of the Spiritualist era—by formalizing a new scientific discipline for the study of paranormal phenomena. It would be based on empirical experiments, statistical measurement, and clinical and experimental mechanisms of behavior. (Some have interpreted this preoccupation with the highly controlled scientific orientation to be the result of a psychoanalytic reaction formation on the part of Rhine after his investigation of the "Margery Mediumship" led him to observations of questionable authority, perhaps trickery, whether perpetrated consciously or not.)

This new discipline, parapsychology, has as its focus three basic areas: *extrasensory perception* (ESP), which includes all kinds of anomalous information reception: telepathy, clairvoyance, precognition, and psychometry; *psychokinesis* (PK), including "mind over matter," teleportation, materialization, psychic surgery and healing, as well as levitation, thought-photography and out-of-body experiences; and *survival phenomena,* including channeling, possession, ghosts and hauntings, reincarnation, and afterlife evidence.[77]

It is within the first category, ESP, that we will find the most useful concept to explain channeling. The third category, survival phenomena, would seem most dedicated to investigating channeling. Rhine called for an abandonment of survival research in 1960, claiming that channeling and related information bearing on survival of death could not be adequately distinguished from information that can be obtained by ESP from living persons. However, Stanley Krippner, a current leader in parapsychology research, believes this aspect should be included in the discipline of parapsychology: "Theta phenomena involve life after death. Any information that is obtained by some unexplainable source but is attributed to entities for me would fall under the category of theta phenomena. I prefer 'theta,' since 'survival' has a bias to it."[78]

Consider a case of ordinary ESP. A woman asks a channel to contact her recently deceased husband. The channel goes into a mildly altered state and relays what he or she claims to hear—clairaudiently or telepathically—from the husband. Or the channel may go deeper into trance and, with deepened voice, appear to speak in the husband's voice. What the channel is hearing or saying as the husband could be explained by the parapsychologist as having been obtained by the channel solely from the contents of the widow's mind via traditional ESP. The channel would be telepathically reading the widow's unconscious mind (or aura or thoughtforms) in order to find the material necessary to compose a convincing presentation of her husband.

In the super, grand, or general ESP theory, material that could be known by channels in no other way is explained by their having telepathically read the unconscious minds of *distant* individuals who are unknown to everyone involved.

Extending this ESP concept even farther, researchers speculate that the mind of the channel may roam other realms in order to telepathically find the right knowledge or nuance of personality to pass for the alleged source. In a computer metaphor, the channel's brain/mind "logs on" to some vast data base from which to access what is needed. In the super ESP model, this data base is composed of all living minds. Perhaps it includes the entire evolutionary mental envelope surrounding the earth, which Jesuit scientist-philosopher Pierre Teilhard de Chardin called the noosphere. Or perhaps it includes Jung's collective unconscious or the ancients' akashic records. The adherence of parapsychologists to such a grand ESP explanation for channeling seems to display an inability to make the conceptual leap to the possibility of nonphysical intelligent beings. Even paranormal debunker Marcello Truzzi is moved to comment that "grand ESP isn't any less extraordinary than the thing it's trying to explain away—channeling."[79]

Just as some parapsychologists choose to explain channeling by an extended notion of ESP, so others choose to explain channeling in terms of an extended notion of psychokinesis (PK). The concept of psychokinesis holds that there is some nonordinary way in which mind can affect matter. The psychokinesis argument for channeling is based upon a basic dualistic notion that mind and matter are different from each other and that all minds are basically of the same nature, whether they are embodied or not, and therefore would have to interact with matter like the brain in the same way.

By this view, we are supposed to wonder how the individual mind can affect its own body to lift a paper clip with its fingers, for example, as much as we are to wonder how the mind might lift a paper clip at a distance and without touching it. The argument is that mind operates brain (and the rest of the body) at all times in a basically psychokinetic manner, although we do not usually think of it that way: we just decide to scratch our nose, or stand up, and then do so. Psychokinesis, after all, is the term for paranormal, not normal, cases of mind affecting matter. Yet, the argument goes, if your own mind can affect your own brain, then the similar nonphysical nature of *another* mind might also be able to affect your brain, giving rise to your hearing a voice, seeing a vision, or having the other mind speak or write by controlling your body the same way you normally control your own body.

Two other contributions from parapsychological research may have a bearing on channeling. First, during research at Maimonides Medical Center in Brooklyn in the late 1960s, Stanley Krippner and Montague Ullman were able to demonstrate telepathic reception in the dream state. An awake subject, while looking at artwork, projected to a sleeping partner certain print images during the REM stage of dreaming. The researchers positively correlated the awakened subject's descriptions of remembered dreams with the content of the prints.[80] In analogy, the channeled source may also communicate to the channel across different states of consciousness and in a paranormal manner. Second, Gertrude Schmeidler showed that "sheep"—persons who have a basically favorable and open attitude toward the new, particularly the paranormal—are more likely to have paranormal experiences than are "goats," those who tend to be skeptical humbuggers. Although there are notable exceptions like *A Course in Miracles* channel Helen Schucman, most channels have tended to be sheep, not goats, prior to their channeling experience.[81]

Conjuring Up "Philip"   In 1973, a group of eight Toronto women and men with no known psychic abilities undertook an unusual experiment.[82] They decided to see if they could create a completely fictitious entity— "Philip"—whom they as a group could then channel. They were aware of the entire channeling tradition: table-rapping seances, ghostly materializations, trance voices, and so on. In addition, as serious investigators, they shared an interest in the collective hallucination theory of ghost sightings. They were aware of the Theosophical concept of thoughtform production. And they were interested in pooling their potential to explore "psychokinesis by committee." They decided to create

"Philip"—his personality, physical characteristics, even a loveless marriage to a frigid wife, "Dorethea," and a new love affair with "Margo," an accused witch. Each of the eight members committed to memory the particulars on "Philip" and company, and tried to see him as a real person.

They reported that a presence began to respond to the people seated around the table asking questions. The presence used the traditional table-rapping code—one rap for yes and two for no. "Philip" answered their questions in a manner consistent with his character, down to the finest detail. They had taken the usual precautions to guarantee that no one present did any table rappings. The conclusion: "Philip" was a production from the group's unconscious mind, which communicated to them by way of psychokinesis, their term for how the unconscious entity could affect the table to make coded raps.

The following year a different group, inspired by the original Toronto experiment, contacted "Santa Claus" and received the correct raps in answer to questions like "number of reindeer?" This research implies that at least some of what was thought to be genuine channeling may have involved sources from the personal unconscious minds of those involved. It seems to stand more as proof of psychokinesis than as disproof of channeling.

Parapsychiatry   One discipline, newly arisen from a marriage of parapsychology and psychiatry, is called parapsychiatry. Its chief clinicians and researchers include Jan Ehrenwald, Emilio Servadio, Jule Eisenbud, Berthold Schwartz, and Helene Deutsch. They aid our understanding of channeling by having contributed evidence to support the view that some of the earlier *DSM III* pathological categories might involve certain more open paranormal processes on the part of patients, including telepathy. For example, many schizophrenics seem to be very psychic and, unbeknownst to themselves or to those working with them, are "tuned" to the minds of those about them, as well as perhaps to other levels of reality, but in a pathological way. Parapsychiatry is in contradistinction to traditional psychiatry with its closed-system view of the human psyche.

Consciousness Studies

Our waking consciousness is but one special state of consciousness, whilst all about it, parted by the filmiest of screens, there lie potential forms of consciousness entirely different . . . No account of the universe in its totality can be final which leaves these other forms of consciousness quite disregarded.

—William James[83]

Each one of us is potentially Mind at Large, but in so far as we are animals, our business is at all costs to survive . . . Mind at Large has to be funneled through the reducing valve of the brain and nervous system . . . Certain persons, however, seem to be born with a kind of bypass that circumvents the reducing valve. In others temporary bypass may be acquired either spontaneously or as a result of deliberate "spiritual exercises."

—Aldous Huxley

The transpersonal perspective holds that a large spectrum of altered states of consciousness exist, that some are potentially useful and functionally specific . . . and that some of these are true "higher" states . . . Since each state of consciousness reveals its own picture of reality, it follows that reality as we know it (and that is the only way we know it) is also only relatively real. Put another way, psychosis is attachment to any one reality.

—Roger Walsh and Frances Vaughan[84]

Charles Tart, a pioneer in the field of consciousness research, has provided a framework for thinking about the topic. He coins the terms state of consciousness (SoC), discrete state of consciousness (d-SoC), altered state of consciousness (ASC), and discrete altered state of consciousness (d-ASC). "When the experiential 'feel' of one SoC differs radically from another, we then talk about an altered SoC, an ASC." Tart believes that "a discrete altered state of consciousness is a radical alteration of the overall patterning of consciousness." Each discrete state of consciousness provides us with a particular reality to experience. Variable consciousness can tune to different realities for itself:

Any d-SoC [discrete state of consciousness] is an *arbitrary* way of working with information, of selectively taking in certain kinds of information and rejecting other kinds, selectively giving importance to it in terms of various kinds of value systems, and doing things or experiencing things in certain ways as a result. So there is no "normal," biologically given state of consciousness that is somehow the natural, optimal state of mind that a person could be in, although there are probably biological restrictions of possibilities. Rather our ordinary d-SoC is a *construction* built up in accordance with our physical, intrapersonal, and interpersonal environments. A d-ASC is a radically different way of handling information from the physical, intrapersonal, and interpersonal environments, yet the d-ASC may be as arbitrary as our ordinary d-SoC.[85]

Jean Houston presents a complementary view. "A great deal of channeling," she says, "comes from the fact that 'In my Father's house are many mansions.' And in the human psyche there are multiple mansions." She expands the metaphor: "We live as if we exist in the attic of ourselves, with the other floors basically uninhabited and the basement locked." When you shift consciousness, as by going into a trance state, she says, you go to a different level of this pluralistic living space. "These other levels seem to have their own aesthetics, their own grammar, their own philosophic content." For Houston, "by shifting levels with different states of consciousness you come up with totally different personae with very different lives."[86]

In light of this relativistic view, Tart offers an intriguing proposal: "That we begin to create various *state-specific sciences,* sciences particular to various d-ASC's. If such sciences could be created, we would have groups of highly skilled, trained and dedicated practitioners able to achieve certain d-ASC's, and able to agree with one another that they had attained the common state."[87] Here, perhaps, lies the possibility of establishing a competing consensus reality with regard to inner or altered states. It could lead, perhaps, to *subjective* consensual validation of phenomena like mystic experience or channeling. There are a number of grounds to suggest a relationship between psychic function and the ability to channel, one of which is a correlation between psychic or channeling performance and the presence of ASCs.

Tart also suggests a state-specific knowledge theory for channeling. "The persons doing the channeling can't get at the information in their ordinary state, so they do some kind of channeling." By channeling, Tart means that "they contact something outside and/or create an altered state at a subconscious level that sets up a tool, as it were, to get certain kinds of knowledge and then expresses it in a way that pretty much will carry over into ordinary consciousness."[88]

In 1977, Tart presented an information-processing type of model to help explain the relationship between psychic abilities (or *psi function*) and altered states of consciousness. In this view, information normally enters the individual's system from the outside world or from body sensations. Input processing includes exchange between the environment, memory, and the subconscious mind. A sense of identity, space/

time sense, and latent functions also bear upon system interaction, evaluation, decision making, and motor output.

As input from the external world is curtailed, either by sensory deprivation or by willfully turning one's attention away from it, the subject begins to take leave of the normal state of consciousness, which by definition is coupled to an external environment. One enters one of the altered states, such as daydream, hallucination, sleep, dream, channeling, or mystical communion. With the silencing of the external input, both the subconscious mind and what Tart calls the psi receptor (one of the latent functions) can be activated, and these may then provide input to awareness. Memory and the body may also provide information to awareness with the weakening of external stimuli.

The psi receptor is especially interesting as a potential site for channeled input. It would appear to be like a window that is normally opaque but becomes clear to mediate outside information in the ASC. We could, of course, as easily point to memory and the subconscious mind alone as the source of all channeled material. But Tart reminds us that the reality of paranormal linkages has been sufficiently documented so that there must be something like a psi receptor capable of opening onto other realms. Once more, we are reminded of the "trapdoor" of F. W. H. Myers's "subliminal mind."

But we are left with the question: Does Tart believe in the existence of other realms in the channeling sense of nonphysical ones? "There's enough evidence that comes in to make me take the idea of disembodied intelligence seriously," he says. "I'm in between those two extremes: I wouldn't say the evidence says it's all nonsense and it's all just the subconscious; neither would I say that you can prove the existence of any of these entities."[89]

Tart's psi receptor, normally latent—a window for certain proven psi activity—could as well be a window for information reception that does not involve the mind of any other person or the physical environment as its source. Tart may not wish to open the window of his psi receptor so wide as to include such channeling. However, the possibility that such a window to the paranormal exists cannot be denied.

8

BIOLOGY AND PHYSICS

This chapter represents the two most traditional hard sciences, as compared to the softer social and psychological sciences. It is important to note two disclaimers here. First, all that can be attempted here is to provide some brief basic background material from these disciplines to enable the average lay reader to understand enough to follow some very tentative speculations regarding channeling. In no way is there enough space to do justice to the tremendous body of scientific literature and detailed understanding that is available in both the branch of biology called psychophysiology (also called physiological psychology), which deals with the structures, functions, and processes of living matter and their relation to mental phenomena, and in the entire realm of physics. Nor is this intended as a technical book primarily aimed at scientists and experts. Second, current science knows relatively little about exactly how the individual brain/mind takes in and processes information from *ordinary* sources, and little about the physiology involved in how we originate thought and imagine things. Therefore we must be humble—and careful—in making any attempts at explaining, beyond this, the psychophysiology of *nonordinary* information generation, mediation, and comprehension.

THE TRADITIONAL VIEW OF THE BRAIN

Psychophysiologists have mapped the route of hearing from external stimuli to the auditory cortex in the brain. Atmospheric waves (or waves conducted by bone in the head) that range from 16 to 20,000 cycles per second vibrate the eardrum and hairs in the cochlea (part of the inner ear). The wave vibrations then become encoded and transduced—changing from mechanical to biologically mediated electromagnetic energy—as impulses traveling along the auditory nerve. On either side of the head, this nerve passes its encoded information, representing sound from the environment, through discrete relay stations of the brain. Finally, the signals reach the auditory cortex, which in turn has connections to Wernicke's area, resulting in speech sounds being heard and understood as language.

Tracing a similar path in the case of normal vision, environmental electromagnetic stimuli vibrating within a perceptible frequency range reach the optic nerves from the retinas and travel through relay stations to end in the occipital region of the cortex. In the traditional view, imaginational, memory, and dream imagery are all generated from within the brain. The definition of *mental image*, for that matter, is an image for which there is no corresponding external stimulus at the time it is being experienced. Other internally acting agents, such as drugs, can cause subjective imagery as well. Scientists say that it requires sophisticated apparatus for a human to see images whose source is in a frequency range outside normal sight. Perhaps clairvoyant channels are able to be their own "television sets" to tune to such higher ranges of information; or perhaps they produce "shows" on their own "channel" by simple bioelectrical self-excitation.

The best speculation that psychophysiology can offer to account for extraordinary or paranormal hearing (clairaudience) is that, because nothing mechanical appears to occur at the outer ear, activation must commence somewhere higher in the system, probably not below the auditory nerve. Wherever in the brain one might care to pinpoint the origin of channeled voices, the self-generated excitations would need to convey the same coded information that is transduced when the eardrum is vibrated by a real voice.

One interesting psychophysiological contribution to explaining the possible origin of clairaudient channeling (or of audio hallucination, depending on your perspective) comes from Princeton psychologist Julian Jaynes. In 1976 he presented his (still highly controversial) theory: that the voices of the gods reportedly heard in Mediterranean cultures prior to 1500 B.C., and reported later in the works of Homer and others, were actually auditory hallucinations generated by the right hemisphere of the brain and received by the left. Jaynes speculates that, until the beginning of written language, human beings lived in a naturally dissociated state. Within this state, the coordination of left and right hemisphere activity that we know today as normal awareness was lacking, leading to a bicameral mind composed of two communicating but separate "houses." A right-brain, idea-initiating, executive function was responsible for the "voices of the gods"; the left brain operated as a passive follower of the directives of the voices.[1]

POSSIBLE EXPLANATIONS

Barbara Honegger, the first person in the United States to receive a graduate degree in experimental parapsychology (from John F. Kennedy University in Orinda, California), presents a view somewhat similar to Jaynes's, which she has in turn focused on channeling. Honegger claims that "each brain hemisphere has a separate and conscious ego," and that "interhemispheric communication" is possible. This is a different kind of communication from the normal traffic of activity that transverses the corpus callosum structure that joins the two halves of the brain and results in normal, seemingly united, self-aware consciousness. "When one of the two centers is active," she reports, "a neurophysiological mechanism actively inhibits the other from expressing its mental contents. This means the 'unconscious' is always thinking and aware. It's self-reflective and it needs to express itself from time to time." For Honegger, mediumship is an expression of what she calls the "alter-ego, the Other entity" to the "normal everyday awake ego."[2] Similarly, French psychoanalyst Jacques Lacan writes of the "discourse of the other" as the expressive unconscious portion of each individual that needs to be attended for self-knowledge and integration.[3]

In contrast to the language *reception and comprehension* functions mentioned earlier, Broca's area in the left cerebral cortex of the brain has been identified as the primary site for language *production* (except in some left-handers). In the traditional view, neuronally encoded programs of motor behavior become activated during speech and writing. In the frontal cortex these programs involve planning, rehearsal, and conceptual organization. In Broca's area they involve the transmission of basic meanings and intentions into the surface structures of verbal composition. This process communicates in turn to the neighboring motor cortex in the parietal lobe, where coded programs of electrical activity lead down through lower coordinating brain centers to the muscular actions of normal speech and writing.

In order to make the human body speak or write, either the person must consciously or unconsciously initiate the act, or some outside agent must initiate and sustain the psychophysiological programs that go from central to peripheral nervous system and muscles. This process would hold true for the other motor automatisms of channeling: the movement of the fingers on the Ouija board marker or the planchette, or the subtle direction given to the pendulum.

A grand mal epileptic seizure is a random discharge of electrical activity from within the brain that is a meaningless manipulation of the "keyboard," resulting in all noise and no signal. Glossolalia (speaking in tongues) and xenoglossy (speaking in a real language that is unknown to the speaker) seem to provide a more organized and interesting activation and output. But glossolalia can still resemble the "word salad" of some schizophrenic language production, with alternating patches of coherence and incoherence. This implies that whatever the real source of foreign "tongues," the initiating excitations only occasionally resonate with established programs of meaningful language-making. Trance voice, however, results in expression that can be—but by no means always is—as well articulated as the speech of normal consciousness. Chapters 1, 2, and 4 present many examples of coherent and even beautiful language production through supposedly channeled means. Whether in the case of hallucination, or of multiple-, sub-, or alter-personality, or of trance voice, it is remarkable that episodes of meaningful expression can be generated in an individual whose chief natural operator—the ego, executive function, or mental operating system—has apparently relinquished control.

Does dreaming hold clues for channeling? Harvard research physicians J. A. Hobson and R. W. McCarley provide the leading theory for how dreams are generated.[4] Blocking environmental input and motor output triggers a desynchronizing of brain waves. Subjective material is then initiated by random firings in the brain stem's reticular formation and in the pons. These signals are relayed up into the forebrain, which then fields and interprets them as best it can. Since the original brain stem activity is relatively random in nature, the decoding interpretations of the forebrain give rise to the rather surreal content of our dreams. This process of attempting to make sense of incoherent signals may be what underlies the bizarre experiences of mentally disturbed people as well. Similarly, channeling may be the way the meaning-making portion of the brain receives signals originating from elsewhere within the system, like dreaming, or from outside the system, like the channeling literature claims. Perhaps conscious channeling is like lucid dreaming in which the dreamer is conscious during the altered state.

THE HOLOGRAPHIC BRAIN

Some neurophysiologists embrace a holographic model, first hypothesized by Stanford's Karl F. Pribram, to describe the coding processes involved in perception and motor behavior. In this model, information is distributed throughout the brain, rather than locally in sites of specific storage. In a holographic photograph, any portion of the film contains the informational image of the whole. In Pribram's model,[5] the brain is pictured as operating in a similar manner. All mind brain activity is seen as complex, mixed-frequency wave forms that can, in turn, be broken down into simpler wave components. Conversely, complex wave systems can be built up out of simpler wave shapes, all in a predictable and elegant manner. These analyses and syntheses are known as Fourier transforms, named after the mathematician who discovered them, and can operate either in space or time. When someone hears music or speech, for example, neurons take part in temporal frequency analysis and synthesis. On the other hand, when one looks out the window or reads a book, spatial frequency operations take place. This view may hold a special interest for us because some of the explanations offered by channeled sources are described in terms of the interrelations of waves and frequencies.

Two basic kinds of neuronal activity are posited. In the holographic model, wave interference patterns spread from slow-graded electrical potentials, especially along the finer nerve fibers called dendrites. In the more traditional model, neuron cells fire in an all-or-nothing pattern along the main (axon) bodies, triggering migrations of chemicals across the synapses (the space between the neurons). The latter model more easily fits the engineer's picture of clearly demarcated programs activating biocomputer "bits" that are either on or off, firing or quiescent. In either case, hallucinating or channeling a voice would have to involve setting in motion complex systems of neuronal activity in one or more parts of the brain attributed to hearing, language memory, and language comprehension.

THE PSYCHOBIOLOGY OF TRANSCENDENCE

The hypothalamus, a small area in the limbic system of the brain, appears to act as a center for drives and motivations such as hunger, thirst, and sex. James Olds found that rats would choose to electrically self-stimulate their brains up to 5000 times an hour via an electrode planted in the hypothalamus, giving rise to the notion of a pleasure center.[6] The hypothalamus also seems connected to sensory information moving to the higher brain. Studies also have shown that injuries to the hypothalamus seem to correlate with the onset of certain paranormal abilities.[7] Listening to some of the ecstatic reports of those who claim to experience the channeling of especially high and loving presences—"love energy," "beings of light," or being "overshadowed by the Christ," for example—gives us the impression that whatever is going on may pass through such a pleasure center.

We have also heard that channeling may involve some kind of self-transcendence. In his article "Towards a Psychobiology of Transcendence: God in the Brain," San Diego neurophysiologist Arnold J. Mandell points to certain other limbic system processes that accompany self-transcendent states. The limbic system is the midregion of the brain between brain stem and cortex that is associated most with emotions and the formation (but not storage) of memory. Mandell is one of many researchers who has found that the neurotransmitter serotonin serves as a built-in insulator against a variety of transcendental experiences. When serotonin-mediated brain activity is temporarily curtailed, and there is a related increase in activity mediated by the neurotransmitters dopamine or nor-epinephrine, certain hallucinatory and other subjective experiences result that can resemble spiritual-type open channeling (see chapter 9). Mandell describes the "releasing [of] the affectual and cognitive processes characteristic of religious ecstacy and the permanent personality changes associated with religious conversion," whether as the result of recreational drugs or internally generated chemicals like endorphins.[8]

There is a close similarity in structure betwen serotonin and the hallucinogenic drug LSD. In his book *Realms of the Human Unconscious: Observations from LSD Research,* medical researcher Stanislav Grof reports many channeling-like experiences of his subjects in LSD-induced altered states of consciousness. "The LSD subject can, for example, suddenly enter a state similar to a mediumistic trance; his facial expression is strikingly transformed, his countenance and gestures appear alien, and his voice is dramatically changed. He can speak in a foreign language, write automatic text." Grof also reports "encounters with astral bodies of spirit entities of deceased persons" among LSD subjects. He even found "the characteristics of spirit possession."[9]

Given that there now appears to be evidence that certain predispositions toward schizophrenia may be inherited, and given that this may involve genetic material for the allocation of neurotransmitters much like those involved with LSD-induced and self-transcendent states associated with channeling-type experiences, then it might follow that some individuals have a built-in brain chemistry disposing them toward channeling.

In the clinical psychology section of the preceding chapter, reality testing was defined as an ongoing comparison of inner to outer reality. Mandell claims that "the association of insight with esctacy, the core of experience of religious conversion, appears to involve the loss of normal hippocampal comparator function [and] the feeling of 'truth.' "[10] The majority of channels report experiencing such a connection to the truth, often ecstatically. Recall, too, that hypnosis (including self-hypnosis) is often described as involving a disengaging of attention from normal stimuli, contributing to a hiatus from the activity of such a comparator function. In this way, normal judgment and reality testing are suspended, and attending to the suggestions of other stimuli, other sources, can take place more easily.

In addition, Mandell found that the high-amplitude slow brain waves from the hippocampus associated with the ecstatic and self-transcendent states "are seen as representing an 'optimal' level of brain activity for energy, orienting, learning, memory, and attention, a positive background state optimizing brain function."[11] This may help explain the often extraordinary altered functioning and intellectual productivity attributed to some channels.

Brain Stimulation

Decades ago, Canadian neurophysiologist Wilder Penfield demonstrated that applying an electrically charged probe to the exposed tissue of the left (language) temporal lobe of a conscious patient elicited self-reported scenes from her past, complete with voices and bits of conversation.[12] This would imply that one need not stimulate areas of the brain down near the beginnings of the auditory circuit in order to evoke the sense of hearing language; it can be done by electrical stimulation to the outer cortical layers.

Michael Persinger, director of the neuroscience laboratory at Laurentian University in Ontario, Canada, reports on experiments that supply small electrical currents via electrodes to the temporal lobe regions of the brain to induce channeling-type experiences in conscious subjects. "The person feels 'floating.' He may feel out of his body," Persinger says. The typical experience "is of profound emotional, profound personal significance, but it's usually given cosmic or religious attributions." He adds that very often there may be "intense auditory experiences, where the person feels messages being given to him in a type of feeling that he knows what's happening to him without necessarily hearing a voice."[13]

Persinger also draws a parallel between these induced experiences and "clinical forms of temporal lobe or limbic epilepsy." Epilepsy involves random, massive brain self-activation. New York therapist Armand DiMele's controversial conclusion, based on work with many epileptics, is that "in epilepsy there seems to be some form of constant channeling . . . They have more of a connection with the universe than other people."[14]

But we are still left with the puzzle of how such stimulation might originate from within that would lead not to conflict and seizure, but to experiences of coherent information. Certainly our brains are stimulated each time we initiate a thought or purposefully recall something. This must either involve self-generated patterns of electromagnetic excitation or be dependent on external stimulus. Where there is apparently no external stimulus, as in channeling, who or what does the stimulation?

If our identity is only physical, based on the material coded within our brain cells, excitation must involve self-excitation or one part kindling another. But if our identity is composed of mental or spiritual substance beyond the physical, then we must account for how we interact with our own physical brain. The channeling sources tell us that we are essentially nonphysical beings using a physical body. This view makes the channeling of nonphysical entities a less bizarre proposition. Still, it would be difficult to distinguish between what comes from one's own nonphysical source and what comes from a nonphysical source other than oneself. And it would be even harder to discern what is going on with someone else claiming to be channeling.

Electrophysiological research explores the brain correlates of subjective events. Event-related potentials, or ERPs, are telltale brain-wave patterns registered at the scalp in response to hearing a sound or seeing an image. The stimulus is repeated until experimenters can average out the wave shape that acts as a signal emerging from background "noise." This wave shape is seen as one of the more precisely defined physiological substrates accompanying the particular subjective perception.

There has been evidence to suggest that such brain waves are continually *self*-evoked. John Lilly, known for his work with dolphins, demonstrated that human subjects in isolation tanks without detectable outside stimulation still produced internally generated images and words. This also recalls the earlier dream-generation hypothesis. Of special interest to us, some investigators have been able to record ERPs when a subject is concentrating on a word that occurs to him before he utters it.

The question remains: Is the telltale electromagnetic activity in response to, say, a word the same whether someone is actually hearing it from the physical environment or only imagining hearing it? Also, is such a pattern the same for all people? And what of differences in local language? These questions cannot yet be answered. But if brain activity can correlate with language and image events and can be evoked both from within and from without, then researchers may yet discover that channeling is just one way of evoking electromagnetic activity from outside the personal mind/brain system that leads to meaningful language experience.

Experiments by Toronto physiological researcher Dr. D. H. Lloyd appear to demonstrate that the psychic projection of thoughts and images by one person can evoke correlatable electroencephalogram

(EEG) brain-wave response in another. While this is useful, it still does not address the crucial issue of whether such paranormally effective thoughts and images can come from a *non*physical source.[15]

Four Pioneers in Brain/Mind Research

Frank Barr and the Melanin Connection   Frank Barr, a physician and interdisciplinary researcher in Northern California's Bay Area, recently completed an extensive survey of medical literature on the naturally occurring organic compound melanin and its brain counterpart neuromelanin. Influenced by the ideas of Berkeley inventor and philosopher Arthur Young, Barr concludes that melanin is a key link between mind and brain. Melanin appears to operate in two basic realms, which might be termed the vertical and the horizontal (my terms and concepts, not Barr's). In the vertical case, he speculates, the molecule may mediate between mind and brain between higher and lower frequencies, while in the horizontal case it mediates, via biochemical processes, between various parts of the brain.

Barr points to the small antennae-like structures (called the glycocalyx) sticking up out of the cell walls, which he sees as having a hand-in-glove relationship with melanin. In his view, these structures may act as antennae to receive electromagnetic radiation of various wavelengths (including light), transducing them to mechanical vibration (called phonons, essentially sound). The vibrations then move through structures called microtubules within the cell to the melanin, which can transduce sound to light and back into sound. But the plot thickens. Barr finds evidence (as Puharich to follow) that extremely low-frequency (ELF) waves may be involved, interacting with, allowing access to, and even activating higher frequencies.

Borrowing from Young's model of an arc (or V shape) to represent a multilevel, interactive, and evolving universe, there are three stages of descending frequency (from pure and originating light), which pivot at a fourth stage (where we may be now as a species), and this is followed by three ascending stages. They see an interplay involving higher to lower to higher vibrations in circulation. Basically, melanin, acting with the other structures, is a phase-timing, information-processing interface molecule, which, as a phototransducer, functionally interacts with light, light being for them the fundamental, initial "quantum of action." A phototransducer can transmute energy across photon to electromagnetic to mechanical states. Photons and other vibrational states within the brain, then, may interact with, or be part of, a larger unified field of such outside energy and the information it could involve. Such a capability may account for the potential of an extraordinary range of frequencies and energy states to interact with one another, connecting the individual brain/mind during the channeling process in ways that researchers are only beginning to understand.

Keep in mind that photons of light can be of a high enough frequency to be beyond the visible light range—ultraviolet rays, X rays, and cosmic rays, for example. When far enough beyond the visible range, the electromagnetic wave packets that we know as light are no longer blocked by nontransparent material, such as the human skull and brain. A great many of the channeled messages tell us that the crucial, wise, spiritual element in the cosmos across all levels of reality is *light*—what Barr and Young call "quanta of action."

A problem arises with such hypothetical high-frequency transmissions that could affect certain brain tissue. When you get far enough from the resonant frequencies of an oscillator such as the neuromelanin molecule (or glycocalyx), little or no energy (and therefore no information as scientists understand it) will be absorbed, according to any currently known process. Therefore the question arises as to how extremely high frequency waves could affect molecules vibrating more slowly than themselves. One possibility is that the oscillations involve the electron or hypothetical subcomponents of the nuclear particles; for it is generally known that the smaller the particle (or "wavicle"), the higher its vibratory rate. Or, as Barr points out, ELF waves may be mediators as well.

On the horizontal level of function, the brain stem reticular formation, running through McCarley's and Hobson's dream-generating pons, is rich with neuromelanin and appears to have a central role for Barr in what Mandell calls the psychobiology of transcendence, including mystical or spiritual states. The horizontal melanin system is also implicated in various psychiatric pathologies (for example, schizophrenia) and in psychedelic/hallucinogenic mechanisms that may be related to the seemingly self-transcending subjective states most associated with channeling.[16]

The pineal gland is considered by occult schools to be the physical counterpart of the crown chakra, through which informing and healing energies from the larger universe are said to enter individuals. The pineal, according to Barr, is known to be rich in neuromelanin and crucial in circadian rhythms and other regulatory activity synchronized with cycles of light and dark. Barr, however (along with Japanese neurophysiologist Hiroshi Motoyama) points to the hypothalamus and the pineal and pituitary glands together—rich in melanin and beneficial in the composition of the diencephalon part of the brain—as the seat of the 6th (brow or "third eye") chakra. They are uncertain about the brain correlate of the 7th (or crown) chakra, although Barr sees the pia mater—the delicate, almost-pure-melanin part of the brain—as a good candidate.

California biologist Colin Pittendrig of Stanford University's Hopkins Marine Laboratory, a leading authority on such circadian rhythms, has recently suggested that a coupling relationship may exist between inner organismic and outer environmental oscillators.[17] Perhaps channeling involves certain invisible electromagnetic light realm oscillations created by nonphysical beings that resonantly entrain (create the same vibration in, or lower the harmonic of) molecular structures commensurate with the channel's altered state of consciousness.

Andrija Puharich: Brain Resonance and the Subatomic Level Parapsychologist, physician, and medical researcher Andrija Puharich has done considerable investigation to develop his picture of human beings as finely tuned "biocosmic resonators" capable of accessing information beyond the self. According to Puharich, and echoing many other researchers (such as Beck to follow), electromagnetic oscillations outside of human systems can resonantly entrain parts of our brains to their frequencies or to lower harmonics of them. We become most capable of coupling with these entraining frequencies at ranges of the upper theta-wave and lower alpha-wave region, specifically at 7.8 hertz (cycles per second). It is at this frequency that we are also coupled with the Schumann resonance, the natural electromagnetic resonance of the earth's ionosphere. Puharich sees this as facilitating our receptive systems.[18]

Furthermore, parts of the human brain generate impulses at specific frequencies based on the predominant neurotransmitters secreted, which are, according to Barr, largely regulated by neuromelanin. Puharich suggests that once the resonance of 7.2 to 8 hertz has been reached, it may be modulated by superimposing other information on it. The lower part of the 8- to 12-hertz "alpha window" has been shown to be the primary brain wave generated during meditative states such as are found in much channeling activity. More recent research has found that psychics generate brain waves in the 8-hertz range while attempting to produce certain psi phenomena. Even more interesting, they do this particularly in the left hemisphere of the brain, which is associated with language and analytical skills rather than with meditative states.

Earlier research by Puharich suggested that subjects apparently able to receive telepathic signals do so by activating the parasympathetic aspect of their autonomic nervous systems. Among other things, this releases the neurotransmitter acetylcholine. This activation and resulting receptivity Puharich terms being in a state of *cholinergia*.

The question remains: Could channeling be a case of information modulation of the 8-hertz region in the channel's brain by electromagnetic oscillations transmitted from an outside source? Or, could such an outside source be nonphysical, yet affect the electromagnetic frequency range that in turn affects our brains? Barr's light-neuromelanin linkage may provide such a mechanism. Puharich's self-other electromagnetic resonance relation may be another.

Yet there is one problem with information transfer via modulation of extremely low frequency (ELF) carrier waves in the 8-hertz region. The modulation frequency, the actual information configuration, should usually be much lower than that of the wave system that carries it (the carrier wave) in order to get reasonable fidelity of reproduction. So we may be talking about operations at much lower frequencies than the range measured in EEGs and commonly accepted as accompanying behavior, perception, and cognition. One answer is that EEGs may represent only the most gross level of hemisphere-wide electrical activity and may not necessarily be of the resonant frequency domain involved in paranormal information-processing. The real activity may lie hidden for now beneath the crude level reflected by the EEGs.

Recently, Puharich has developed a new model based on what he calls preons—hypothesized structures smaller than quarks, with quarks being the particles hypothesized by physicists to comprise protons and neutrons in the atomic nucleus. Three preons are thought to comprise each quark, with three quarks in turn comprising a proton or neutron. Puharich speculates that the preons in the genetic DNA and other molecular material in every human cell are of such a size, and cooperate in larger structures in such a way that they are able to interact with the extremely small-wavelength electromagnetic (or other) information existing across other dimensions of reality. Here we may have both the home of the alleged channeled sources and the way they interact with those who channel (potentially *all* of us, via our DNA).

Puharich has most recently focused on how ELF electromagnetic waves affect the chemical bonding between hydrogen atoms in organic tissue, especially at the level of DNA and RNA. He sees the proton as being crucial to how some communication comes into, and other communication interacts within, organic material. He has narrowed his focus to the resonant frequency, the magnetic properties (called magnetic moments), and the spin states of the proton (each particle is said to be like a little spinning top). He is specifically studying the interaction of protons, involving processes known as spin coupling and magnetic resonance. He has concluded that the brain is a vast set of interference patterns of magnetic waves generated by the ELF frequencies of protons according to their magnetic and spin properties and according to what is called their precession. (*Precession* means the frequency of the gyrations of the rotational axes of spinning bodies.) These interference patterns, Puharich believes, cause all human subjective experience and dynamics of brain/mind.

According to Puharich's research, when other electromagnetic noise that comes into or arises within the nervous system is shielded out or quieted, the protons in the hydrogen comprising the water that is in the neurons and the adjacent glial cells—when in the presence of slow oscillations (8–14 hertz alpha waves) and via resonant entrainment (especially at 8 hertz)—become receptive to similar signals operating *at a distance*. Such at-a-distance proton ELF resonance, then, may possibly be at the heart of channeling interactions. As Puharich points out, about 63 percent of the human body is comprised of hydrogen (each atom with one proton as its nucleus), while protons fill the entire cosmos—almost one per centimeter on the average (as a part of the dominant universal element hydrogen). This provides what Puharich calls a permeating "proton matrix" for "proto-communication" throughout the universe. But then we are still left, in the case of channeling, with the question of from who or where do the transmissions come.

Bob Beck and "Brain Tuning"   The brain "talks" to itself constantly, with various oscillating domains inducing vibrations in one another (entraining) or remaining isolated in complex fluctuating patterns of excitation and quiescence. New research shows that external wave systems can "talk" to internal ones. Neuroscientists have found that externally oscillating fields can resonantly entrain oscillating living tissue such as the brain. Researcher Bob Beck of Los Angeles, a pioneer in brain-wave experimentation and "new science" theory, has found that Puharich's brain-wave "window"—7.8 hertz—makes subjects more open to a variety of information sources, including those associated with paranormal phenomena. Beck claims to have recorded an EEG 7.8 hertz of almost pure wave coherence in one Hawaiian *huna* master (a spiritual adept). He also developed a "brain tuner" device whose battery-operated magnetic oscillations in this frequency range can induce vibrational change in the brains of hundreds of subjects, leading, he claims, to altered states of consciousness, improved memory, weaning from drug addiction, and production of pain-killing endorphins.[19] Perhaps ELF fields, which can induce in the brain patterns of vibration similar to their own, may be a medium for the paranormal information-processing involved in channeling.

Given this range of research, we can speculate that we are no longer closed physical systems. Rather, we are vibratory systems capable of being affected by other such systems. The physics section to follow will explore a number of vibrational influences from outside that might possibly account for channeling.

Jack Schwarz   Jack Schwarz, founder and president of Aletheia Foundation in Ashland, Oregon, is the author of a number of books that reflect his decades of research involving psychoenergetic states, including *The Paths of Action, Voluntary Controls,* and *Human Energy Systems* (published by E. P. Dutton in 1977, 1978, and 1979). His own self-regulating paranormal abilities have been successfully demonstrated to researchers at the Menninger Foundation (Topeka, Kansas) and elsewhere. (The following material stems from my personal interview with him on June 8, 1987.)

Schwarz is especially interested in the way an individual can reach an altered state of information-processing ability by "actually exciting the electrical potentials that are in the brain." This involves escalating energy exchanges between incoming energies to the pineal and pituitary glands of the brain (via subtle energy currents entering the head at the posterior fontanelle region) and the pelvic gonadal region long associated with the "root chakra" human energy center. This heightened energy increases cell activity, especially in the hippocampal area implicated by Schwarz in sensory activity. This produces what he calls a "hyperaesthetic" state, which allows the senses to reach into the paranormal range. The brain state for this increased sensitivity and receptivity is *high-amplitude and low-frequency,* which jibes with Mandell's finding that slow, high-amplitude hippocampal waves correlate with transcendent states.

Schwarz contends that the key to understanding channeling, which he agrees may involve interaction with high-frequency domains unknown to current science, lies, paradoxically, not with the eight-cycle alpha region of brain-wave activity already mentioned by others, but with still *lower* frequencies (but higher amplitude), especially the lowest—or Delta—wave region of zero to four cycles per second. He believes that trance channels, such as Jach Pursel (with whom he has worked), operate in this lowest of all frequencies, but at high-energy amplitude ranges, measured in millivolts. Schwarz claims that in the near-zero brain-wave region, "spontaneous expression" can take place involving what he calls the "paraconscious" of transpersonal activity in interaction with currently unknown energy fields.

"If you go below one cycle per second in brain activity," he speculates, "you go into the infinite. You go absolutely above the speed of light, and you can then interact with information in that range." This means that "when we talk about higher dimensionality and their extremely high frequencies, we will have a greater chance to pick up a greater amount of, a greater quality of, this information via our low frequencies and high amplitude." How does this work? According to Schwarz, "it is because the extremely high-frequency substance itself is less dense when approached that way. It's easier to have access to it." He points out that if there is enough amplitude energy and enough momentum, time slows down, as in Einstein's relativity theory. Increasing the energy while lengthening the wavelength of the brain waves of the receiver/perceiver—who is operating as a frame of reference in regard to the extremely high-frequency information with which he is hoping to connect—can act as both a magnifying lens and an amplifier, zooming in on the very-high-frequency wave system of the information so as to have it appear more diluted or spaced apart, and therefore be more accessible to the individual.

Brain Synchrony

In his Ph.D. dissertation, Fairfax, California, research psychologist James Brown looked at the relationship between EEG patterns and experiential reports of channels, meditators, and controls (who were neither channels nor meditators). EEG signals were recorded with electrodes over the left and right parietal lobes of the brain. He found the most consistent EEG correlate of nonordinary consciousness was a combination of amplitude and interhemispheric synchrony increase in the alpha range. Synchrony means that the peaks and valleys of the brain waves in both brain hemispheres occur simultaneously. He also found EEG readings in those capable of nonordinary states to be different than those of the controls, even in baseline measurements when they were all asked to solve mental problems in an ordinary state. This implies that those capable of nonordinary consciousness, like channels, either naturally have nonordinary brain-wave function or have developed unusual brain-wave production during normal conditions due to their altered-state experiences.[20]

Researcher Jean Millay has pointed out that every time an individual shifts focus of attention, the entire frequency pattern of the brain shifts to other frequencies. This shift is of particular interest when it involves synchrony between the hemispheres. She and other researchers are finding that a shift involving the presence of such EEG synchronization in *any* frequency—not just the alpha-wave "window"—precedes or accompanies nonordinary states of consciousness associated with meditation and channeling-type trance experiences. Of these experiences involving synchrony, Millay writes, "Some seems to be trance-like. Some seemed to transcend space and time limitations."[21]

San Francisco researcher Tim Scully has developed a phase comparator that signals with a tone when the EEG alpha-wave readings are the same in both brain hemispheres. Scully and others have found that alpha-wave synchrony in both hemispheres is a better indicator of meditative and other nonordinary states of consciousness than alpha measured only in one hemisphere. Furthermore, the abilities to focus attention and to achieve flashes of intuitive insight have been correlated with increased phase synchrony.[22]

Millay has joined with physicist James Johnston, who has designed new computer biofeedback approaches, in studies to monitor brainwave synchrony *between* people, which is correlated with "intense, nonverbal 'feeling' states" recorded between subjects. There has long been evidence that identical twins are capable of paranormal communication with each other; this now may be conjectured as due to a natural brainwave synchrony between them.[23]

Robert Monroe, author of *Journeys Out of the Body,* and his research colleagues at The Monroe Institute in Faber, Virginia, have developed what he calls hemi-sync, which can lead to a variety of nonordinary experiences including channeling. It involves

a system of "binaural beats," feeding a separate signal into each ear. By sending separate sound pulses to each ear with stereo headphones, the two hemispheres of the brain act *in unison* to "hear" a third signal—the difference between the two sound pulses. This third signal is not an actual sound, but an electrical signal that can only be created by *both brain hemispheres acting and working together,* simultaneously.[24]

There appears, therefore, to be evidence that unusual levels of hemisphere synchrony at various frequencies may be implicated in states of consciousness associated with channeling-type activity. The average frequency of brain waves during such activity was found by Brown to be around 10 hertz. Berkeley, California, research physicist Elizabeth Rauscher speculates that currently unmeasurable EEG frequencies may exceed 1000 hertz.[25] We may speculate that individuals who are capable of intentional generation of brain synchrony can bring on a brain/mind state conducive to paranormal activity, one form of which may be channeling. We may also speculate that there may be some form of synchrony taking place between the source and the channel, perhaps in a frequency range well above the level that current technology is able to detect.

Again, however, this does not help to establish the plausibility of the existence of a conscious source that is not physical as we know it that could transmit communication signals. For the present, we can only conjecture that, if there is such a source, it would transmit signals that either induce brain-wave synchrony in the channel, or connect to the channel because of his or her synchrony, or connect because of resonance due to a harmonic relation between the two systems. To proceed any further along this line of speculation, however, we must turn to the science of physics.

PHYSICS AND PARAPHYSICS

Like the preceding section, the following consists not so much of new scientific ideas about channeling, but more of a restatement of previous ideas in new terms. We will examine some of the physicist's descriptions of the world to see if they help us better understand what channels report experiencing. What is to be gained by this borrowing of modern science concepts? It may give us new precision and thereby lend more credibility to a phenomenon that at first glance might seem outrageous to many. Yet we must weigh as we go along whether physics is the proper discipline to give us insight into human nature, ordinary or nonordinary, or whether this is better left to psychology, the humanities, and religion.

The kind of speculation that follows is interesting, but it risks alienating those who might see it as an attempt to borrow science's legitimacy as well as its terminology. Therefore, I reiterate the point established at the outset of the last section on biology: This is in no way intended to be a rigorous treatment satisfactory to the trained scientist. This must remain a book for the lay reader. All we can hope to do in this section is provide a modest groundwork in the concepts of present-day physics so that the reader can understand the various highly tentative speculations about channeling that follow. One thing is certain: the concepts of physics must be stretched if we are to use them to understand nonordinary phenomena such as channeling.

We will explore some expansions of the tenets of current physics, as well as recent speculations from the "new physics," or "paraphysics," in an attempt to understand channeling with physics-like terms. This larger frame of reference could be used to explain how the physical domain and the apparently nonphysical domain—the body and the mind—can coexist and interact with each other.

In order to do this, we must explore the prevailing Cartesian distinction made by seventeenth-century philosopher Rene Descartes between what he termed the extended substance of physical matter and the unextended thinking substance of mind. In the centuries-old debate over the mind-body problem, *dualists* are those who believe that the fundamentally different substances of mind and brain are needed to understand consciousness and reality. *Interactionists* hold that the two domains, though different from each other, can affect each other. We can resolve some of the mysteries surrounding mechanisms of interaction between these realms by taking what is sometimes called a *monist* position, placing all mental and physical phenomena on one spectrum of one kind of substance. We can create this single unifying context either by "mentalizing the physical" or by "physicalizing the mental."

Physicalizing the mental means considering everything in the universe—including thoughts, feelings, and spirits—to be physical in nature. Everything is made from one kind of substance. This substance is differentiated into all the diverse, multileveled objective and subjective manifestations that we can experience. (This is similar to the astrophysicist's big bang theory, which explains how the present universe may have come into being from an undifferentiated, primordial material billions of years ago.) Within this physical context, individual minds—even discarnate spirits—would be described in terms of structures and functions, forces and fields, potential and kinetic energies, particles, frequencies, and wavelengths of the one all-pervasive ground of being. For the duration of this section, then, we need no longer talk in terms of how nonphysical phenomena (like channeled beings) could exist and interact with our physical reality. At most, we might need to reactivate older terms like *subtle energies* or the *higher physical,* or just speak of *energies, entities,* or *information,* designating their respective "home" planes or dimensions as we go.

Mentalizing the physical, on the other hand, means considering everything ordinarily deemed physical to consist entirely of mind or spirit, only in a denser form, via a shift in perspective. By this view, physicality—whether of energy and matter, time and space—is the product of the activity of mind: human minds or a superhuman Mind or both. This recalls eighteenth-century philosopher George Berkeley's view that all things are "ideas in the mind of God." Similarly, Baruch Spinoza pictured the entire cosmos as made of spiritual substance: "Matter is an extension of God." And G. W. F. Hegel wrote that all is basically Absolute Spirit, which gets differentiated into the antithetical state of the apparent qualities of consciousness on the one hand, and matter as the objects of consciousness on the other.

We must weigh carefully how, by physicalizing the mental, we may be coloring the nature of spiritual reality in such a way as to make it something other than it naturally is. John White, author and researcher of paranormal and spiritual topics, warns of what he calls a New Age fallacy:

States of consciousness can certainly be *correlated* with states of energy, but they cannot be equated. Consciousness is wholly outside the realm of matter and energy, although it is wholly co-extensive with it . . . Consciousness is an aspect of God—one of the two primary aspects, the other being substance in all its forms, from subtle matter to subtle energy. Consciousness wholly transcends the cosmos, including energy in all its forms.[26]

Likewise, Ken Wilber, whom White refers to as an "Einstein of consciousness," would have us think carefully before using the latest fashionable scientific theory to explain what may be the nonphysical realm of spirit. Here he refers to the use by many of the holographic model of physicist David Bohm and neurophysiologist Karl F. Pribram:

A highly speculative, tentative system of physics was linked together with a partial but accurate theory of brain physiology and the result was supposed to be equal to God. Probably not true at all. The other thing you have to remember when you're trying to use recent scientific theories to validate religious insights, is that scientific theories change approximately decade by decade, and religious insights, to the extent they're true, are supposed to be timeless.[27]

Forewarned, then, we will try a brief experiment in physicalizing the mental, to see if physics concepts can contribute to our understanding of channeling.

First, a bird's-eye view of physical science's attempts to be inclusive and universal. Many physicists have attempted to bring together what once were considered separate aspects of the cosmos. Albert Einstein attempted to discover a "unified field theory" to explain all that takes place within the physical universe. More recently, theoretical physicists have made attempts to develop a Grand Unified Theory (G.U.T.). These theorists are looking for a way to coherently integrate the four known basic forces in nature, using three basic systems of thought. The four forces: *electromagnetism, gravity,* the *strong* or *nuclear force* that holds nuclear particles together, and the *weak force* that is responsible for radioactive decay.

Nobel prize–winning theoretical physicist Steven Weinberg points to a need to posit more than the current three spatial dimensions plus time in order to account for how the physical universe operates. He and others see these extra dimensions as curled up smaller than an atom. "But even though we cannot see the extra dimensions directly, we can detect the effects when the dimensions wiggle." For example, he says,

"A wiggle in the fifth dimension is perceived as the electromagnetic force, responsible for things like light, magnetism, and radio and television waves."[28]

Much of channeling literature is predicated upon an extradimensional universe, one that allows messages to be sent from other levels of reality to ours. The recent multidimensional unification theories of physics seem to lend at least some credence to such a possibility.

Physicist Saul-Paul Sirag speculates on the possibility of as many as 48 to 192 dimensions (and Puharich has 500 plus!), agreeing with Weinberg and others that our "space-time is a projection from a space of more-than-four dimensions." And he adds, "It is plausible, then, that the present-day hyperspace unification of the forces will lead to the understanding of some phenomenon analogous to light." The channeled literature is rich with references to the one living light of the universe (God). Sirag speculates, "The current hyperspace unification of the forces may well lead to an understanding of the mind just as Maxwell's unification of electricity and magnetism led to an understanding of light."[29]

Besides the four known forces of nature, there are three basic areas of application in physics: classical, relativistic, and quantum. The vigorous efforts now under way to develop a grand unified theory continue an endeavor initiated by Albert Einstein, who spent a good portion of his later years attempting (unsuccessfully) to unify gravity and electromagnetism. Both relativity theory and quantum theory enter these efforts. Relativity theory deals with how space and time, the fundamental ingredients of physical theory, are affected by the relative motion of an observer at velocities close to the speed of light. Quantum theory deals with the behavior of the smallest constituents of nature, the elementary particles. The rest of the physical domain, where objects are big and velocities are slow, is subsumed under the umbrella of classical physics, the theories that were established prior to the twentieth century.

As we progress, we will find that channeling can possibly be explained in some of the terms and concepts of at least some of these four forces of nature and three areas of application when we extend them to limits that many physicists might find objectionable. (For example, almost all physicists would choose the electromagnetic domain as the only one holding any promise of being implicated in channeling.) Therefore we must keep in mind the highly speculative nature of this enterprise of physicalizing the mental.

During the last ten years, numerous books, such as physicist Fritjof Capra's *The Tao of Physics,* have tried to make the basic concepts of contemporary theoretical physics accessible to a broad base of nonphysicists. As a result, many people are familiar with a view of the physical universe as composed of *immaterial* energy fields in constant motion and vibration. Physicists discovered that any solid matter is temporarily entrapped radiant energy and, conversely, any potential energy can be "written into" material constraints.

Physicists have assigned to each of the four universal forces an experimentally proven or hypothetical particle (or *wavicle* or *wave packet*) that is said to be responsible for the interaction of phenomena operating within its domain. For example, a *photon* of light is the particle for the electromagnetic force. Its electrodynamic interactions with the outer electron shell of material atoms account for much of what is studied in physics and chemistry. Most of the "grand unified" theories predict a single underlying constituent that, depending upon its orientation to a larger frame of reference, is responsible for all particles in nature, including massless, radiant-energy *bosons* and the *fermions* of mass and matter.

Furthermore, within many of these theories, *local symmetry breaking* is seen as the process that brings into manifestation both fields of particles and the forces operating between them. While the theory of symmetry breaking refers to the generation of subatomic particles and forces, it may be conjectured to be the micro reality responsible for our everyday macro level. Each particular configuration of forces and particles, such as those that make up a large object like the human body, may require symmetry breaking in a certain complex and detailed way. Still, any physicist will tell us that we are stretching the concept quite a bit to conjecture in this manner.

The question remains: Besides the particles and forces understood by current physics on this level of reality, can any other manifestations be liberated from symmetry breaking? Could such a process account for the bodies, voices, visions, and movements attributed to channeled sources and their messages? If the symmetry of this dimension of reality can be broken into subjectively experienced objects, could there be other dimensions within which symmetry breaking leads to other environments and their inhabitants? And, if so, could autonomous beings in these dimensions communicate with us?[30]

Physicists tell us that all known particles are in ceaseless vibration and, depending on the way one observes them, they are packets of pure waves or are particles. Essentially, as long as it is unobserved by us, anything and everything is only a probability distribution of waves until a measurement or interaction of direct experience is made with regard to it, whereupon the experienced result takes particle form. All particle structures built up out of such components are vibrating: from electron to atom to molecule to cell. The larger the object, the slower the vibration. For example, the entire planet containing all of these faster-paced components has a natural vibrating electromagnetic field frequency (or resonance) near 8 hertz (cycles per second). As already mentioned, this frequency is in the alpha brain-wave range associated with the vibrations of millions of brain neurons and is implicated in meditative and psychic states. Each human being is a superimposed hierarchy of different wave vibrations existing within an environment of vibrations. This idea will be crucial to the remainder of this chapter.

Whether we consider the particle or the wave to be the basic form of nature's building blocks, such a basic form is known to oscillate at a telltale frequency that is the "voiceprint" of its identity. More complex wave systems have more superimposed, "choruslike" vibrational patterns, out of which it is possible to differentiate constituent "voices" (via Fourier transforms). Are there beings who are composed of, and exist within, the same universe of substance but at higher vibrations, who are able to communicate with some of us by the process of channeling?

Developing a Spectrum of Being

Earlier we spoke of the need to expand the spectrum used by physics to explain ordinary physical reality in order to view mental activity and anomalous phenomena like channeling. The spectrum most commonly used by physicists is the electromagnetic one, including wavelength and frequency. This is not to be confused with the spectrum of sound waves, the medium for which is air molecules in mechanical vibration. The electromagnetic spectrum involves the vibration of a medium composed of electromagnetic energy. Still, there may be ways in which the cycles-per-second rates of vibration may affect one another across kinds of media, or in which a vibratory rate may transduce from one medium or quality to another.

The extremely low frequencies (ELF waves) include the known cycles per second of brain waves that have been recorded by EEG, from a few cycles per second (deep delta-wave sleep); to a few more per second (theta, associated with creativity, learning, and reverie); to 7–12 hertz (alpha-wave relaxation, meditation, and reported psi functioning); and from 18–30 hertz (the "chatter" of beta-wave activity, the waking state, analytical processing, and perceptual and motor interaction with the environment).

Along the spectrum, AM and FM radio waves come next, followed by television, microwaves, radar, infrared light, visible light, ultraviolet light, X rays, gamma rays, and cosmic rays, and the end of the known spectrum. The stretch from ELF to cosmic rays spans a range from waves hundreds of thousands of meters in length to those smaller than the diameter of a subatomic particle, and from a few hertz in frequency to numbers so high they require 25 zeros after them.

Finally, we need to imagine that we collapse the linear spectrum we have been considering so that we have what physicists tell us is actually the case: a simultaneous continuum within which the hierarchy of wave bands—different vibratory rates within the medium—is superimposed. This superimposition provides an interpenetrating single system that is neither spatially nor temporally separated. The different bands of the spectrum are not side-by-side or end-to-end.

Cross-band Communication

We then transmit through the cosmos in the various levels that enter your reality through the mental planes, then drifts down in its way to the physical plane, much as the television signal to the antenna and then it is amplified. We transmit blips and bleeps that through their amplification sound like words. You absorb the ideas and thus we communicate.
—the channeled source "Lazaris"[31]

The resonance frequency used by the guides cannot be detected with our physical senses, so it is broken down in stages. There may be as many as fifteen or twenty links between you and your guide and yet there is no time lag when you speak with him. You do not have to wait while your words travel along a network of links because outside the physical there is no time; there is only one continuous *now*.
—channel Dawn Hill[32]

The force of the intelligence that has created this book is within the periphery beyond your limited senses which are contained within a frequency band lower than that in which we operate. It is necessary then to reduce or reform this frequency so that it is contained in a lower frequency band than from its original basis. So another instrument is used for this purpose; this instrument [the channel] is one that is necessary to receive the frequencies of these intelligences.
—a "source" through channel Ruth Norman

I am but the spiritual energy upon the sounding board of all vibratory forces throughout the universe. I enter the computer of this instrument [the channel Elwood Babbitt] and pick the words needed to give energy expression. I am likened to your cosmic ray. I am a primary energy needed to expand the force of mind.

—the Hindu god Vishnu, through channel Elwood Babbitt[33]

Here in this world of matter in which we function, we are only conscious of a lower scale of vibrations, whereas in the etheric world, where life also functions, consciousness is affected by a higher scale of vibrations. The ether is as much to other life in the universe as it is to us. To this other life its surroundings are just as substantial and real as ours are to us. Life functions in the ether, and it is just as much able to do so when free of matter as it is when clothed in matter.

—channel Arthur Findlay[34]

The Spirit of God tries to speak to His children using the earthly language . . . The Spirit of God flowing in the instrument [to] irradiate another brain cell in which will vibrate a word that comes close, in its frequency of light, to the meaning the Spirit wants . . . God is Spirit, and His Language is High Vibrations of Light . . . [the] writing instrument may record part-truths for some time, because the soul and the person are not yet totally aligned with the inner light, with the Word of God . . . not yet totally irradiated.

—a "cherub" through channel Gabriele Wittek[35]

Many of the channels and their sources speak of the channeling process in similar terms suggesting broadcast radio waves. Let us consider how the physicist might view some "cross-band" interactions within this spectrum. We know, for example, that a communication source operating within the AM radio frequency band of 540,000 to 1,600,000 hertz (cycles per second) could initiate a transmission of information that would be nonexistent for normal hearing—which initially must operate within an acoustical, not an electromagnetic, medium and in a range of 20 to 20,000 cycles per second. However, we know that with the proper radio tuning, transducing, and amplification apparatus, normal human hearing can receive such higher-frequency information. We have the apparatus capable of detecting X-ray and cosmic ray frequencies, yet the sources responsible for such *extremely* high-frequency wavelengths seem to be only the natural occurrences within the inanimate realm of stars, nebulae, and galaxies.

POSSIBLE EXPLANATIONS

In the case of channeling, we are interested in the possibility of *animate*—that is, conscious, sentient, intentional—beings who reside within and communicate from extremely high frequencies. By this view, a supposed disembodied human spirit might surpass cosmic ray vibrations in frequency, and an "ascended master" in turn might be ten times that frequency. A great many channeled sources speak of this hierarchy of increasing vibrations within the one universal substance. Changing vibrations is not an easy matter to conceptualize, however. While we can talk about a generic frequency when describing vibrations at different levels, to speak of "cycles per second" implies that the time scales for different levels are the same—and this, scientists know, is not the case. For example, changing frequencies can be accomplished by varying the rate of passage of time instead of the number of events per unit of time.

Jean Houston speculates on the kinds of embodiment that might exist across such levels of reality:

> I think the universe is filled with intelligence. Some is embodied, some is disembodied, and ultimately probably none of it is disembodied. It may have minus n-dimensional structure or go through a black hole to a negative particle structure. But I think everything has structure or pattern. And I think it is how you define embodiment. If it's embodiment of protein or computer or chemicals, then we have a problem. If you think of embodiment as perhaps of frequency which is pulsed, they may not even be in space, they may be across time.[36]

Consider the case of communication between two individuals sharing the same frequency domain. When I vibrate air with my vocal cords, I make acoustical waves that strike your eardrums, resulting in audible, intelligible sound for you as listener. We are both functioning within the same frequency range of acoustical waves. Still, your brain has to take the frequencies of those sound waves and transduce and encode them into bioelectric frequencies involving nerve impulses before you can have the conscious sensation of hearing me. When we communicate back and forth on ham or CB radios, we again hear each other within the same frequency domain as when standing together. But this radio-mediated experience is the result of an apparatus transducing the mechanical forces of our voices into much-higher-frequency electromagnetic waves that can be broadcast wirelessly at the speed of light. It involves, as well, the same apparatus tuning to and transducing such electromagnetic waves into slower mechanical waves that affect the ear; the mechanical waves, in turn, must be transduced into the brain frequencies required for speech comprehension.

So, we have learned to overcome certain physical constraints by communicating *across* a commonly shared higher-frequency wave band, which can be stepped up for transmission and stepped down for receiving. This operation, as we are familiar with it, always requires some kind of transducing apparatus from the same frequency range as those wave bands using it.

With channeling, we are interested in the possibility of *cross-band* communications in which the bodies—or at least the loci of consciousness—of both parties at the time of communication are *not* within the same frequency range. Nor do they possess a transducing apparatus made from the same shared frequency range.

On one end of the communication line, imagine a human being, the channel, with no other "apparatus" than a mind, brain, and body. On the other end, imagine someone who claims to have died and to be living without a physical body in a realm of higher frequency. We can speculate that this disembodied being can transduce information from its native frequency range to the lower range inhabited by and comprising the brain and body of the channel. In this way, the channel's brain and body could be contacted.

To continue speculating in this vein, consider that the mental activity of any human mind, regardless of the frequency domain of its bodily vehicle and native environment, excites waves on one band of the extended spectrum. At the limits of our speculation, we might consider that *all* minds in the universe share this common band. Let us call this band the mental plane, as it has been designated throughout ancient wisdom and channeled literature. Having physicalized the mental, we can see such a plane as a specific band of vibration of the one "physical stuff."

Each individual is a superimposed set of vibrations: the mental level vibrates at a higher frequency range than do our bodies and brains. It is the one medium within which to transmit and receive messages of intentional acts of will of individual minds.

The life of any physically embodied mind shares this mental band of the spectrum with the life of every other embodied mind. But, more importantly, we can conjecture that this mental band can be shared with us by the alleged sources whose bodily vehicles are said to be of higher frequency than ours. The minds of these sources, however, operate within the same bandwidth as incarnated minds do.

The mental band is only one of a number of simultaneous bands at work in the human being. In our current culture we tend to identify individuals primarily in terms of the frequency band in which physical bodies have their existence, rather than in terms of their mental band and behaviors. The channeled sources identify themselves as being from frequency bands higher than the physical one: the etheric, astral, mental, causal, or higher ranges. An alleged resident of the mental plane, for example, would live within and communicate from the same frequency range as the human mind. So, in a channeling relationship between a mental-plane being and a physically embodied being, the mental being might perturb his environment, creating what are often called thoughtforms. Since the thoughtforms are on the same universal bandwidth as the channel's own mind, a kind of coupling might take place at whatever velocity mind operates.

Channel Elwood Babbitt describes his experience of receiving nonordinary information from other people:

A psychic vibration operates like a sound, or like waves in water. That is, you throw a stone in the water and you see the ripples go from it. Similarly, there are these waves or vibrations from people that come in bars and lines, either horizontal or vertical. They come in different degrees of vibration—at different vibratory rates, or frequencies; they look like lines. Each one is different in thickness. They'll expand and contract according to how or what you are thinking.[37]

Similarly, contemporary Oakland, California, channel Duane Packer speaks of "trying to decipher images of wave patterns. The patterns challenge me to pick a word from my vocabulary to describe waves. I experience an energy being directed."[38]

Babbitt's and Packer's descriptions sound like the scientific process known as spectral analysis, where the line bands emanating from various radiating systems, such as stars or heated metals, can be analyzed to identify the elements they contain; or the way the laser-flashing device at the supermarket checkout counter scans the set of parallel lines of the Universal Product Code on each item—a kind of two-dimensional wave system.

Babbitt here describes the process that takes place when he channels information said to be from other levels of reality. In such cases, the encoded vibratory information must step down through dimensions:

To lower the current it has to form like the funnel of a tornado, with a rapid rotation developing centrifugal force. It spirals down and it decreases its intensity as it reaches each successive ring or progression. As it reaches the bottom of the funnel, which is the earth level, the current exhausts itself and lowers itself through the resistance (or inertia) of the earth level.[39]

In physicalizing the mental, then, we have considered a framework within which the concepts of today's physics might be extended to describe the cross-band communication phenomenon called channeling. In addition, it might allow us to entertain the possible existence of higher-frequency life forms whose vehicles are constructed from the level of their environmental vibration, just as our bodies are constructed from the physical realm.

The "melodies" of vibratory wave forms created within different frequency ranges also would have some cross-band relationship with one another. They might stand in harmonic or resonant relationship with other levels that are capable of inducing in lower-frequency wave forms their melodic, informational signature by the process of sympathetic resonance.

Psychologist and channel Jose Stevens describes his experience of the channeling process, which includes the mechanics of our cross-band view:

> There's a great deal of interplay and dialogue across the barrier, which is very permeable. And the phenomenon of channeling is simply the ability to raise the frequency level that allows communication across that barrier to take place. And usually what that involves is increasing the frequency on the physical plane and decreasing the level of frequency on the nonphysical plane, so that the two can meet.[40]

Thus far, we have been considering an electromagnetic spectrum composed of the superimposed wave bands of the different vibratory rates taking place within it. We extended this concept to include higher-frequency activity such as that hypothesized to be mental vibrations. To complete our physicalizing of the mental, we also need to add the other earlier-mentioned forces of nature to make one all-inclusive continuum composed of all the vibrations of all the different qualities of the one ground of being. We must superimpose in our thinking all wave bands of all kinds of spectra: radio waves, TV waves, hypothesized gravitational waves, cosmic rays, waves involving the strong nuclear force and weak force as well. In our speculation they are all composing and interpenetrating the minds, emotions, and bodies of each of us. And this is true of the beings hypothesized to exist on other levels of reality as well.

In our speculation, all spectral bands—which might also be described as dimensions—are superimposed on one another at every moment and are not side-by-side, end-to-end, or separated by time. Therefore, cross-band channeling does not necessarily involve covering any distance or communicating across space. It more likely involves transformation, transduction, and interaction of frequencies in the here and now. And this is just what many of the channeled sources tell us is happening.

While we have been talking throughout about *frequency* of vibration, there is also the matter of *velocity* within our extended unified field obtained by physicalizing the mental. As we have extended the traditional electromagnetic spectrum by speculating on higher frequencies than are currently known, we may also wish to extend the ceiling of the speed of light, which is understood by physics to be the upper limit for known activity. We speculate that wave systems of different velocities, as well as of different frequencies, may interact during the process of channeling. Indeed, there is recent channeled material making just such claims for the reality of higher velocities and higher frequencies than we currently understand. Time must enter into our picture as well as frequency and velocity. In realms based on a different frequency than ours, time runs slower, or faster. Time stops when the "now" persists. Speed, then, would be infinite, implying no spacelike separation. (Also, recall the suggestion of Jack Schwarz in chapter 8 that, paradoxically, one may couple with and access superluminary material by slowing brain waves.)

Variations on the Theme

Stanford engineering professor William Tiller has been a pioneer in paranormal research as well as a highly respected material scientist and authority on crystallization. His basic view is founded on a set of *superluminary* dimensions (planes or bands) adjacent to our own, involving extraordinary frequencies and velocities that exceed the speed of light. In Tiller's model (reflecting systems from channels such as Blavatsky and Bailey), universal process moves from Spirit to Spiritual Mind, to Intellectual Mind, to an Astral level, to an Etheric level, and down to the known Physical level. When physically embodied minds initiate any thought or intention, events occur in the mental domain as excitations within that wave system. A cascading wave flow of stepped-down velocity and frequency then takes place, as mental action manifests across descending levels. Tiller has not ruled out the possibility that other beings may inhabit the higher realms of the hierarchy, setting in motion cascades that reach our minds and affect our perceptions. (Keep in mind, once more, that all such hierarchical models are spread out to show their various component bands or layers; but when we are dealing with wave systems they are, in fact, superimposed on one another and are therefore spatially coexistent.)

We live in an "integrated circuit," Tiller believes, energetically coupled in ways that transcend currently accepted scientific understanding.

In a frequency-dependent way, we tune and filter the incoming radiation of signals from "on high." Channels may just tune differently, or filter less, than the rest of us; we, too, have the potential of doing so.[41]

Louis Acker, a little-known independent researcher in Chichester, New York, presents a related view in unpublished, privately circulated papers. Based on his research on what he calls the "fire crystal technology of fabled Atlantis," he also envisions human beings in constant interaction with a number of simultaneous superimposed levels of reality, each with its own frequency range. Acker emphasizes certain "geometrically organized wave length harmonics" (as found in crystals and "sacred geometries"), which act as wave guides that line up the physical with higher-frequency and higher-velocity domains. Once this alignment occurs, he says, the higher-wave systems can implode into this level of reality: they are literally channeled. During this process, there is a transference of energy from higher to lower dimensions by way of resonance and harmonics among common structures.[42] Building on this theory, holographic thought forms that exist on higher frequencies, such as those from channeled sources, could be reflected down to subharmonic carrier frequencies and thus reach the channel.

T. B. Pawlicki presents a view similar to Acker's in his book *How You Can Explore Higher Dimensions of Space and Time.* Pawlicki is an Olympic-class athlete, commercial artist, and author of the earlier *How to Build a Flying Saucer.* Since "crystalline resonance is the physical basis of tuned electromagnetic radiation and absorption," he writes, "the human body must be a radio broadcaster and receiver." Just as squares in a two-dimensional world may be the result of projections of cubes into it, so the reality we experience, according to Pawlicki, is the result of interaction with many other dimensions than the usual three or four (including time). Space, for him, "is filled with the vibrations of the universal hologram." This hologram he refers to as "hyperspace," and 90-degree-angle rotations through this hyperspace define one dimension from another.

In the following passage from Pawlicki, keep in mind that *phase* is a term used when working with recurrent wave structures. For example, if the magnitudes of different wave systems match up at the same time, the two systems are said to be "in phase" with each other. A *node* is the point of least (or no) motion within any wave pattern or oscillating system. And *superconducting* means the ability to conduct a flow of current (or information) with no resistance. Pawlicki writes:

> Detection and measurement are possible only by the contact of one wave against another . . . Our reality is created by the mutual opposition of infinite numbers of electromagnetic waves. We coexist

in the same hyperspace with all other possible realities (our past and future) and each reality is defined from every other reality by the specific phase alignment of its generating waves . . . There really are windows into higher/lower dimensions of space-time and you really can pass through the windows at the nodal points of the dance of life. To find a window through hyperspace, you must learn how to become absolutely still. At the still point, you become superconducting, and you then pass through the eye of the needle into Heaven, just as all the mystic Masters describe . . . When you pass through the still point, you therefore enter another reality defined by waves of another length, another frequency, and another velocity on another harmonic scale.[43]

Pawlicki's description seems to closely fit our cross-band communication model of channeling; he speaks of hyperspace "crosstalk." His view also allows for the possibility of beings existing on other dimensions of reality than ours—beings who are made, just as we are, of different frequencies and velocities of phase relationships of waves of the one hyperspace. And certainly the "nodal point" stilling of oneself to make a transdimensional window fits the meditation-type procedures reported by so many channels.

As we draw the different kinds of dotted lines across the bands of our spectrum of being that might represent avenues of normal and paranormal communication, consider another perspective. In his recent book *A New Science of Life: The Hypothesis of Formative Causation,*[44] British plant physiologist Rupert Sheldrake advances the idea that the structure and behavior of organisms are governed by self-replicating morphogenetic fields. Though more dynamic, these are somewhat like Plato's transcendental forms existing outside of space and time and said to be responsible for all physical forms. Sheldrake's fields program an organism's development via its genetic mechanisms through resonance (Puharich's recent research seems to be in this area as well). His fields, too, are said to lie outside of time, space, and energy as we know them, acting as blueprints for the acquisition of an organism's programs for action and for its patterns of understanding.

According to Sheldrake, these morphogenetic fields have been built up by a sufficient number of "real" individuals projecting intentions, thoughts, and actions—a sort of modern-day akashic records, at least of the most dominant and perhaps archetypal patterns. We might then conjecture that these fields may be channeled by individuals who are able to quiet their habitual mental activity and entrain, or be in sympathetic resonant vibration, with the new information. For example, Jesus Christ or other great spirits might have, by thought, word, or deed, left a legacy of powerful morphogenetic fields. And in channeling, we may open ourselves to this extradimensional resource.

French biologist Rene Thom seems to present a variation on this theme. According to Thom, at each catastrophic stage of growth, the contents of an individual system, thrown momentarily into flux far from equilibrium, become susceptible to the effect of what he calls attractors. These hypothetical attractors, lying outside the system and providing information, reorganize the momentarily chaotic material along their lines of force attraction, much as the randomly scattered iron filings on a sheet of paper will rapidly conform to the magnetic field of a magnet placed underneath.[45]

Perhaps shifting from a normal to a meditative or altered state of consciousness is like a subtle but effective psychophysical catastrophe, a move toward a loosened state that can be affected by the subtle attractors, fields, or other influences in the surroundings. It is known in related "chaos theory" that fluctuating, highly unstable systems (such as the brain) can be extremely sensitive to very small, or subtle, inputs. In this speculation, the entities or sources in channeling may operate like Thom's attractors (which in turn may act like, or be, Sheldrake's morphogenetic fields). Or perhaps the entire species is going through a growth-spurt "catastrophe" that is opening increasing numbers of us to the possibility of paranormal interaction with the larger "attractive" system. Certainly the recent channeled material says as much. In the following section on paraphysics, we will find even more variations on the theme of other wave-band field phenomena that are said to interact with and affect our level of reality through normal and paranormal kinds of communication.

Recall the earlier argument that we are *not* closed systems, either psychologically or physically. Belgian physical chemist Ilya Prigogine has put forth a notion of "dissipative structures"[46] that may shed light on paranormal information-processing and the experiencing of outside presences other than our own and other than our usual reality. Prigogine sees open systems as structures that exchange energy with the environment. The more complex the structure, the more it must dissipate its energy into the environment in order to maintain its complexity. This flux of energy makes the system highly unstable, operating far from equilibrium, and it is then highly susceptible to internal fluctuations and sudden change, and susceptible to external stimuli. This seems to be a good model for the human brain/mind. In one interpretation, the more complex the system, the greater its potential for self-transcendence, the more it can let go or give (dissipate), and thus the more it can take in from the environment. Perhaps we are, as the channeled literature keeps saying, evolving toward ever more intercourse and unity with the larger multidimensional, living, populated universe. Perhaps all of these reported channeled messages are part of the influx that we as a species are starting to experience as our evolving beings dissipate and receive more energy than before.

Another view takes our multiband spectrum of being and puts it through a sort of blender, reducing it to a single wavy, building-block mix of everything that is. British physicist David Bohm presents a model of the universe as an immense moving sea of multidimensional but ordered frequencies—a mixed-frequency domain in which the bandwidths are superimposed. The universe, for him, is like a vast hologram in which "a total order is contained, in some implicit sense, in each region of space and time." And, as in the all-inclusive spectrum, "matter and consciousness have the implicate order in common."[47] This means that the common denominator both share is the one non–space-time mixed-frequency domain.

What Bohm terms the implicate order is the realm containing all differentiation and form as yet undifferentiated and unformed for local experience. It is the creative ground for phenomenal being. Locally experienceable phenomena are of the explicate order derived from the implicate. Consciousness and what consciousness experiences are inextricably caught up together in wave systems of causal, transformative interaction. Bohm writes, "Consciousness is to be comprehended in terms of the implicate order."[48] What consciousness experiences and manifests is described as a "creative inception of new content as projected from the multidimensional ground," a ground that "is still in a certain sense enfolded in our consciousness."[49]

On the basis of this model, we can speculate on communication processes. We generate experiences by the way our respective wave systems, both implicate (consciousness) and explicate (bodily), interact with the larger implicate- and explicate-order wave system. All voices heard from without or within, from embodied or disembodied sources, are derived from universal background implicate order. There are all kinds of "embodiments" that have been explicated out of the implicate order and that dwell within many of its frequency domains. These are the vehicles, like our bodies, for the one implicate-order stuff of consciousness that *all* beings share and are. Channeling is the ability to connect one station within the implicate-order sea of consciousness with another, in spite of the differing frequencies of embodiment and differing frequency domains as respective home planes for those involved in such communication.

Jean Houston presents a picture of channeling as a sort of accessing of the Universal Mind based on this holographic model:

If the holographic theory has any proof to it, then it suggests that everything is ubiquitous [omnipresent] with everything all the time anyway in this simultaneous-everywhere matrix universe. And that would take care of a great deal of the channels . . . Certain individuals are able to raise the gates or lower the ice or become diaphanous, be stretched very thin, so that this ubiquitous, simul-taneous-everywhere-all-the-time information is available to human beings . . . Then you've got to project a persona [a source] to con-tain the ubiquity of the information, otherwise you're not going to take it.[50]

Whether it is Houston's holographic ubiquity or "the Law of One"—the constant message of the "space brother" group being "Ra" —we seem to be finding a common theme. It is suggested in the work of physicist John Bell as well. He demonstrated that any pair of particles (photons of light that share a common origin) that become separated in space remain connected in ways that violate what physicists call locality (normal causal connectedness). Bell proved a mathematical theorem that implies that an observational interaction with one of the twin parti-cles automatically and instantaneously affected the state of the other one, even if they were separated by great distances. His conclusion: something nonlocal seems to be at work that transcends the usual causal mechanisms understood by science.[51] This is another view of the pos-sible unity of all aspects of Creation (if all aspects are seen to share a common origin). Channeling may be just the beginning of establishing human reconnection to our fellow beings with whom we are connected in ways that appear to transcend normal space and time.

It is now a well-established notion in quantum physics that the experienced nature of the observed is at least partially a function of the observer's interaction with it. There may be no innocent realm of con-crete observables irrespective of the conscious realm of observations responsible for them. In the quantum view of physics, all unobserved, unmeasured existence exists only as a probability distribution of waves until interacted with by consciousness or instrumentation that essen-tially measures it. The observation or measurement is said to collapse the wave function used to represent the until-then only partially focused realm of probability. Only with measurement does the experience of material existence occur; and perception is a form of measurement.

According to physicist Eugene Wigner, "It is the entering of an impression into our consciousness which alters the wave function, be-cause it modifies our appraisal of the probabilities for different impres-sions which we expect to receive in the future."[52] Perhaps here we have a mechanism for understanding the often-repeated claim in channeled literature that we create our own reality. Fellow physicist Fred Alan Wolf, in his book *Star Wave: Mind, Consciousness, and Quantum Physics,* claims that the universe we know is constructed "through the interference patterns between the mind and the physical frequencies."[53] For Wolf and others, the observer-observed interaction is a multidimensional, or at least multifrequency, interference pattern of waves. We can see the similarity, at this level of approximation, between Bohm's implicate holographic view and the older quantum picture.

In the interview with contemporary channel Jach Pursel's alleged entity "Lazaris" at the end of chapter 1, there is an extraordinarily lucid passage in which "Lazaris" presents a quantum physics type view of how channeling takes place between "himself"—a supposedly nonphysical and multidimensional group being—and the channel, Pursel. It nicely summarizes and epitomizes the "spectrum of being" and "crossband" views as well as the holographic and quantum pictures.

Paraphysics

Paraphysics is to physics what parapsychology is to psychology. Brendan O'Regan, vice president of research at the Institute of Noetic Sciences in Sausalito, California, has defined paraphysics as "the study of the physics of paranormal processes."[54] California physicist Charles Muses writes, "Scientists who are seeking to enlarge their scope of scientific thinking use the term paraphysics to denote the field of phenomena covering interactions of non-physical things (such as consciousness) with physical bodies and objects. Terms such as psychotronics and parascience have also been suggested."[55]

Scientific attempts to physicalize the mental, though varied, have tended to seek a crucial "ether" underlying physical manifestation and energy and responsible for the "life force" itself. There has been a curious history of attempts to understand energy relations that have fallen outside of mainstream scientific thinking. In the eighteenth century, the Frenchman Franz Anton Mesmer proposed a universal magnetic fluid, which he claimed he could manipulate to induce "mesmerized" hypnotic states. Baron Karl von Reichenbach preferred an "odic" magnetic force. In 1878, Edwin S. Babbitt presented new ways of studying the effects of light on living organisms.[56] At the turn of the century, Albert Abrams laid the groundwork for the much-debated science of radionics, and was followed by Malcolm Rae, George Delawarr, Ruth Drown, David Tansley, and others. Meanwhile, psychosomatic medicine for the first time looked at the effect of the mind on the body.[57]

Harold Saxton Burr and F. S. C. Northrop, professors at Yale, discovered what they took to be *prephysical* states, which appeared to organize and influence the bodies of living organisms. This led them to formulate an "electrodynamic theory of life." Edward W. Russell and others developed variations on this theme.[58] Soon, a set of interrelated terms sprang into use, including *organizational fields, life fields,* and *thought fields.* Wilhelm Reich conducted research to prove the existence of an all-pervasive *orgone* energy. All of these seem variations on the same theme tapped by Plato, Bohm, Sheldrake, and Thom.

More recently, Soviet researchers developed the concept of *bioplasma,* recalling Spiritualism's ectoplasm. Another Soviet contribution was the cold electron emission measurements of Kirlian photography. The Soviets have also studied what they termed biological radio communication. This was epitomized by a famous experiment in which baby rabbits were killed in a submerged submarine and the correlated brainwave reaction of the mother rabbit was observed in a laboratory on land. Numerous parapsychological experiments have studied how ESP or telepathy may be propagated and in what medium. Placing a "sender" or "receiver" in a metal Faraday cage, which screens out radio and other electromagnetic waves, for example, seems not to affect paranormal communication. Some researchers have speculated that, because some paranormal communication is unaffected by material obstruction, perhaps the information signals involve massless neutrino particles, which are known to pass through the entire earth unaffected.[59]

Retired IBM senior research scientist Marcel Vogel has studied the use of crystals as conductors, tuners, condensers, and amplifiers of subtle-energy fields, perhaps even beyond the known electromagnetic spectrum. Research with crystals has shown that quartz is preferable to glass for working with subtle energies, since glass is known to block frequencies higher than visible light, such as the ultraviolet range. Vogel and others appear to have discovered that crystals can mediate *mental* energy as well. For example, Vogel claims to be able to focus his intention into and through crystals, causing them to resonate, hum, and glow in the process.[60]

In his studies of paranormal communication, Cleve Backster used a modified lie detector apparatus to measure the difference in electromagnetic potential across a gap. By wiring plants up to the device, he discovered that they responded to the feelings and intentions of human beings present. Taking this approach a step farther, researcher Julius Weinberger decided to use a Backster-like apparatus to try to detect the presence of nonphysical beings. Choosing a Venus's-flytrap plant as his detector, he used a vacuum-tube amplifier to detect minute electrical changes between two points on a leaf. By asking questions and noting the coded response by way of the plant, Weinberger was able to engage in what he believed was actual discourse with discarnates. Farfetched as it seems, this may be a plant-mediated version of the Spiritualist seance process.[61]

In 1971, Latvian psychologist Konstantin Raudive published *Breakthrough: An Amazing Experiment in Electronic Communication with the Dead*.[62] By using ordinary tape recorders, sometimes augmented with other ordinary electronic equipment, he said he was able to record and play back voices claiming to be human spirits. More recently, George W. Meek at his Metascience Foundation research lab in North Carolina claims to have developed a cross-band transducer, an instrument that, he says, has permitted him and his co-workers to carry on two-way conversations with deceased human spirits. Meek's device is technically called a transceiver, a sort of radio receiver, which is a piece of instrumentation for electromagnetic wave frequency modulation that functions in the 30- to 130- megahertz range. The crucial ingredient of this technology, however, according to Meek, seems to involve the psychic energies of the person who operates the physical hardware. This combining of known energies with etheric or other conjectured subtle energies is similar to radionics, which we will discuss shortly.[63]

The concept of chakras—said to act as wheels or vortices in the human subtle-energy body for the movements of psychoenergetic flow between levels of reality—has long been a topic of channeled material. The throat (thyroid), brow (pituitary), and crown (pineal) chakras have all been implicated in the inception of channeled material. Soviet paraphysics researcher Victor Adamenko and Japanese neurologist Hiroshi Motoyama both claim to have developed instruments to measure the bioplasma, prana, or chi moving through the chakra and acupuncture meridians.[64] And former UCLA professor Valerie Hunt reports having obtained amplified sound recordings of the chakras.[65]

Radionics and a Possible Universal Tongue Of all the purported sciences dealing with the paranormal realm, perhaps the one most associated with the interaction of mental and physical (or cross-band) patterns is radionics. In the earlier part of this century, Stanford neurologist Albert Abrams, California chiropractor Ruth Drown, and the Englishmen George Delawarr and Malcolm Rae were united by their interest in discovering the subtle energy or mental levels underlying organization on the physical level. Anticipating Sheldrake, and perhaps Thom, some of the radionics pioneers believed that such fields might be nonphysical—organizational, informational, or mental—and yet somehow be able to affect what is known as the physical. Radionics became the science of the detection and manipulation of these paranormal fields in interaction with living organisms.[66]

In the view of radionics, all things in the universe are made of substance in vibration. Every kind of thing supposedly has a telltale natural rate of vibration, like an identifying voiceprint. The wave form of the transmission (the natural emanation given off by its nature) will be a function of the kind of vibrating structure and substance. A radionics device is said to operate only with the higher, apparently mental or intentional level energies of the human operator in interaction with those of other persons or objects. The process seems to involve some kind of cross-band resonance relationship between an object, what is often termed the etheric subtle energy level of that object, and the thought of that object.

Radionics—like the theories of Bohm, Sheldrake, and Plato—seems to imply that physical reality may have a higher-octave or nonphysical counterpart that can affect it. The mind's wave structures may affect and be affected by the harmonics of resonant tuning within and across levels of reality. Returning to our earlier cross-band "spectrum of being" communication model, channeled sources may have energy bodies of some kind, whose "organs" might perhaps be something like chakra vortices. The sources would live within environments in these higher realms, while their mental wave structures may be no "higher" than our own. In channeling situations, the sources overcome the cross-band differential by establishing resonance relationships with the minds, brains, and bodies of physical-level channels. This would all seem farfetched indeed if it were not for the fact that a great deal of the channeled literature presents just such a picture.

Neuroscientists tell us that the brain is a complex set of resonators, able to decode and encode a wide range of frequencies. Its myriad resonators can be tuned independently to the diverse components of a radiating wave. Each of us is a sophisticated wave analyzer that can take complex oscillations and isolate components by way of bioelectric circuits tuned to several frequencies. What radionics would add to this picture is this: the frequency domain for encoding and decoding appears to be operating on unknown bands of the traditional spectrum. In order to deal with the informational nature of channeling, we still need to account for how an idea of a thing, as in radionics practice, apparently can act as a medium for wave information.

We seem to be approaching a model within which each object (including thought) in the multidimensional universe operates like a little transducer, or two-way radio, capable of mediating a number of different wave bands. Thus a strand of hair, or the light reflected from it, for instance, has a radiation that reaches the normal perception and instrumentation, but it may also transmit information within etheric or mental planes as well. Furthermore, there is a consensus in the channeled literature that the higher levels are responsible for the physical level. This top-down chain-of-command scheme is at the heart of a constellation of alternative technologies and healing approaches. It may be at the heart of channeling as well. To use novelist Upton Sinclair's term, "mental radio" (a term he coined while studying his psychic wife) may be operating between dimensions in the process of channeling. According to radionics, the common language used would be related by resonance across all bands of the spectrum and would be composed of a vocabulary of the natural rates given off by thoughts and the objects with which they are associated.

CONCLUSIONS

In the last two chapters, we have considered a variety of descriptions and explanations drawn from different disciplines: experimental, cognitive, and clinical psychology; parapsychology and consciousness research; psychophysiology; and physics and paraphysics. We have done this in order to mount a series of speculations based on these disciplines in order to gain a better understanding of the nature of the channeling phenomenon.

At the same time, with psychophysiology and, especially, physics, we have taken into account various warnings regarding the appropriateness of using physically oriented *objective* science to try to shed light on the *subjective* realms of consciousness, knowing, and the spirit—realms that may well not involve the physical at all.

While physics has ample empirical evidence to support most of its theories about the physical universe, it has little or none with regard to such highly speculative areas as: (1) whether mind or spirit has anything to do with the physical or could be contained within any kind of grand unified theory; (2) the existence of information-carrying frequency domains beyond the known electromagnetic spectrum; (3) anything like a mental domain involving thought waves; (4) signal propagation operating beyond the speed of light; (5) the existence of nonphysical dimensions beyond the three of space and one of time; (6) whether there could be any such thing as disembodied intelligence living in and communicating from such dimensions, either completely nonphysical life forms or life forms whose bodies are of a higher physical or subtle-energy sort compared to ours.

All six of these areas are largely speculative at this point. There are two things to bear in mind, however. First, mainstream physics does give us *some* grounds, at least, from which to make these speculations. Second, there appears to be a strong consensus within the channeled literature, especially in the past thirty-five years, for an explanation of channeling very much along the physics lines suggested in this chapter.

While nothing conclusive or definitive may be drawn from this exercise, hopefully it has opened some new avenues of thought and possibility. Perhaps, as well, some seeds for future research into channeling and related phenomena may have been planted by this chapter. It is at least a start.

A CONCLUDING METAPHOR

As my own attempt to come to terms with and integrate the various explanations and speculations of the last two chapters, I would like to present for your consideration a metaphor that I find works for me with regard to channeling. I think that this metaphor can be entertained by the atheistic materialist and the devoutly spiritual person alike.

In the first stage of the metaphor, each of us is an individuation out of the one universal physical energy ground of Being (physicalizing the mental), or out of the one Universal Mind or spirit (mentalizing the physical), depending on your perspective. Or, in a third, dualist, view, the entire physical energy universe is like one universal Brain/Body, and the consciousness that exists dependent on and in interaction with it is the one Universal Mind. Yet in any of these three accounts, each of us is an episode of individuation temporarily welled up into local, seemingly separate being. And we each appear to be surrounded by a semipermeable membrane that marks us off from the stuff that seems to be not us (including one another). These membranes may be molecules of skin, electromagnetic force fields, ego boundaries, or any other material or immaterial stuff derived from the same basal substance that one sees as being subdivided by such membranes in the first place.

From the larger perspective of this metaphor, such separateness would not be ultimately true, since the one ground of Being is the true unifying identity and organicity of the separate individuations out of itself. As "Seth" says: "There are no closed systems to reality . . . consciousness can never be a closed system, and all barriers of such a nature are illusion."[67] We are each something like localized events of self-reflective function taking place within one universal Godhead or cosmic ground of Being.

This brings us to the second phase of the metaphor. Recall both the definition of multiple-personality disorder (MPD) and the non-pathological notions of co-consciousness (Beahrs) and multimind (Ornstein) that might possibly serve as parallels or replacements for MPD. Consider, now, that *we are all sub- or alter-personalities within one Universal Mind, or Godhead.* The subpersonalities within an individual MPD (or co-conscious) subject usually believe that they possess an identity separate from their host or parent mind. Similarly, in our metaphor, most of us human beings in our present states of mind take what we identify as ourselves to be separate from one another and separate from the host and parent Mind from which we have arisen and with regard to which we maintain a dissociated state. This dissociated state does not allow us to realize the identity condition that joins us with that Source, which is our own larger Self.

Continuing this metaphor, we subpersonalities of the one Universal Mind maintain our dissociated states, relatively unconscious of our deeper identity, and in a kind of involuntary or autonomic state with regard to the possibilities of access and interplay with the parent ground. Channeling, then, as well as normal interpersonal communication, is the activity of different kinds of subpersonalities communicating with one another. Depending on our perspective, we subpersonalities may be made out of embodiments of neuronal cell assemblies, firing patterns or programs, or complex wave systems or thoughtforms, interacting across semipermeable membranes within the one Universal Brain/Mind. To say that one communicating source, because it is said to be "channeled," is only "made up" by the one receiving it, would then be a relative matter; for both sender and receiver are "made up" within the larger creative Mind/Brain anyway. In this metaphor, the one Mind makes up its minds out of itself, and they, or we, in turn, make up our minds and mental content in a nesting system of cross-talk interplay that is the living Godhead's house of many mansions.

In both clinical and cognitive psychology views of the human being, there is something like a core identity, true self, executive ego, or executive function, depending on one's terminology. And no matter what is going on with the broken-off and autonomously acting subpersonalities or subsystems of that individual, there is supposed to be some kind of rightful pretender to the throne of that individual's personhood—his or her consciousness, control, and identity. In the psychological hierarchy, this primary self sits at the apex or center of the individual's multifaceted structures and functions.

This central, managerial ego, or self-identity, does not usually seem to possess the kind of exalted awareness attributed to the "higher Self," "God within," or "I Am" presence that is said by so much of the channeled literature to be our true identity. The current, day-to-day self-aware conscious part of each of us, rather, appears to be markedly more stupid, less conscious, and more in a state of dissociation and amnesia with regard to all that is going on within and apparently outside of its own multifaceted system than is such a fabled higher Self. Our normal self-conscious aspect is also usually relatively unaware of the larger Universal Brain/Mind within which our metaphor says that it and others like it exist.

Within our metaphor, then, what many of us tend to call the Supreme Being or God is the omniscient apex of the Universal Brain/ Mind. Only *it* can fully understand and coordinate all of its own brain-children, its own subpersonalities. As these subpersonalities, we are shards of its own mind living out our existences—and living out *its* existence—with varying degrees of dissociation and forgetfulness with regard to our true identity and possible integration and expansion.

Clinicians try to help their clients who are suffering from dissociative conditions to get their subpersonalities to see their true place in the scheme of things. They also try to help the "real" person involved—the executive ego or host conscious self—to understand, control, and integrate the subpersonalities in order to reestablish a cohesive and coherent identity that can function in a healthy, productive manner. In this metaphor, God, or the Universal Being, is trying to help us do this for ourselves and for itself as well.

The subpersonality that is "me" talks to the subpersonality that is "you." Neither of us may realize that we are in fact subpersonalities of the same underlying Mind. We are not lucid enough yet to realize it. Or I may "channel" some other subpersonality for the consideration of your subpersonality. The subpersonality that I channel may reside on any of a number of levels of reality within the one Brain/Mind. And, depending on your state of mind, perspective, or degree of lucidity, you may deem it as a "made up" figment of the imagination, as disembodied, as part of a person, as all of a person, as not a person, as an archetype; and so on. Just remember that, by our metaphor, each and every one of them (and of us) is the contents of—is the interacting wave patterns within—the one Brain/Mind.

From the perspective of each of us subpersonalities—whether we are considered brain/minds, psychic centers, spirits, or evolving souls— it may appear *to us* that the one Universal Being is, therefore, schizophrenic by reason of its apparent dissociation from itself. But from the perspective of our own supposed higher Selves, let alone from the perspective of the parent Mind itself, the experienced dissociation is strictly a state-specific function of a less-aware or lower level of consciousness. In our metaphor, it is up to each of us subpersonalities to realize our true place and identity in the greater scheme, and to become integrated back into the one Brain/Mind.

The dreamer becomes lucid and realizes that the dream is taking place within a still-larger frame of reference that is equally (or more) real. Similarly, the subpersonality in our metaphor may realize that it— he or she, you or I—is functioning within something like a dream that follows from its own state and view, and yet at the same time it is functioning within the larger identity and Being as an individuation of it. Once this is realized, according to this metaphor, the true nature and possibility of channeling quickly dawns on the subpersonality:

> Ah, I potentially have access to the rest of my own Mind! Everything of which I was earlier not conscious—all the rest of the larger Brain/Mind of all Creation—was, by definition, my own unconscious. Now I wish to allow it into my consciousness, or to allow my consciousness into it. In the larger reality, I am both *part* of the one Brain/Mind, and yet I am potentially (and on another level of consciousness already am) *all* of it. I am connected to and at one with it, with both its Brain (physicalizing the mental) and its Mind (mentalizing the physical).

Channeling, then, is the growing awareness of any part of the one Being that it can access any of the rest of itself. And this may include the sense that each of us may receive, into our current cloud of unknowing, waves of cognition like light streaming from the seat and source of omniscience, omnipotence, and omnipresence.

Three ideas may be derived from this extended metaphor. First, there is what I will call a kind of relativity theory that may help us better understand consciousness and what, in each of our cases, consciousness experiences as real for itself. The frame of reference used by any of us subpersonalities is a function of the state or level of our consciousness, of our respective degree of lucidity, and provides a degree of access to the larger parent Consciousness. By means of that individual frame of reference, we each experience a particular kind or level of reality, a slice of "truth" from the Universal Brain/Mind accordingly and in a state-specific manner. Whether or not you channel, and whatever you make of the channeling phenomenon, are inevitably results of your local state. This is true for all of the minute-to-minute reality you experience and for what you make of it as well. Eventually, by our metaphor, all roads or taos and all perspectives lead us, through a kind of spreading activation in the one Brain/Mind, to return to the truth of truths: that we are of the one Universal Being; or, as some say, that we are God.

The second idea is that we are currently undergoing what I will call a spiritual *reformation*. All of us—atheist and devout alike—now have the possibility of giving ourselves permission to renegotiate our own most-meaningful relationship with the living ground of Being: to variously knock upon it and to have it open to us. And it appears that this is to be done with less guidance than ever before from either the churches of organized religion, or from the "church" of organized science. It seems to be a most personal affair.

We have become untied into the dissociated subpersonalities that we are, each of us with his or her own brand of identity and thought disorder (with regard to the larger truth). As a result, many of us seek understanding and meaning, healing and atonement. Here may lie the key for the return to the at-one-ment that is available to us, who are our Source's own wayward and prodigal offspring. We can intentionally seek to reestablish ties and to align and identify ourselves with our parent Consciousness and the ground of our being. Each new wave of channeling seems to be part of this movement. Indeed, the channeled material echoes this theme over and over.

As Martin Luther's sixteenth-century Reformation tried to give the individual the freedom to interpret the Bible according to his or her own personal spiritual guidance, so we are each perhaps faced with a renewed opportunity to reform our method of operating into an active, personalized participation in seeking the goal of all religion: making for ourselves the deepest possible meaning to our existence, together with the establishment of a true identity condition with All That Is, personally experienced in both our knowing and our doing. To the extent to which the current organized religions truly support this individual relationship-making and meaning-making with source identity, they will be part of this new reformation. But, just as in Old Testament times, to the extent to which the churches seek exclusive rights to contact with that which transcends day-to-day reality and consciousness, and to the extent to which they brand and prohibit channeling as demon worship and consorting with "unfamiliar spirits," they will be abdicating what should be their role: to help us reconnect ourselves in our own way with our common Source as underlying Reality.

The third related idea is that we are now entering a new kind of *cognitive revolution*. *Cognitive* simply means knowing. I could have said "information revolution," but that phrase has been most recently associated with the computers, programs, and data bases instrumental in perpetuating the current materialist-oriented consensus reality in contradistinction to channeling, which seems to presage the transformation of that reality. By *cognitive revolution,* I mean simply that we human beings appear, through the processes of channeling, to be becoming more able to access the larger, Universal Mind at will. The membranes between our subpersonality, or spirit, selves and the larger Mind or Spirit that we exist within are growing more permeable. Thus we seem able to talk with one another more easily across kinds of consciousness and dimensions of reality, as well as to talk with the parent Mind. What we were previously unconscious of is entering our individual consciousnesses in a variety of ways and in the forms of a variety of other subpersonalities.

"Each of us," wrote Aldous Huxley in his *Doors of Perception,* "is potentially Mind at Large."[68] A "space brother" tells us: "[Your] vibration or frequency is the only important part of your being, since it is an index of your consciousness with respect to the original thought." When any one of what I am calling the subpersonalities "is aware of life in its infinite sense, he is also aware of the benefits of matching this vibration of the original thought of the Creator."[69] As the source of channel Ken Carey's book *Vision* puts it:

> My intelligence encircles the Earth in a band of spiritual frequencies that daily increase in amplitude. You need only to turn your heart in my direction, be still and listen. In love, you shall receive my intelligence. The more you love, the more you will understand. The shift back to internal guidance has begun. Truth is penetrating human minds and hearts. Broken and intermittent contact is increasingly giving way to a true sharing of intelligence, a true sharing of wisdom between Creator and Creation.[70]

This internal guidance is emphasized over and over within the recent channeled material. This would fit our metaphor that in our heart of hearts we are at one with our source identity, and that our higher Self is just another term for our consciousness as it blends back into the Universal Mind from which it arose and within which it is sustained. So we are told to trust the Universal Mind within each of us; for are we not that very Mind beneath the delusional and dissociated conditions of our subpersonality wave patterns and perspectives?

The group-being "Michael" counsels us that "the correct source is within you, in the soul that is eternal. That is your only source of assistance in the physical plane or any other."[71] "Seth's" variation on the theme is that "the answers to the nature of reality, the intimate knowledge of All That Is that you seek, *is* within your present experience. It will not be found outside of yourself, but through an inner journey into your self, *through* yourself."[72]

The cognitive revolution means that each of us, by reason of our being subpersonality wave patterns (or spirits) of the one Brain/Mind (or Spirit), can potentially and at will access the "data base" of All That Is. How to do this? Again, in "Seth's" terms, it is

> an ability to look inward, to concentrate deeply, to lose the sharp edges of the physically-oriented self in contemplation, and an intense desire to learn. These must be coupled with the inner confidence that pertinent knowledge can be directly received. To those who believe that all answers are known, there is little need to search . . . There is a fine impatience, a divine discontent that drives them on until the frontiers within their own personalities are finally opened . . . The energy generated by some such experiences is enough to change a life in a matter of moments, and to affect the understanding and behavior of others. These are intrusions of knowledge from one dimension of activity to another.[73]

FOUR
THE POTENTIAL

9
OPEN
CHANNELING

St. Teresa, by her relationship to the beloved of the soul, had a lensing system that permitted her to gain access to a certain kind of knowledge. I think of Einstein, who by virtue of his relationship to Being Itself and to subtle and very abstract concepts of God, was given the creative potency to be able to screen through a whole different relationship to the whole nature and structure of the universe. The lensing system that one has, that is often culturally conditioned, allows one to create those particular archetypal structures that will be certain kinds of information.

—JEAN HOUSTON[1]

Could we each have our own version of what Houston calls a lensing system to focus extaordinary information and experience out of the ground of the one Being? I believe so, although we are not all using it, or at least not using it in a way to get anything extraordinary in return. The theme of this chapter, and of the remainder of this study, is that we each have a relationship to the larger ground of Being; what we focus out of it is up to each of us.

So far in this book, we have for the most part explored *classic* channeling, which is said to involve supposedly identifiable nonphysical or other paranormal sources from outside the channel. In Houston's sense, the channels' lensing systems in these cases focus into expression individual beings, beings other than the kind most of us are used to. Although polls cited earlier reflect that the majority of us have reported some kind of contact with the deceased or with other paranormal information sources, classic channeling involves a small percentage of the population on an ongoing basis. But there is one form of channeling that is arguably a *universal* experience, occurring within the mainstream of our everyday lives: open channeling.

Open channeling may include intuition, inspiration, and aspects of the creative process. Due to the acknowledged universality of these notions, we can see channeling along a continuum—from the most exotic classic kind (parataxic) to the most ordinary, everyday sort (syntaxic)—with each human being, to varying degrees, an open channel.

Open channeling is the ability to act as a vehicle for thoughts, images, feelings, and information coming from a source that is beyond the individual's self and from beyond ordinary reality (as we know them)—*a source that is not identifiable and does not identify itself.* Open channeling occurs in an apparently ordinary way, with none of the uncontrolled, alien sensations usually attributed to other channeling phenomena.

According to Earl Babbie, many of the classically channeled entities he has interviewed share the following view of open channeling:

> A lot of the entities say that much of their purpose is simply to train us to use our intuition and creativity—that we have all this material available to us, and we're not using it and not trusting it. And their purpose, they say, is to get us more in touch with that so that we're not getting dependent on entities, but are learning to trust our own intuition.[2]

Los Angeles author and channel Alan Vaughan refers to this having taken place with his own entity, "Li-Sung": "He showed me how to channel my own higher Self with its higher levels of creativity—something that everyone can learn."[3]

Intuition and creativity are the two most universal kinds of open channeling. Intuition, although it is an interaction with larger Being, is a more passive and receptive process, while creativity is more active and inventive. But, as we shall see, it's not so easy to keep these two interrelated phenomena distinct, or to exclude the closely related notions of insight, inspiration, and imagination.

What is crucial for the remainder of this chapter is to weigh the importance of these processes and their fruits in light of our universal need to solve pressing problems. The human mind has unlimited resources from which to draw. Although intuition and creativity have long been associated by some with whim and fancy and have been considered as playthings of the leisure class, these topics need to be explored in a more serious light. For now as never before, our collective quality of life depends on our best intuitions.

Keep in mind the following questions in an effort to account for the ultimate source of intuitions and creative expressions: Is the source of creativity and imagination within our unconscious minds, or is it external to us? Is it "the God within," or our own mental raw material? Or is it divine inspiration from without, divine or otherwise? Is intuition some kind of resonance with ideals, forms, fields, or records that lie within us? Outside of us? Or both? Or are our usual concepts of *inner* and *outer* antiquated and in need of being replaced by some kind of unified field theory that would unify individual mind with Universal Mind, as suggested in the previous chapter?

In investigating open channeling, we must try to leave behind the outdated notion that we are closed systems. The knowledge from several academic disciplines tells us that we are relatively open systems, some of us more so than others. Being an open system means that we are capable of mediating energies and information from outside our local systems in ways that Freud's closed psychodynamic model of the psyche, for example, would not tolerate. By open channeling, we might say, we can drink from larger waters than our own.

In the physics section of chapter 8, we explored the process of physicalizing the mental. Here we will reverse the approach and try to *mentalize the physical.* Consider a first step taken by author-researcher John White as he makes some conjectures based on Edgar Cayce's channeled idea that "thoughts are things." White writes:

> Thoughts are things—real but non-physical energy configurations, produced by human consciousness, that exist objectively in space outside the human beings who produce them . . . A thought form is the energetic embodiment of an idea . . . Thought activity extends beyond the physical body, partaking of a "field of mind" surrounding the planet and extending into space for an unspecified distance. This mind field is composed of the collective experiences of the human race—our thoughts, feelings, and actions . . . Thoughts of a similar nature tend to coalesce over time, to gather into what could be called thought fields . . . People may "receive" from the planetary mind field . . . as well as "give."[4]

Expanding this point of view, we might see our bodies and the body of the planet as merely more dense, coalesced thoughtforms. The "ether" from which everything is made, in this world view, is living, knowing *mind,* rather than a physical wave system. We would live within a vast Universal Mind, which some call God. As British astronomer Sir James Jeans put it, the universe seems more like a great thought than a great machine. Fellow astronomer Sir Arthur Eddington concurred: "The stuff of the universe is mind stuff."

If all is Mind, then everything outside the scope of individual conscious mind is part of its unconscious. The rest of the universe could be likened to the collective unconscious—temporarily inaccessible but theoretically available as part of the one Mind in which we participate.

From this point of view, open channeling would mean individual awareness gaining access to its potentiality by becoming more aware of itself, like a leak of the larger Mind into the local minds (like author Joseph Chilton Pearce's "Crack in the Cosmic Egg"). The question arises, Does the larger Mind leak into us or do we leak into it? Entire philosophies address this issue—and probably, in the end, will find it unanswerable.

As transpersonal psychologist Ken Wilber put it in a recent interview with me:

> The idea is that ultimately there is only one consciousness, or one source of consciousness, and it's taking on various stepped-down versions of itself in all these other dimensions of reality. So when I say "one of the unidentified sources of channeling"—when somebody gets an inspiration or influx and it's not identified—I think that can be a transcendental source being translated into language. And I think that does happen. I think it's very close to artistic inspiration.[5]

Of course, we need not turn to such extreme picturizations to explain open channeling. It may be *merely* the product of the unconscious.

Let us now examine how the notion of open channeling, within a context of all-as-one-Mind, works in relation to three basic contexts: intuition, creativity and the arts, and spiritual experience.

INTUITION AND CREATIVITY

> Intuition is the vehicle that moves you closer to God/Goddess/All That Is, and it is the fuel that propels that vehicle as well. Your job is to discover yourself, becoming ever more of God/Goddess/All That Is.
>
> —the channeled entity "Lazaris"[6]

> If we open to these sources of inspiration and creativity, we open a window to a universe that is going to be becoming better. Someone once asked me about which model of the universe I favored. I said, "To hell with the model, let's just channel the universe. Let's become one with it. That way we don't have to play little games."
>
> —channel Alan Vaughan[7]

What is referred to as channeling might be one of the means by which some types of creativity take place. Channeling may also be one of the means by which an intuitive judgment could occur. It

will be easier to study the interface of channeling and human cognition if more research is conducted on the channeling *process* with
less speculation about the nature of the purported entity whose
message is channeled.

—psychologist Stanley Krippner[8]

Intuition

Those of us who may not call ourselves channels, psychics, or mystics
may still consider ourselves capable of acting as open channels by way of
intuition. *Webster's Third New International Dictionary* defines intuition as
"the act or process of coming to direct knowledge or certainty without
reasoning or inferring: immediate cognizance or conviction without rational thought: revelation by insight or innate knowledge." All of us, at
some time and to some degree, are intuitive.

"I call intuition cosmic fishing," wrote the late inventor R. Buckminster Fuller. "You feel a nibble, then you have to hook the fish."[9]
Again the question arises, What is the nature of the fishing hole from
which intuition draws?

Besides bypassing normal thought processes of inference and reason, intuition is also thought to bypass normal senses. There is debate
among leading researchers as to whether intuition is a kind of extrasensory perception. Frances Vaughan claims, in *Awakening Intuition,* that
"ESP, clairvoyance, and telepathy are part of the intuitive process."[10]
Philip Goldberg, author of *The Intuitive Edge,* writes, "Telepathy and
clairvoyance are not intuition; they are ways of bringing in information
that intuition may work on."[11] Many so-called psychics prefer to call
themselves intuitives or sensitives.

We know that we get hunches from intuition that seem suddenly to
appear to consciousness. For the individual mind there is a differentiated something that presents itself out of undifferentiatedness. Figure
arises out of ground, so to speak. We think objectively that we can know
only the figure; perhaps intuition can know the *ground* as well. In this
sense, intuition tends to involve knowing in terms of essences or wholes
rather than particulars, and as a result may have a rather ineffable quality
to it. Perhaps direct knowing of, or by way of, this ground, these essences,
has something to do with Bohm's earlier idea of the multidimensional
ground that is "in a certain sense enfolded in our consciousness."

Most cultures have had their version of the mythic Pierian spring,
which gave instant knowledge and wisdom to those who drank from it.
Intuition is often considered veridical—connected to or providing direct knowledge of basic reality. As Frances Vaughan puts it, "Intuition is

true by definition. If a seemingly intuitive insight turns out to be wrong, it did not spring from intuition, but from self-deception or wishful thinking."[12] This reputed directness often involves the sensation of being united with that which one has intuitively experienced. There is an apparent transcending of the old distinction between self and other, subject and object. This is sometimes referred to as knowledge by identity, or knowing by becoming identical with the known. Here we have, perhaps, the deliciously convoluted concept of "drinking from larger waters" that we are, so to speak, at sea within, and out of which we are made.

Such was the view of the Greek philosopher Plotinus. "This [intuition]," he wrote, "is absolute knowledge founded on the identity of the mind with the object known."[13] We find much the same idea in the translation of the ancient Chinese philosopher Seng-t'sam: "In the higher realm of true suchness/ There is neither 'self' nor 'other':/ When direct identification is sought,/ We can only say, 'Not two.' "[14] Similarly, the Indian scripture *Chandogya Upanishad* tells us: "An invisible and subtle essence is the spirit of the whole universe. That is reality. That is truth. *Thou art that.*"[15]

From a somewhat different perspective, Buddha believed that intuition, not reason, was the source of ultimate truth, and because the Buddha Nature is in all things, including oneself, self-transcendence by intuition is, at the same time, self-discovery of an ever-larger order.

As the modern Indian philosopher Sri Aurobindo wrote, "Intuitive knowledge is a lightning flashed from the silence and all is there, not higher or deeper, in truth, but just there, under our very eyes, awaiting our becoming a little clear. It is not so much a matter of raising oneself as of clearing obstructions."[16]

What might allow for this direct connection to, or oneness with, the object of intuition? Again, the holographic model suggests that the whole may be distributed in wave forms throughout its parts, and each part may be on a connected wave relation with each other part *and* with the whole. I am suggesting, further, that we try trading in the waves of the hologram for the waves of living mind.

Another key element in intuition is *receptivity*. For Frances Vaughan, "a noninterfering, alert awareness maintained in the midst of the inner world . . . is the key to expanding intuition."[17] In Patanjali's *Yoga Sutras,* we are told that one must make one's self as still and clear as a crystal in order to experience unadulteratedly that which lies beyond oneself.

The philosopher Rene Descartes wrote:

Intuitive knowledge is an illumination of the soul, whereby it beholds in the light of God those things which it pleases Him to reveal to us by a direct impression of divine clearness in our understanding, which in this is not considered as an agent but only as receiving the rays of divinity.[18]

F. W. H. Myers emphasized the quality of genius potential in all of us, which is able to receive "the vague supernormal content of moments of inspiration." This "inspiration of genius," he wrote, "will be in truth a subliminal uprush, an emergence into the current of ideas which the man is consciously manipulating of other ideas which he has not consciously originated, but which have shaped themselves beyond his will, in profounder regions of his being."[19]

Yet that which proves to be the raw "first draft" of intuition must be "edited down" in order to find what, if anything, is useful and meaningful in it. In this respect, each of us is a creative artist whose seeds of intuition must be nurtured and pruned in order to bear fruit.

Discernment is called for, whether the intuited material comes from one's own unconscious or from beyond oneself. One must look the gift horse in the mouth in each case in which the gift is not clearly accurate or useful, and one must do this regardless of source. We were told earlier by many of the channeled sources not to accept messages just because of their seeming otherworldly status. Test what we tell you against experience and weigh it within, they said. The same holds true with intuition as a form of open channeling.

In addition, Philip Goldberg warns us that what we call intuition may be only unconscious inference, reaction to subliminal stimuli, impulsiveness, imagination, rebelliousness, intellectual laziness, uncertainty, or simple emotion. Further, the person most susceptible to "intuition" may be the one most likely to "make things up."[20]

Creativity

Open channeling has two sides: Intuition is the relatively passive reception of knowledge from an unknown source. Creativity is a more active process of seeming to *make up* something that did not exist before. To create is, according to Webster: "To bring into existence; to make out of nothing and for the first time; to cause to be; to produce . . . along new or unconventional lines."

Creativity requires a process that allows something new to be created in the world, either a generation of new information or a recombining of existing information with a new result. Novelty, according to creativity experts, however, is relative. Some make a distinction between *discovery* and *invention*. Discovery implies the uncovering of something that had been in existence but had been hidden; while invention brings into existence something that did not exist before. Intuition may better fit discovery; creativity, invention. Yet invention, too, may be discovery.

Philosopher Huston Smith wrestles with some of the difficulties that arise from thinking about the creative process:

> Channeling assumes the arrival of information from discarnates who already possess that information. Creative insights do not require this assumption. The novel thought or hypothesis simply emerges. Today "emergence" is widely invoked as an explanation of how novelty takes place. It is doubtful that it does actually explain the occurrence; the word looks more like a verbal fig leaf to cover our ignorance. How something that has no existence at all can acquire existence is so totally mysterious that it seems more reasonable to assume that somehow, in some way, it existed in advance. It arrives, not from nowhere, but from a different quarter.[21]

This "different quarter" may be one of the bands of the spectrum of being discussed in chapter 8. Or creativity may be the way part of the Universal Mind, perhaps under some kind of amnesia, accesses awakening material from elsewhere in itself, all within the ubiquity of the one Being.

Plato was one of the earliest thinkers to conjecture that when we make or experience something new to us, we are only remembering something that we already knew but had forgotten. For Plato this explained why "we know more than we should." He wrote, "The soul, then, as being immortal, and having been born again many times, and having seen all things that exist, whether in this world or in the world below, has knowledge of them all."[22]

The channeled literature repeats, in many forms, the idea that we are co-creators with God. That is, we create our own reality. On the physical and ego levels, we have forgotten our true nature and the true nature of the multileveled spiritual universe. But, we are told, the higher Self has not forgotten and is at one with these larger truths; and often it is the higher Self that lets us know this.

The sources tell us it is meaningless to think we can create something out of nothing, because the universe *is* the living mind of God. So, they say, we all have access to the same source and are parts of the one God, the source of all creativity. By our respective individual creativity, we are the way God has individuated itself to experience itself and explore its creative possibilities. All life, the sources say, is an exploration of the infinite possibilities within and of the one "house of many mansions."

However we define creativity, it still—like intuition—requires *verification*. The individual must always weigh and test, adjust and adapt what flows from the creative process in order to see what fits, works, or means something. In the end, creativity must do good in daily life.

One of thousands of striking examples of the benefits gained from creative open channeling is the case of Chester Carlson, inventor of xerographic copying and founder of the Xerox Company. He believed that the information for his development of the photocopying process "came from the spirit realm." He wrote:

> I early learned not to anticipate the source from which verifications would come because the conscious, logical mind was usually wrong when it tried to interfere with an area of the deeper self which seemed to know more than this so-called "logical" mind. I early learned that paranormal experiences flowed more easily and with less distortion when body and mind could serve as an open, unobstructed channel without interference from preconceived notions or opinions.[23]

THE CREATIVE ARTIST

All the research we did with artists in channeling the creative process showed us that you reach levels where it's interesting that the experience of the artist and the experience of the religious figure become almost indistinguishable from each other.
—Robert Masters[24]

I have contended that we are all capable of being open channels because of the universality of the creative process. Therefore, it may be useful to look at the testimonies of creative artists to better understand our potential in this area. While intuition fits the image of drinking from the Pierian spring,[25] the creative artist has the equally time-honored muse: goddesslike helper, midwifing new creation into being, or simply an anonymous inspirational spirit that guides the creative process. We each have the spring and the muse available to us. Indeed, they may be one and the same.

Let me begin with myself as a witness. What can I possibly say in a few sentences that can do justice to thirty years of actively courting and immersing myself in the creative process? As I said in the introduction to this book, for a good part of my life I was primarily a poet and visual artist. I have had my own version of virtually every one of the experiences described in the next few pages. I have had the wondrous goose-bumpy sensation of being gifted, over and over, from a living presence that is beyond me yet seems to well up from within me. I've been humbled under the onslaught of images, thoughts, and words coming so fast, like heady wine splashing into the chalice of me, that I have over-flowed at times and even "lost my mind" entirely for stretches of my life. My system has streamed with incoming energies in a kind of extra-dimensional intercourse where I have felt that something has made love to me, and I am left weeping and in love, with the seeds of new creation growing in me. Yes, I can attest to the reality, for me, of what I have defined as open channeling.

Poets and Writers

As Percy Shelley, the nineteenth-century Romantic poet, describes, "Man is an instrument over which a series of external and internal impressions are driven, like the alterations of an ever-changing wind over an Aeolian lyre. It is as if the lyre could accommodate its chords to the motions of that which strikes them." This may remind us of the vibration concepts of rhythmic entrainment and resonance explored in the physics section of chapter 8. Perhaps Shelley referred only to normal environmental stimuli and "internal impressions" from the personal unconscious. However, he added, "A poet participates in the eternal, the infinite, and the one."[26]

In the *Republic*, Plato claimed, "All good poets composed their beautiful poems not by art, but because they are inspired and possessed. There is no invention in him until he has been inspired and is out of his senses." And, again, from Plato:

> And for this reason God takes away the minds of these men [poets] and uses them as his ministers, just as he does soothsayers and goodly seers in order that we who hear them may know that it is not they who utter these words of great price when they are out of their wits, but that it is God Himself who speaks and addresses us through them.[27]

The English poets Samuel Taylor Coleridge and William Blake con-cur. Coleridge experienced imagination as "a repetition in the finite mind of the eternal act of creation in the infinite I AM. Imaginative man is a creator; through him God creates and knows and loves."[28] Blake claimed: "The eternal body of man is the imagination, that is, God Himself . . . It manifests itself in his works of art."[29]

Some writers report feeling as if they are engaged in something like automatic writing or taking clairaudient dictation. Novelist Robert Louis Stevenson, for example: "The whole of my published fiction should be the single-handed product of some unseen collaborator." Stevenson believed that he was often aided in his writing by an "unseen collaborator," that he was in communication with what he called "my brownies . . . the little people," and that he was given the plot for his novel *The Strange Case of Dr. Jekyll and Mr. Hyde* in his dreams.[30] In his *Roundabout Papers,* English novelist William Thackeray wrote, "I have been surprised at some of the observations made by some of my characters. It seems as if an occult power was moving the pen."[31]

Poet Amy Lowell described the occasional trancelike state of her creative process. "I do not hear a voice," she recalled, "but I do hear words pronounced, only the pronouncing is toneless. The words seem to be pronounced in my head, but with nobody speaking them." She used a now-familiar analogy: "A poet is something like a radio aerial: he is capable of receiving messages on waves of some sort; but he is more than the aerial, for he possesses the capacity of transmuting these messages into those patterns of words we call poems."[32]

Often the writer can feel overwhelmed. "It was something that took hold of me and possessed me," novelist Thomas Wolfe wrote. "It was exactly as if this great black storm cloud had opened up and, amid flashes of lightning, was pouring from its depth a torrential and ungovernable flood. And I was borne along with it."[33] Similarly, writer-philosopher Friedrich Nietzsche told of receiving the material that was to become *Thus Spake Zarathustra* in one of these uncontrollable floods of creative inspiration. "It invaded me," he wrote. "One can hardly reject completely the idea that one is the mere incarnation, or mouthpiece, or medium of some almighty power . . . One takes; one does not ask who gives. A thought flashes out like lightning, inevitably without hesitation. I have never had a choice about it."[34]

A few years ago, author Marilyn Ferguson met R. Buckminster Fuller, who told her he had been reading her book *The Aquarian Conspiracy* half the night. "You know," he said, "the spirits of the dead helped you write that book." "I laughed," she recalled, "and I said, 'Well, I sometimes thought so, but I wasn't about to tell anybody.' "[35]

Many other contemporary writers and speakers also describe what might generically be called inspirational writing and inspirational speaking: a kind of relatively unthinking, spontaneous, improvisational flow of discourse that doesn't seem to be coming from the usual place we experience normal writing or speaking as coming from. Jose Stevens's description in chapter 7 of his teaching experience is a good example of this. I, too, have experienced this is a great deal during the last ten years in my own teaching as well as in regular conversation.

Finally, prize-winning poet James Merrill has incorporated material received through the Ouija board into his recent works. Here he describes a kind of co-creator view of how he gets his "figures":

In a sense, all these figures are our creation . . . The powers they represent are real—as, say, gravity is "real"—but they'd be invisible, inconceivable, if they'd never passed through our heads and clothed themselves out of the costume box they found there. *How* they appear depends on us, on the imaginer, and would have to vary wildly from culture to culture, or even temperament to temperament.[36]

Musicians, Dancers, and Artists

The composer Johannes Brahms thought that on occasion he was "in tune with the Infinite." Brahms also said that in the composing process, "when I feel the urge I begin by appealing directly to my Maker. I immediately feel vibrations which thrill my whole being. In this exalted state I see clearly what is obscure in my ordinary moods." He continued, "I have to be in a semitrance condition to get results, a condition when the conscious mind is in temporary abeyance." On another occasion, he wrote: "Straight away the ideas flow in upon me, directly from God . . . measure by measure, the finished product is revealed to me when I am in those rare, inspired moods."[37] Similarly, the Russian composer Pyotr Ilich Tchaikovsky confided, "I forget everything and behave like a madman. Everything within me starts pulsing and quivering."[38]

Composer Richard Strauss described a similar experience: "While the ideas were flowing in upon me, the entire musical, measure by measure, it seemed to me that I was dictated to by two wholly different Omnipotent Entities." Strauss described the feeling of "being aided by more than an earthly Power."[39] Giacomo Puccini believed that his great opera *Madame Butterfly* "was dictated to me by God; I was merely instrumental in putting it on paper."[40] Gustav Mahler claimed, "I don't choose what I compose: it chooses me."[41] And Ludwig van Beethoven concluded that "music is the mediator between the life of the senses and the life of the spirit."[42]

Contemporary composers have reported their own versions of the inception of the creative process, which we're calling open channeling. American composer George Gershwin described how, riding on a train to Boston and under pressure to complete *Rhapsody in Blue,* "I suddenly heard, even saw on paper, the complete construction of the *Rhapsody,* from beginning to end."[43]

Operetta composer Rudolf Friml described his experience: "I sit down at the piano, and I put my hands on the piano. And I let the spirit guide me! No, I never do the music. I never compose it; oh no, no! I am a tool. I am nothing. I am being used. It comes from someone, a spirit perhaps, using me."[44] Harlan Howard, composer of hundreds of country and western songs, thought he could not really take credit for his hit song "The Blizzard." "The pencil kept on moving and I didn't know how it would end. Did some great song-writer in the sky use me as a medium?"[45]

The late Jesse Shepart, born in England and raised in the United States, began at age nineteen to do a kind of spontaneous piano playing, an automatism of the musical keyboard. Throughout his highly successful tours of Europe, it was reported that he played musical improvisations "unlike anything in the world." After a particularly entranced (and entrancing) performance, one critic wrote, "Something more than sound issued from that piano . . . I felt there was an image that wanted to break through, a consciousness of some mighty presence."[46]

Northern California New Age music composer Steven Halpern recalls: "Amongst the redwoods, I very clearly heard this music—what sounded like *Spectrum Suite* [what would later be his first major published work]—and I heard instruments that had not been invented then and I was basically told this is what you're supposed to work with." He remembers, "It was not a voice, but it was knowing." Then, "I started recording what I received in trance or altered states." Halpern concludes, "I had known that there should be music that would help and heal. I ended up being guided."[47]

In her book *Sacred Dance: Encounter with the Gods,* Maria-Gabriele Wosien conducts a sociohistorical study of the roots of dance in which she echoes many of the themes of open channeling. In Hindu mythology, for example, the creation of the world is the dance of God in the form of Shiva Nataraja, Lord of the Dance. Once the cosmological dance begins, everything is vibration, throughout Creation. All *human* dance is the communing with larger realities, ultimately with God, in an attuning to and expression of the *universal* dance. One must give oneself to the dance, Wosien says, for it is an identification with the manifestations of Divinity. "Through his ecstatic dance-journey to the beyond," she describes a shaman dancer, "he achieves communion with the supernatural. The meeting with the other world is the result of an expansion of consciousness."[48] Although the great Russian dancer Nijinsky went mad in the throes of this kind of experience, many improvisational dancers today can identify with Wosien's description.

Many visual artists, too, have reported receiving anomalous visual information as part of the creative process. They see visionary material, they say, which serves as the model for the mind's eye. These nonphysical models inform and inspire their creation; however, we cannot know for certain their source.

Two of the greatest twentieth-century painters have been the Russian-born abstractionist Wassily Kandinsky and the Spanish surrealist Salvador Dali. Drawing on Rene Thom's concept from the last chapter, we might see these men as allowing themselves to undergo some kind of loosening-up "catastrophe" in consciousness that would leave them open to the influence of transcendent "attractors." "Everything 'dead' trembled," Kandinsky recalled, "not only the stars, moon, woods, flowers of which the poets sing, but also a cigarette butt lying in the ashtray . . . everything shows me its face, its innermost being, its secret soul, which is more often silent than heard."[49] And Dali lived for "the moment when delirious instantaneity is produced" by an "active, systematic . . . cognizant attitude to irrational phenomena."[50]

There are hundreds of examples in which an artist derives inspiration, guidance, and subject matter apparently from beyond his normal self or from some other level of reality. For example, some paint pictures of nonphysical worlds and beings they claim to have seen with the mind's eye, including science fiction and fantasy-type scenes, UFOs and Atlantean landscapes, as well as fairies, elves, plant devas, angels, and other spiritual beings. Today these artists are labeled visionary. Other artists report going into altered (parataxic) states of consciousness in order to receive their images or to open themselves to some degree of automatic painting.

RECEIVING SPIRITUAL EXPERIENCE

He [my guru] asked me to pray, but I could not pray. He replied that it did not matter, he and some others would pray and I had simply to go to the meeting . . . and wait and speech would come to me from some other source than the mind [I did as I was told].

The speech came as though it was dictated, and ever since all speech, writing, thought and outward activity have so come to me from the same source.

—Sri Aurobindo[51]

I will call this higher part of the universe by the name of God. We and God have business with each other; and in opening ourselves to his influence our deepest destiny is fulfilled.

—William James[52]

It is God which worketh in you both to will and to do of his good pleasure.

—Phil. 2:13

He that believeth in me, from him shall flow rivers of living water.

—John 7:38

There is a deep need in the world just now for guidance—almost any sort of spiritual guidance.

—C. G. Jung

Open channeling of the spiritual kind involves receiving knowledge or understanding, ineffable though it may be, which includes the sense of revelation and the uplifting of one's spirit, and feelings of oneness with the Universe and all it is. Although most of us don't normally think of ourselves as channels for spiritual or religious thought, this phenomenon is obviously closely allied with inspiration and intuition, which we all possess. Moreover, most of us will admit to having felt some sense of reverence or spiritual uplift at some time. So it is really only a matter of degree.

In chapter 5 we discussed God as a reported source of classic channeling. Typically this experience is characterized by a personal flavor: God as an individual communicating his word to the channel. For purposes of this book, however, spiritual *open* (as opposed to *classical*) channeling can be seen as a more diffuse, mystic affair, a communication with the absolute, impersonal aspect of God. To channel the "Christ consciousness," "Buddha wisdom," "God's love," or the "all-knowing light," for example, is not simply to be irradiated by some kind of cosmic rays. Rather, the channeled literature implies, such spiritual channeling opens one's mind to larger Mind, one's heart to larger Heart, and one's spirit to larger Spirit. The result is reported to be some degree of enlightenment, direct knowing, or uplifting that involves spirit as well as mind.

The word *religion* comes from *ligio,* meaning to tie, and *re-,* meaning back. Religion, then, is a way of tying ourselves back into something from which we have disconnected. Spiritual open channeling might be the term for the actual experience of this personal reconnectedness, this celestial umbilical cord between the self of the individual and the Self of God. Personal *meaning* must be a crucial ingredient of such experience. Apparently this meaningful experience of tying back in is more widespread than some might think. In a recent poll, 35 percent of Americans said they had had a "mystic experience" at some point in their lives.[53] (And recall the polls cited earlier: 71 percent believe in life after death;

94 percent believe in God or some Universal Spirit; 69 percent feel guided by this God; and 36 percent claim God has communicated to them.)

Spiritual open channeling, of course, is really only a new term for an age-old process that runs throughout world religions and spiritual practices. A few other terms for this process: *Afflatus* is a divine imparting of knowledge or power; a supernatural or overmastering impulse. *Effulgence* is the strong radiant light, the glorious splendor so often reported in mystical and transcendental ecstatic states, as well as in near-death and out-of-body experiences. This light is often described as possessing and conveying an all-knowingness. *Sufflation* is the breath of divine inspiration, which creates the feeling of being overshadowed by spiritual presence and absorbing from it a heightened awareness and understanding. *Revelation* involves divine impartings, gifts, and blessings to us. *Prayer* and *communion* involve the ability to communicate with a self-transcending spiritual presence.

William James, in *The Varieties of Religious Experience,* and Richard Bucke, in *Cosmic Consciousness,* each made the point that, as ineffable as spiritual experiences have tended to be, many of the individuals involved were able to articulate at least an approximation of what occurred. Therefore we can compare and contrast their descriptive self-reports. When we do, these authors said, we see a remarkable similarity among the experiences described. This allows us to make an argument for a degree of subjective consensual validation of this reality.

In his recent book *Opening to Inner Light,* Ralph Metzner, dean of San Francisco's California Institute of Integral Studies and a pioneer in research on spirituality and consciousness, must have been inspired himself when he described "the greater multidimensional tree of life energy and wisdom, the divine foundation and axis of our physical and spiritual life . . . whose crown reaches up to the heights and absorbs into itself the radiating energy essence of light, awareness and spirit."[54]

In one of the Stuart Edward White books of channeled material published forty years ago, one of the "Invisibles" says through the channel:

A human being can be, according to his own desire, unaware of life forces passing through him in which he is immersed, but he can also voluntarily incorporate himself with them . . . The sensation of being in this spiritual blood stream pouring on earth conditions is not to be contained in words. I long intensely to work out for you some concept of the spiritual blood stream. It has always been inadequately screened by the word "God."[55]

Finally, here is how two of the giants in this field chose to end their major works. In the closing words of F. W. H. Myers's *Human Personality and Its Survival of Bodily Death:*

> We are standing then at a crisis of enormous importance in the history of life on earth. The spiritual world is just beginning to act systematically upon the material world . . . In this complex of interpenetrating spirits our own effort is no individual, no transitory thing. That which lies at the root of each of us lies at the root of the Cosmos too. Our struggle is the struggle of the Universe itself; and the very Godhead finds fulfillment through our upward-striving souls.[56]

Evelyn Underhill concludes her great effort, *Mysticism: A Study in the Nature and Development of Man's Spiritual Consciousness:*

> When the "new birth" takes place in him, the new life-process of his deeper self begins, the normal individual, no less than the mystic, will know that spiral ascent toward higher levels, those odd mental disturbances, abrupt invasions from the subconscious region, and disconcerting glimpses of truth, which accompany the growth of transcendental powers . . . Only by this deliberate fostering of his deepest self, this transmutation of his character, can he reach those levels of consciousness upon which he hears, and responds to, the measure "whereto the worlds keep time" on their great pilgrimage toward the Father's heart . . . The story of man's spirit ends in a garden: . . . Divine Fecundity is its secret: existence, not for its own sake, but for the sake of a more abundant life.[57]

Today we are faced with much that is stale, stuck, or constrained, both inside and outside of us. Personal and global problems abound. Many are searching for a deeper meaning to their lives. Open channeling, through its connection to what many believe to be a spiritual source, and by its processes of intuitive insight and creative flow, can provide the very lifeblood of the new and helpful for us, if we will only allow it in ourselves.

In the next, final, chapter we will explore ways in which to experience both classic and open channeling for ourselves.

10
YOUR TURN

If you are now willing to grant the possibility that channeling is part of a spectrum of abilities we may all possess, you may well be asking how you might attempt to tap into these abilities yourself.

If you prefer, however, you can use the suggestions here simply as a tool system with which to explore your own creativity, your own consciousness, and your own unconscious—without believing in the truth of any of the claims made on behalf of channeling throughout this book.

There is no one way to become a channel. Contemporary channels present a colorful array of different stories about how they began, what works best for them, and, if they teach channeling, what methods they use with their students. Nonetheless, certain patterns and common denominators emerge that will be highlighted in the subsections that follow. You are welcome to stop and taste them experientially as you go along, or to select your own combination to try later. The chapter will end with a series of examples that demonstrate approaches used by experienced teachers of channeling or related areas. You are also welcome to try these approaches for yourself. But remember, no two people are alike, and no two people learn best in quite the same way; nor do people experience things in the same way.

The steps involved in preparing for any kind of channeling are very similar to those associated with traditional meditation and spiritual practices throughout the world. They also reveal a close kinship to many approaches used in altering consciousness, to self-hypnosis, and to methods used for developing psychic abilities.

Both trance channel Jach Pursel and his source "Lazaris" separately tell us that channeling isn't for everyone; it just may not suit you at this point in your own development. You may require other kinds of inner and outer experience. Then again, you may be ripe for channeling. But even if you feel you are ready, know that patience and trust can be critical. Many channels report that it took years after they first desired to channel until they obtained positive results.

You may be comfortable with the concept of entities as discussed in the Introduction and chapter 5, or you may not. Entities need not enter into our thinking about, or into our own experience of, open channeling. Drinking from the larger waters that lie beyond us is strictly a matter of the relationship between us and those waters. Like religion, it is a personal matter, and, as Christ suggested, each of us can enter privately into our own form of communion with the larger Being, and then see what the result is. No need to posit other entities bobbing around out there sending us signals, if we don't want to.

Similarly, we should be able to feel that we can safely go alone to draw our inspirations from the starry night sky, or our fresh intuitive knowings from the Pierian spring that lies deep within us yet is connected to all other inner and outer being. And we can fill ourselves with the flow from the wellsprings of the creative muse that may have no more individuality than the sparkling ocean waves. In addition, if your desire is to tap new, deeper levels of yourself—higher Self or whatever else—feel free to do so. Universal Mind and the collective unconscious may also be at your disposal if you wish them. So remember, not everything you may be after, and not everything you may get, comes through the proverbial deceased loved one, spirit guide, angel, extraterrestrial, and so on.

If you do choose to try classic channeling, what or who can you expect to contact in your first attempts? Echoing speculations by many skeptics regarding the authenticity of the phenomenon, channel Alice A. Bailey provided the following data from her source, "the Tibetan." Two percent of the material purported to be channeled comes from "masters" to their disciples; 5 percent is from more advanced disciples in training on the inner planes; 8 percent is from the channels' own higher Selves or souls; and some 85 percent is from the personal subconscious of the channels.[1] Experienced channeling teachers, such as Canada's Joey Crinita, are the first to tell us that most of what novice channels think is channeling is rather the product of self-delusion brought on as a result of psychic immaturity. Or, through a kind of self-hypnosis, some so-called channeling is simply imagination creating its own characters.[2] Most of the material in chapter 7 echoes the same theme.

Therefore, much, if not all, of what you may be getting yourself into by attempting to channel is simply you—your own larger, inner creative unconscious—sometimes standing forth and speaking as what seems to be someone or something other than you. If this is so, then the primary prerequisite to all that follows is: know thyself. Hal Stone's technique, explained toward the end of this chapter, is one example of an approach that allows you to work on and learn the larger you as well as perhaps contact other sources through channeling.

DISCERNMENT

Virtually all channels and their sources tell us that *discernment*[3] is crucial. As inner information wells up, you may wish to be able to discriminate whether it is coming from the self or from elsewhere, and if from elsewhere, then from what or whom. While most conscious channels say they don't have a problem knowing when the thoughts, images, or sensations they experience are externally derived, many have said it took time for them to reach that point. Part of discernment, then, is learning what the truth feels like for you. In a kind of psychic biofeedback process, you learn at the same time what it feels like to experience a "miss" (self-generated but dissociated material)—which may be perfectly useful—as well as a "hit" (an authentic channeling experience). As California psychic and channel Anne Armstrong puts it:

> On a conscious level we begin to align ourselves with everything that is truth. By discrimination we learn to set aside that which is not truth to the best of our abilities. We move closer and closer to a pattern of alignment . . . So we must eventually cleanse the centers of all except that which registers the truth.[4]

Channel Laeh Maggie Garfield, co-author of *Companions in Spirit: A Guide to Working with Your Spirit Helpers,* describes some of the subtle phenomena that may be experienced accompanying the channeling process:

> You may hear your guide: your name spoken aloud, a line of song, a distinctive vocabulary and style of delivery. You may notice a characteristic scent, a whiff of tobacco or perfume, or perhaps a more subtle aromatic tone. You may feel a certain presence, much as you sense the vibration of someone coming up behind you. Or you may have an intuitive perception similar to that of entering a crowded room and knowing that somebody you love is in there somewhere.[5]

Others describe a variety of sensations: a coolness or tension in the air; a vibratory presence not normally felt; a sense of being brushed by a breeze; a lightness, numbness, tingling, glowing, or pressure in the head. Often there is a swooning sense of drifting away from normal consciousness with unfamiliar stimuli replacing familiar ones. Trance channels like Jach Pursel and Kevin Ryerson simply "go under," as if nodding off on cue. Ryerson describes it as a "falling *backward* into sleep." Such are the kinds of telltale sensations you must alert yourself to in order to learn which correlate with which experiences, channeling or otherwise.

Further, if channeling distinct entity-type personalities is involved, we are told that we need to discern the nature, quality, and trustworthiness of the source. As Pursel's entity "Lazaris" describes it, "People assume that if it's a channeled entity, then it's got to be speaking the truth, the highest truth . . . [but] there are good entities and bad entities, as far as the quality of information goes."[6] We must guard against the charisma of authority. As you have heard numerous times before, just because we may believe that information comes from some glamorous paranormal source, we should not fail to scrutinize its content and weigh our response to it as carefully as if it came from a more pedestrian source, such as a workshop leader or university lecturer.

Two well-known modern speakers in the United States, Judith Skutch and Marilyn Ferguson, quoted earlier, say that the questions most often asked of them when lecturing on New Age topics involve discernment. In her fifteen years of public speaking, Skutch says, the most common question has been, "How do you know what voice is speaking to you when you're asking for your inner voice to talk? How do you know if you should believe its guidance? Her answer, she says, is always the same: "Try it and see if it works. If it works for the better, you're going to be sure you want to follow it."[7] Similarly, Ferguson reports:

What people very often ask me is, "How do you know your intuition from impulse or wishful thinking?" We can learn many voices inside. To learn *the* voice is the secret, and here's where you have to be scientific. You really have to pay attention to which voice gets you into trouble.[8]

Pursel's channeled entity "Lazaris" proposes scrutinizing the messages from himself and other sources:

First, are the teachings limited? Are the teachings giving you the sense that you are less than you are? Second, can I apply this? Can I use this? What's it going to do for me? Third, as I apply what's being said, am I happier? Am I more myself and is my life working better? Fourth, when I come away from the experience, am I feeling and am I thinking more positively?[9]

Now that we have this tentative set of guidelines for responding to whatever it is that may result from trying to initiate channeling, we will proceed with some well-agreed-upon generic approaches, followed by a sampling of specific approaches.

PREPARING YOURSELF: BELIEFS AND ATTITUDES

To begin with, once again, follow the old adage: know yourself (as best you can). Center and ground yourself. Be open and honest. Ask yourself why you are seeking the channeling experience.

Your attitude is crucial. If you are serious, dedicated, and genuinely desirous of positive results, we are told, the chances are good for success. As noted parapsychologist Charles Tart points out, many different routes can lead to the same goal; it's a matter of positive thinking:

> Whenever someone has any kind of cognitive framework to legitimize what they do, they do it better than if it's meaningless. If you believe in quantum events collapsing in your brain and that makes it all right to be psychic, that will help you do it. If you believe that spirits do it, that'll help you do it. If you believe glial [nerve] cells do it, that'll help you do it. It's clear that when people believe in a theory, it's good for them in terms of mobilizing energy.[10]

At the same time, Tart's research into psychic development showed that some subjects were sometimes working at cross-purposes with themselves because of fear of their own psychic or channeling abilities. "On an unconscious level they're afraid of it, and so you get a funny kind of conflict going where you get very inconsistent kinds of results, results that are self-defeating in the long run. It's a way of being interested in it, trying to control it, but not facing its reality."[11] Clearly, if you want to try channeling, then you want to minimize being at cross-purposes with yourself.

Berkeley, California, psychologist Freda Morris, whose hypnosis training techniques have helped a number of her students develop into channels as a side effect, also emphasizes the role of belief:

> If you could just get to believing . . . The more you can really believe it's totally outside of you, not just your subconscious, the more remote you make it. Then it will more and more free you of your anxious ego concerns and you can get better and better advice.[12]

Try to channel for the highest good of all concerned, we are told.[13] Set out by being honest with yourself in your innermost soul.[14] Do not use the phenomenon for the sake of commercialism or self-aggrandize-ment.[15] It is suggested that we channel with the awareness that we are essentially spirits within the loving, learning ecology of an essentially spiritual, hierarchical universe. Also, while channeling, trust in life instead of focusing on communication with the dead, and bring as much as you can by your channeling back into the world for the benefit of real people and their (and your) struggle for meaning.

RAISING VIBRATIONS AND CLEANSING EMOTIONS

Like attracts like, the channels and sources tell us. "Where you are on the pathway, that is the nature you will attract to yourself," counsels the entity "Kuthumi."[16] To put ourselves in the best state from which to channel, we are told by many sources to raise our vibrations by focusing on the spiritual—to *be* spirit, not just body or ego. Identifying the self with the highest Self, the "I am" presence, the God within, is a common theme. Practice thinking of becoming coherent—every cell in phase with every other—a living human laser light of ever-purer, ever-higher frequency.

One suggestion is to imagine a dial attached to yourself with a calibrated gauge numbered one to ten. Then imagine starting with the indicator on "one." As the knob is slowly turned, it raises your vibratory rate, with each number indicating a tenfold increase. Feel the increase as the dial rises; see and feel yourself glowing ever-brighter, clearer, lighter, wiser, and more loving at each increment. Such exercises share common processes of self-suggestion and the self-modulation of one's energy system. However, we may wish to do this exercise in order to raise power, rather than vibratory rate. Bear in mind that the research of Jack Schwarz (chapter 8) suggests that, while we should raise the energy or amplitude of our brain waves, we should actually at the same time be *lowering* their frequency in order to access higher frequency or super-luminary sources.

Have your heart in the right place, as the saying goes. "Lift loving thoughts to us," one source counsels, "and we can return to you along the same energy pathway."[17] "Fear will attract that which is feared. A strong cocoon of love energy is vital," says another.[18] And a third: "Anyone covered with light and filled with the love vibration faces no danger in telepathic communication with the higher levels."[19] Still the emotional body; cleanse it with peace and love.[20]

Anne Armstrong prescribes: "Imagine the spiritual essence at the base of the spine. Begin to feel its warmth, because it is a flame." She then asks us to feel and trace this essence with our inner senses as it rises, spinning clockwise and counterclockwise around each chakra center. "In this process," she says, "we mentally burn away all the confusion, all the residue that has been stored in the spiritual centers by the thought patterns and stimuli we have allowed to invade our emotional body." We then can keep these centers cleansed and lower the likelihood of attracting unwanted, random emotional patterns.[21]

WORKING WITH YOUR PHYSICAL BODY

> Know ye not that ye are the temple of God and that the spirit of God dwelleth in you?
> —1 Cor. 3:16

The physical body is a central part of the channeling instrument. We are told that we should cleanse, purify, and ready the body as a worthy and unpolluted channel. Many of the sources stress good nutrition. Red meat, excess fats and sugars, alcohol, drugs, and tobacco, they say, slow the vibrations of the physical and subtle bodies. (Although, in many cultures, drugs and "teacher plants" are ingested in order to enter channeling states.)[22]

To relax the body also means to clear the mind. Different channels have different ways of relaxing. Most just will themselves to relax, to let go. As they relax and release, some, such as J. Z. Knight and Elwood Babbitt, claim to see a light in the mind's eye. They feel themselves drawn into it, going through a kind of tunnel. In this process of entering the light, they lose consciousness and enter the state necessary for trance channeling.

Be as comfortable as possible and close your eyes. Breathe deeply and slowly. Breath, many tell us, is very important. Practice deep abdominal breathing—drawing the breath into and exhaling it out of the lower body. Many people concentrate on the single object of each breath as part of focusing and quieting the noisy mind. Some suggest and imagine to themselves, for example, that with each exhalation there is a release of pent-up tensions and concerns, and with each inhalation there is a drawing in of golden vapors of loving light that infuse the body, causing it to glow, soften, and float.

San Francisco Bay Area trance channel Jon Fox asks us to be aware of "a brilliant star of white light at the center of your chest and to draw it in with each breath." He says that "by increasing this light that is your being, there is an interaction with greater numbers of the higher vibrational beings as well as interaction with your higher Self."[23]

Various muscle relaxation practices are espoused. Some follow Edmund Jacobson's progressive relaxation technique, which is used in various therapies, as a dependable approach to stress reduction and the altering of consciousness. In this version, one focuses on each muscle group, tensing and then totally relaxing it, moving progressively from toes to scalp. Others prefer to relax their bodies by repeating suggestive phrases and accompanying mental imagery, such as "my body is growing more and more relaxed."

GROUNDING

Los Angeles psychoenergetic researcher and former UCLA professor Valerie Hunt suggests a mental-imagery approach to working with the body's subtle-energy system in order to "ground" yourself prior to channeling or other psychic work:

Imagine that you can move your energy field, that as you breathe, your nose is down by your left foot. Breathe in through your left leg across the back at the hip level and down through the right leg, and you are grounding the electromagnetic field to gravity.[24]

Here is another grounding approach, by Petey Stevens of the Heartsong organization in Berkeley, California:

Place your attention in your pelvic cradle at the base of your spine. Now with every breath that you breathe in, postulate that you are drawing into your pelvic cradle long threads of golden energy. Reach into the very depths of your Soul for this energy. As these threads meet, they become fused into a long golden rope and rolled into a large ball. Feel the power and strength of that energy.[25]

Then, with each exhalation, imagine this gold ball dropping down so that "there is a golden energy beam from the base of your spine to the center of the Earth." According to Stevens, this grounding cord "is a statement of commitment to your Body, the Planet Earth and the reality you are experiencing."

As you proceed with channeling or other altered-state work, many teachers believe that grounding minimizes the chance of problematic disconnection from the body. Establishing this kind of grounding, together with seeking guidance and protection, forms the heart of preparation for channeling.

STILLING THE MIND AND LETTING GO OF THE EGO

Virtually all channeling practitioners tell us to *turn from the outer to the inner world* by ceasing to pay attention to external stimuli. Closing the eyes is usually the first step. *Still the mind*—the usually busy mind, running around in its small, automatic programs and preoccupations—in order to make it receptive to paranormal impressions and information from beyond itself. Do this by focusing on a single object or on the goal of consciousness without an object, or mind without content. Quieting the mind is very much interrelated with relaxing the body. As the inwardness and stillness grow, make yourself as positive, peaceful, and receptive as possible. Possess an "effortless intention to succeed."

The great German psychic and channel Rudolf Steiner suggests:

> Persevere in silent inner seclusion; close the senses to all that they brought you before your training; reduce to absolute immobility all the thoughts which, according to your previous habits, surged within you; become quite still and silent within, wait in patience, and then the higher worlds will begin to fashion and perfect the organs of sight and hearing in your soul and spirit.[26]

Learn to set aside the logical and measuring faculties and the comparing function of the lower mind[27] to clear the path for inspirational flow. Intellect and reason, we are told, can sever the telepathic thread. The more disinterested we become in ourselves as a personal ego, the finer our perceptions become.[28] As Theosophist channel Annie Besant put it, we must stop the ever-changing fluctuations of the "mental body" by dropping the objects of consciousness of the lower world and replacing them with the objects of consciousness of the higher world.[29]

The sources, as well as their channels, speak of the more troubling theme of self-surrender, of relinquishing conscious control over the play of mind. We hear the call for ego to efface itself, to give way to a deeper, larger, wiser presence, whether that be the higher Self or an opening into the collective unconscious or the Universal Mind. The clamping down of the ego in the face of its own loss of authority is often called "the guardian of the threshold" in the occult literature. For many of us this is tantamount to inviting the dissolution of the only self with which we are familiar, even though the channels and their sources tell us that we are more than our normal waking consciousness (as "self").

SETTING INTENTION AND
VERBAL SELF-PROGRAMMING

The next step in channeling is to set and register one's intention. We have already mentioned the use of phrases repeated aloud or quietly to oneself, such as "My body is growing more and more relaxed," or "I desire to contact my spirit guide now." One channel always begins his sessions with, "I wish to be made an instrument of the manifestation of my highest Self."[30] Self-induction into the channeling process usually involves both self-talk and mental imagery. Verbal accompaniment may include self-suggestion, programs for inner or outer action, affirmations,[31] invocations and evocations,[32] decrees,[33] invitations, and prayers. No matter which tack is taken, many of the teachers say that you need to announce yourself and to frame clearly the "other" with whom you seek contact, and why. This is part of unequivocally stating, or setting, your intention. Again, the "other" with which you wish to communicate may not be any kind of personality, but rather may be your own higher Self, Universal Mind, or the Pierian spring of intuition, or the muse for creative flow.

An *affirmation* is an assertion that the channeling process and its other levels of reality exist. This may involve articulating clearly and with conviction what you wish to have happen.

Programming yourself as a form of autosuggestion is part of this process. For example, you may activate a particular "program" prior to going into a dream state, trance state, or a hypnagogic state of consciousness (the condition of reverie between waking and sleep). This may involve asking your higher Self or spirit guide for particular things to happen. You can, while still awake, program your dream self to have certain kinds of experiences, to receive certain information, or to meet certain characters while asleep. In the same way, we are told, we can program specific suggestions for certain procedures to take place prior to entering the altered mental states connected with channeling.

Hypnotists claim that no one can be controlled in hypnotically induced states to do anything against his or her will. You need not worry, they say, about doing anything against your own basic welfare. (A self-hypnosis procedure will be presented later in this chapter.)

An *invocation* is another way to set intention or to state purpose as you go into the channeling situation. "From the point of Light within the Mind of God/ Let light stream forth into the minds of men," begins the "Great Invocation" provided by Alice A. Bailey's source "The Tibetan."[34] Ask and you shall receive, knock and it shall be opened unto you. Each person has his or her own way of knocking.

THE USE OF MENTAL IMAGERY

As we have already seen, there are many forms of active imagination in preparation for channeling. You simply use your imagination to create a clear image of something you wish to manifest. Shakti Gawain, in *Creative Visualization,* suggests that first we set our goal, then create a clear picture of it in our minds, focusing on it often and giving it positive energy.[35] Some suggest imagining a tube of light joining yourself with your target source. Max Freedom Long, authority on the Hawaiian *huna* system, tells us to imagine setting up a sticky communication thread of telepathic connection between sender and receiver.[36] Others picture their version of an inner advisor, such as an archetypal wise old sage, or a guardian angel complete with halo and wings, or a deceased loved one as remembered.

In *Mind Games: A Guide to Inner Space,* Jean Houston and Robert Masters suggest their own kind of mythic-type guided fantasy episodes in order to help us get in contact with our nonordinary and often archetypal sources.[37] Psychic teacher and channel Jean Porter, for example, imagines an inner sanctuary where she goes for contact with her higher Self, which in turn may connect her with other channeled sources:

> Close your eyes and relax. In your mind's eye, see or sense yourself projected into a natural scene. See a place unfold before you, as if on a screen, a place which gives you a strong feeling of warm, comfortable, peaceful, relaxed safety. It might be a setting at the seashore, in the mountains, by a lake, in a meadow, etc.

Then, Porter continues, "As you look down the path or off in the distance you become aware of a radiant, blue-white glow which is moving slowly toward you." As it nears, you see a human form; closer still, you see the face. "When you are quite close, you reach over and swiftly peel off the face as if it were a mask." If the face underneath is frightening, demand that it leave, and let it go. Again see the glow on the path nearing you. Repeat the process. "If, after the mask is pulled off, the face remains essentially the same, this being is your guide." Porter sees this being as "a non-physical part of yourself but not a product of your imagination. It is the expression of your higher consciousness, perceived as a form by the subconscious, psychic mind."[38]

ATTUNEMENT

Remember that a growing number of scientists tell us we are composed of bio-resonators or tuned oscillators. The more finely tuned we are, the

more subtle are the signals we can pick up or with which we can resonate. Like a radio receiver tuned to a broadcast beacon, we want to
establish resonance between the brain/mind "antenna" and the vibrations of the sender or the information source. As suggested in chapter 8,
this may be a cross-band or interdimensional proposition. By becoming
stilled enough to be in a potential state for attunement, the channel as
receiver can allow himself or herself to be rhythmically entrained to
vibrate at the same frequency, or a lower harmonic of it, and in the same
wave forms as the sending source. (Both Itzhak Bentov's *Stalking the Wild
Pendulum* and Steven Halpern's *Tuning the Human Instrument* are good
resources in this area.)[39]

So: Still yourself. Will. Intend that it be so. Focus on what you're
after. As radionics speculates, each being, each thing, has its own fundamental frequency, its natural rate. Your rate will best connect with that
of your intended information source if you focus yourself and focus on
your source, clearly and calmly.

The sources in the channeled collection *Seasons of Change* describe
something very similar, which also echoes the way "Lazaris" started off
his interview in chapter 1. They say:

> Then when the name and the birthdate of an individual would be
> given, the collective consciousness, being One with *all* that is, *vi-
> brates* with that particular individual, with that particular vibration
> of that individual, and signals, as a radio signal . . . By tuning in
> on this particular vibration, every individual has his own song
> and is singing it. That they are in harmony. And it is a question
> of picking out one particular song, on one particular level of
> harmony.[40]

BECOMING AN OPEN CHANNEL

Many books, courses, workshops, and consultation activities have
sprung up in the last few decades that claim to help the individual
develop innate intuitive and creative abilities. There is no way in the
space allowed here to do justice to this growing field, which had its
modern origins with Carl Jung's *active imagination* and Roberto Assagioli's *psychosynthesis* and with humanistic and transpersonal kinds of
educational, therapeutic, and personal-growth concepts and techniques.
Most of my professional life has been involved in helping students,
teachers, therapists, children, and adults learn to open channel, and to
do this for specific problem-solving reasons as well as for pleasure and

personal growth. There is a rich assortment of tools and approaches available to you.

Forced to speak generally here I can say that I have found those activities are best that free the individual to allow the natural creative flow. Inhibition, fear, and negativity must be quelled. Consciousness need not be altered; and a dissociated state or loss of consciousness should not be part of open channeling. To state it simply, you must learn to become spontaneous, playful, and open enough to permit improvisational expression. Either "the child within" should reign, or you should experiment with expressing yourself from a region that feels more open than that part you usually use.

The difficulty of articulating this process may lie in the fact that it is so natural. It is the superimposition of layers of beliefs, fears, and habits on our natural state as open channels that has led us to require artificial activities in order to reestablish that natural openness. We are reminded by the ease of that flow, once it is allowed to occur, that it is a most *natural* openness to the rest of our beings and to the living creative mind of the universe.

The entity "Lazaris" speaks frequently on the nature and development of intuition, which is "the energy boost to get out of orbit going around and around the personal and collective unconscious." According to "Lazaris," one must first wrestle with the various internal objections to being intuitive: fear of the message ("I don't know if I want to know"); fear of being wrong; fear of losing one's self-image as rational, stable, and intelligent; lack of self-love; fear of risk-taking; and fear of making choices and decisions. The answer, according to "Lazaris," is to develop the seven values: self-awareness, self-worth, self-esteem, self-confidence, self-respect, self-realization, and a path toward unconditional love and connection with the higher Self.[41]

SOME SAMPLE PROCEDURES

Self-Hypnosis

In his book *Self Hypnotism,*[42] Leslie LeCron, a clinical psychologist and leading authority on therapeutic hypnosis, recommends that you begin by concentrating attention on a single stimulus, such as a candle flame or fireplace. Soft, peaceful music in the background is helpful as well. Comfortably sitting or lying down, take slow, deep breaths while you watch the stimulus. Then, begin the suggestions: "As I watch this candle, my eyelids become heavier and heavier." Soon they become so heavy that they close. Now begin progressive muscle relaxation throughout your body, continuing suggestions like "I am drifting into hypnosis and relaxing more and more." He also suggests image making, starting at the top of a staircase or escalator and feeling yourself slowly descending ever-deeper.

If you can remain conscious, you can make further suggestions for channeling, such as, "I am now going to meet my spirit guide" (alter personality, higher Self, etc.), or "I will now make myself available as a channel for my best and highest good and for the good of all concerned. May no negative forces be allowed to interfere." In order to come out of the self-hypnotic state, LeCron suggests that one simply say, "Now I am going to wake up"; then count slowly to three and come out of the altered state relaxed and refreshed.

LeCron suggests that you can be your own pendulum under self-hypnosis by setting up the procedure for response by finding which finger will move to signify "yes," which one "no," and which one "I don't know." Then you can proceed to interrogate your own unconscious mind, or your channeled source.

For clairvoyant work, he suggests that you, again under self-hypnosis, imagine a blackboard on which writing appears to the mind's eye in response to questioning. And for clairaudience, simply ask to hear within yourself the voice of your channeled source, and then quiet yourself to hear it.

For automatic handwriting under a self-hypnotic dissociated state, LeCron suggests comfortably sitting with a cutting board across the knees. The board's surface is covered with a piece of shelf paper that can be rolled out if more is needed. Use a very soft pencil or colored marker for writing. Hold the instrument as you normally would, or straight up and down between thumb and forefinger. Now tell your subconscious mind, or your targeted source, that you would like to have it control your hand. Experiment with circles, scribbling in loose, random motions. Or watch your motionless hand and anticipate that it will move at any moment. You may feel a tingling or a loss of feeling. Do not try to consciously think of subject matter, thoughts, or words. Many suggest engaging in another task, such as reading or figuring out math problems, while the hand lies ready, or moves loosely, after the suggestion has been made.

Hal Stone's Voice Dialogue

Psychologist and consciousness teacher Hal Stone's approach to working with people's subpersonalities was described in chapter 7. After doing voice dialogue (that is, contacting and talking) with the subpersonalities, one can move on to the archetypal level:

> For example, somebody is a mental plane type identified with an Apollonian energy. Then we will work with the Apollonian side. We always work with opposites, so that people start to become familiar with these energies which we call archetypal energies. What this process gradually does is help us develop an awareness level of consciousness. It's what the meditational systems do. Then we also develop the experience of the different parts of ourselves and we make the discovery that a lot of choices are being made by a dominant subpersonality . . . You begin to discover who's driving the car [of yourself]. And there gradually begins to develop an aware ego . . . that can be aware of these parts and that can hold the tension of the opposites.[43]

Stone also admits to the existence of outside energies—what we have been calling entities or actual channeled personalities as sources—that can be contacted during work with one's own subpersonalities and with archetypal energies. He warns against bonding to, or becoming overly identified with, either inside or outside energies. "Embracing ourselves" is crucial; the goal of the aware ego is "the honoring of all energy without being identified with it."

In the following description of Stone's process, notice the resonance, attunement, and entrainment components we have emphasized earlier:

> Let's say that somebody is cut off from the energy of the vulnerable child. They've been wounded as a youngster for whatever reason, and they've had to become strong in order to develop power, go to school . . . And that vulnerable child is still living inside them . . . We talk to that side of them, so that voice has its say . . . And I go into that part of me and literally enter a resonation with that energy. We make contact. By being in touch with *my* child I can contact that child from the unconscious. It is like two vibrating systems. Because I am one with that vibration, I can hold that energy for the other person until that vulnerable child appears . . . [Or] by getting in touch with my *own* free spirit, I trigger that free spirit in her [the client], and I'm in touch with this totally different being in her. And then we may talk.

Based upon this approach, outlined in *Embracing Our Selves,*[44] it may be possible for you to pair up with someone else and to draw forth expressions from each other's subpersonalities, archetypal material, or even to contact genuine outside energy sources (although there's no inside/outside, in the sense that the nonphysical consciousness part of us is interrelated with all other nonphysical consciousness and reality). Working alone, it is still possible to adapt the voice dialogue, as in the Gestalt manner of identifying and temporarily separating out from yourself a subpersonality or other source (a dream component, for example) and questioning it, and then listening within for the response. Just know that when you venture inward in the channeling quest, your own subpersonalities are liable to be part of (or all of) the picture. Developing yourself as what Stone calls an aware ego can only help you with the channeling process. Indeed, he would say it is a prerequisite to channeling.

Opening to Channel: Sanaya Roman and Duane Packer

Northern California channels Sanaya Roman and Duane Packer (and their sources "Orin" and "DaBen") have trained over two hundred people in channeling in the past four years. Their procedure is detailed in their book *Opening to Channel.*[45] You will notice that their system includes virtually all of the different methods presented thus far in this chapter.

First is the process of *relaxing and focusing.* Create your own enjoyable, soothing environment, breathe deeply and easily, letting concerns fall away, relaxing your body all the while. Put an imagined, protective bubble of white light around you. Then learn to *quiet your mind,* concentrating on only one thing at a time. Next, *attune with life-force energy,* learning to sense the subtle energy presence of crystals, plants, and eventually your guide. Learn your best trance position as you explore relaxing deeper yet remaining conscious. *Imagine* going to higher realms of light and love. Imagine a golden light coming to you, entering the back of your neck and head. Imagine beings of light coming to you, and you welcoming them and them you. See a doorway, and know that there is a world of light beyond it, of higher frequency, of accelerated growth for you. When you are ready, imagine entering it. Little by little, you will learn how to invite and experience your guide. Eventually you will be able to allow him/her into your aura or energy system. Imagine the connection between you growing stronger. Now you are ready to ask your guide questions.

Shawn Randall

Shawn Randall is a Los Angeles area trance channel and channeling teacher. Her entity "Torah" also works with people while she is in trance. Randall/ "Torah" approach the channeling process as a tool for personal growth. As "Torah" puts it, "Learning to communicate with interdimensional consciousness can be a powerful tool for growth and an unlimited source of unconditional love." Randall says, "I do have an outline that I follow" for the twelve-week courses she offers. Her approach[46] is to first acquaint people with meditation and visualization (imagination/mental imagery) techniques; to help them realize that they "create their own reality"; and to work with them to put aside negative ego in a process of "integrating." There are a number of exercises for opening the physical, emotional, intellectual, and psychic-intuitive "bodies," as she calls them. Part of this involves pairing off and working with eye contact communication; and standing back-to-back and learning to sense each other's energies, tuning for images, thoughts, and feelings.

Early on, Randall reports, "Torah" assists the participants in getting in touch with their higher Selves. Part of the reason for this is "to let the subconscious know you are choosing this agreement to channel—to get the subconscious to more fully cooperate." Next she involves her students in "semi-automatic writing," claiming that often "the non-physical consciousnesses start connecting in the writing." The important thing, she says, is to develop a relationship with these new sources, just like with embodied people, a process that involves honesty and integrity. Then there is work with putting oneself aside; setting thoughts aside, along with physical relaxation exercises that help in instilling a feeling of letting go. Then an acknowledgment and invocation "that you are creating a safe and loving space within your meditative state and invoking and inviting energies into that space."

During part of each session while Randall is in trance, "Torah" works with the trainees, "opening their electromagnetic energy fields to fields beyond them, to invite external energies to blend with theirs." Eventually, she says, most of her students reach at least a semiconscious altered state within which information begins to appear to them. She reports that, with very few exceptions, those who work with her learn to trance channel. Throughout this process, there is "personal processing" to be done, she adds: you must learn to love yourself as you are growing and blending with other-than-self. Randall sums up the process as "learning to let in the love." "The more you allow yourself to love yourself and let in the love of All That Is," she says, "the more you are able to receive loving energies and information from the nonphysical realms."

"Lazaris"

In his many workshops and on various video and audio tapes, Jach Pursel's source "Lazaris" tries to involve people in an opening, growing process that, while it does not formally teach them to channel, seems related to channeling. In the following example, "Lazaris" guides the audience into their deeper intuitive ability:

> Relax. You are in control. You can accept or reject anything that comes to you. Now go deeper, let yourself go, tension going, replaced with quiet beautiful relaxation. Let the natural electric tension in your muscles go. Let that survival tension go. Know that you are safe.

"Lazaris" suggests trying to imagine that you have no body or form as the relaxation continues. Counting backward from ten to one, allow your consciousness to become more condensed with each number until it is pinpointed "like a laser beam." Then slowly move this self-focus through the body, passing through the chakra centers, exiting out the crown of the head as a bubble of consciousness that floats up and away from the body.

Next, imagine being on a pathway and coming to a place where it forks. Decide which direction to go on the basis of right-feeling intuition. A wall appears, impeding further progress. Imagine dismantling it, layer by layer. Experience one level being cleared; know that it is your self-image as a rational and realistic individual that has been reinforced by others. Another level to be dismantled is the refusal to be loved; another is the fear to risk. See yourself dismantling the blocks to your freer, fuller life.

Once the wall is gone, if intuition bids you to move forward on the path, you will come to "the place of intuition." When you reach it, "Decide how intuition is going to come to you. Through a picture, a printout, or through words that echo round the characters of your brain." Then ask questions to which the answer can be yes, no, or blank. Begin with, "Will I allow my intuition to work?" If the answer is yes, proceed to other questions, awaiting each response from the imagination domain, and believing it when it comes. You can return to this place, "Lazaris" says, and continue the process at will.[47]

WARNINGS

Problematic psychological states of mental dissociation or breakdown can result on occasion from insensitive experimentation with altered consciousness or from prematurely altering one's consciousness when one does not yet have a well-developed ego. Stern warnings are called for regarding any attempt to seek out loss of control, to weaken ego boundaries, or to solicit material from the deepest unknown sources. All have been known to lead at times to the erosion of individual security and integrity and to the disruption of healthy functioning with regard to consensus reality. Yet, while many psychologists warn against experimenting with such processes, others claim that only such experimentation can lead to personal growth and self-knowledge. Clearly, we must heed the warnings as well as the enticements that accompany the formulae for channeling, self-transcendence, or enlightenment.

Some psychologists use the concept of *developmental forcing,* which has been associated with schizophrenia, possession, hypnosis, drugs, and biofeedback, to describe the artificial introduction of an individual into a stage higher than he can function effectively in. This, they say, may create trauma; it is contrasted to *developmental escalation,* which results in healthy progress.[48] Each individual can only evaluate for himself whether his experimentation with channeling is developmental forcing or escalation.

The attempted communication with other levels of existence is not to be treated lightly, we are told. To the extent to which channeling is said to be taking place within a spiritual universe, approaching it in less than a spiritual manner may be tantamount to sacrilege. For others, conjuring paranormal phenomena with insufficient preparation or misdirected awareness can lead to associations with the demonic or "left-handed path." The English psychic and channel Aleister Crowley reportedly pursued this darker path deliberately, sometimes resulting in problems for himself and others. And, of course, the Bible admonishes against channeling anything less than God. Still, there are divergent views regarding the acceptability and efficacy of channeling, depending on the historical period, the local culture, and the personal belief system within which one is operating.

In his definitive book on the Ouija board, subtitled *The Most Dangerous Game,* Stoker Hunt devoted almost one-third of the text to assorted "rapes," demonology, and spirit obsession and possession attributed to beings attracted to people using the board. Some in the channeling subculture think Hunt paints too dark and unrealistic a picture; others think he sounds a healthy warning. But most would concur with the age-old esoteric adage, like attracts like: to the extent to which the "players" treat the channeling experience lightly, as a game, they tempt and draw to them what are supposedly their fellow players on the "other side."

CONCLUSION

I would like to end this chapter on the all-important theme of self-empowerment. It has to do with what psychologists call an internal locus of control and an internal locus of responsibility. In all the mysterious and fascinating otherworldy, populated scenarios we have been through together in this book, *you* are that focus of God or Universal Being in human form, evolving in understanding and in love. Take back your power. Be responsible for the way you steer your God-power through the universe of others doing the same.

Nineteenth-century Spiritualist channel Andrew Jackson Davis, late in his life, had the following observation:

Spiritualism is useful as a living demonstration of a future existence. Spirits have aided me many times, but they do not control either my person or my reason. They can and do perform kindly offices for those on earth. But benefits can only be secured on the condition that we allow them to become our teachers and not our masters, that we accept them as our companions, not as gods to be worshipped.[50]

Recently James B. DeKome of El Rito, New Mexico, wrote a letter to the editor of the journal *Common Boundary,* which focuses on the relationship between psychotherapy and spiritual matters. In it he said:

I question the relatively uncritical acceptance of what is essentially the product of someone else's unconscious psyche. Each of us has the ability to get information specific to our life situation from our personal inner source. It is dangerous to rely upon the inner voice of someone else, as it is to accept our own without careful evaluation.

The world has had enough saviors; what is needed for the New Age are individuals who willingly embrace the burdens of individuality. We will never achieve our true potential or true freedom until we are able to be critically self-governing from our own inner source.[51]

CONCLUSION

One thing seems clear: The various phenomena we have been discussing under the general rubric of channeling take us to the edge of human experience and understanding. They involve a variety of as yet largely unexplored fields as well as processes including consciousness itself; the cognitive and psychic sciences; transcendental, transpersonal, and mystical experiences; near-death and out-of-body experiences; lucid dreaming; the creative imagination and the intuitive processes in general; and, of course, the whole ages-long debate about matter and spirit.

At the end of decidedly skeptical study, *The Spiritualists,* researcher and author Ruth Brandon concludes, "Ever since Darwin seemingly staked out their territories in such clear and discrete opposition, the roles of science and religion have been getting more and more intermingled." Brandon seems to be speaking to those who engage in this kind of study when she laments: "Why do they do it? Why go to all this bother to dress something up as science when it is clearly not science but . . . magic?" For Brandon and those who share her perspective, "the act of faith is transferred to the realm of science," and as what passes for science "progresses into ever more arcane and unimaginable spheres, there is a deep wish for the irrational to triumph."[1] Yet even Einstein sought to embrace the rational *and* the spiritual, claiming that "God does not play dice with the universe." Elsewhere, he wrote, "The most beautiful and profound emotion we can experience is the sensation of the mystical. It is the sower of all true science."

I do not think we can afford to either ignore or too quickly explain away the chief anomalies that remain for us in science today. I believe that these unknowns exist to stimulate us individually and as a species into the restructuring of thought and action that inevitably accompanies true learning, growth, and even self-transcendence. Channeling is one of the most visible and perplexing of these anomalies, and implicates most others in its possible nature.

The explanations offered here have been varied. Sometimes they have even been mutually exclusive. On the one hand, new research in any of the branches of science may invalidate much of what is presented in this book. But, on the other hand, new research may also invalidate some of the scientific thinking that thus far dismisses channeling as a phenomenon not worthy of serious study. Yes, channeling may only be the creative pretense of an unbridled conscious or unconscious; or it may only be a form of clinical disorder. But based on the evidence, it does not seem possible to conclude that all channeling can be put to rest solely in terms of such explanations.

We then have to ask what kind of physical reality or what kind of psychological or nonphysical reality might have to exist in order to explain the remaining cases. None of the possible scientific explanations provided in this book is meant to represent more than the first tentative guesses that scientists are now able to make. None may be exactly true, but all point the way to areas that need further research. For, with channeling, we find ourselves facing the most crucial questions: *What are human beings? How are they constructed? Is there more to the universe, and to us, than physical reality as we know it? Are we alone in the universe, or are there others on nonphysical as well as physical levels? What is the nature of the spiritual? Why are we here? What happens when we die?*

Scientists still have little understanding of what lies at the deepest heart of matter, of what is responsible for life itself, or of how the brain is related to consciousness, let alone what consciousness is. Humility within a larger perspective, as well as rigor and caution, are called for. The coming years are likely to bring further restructurings of many of our present understandings. This book is offered with the hope that it will stimulate further exploration and research.

How is it, for example, that the content of channeling seems so consistent from culture to culture and individual to individual, across so many millenia? Does this similarity offer clues about the makeup and structure of the brain or of consciousness itself? Does the fact that the oft-channeled theme of beings evolving through a hierarchically struc- tured cosmos—in which more evolved beings are teaching the less evolved—have anything to do with the fact that the brain, according to Paul D. Maclean and others,[2] is made up of a hierarchy of structures, some of which are at more advanced states of evolution than others and in control of them?

A close examination of channeling also makes it difficult to accept the double standard which holds that the beliefs and practices of organized religion are acceptable, while belief systems and practices outside organized religion—such as channeling with its claim to com- munication from nonphysical and spiritual realms—are not. Indeed, his- tory presents a picture that shows us how deeply interconnected chan- neling-like phenomena are in the roots of most of the world's great religions. At the same time, I do not think that channeling should be associated only with the current wave of Charismatic and Pentacostal religious movements with their reported speaking in tongues, prophesying, and receiving spiritual gifts from God. Rather, channeling should be treated as an expanded type of information-processing capacity potentially available to us all and amenable to scientific investigation as well as soul-searching. It may prove useful not to allow the current consensus reality and its acceptable role models to be held up to us as automatically superior to the realities presented by channeling. In our troubled times, we cannot afford to pull the blinds upon alternative sources of information and guidance. Our times may be so troubled at least in part because our innate desire for deeper, truer values and a richer meaning to our existence has not been adequately met by the usual avenues of information and experience.

I firmly believe that a Grand Unified Theory for *everything* lies just ahead for us. Such a theory would have to include not only an integration of the various forces of Nature known to physicists but an integration of those forces with the dimensions of mind, heart, and spirit as well. The paranormal, and channeling specifically, may just be another name for the place where outer and inner, objective and subjective reality (as we have called them) meet and shade into each other. Theoretical physicists and channeled sources alike ask us to consider that the mind may directly contribute to the nature of what it experiences and that there may be more dimensions to existence than the three of space and one of time to which we are accustomed.

We stand in wonder on the shore of a vast sea of consciousness. Both the star-filled reaches of the supposedly external Universe and the unfathomable inner reaches of our own beings await us now as two aspects of a single, encompassing truth. Channeling holds out to us the possibility of an incredibly complex, multileveled universe, filled with fellow consciousness, a universe with which we can *all* interact in new and meaningful ways, each of us taking ultimate responsibility for our respective growth. Rather than following some voice of authority from beyond ourselves, most of the channeled sources stress self-determination, guided from the highest levels within ourselves. We are given messages of self-empowerment, love, and the oneness of all beings, of all Creation. We are told by the channels, and it is echoed by their sources, that we can do what they do (even, for that matter, as Christ said that we would be able to do as he had done). And as we have seen, we are all channels—*open channels* anyway. It is only a matter of degree, not kind.

Our individual identities seem to ride, like wave patterns, on the surface of the vast deeps from which all identities arise. In these liquid fathoms of being, as we continued to learn and evolve, the boundaries are likely to increasingly dissolve and reform in ways that inform, challenge, and redefine us. As we drink from the deeper waters of our own larger identity, we may come to understand the true meaning of the sayings "The Kingdom is within you" and "Your life is in your hands."

An audio cassette entitled "Channeling," which further explores the ideas in this book and includes interviews with Jane Roberts, Jach Pursel, Iris Belhayes, William Rainen, Neville Rowe, Carol B. Simpson and Tom Massari, is published by Audio Renaissance Tapes. The cassette is available at your local bookseller or directly from Audio Renaissance Tapes, 9110 Sunset Boulevard, Los Angeles, CA 90069, for $9.95 plus $1.50 postage and handling.

GLOSSARY

Afterlife. A multileveled nonphysical reality that one is said to enter following death of the physical body. Sometimes called *bardo* or *devachan,* it is where human spirits dwell between (and following all) earthly incarnations.

Akashic records. Said to be the nonphysical "cosmic memory bank" of all that has occurred, which can be tapped by certain individuals, physical and nonphysical.

Alter personality. An autonomous personality or seat of consciousness operating in a person that is different from the one usually taken to be that person; a subpersonality.

Altered states (of consciousness). States other than ordinary waking consciousness, such as daydreaming, sleep dreaming, hypnotic or trance, meditation, mystical, or drug-induced states, or half-unconscious (hypnagogic) states or half-waking (hypnopompic) states.

Amanuensis. One who copies what another has said or written; therefore, often a term used for automatic writing or clairaudient channels.

Ascended Master. A highly evolved individual who is no longer required to undergo lifetimes on the physical level for spiritual growth.

Astral. The nonphysical level of reality characterized primarily by emotion and considered to be where most humans go after they die and where they exist not only between earthly incarnations but after incarnations as well, prior to ascending higher.

Automatic writing. Handwriting (or typewriting) done without conscious control, the source of which is apparently not oneself.

Automatisms. Behaviors conducted without conscious control, such as automatic writing.

Book test. A way of attempting proof of survival of physical death whereby a discarnate spirit communicates through a channel directions to locate material within a particular book that implicates the spirit as sender.

Channel (noun). (also **Channeler**)   Someone who is able to receive or transmit information that originates from a level of reality other than our physical reality; this includes all paranormal information reception except for communication with one's own conscious or unconscious self or with that of another who is also in a physical body. Excluded, then, is telepathic or clairvoyant contact between one physically embodied individual and another or between one and the physical environment (like remote viewing).

Channel (verb).   To receive and convey information (or energy) that is said to come from neither one's own self nor from other embodied minds, nor from physical reality (as defined by current physics and psychophysiology).

Channeling.   The process of receiving information from some level of reality other than the ordinary physical one and from beyond the self as we currently understand it. This includes messages from any mental source that falls outside of one's own ordinary conscious or unconscious and is not anyone else incarnate on the physical level of reality.

Classical (or **classic**) **channeling.**   Any channeling in which there is an identified (or self-identified) source said to be responsible for the information coming to or through the channel.

Closed system.   In this book, used to mean a biological or psychological system that appears to operate with no information or energy connection between itself and the rest of reality other than by way of ordinary perception and the matter and energy interactions accepted by current physics.

Collective consciousness.   A term for the Universal Mind, or for a conscious version of something like the Jungian collective unconscious.

Collective unconscious.   Jung's term for the shared memory and accrued archetypal dispositions of the human species.

Co-consciousness.   The concept that there can be more than one seat of consciousness operating within a person at the same time, independent from one another, and considered to be a *natural* way of being and operating. This is distinguished from multiple-personality disorder, or dissociation, which is seen as abnormal and problematic for the individual.

Consciousness.   Mental awareness or present knowing; awareness or perception of one's inner self (of psychological or spiritual material), or inward awareness of external objects or facts.

Consensual validation.   The process by which members of a group or culture provide for themselves, by their joint (consensus) agreement, validation of the existence or truth of a belief or experience.

Consensus reality. The ordinary day-to-day physically-oriented public reality shared by most people and experienced by them as being similar enough among them that they agree on it as the primary (as well as consensus) reality.

Control. The main entity on the nonphysical end of the channeling process, said to act as "master of ceremonies" or "traffic controller" for others who also may wish to communicate through the same channel; sometimes used for any being controlling the channel during channeling.

Cross-correspondence. A method of proving survival of physical death whereby a spirit communicates parts of a complex message through a number of different unconnected channels; the message can only be understood when all the parts are brought together.

Deceased. Having left one's physical body by the process called death.

Discarnate. Not incarnated in a body living on the physical plane.

Discernment. The process of seeing, recognizing, and deciding for oneself.

Disembodied. Not having a body as we know it; discarnate.

Dissociation. An alteration in the normal integrative functions of consciousness, identity, or motor behavior, such that part of oneself appears to be split off and operating independently.

Entity. The core identity of any individual existing being; especially refers to a being that exists on a level of reality other than the physical and beyond the mind of the channel, and that operates as a source in the channeling process.

Entrainment (or **rhythm entrainment**). The process whereby a stronger (or possibly higher-frequency) rhythmically vibrating system induces the same rate of vibration in another vibrating system susceptible to such a process.

Etheric. Said to be the nonphysical, or sometimes the "higher physical," level of reality above the physical level as we know it but below the astral level.

Executive function (or **ego**). That part of a person's brain/mind that operates as the centralizing identity, or the executive; it integrates and coordinates the components that compose the psyche and is responsible for planning and goal-directed behavior (according to current Cognitive Psychology).

External reality. The environment that one experiences as existing outside of one's own body and mind.

Extraterrestrial. Not of the physical earth; usually associated more with physical, rather than nonphysical, planets or environments other than Earth; but in this book tends to refer to nonphysically based locales.

Factitious disorder. Mental disturbance that involves behavior under conscious, voluntary control that is used to pursue unconscious or involuntarily adopted goals; this could account for fraudulent cases of channeling in which a person pretends to channel but is not consciously aware that it is a pretense.

Frequency. Any wave system is composed of the repetitions of its characteristic wave shape; the rate at which a series of wave shapes passes a given point is its frequency. Human hearing, for example, can detect sound waves in a frequency range of 20 to 20,000 cycles per second.

Glossolalia. Speaking in unknown tongues.

Hidden observer. In hypnosis, according to Ernest Hilgard, that aspect of the subject that appears to know everything that is taking place but is not part of normal waking consciousness or part of the hypnotized self.

Higher Self. The most spiritual and knowing part of oneself, said to lie beyond the ego, the day-to-day personality or self, and beyond the personal unconscious, and which can be channeled for wisdom and guidance; variations include the *oversoul,* the *superconscious,* the *Atman, Christ* (or *Krishna* or *Buddha*) *Consciousness, the God within,* or *the God Self.*

Hypnosis. A relaxed, altered state of consciousness induced by suggestion; characterized as being like reverie or sleep yet open to suggestion and able to be focused by suggestion away from the external environment and consensus reality.

Incarnate. Living in a body on the physical plane.

Medium. An earlier term for a channel; some use the term only to refer to trance mediums, while others use it only for mediums who communicate with deceased (discarnate) human spirits.

Mediumship. The practice of being a medium or channel; specifically, the practice of communication with the dead.

Nonphysical. That which falls outside of the definition of *physical* established by a consensus of contemporary physicists; that which is considered neither matter nor energy (nor objectively real) as detectable by the normal senses or their extension by way of instruments of measurement acceptable in current scientific practice.

Occult. Hidden or secret; as the knowledge possessed by traditional mystery schools throughout history dealing with nonphysical levels of reality.

Open channeling. Receiving information from an *unidentifiable* source, experienced as self-transcendent and as coming from a dimension or level of reality other than the consensus reality, the physical, sensible world, or from one's own psychological being or self, conscious or unconscious; this includes mystical experience, aspects of the intuitive, creative, inspirational, and imaginative processes, but does not include the parapsychological processes of telepathically receiving material from other incarnate persons' minds or clairvoyantly receiving from the physical environment.

Person. Similar to *Self* or *Entity* (elsewhere in glossary); or defined as an individual in terms of having a *personality,* i.e., possessing a particular identifying set of traits, characteristics, behavioral dispositions, attachments, identifications, memories, programs, and beliefs acquired by a combination of genetic inheritance and learning (conditioning) through experiential interaction with the environment (and in metaphysical terms, accumulated through past lives via reincarnation).

Physical reality. The realm of matter and energy that is agreed on as objectively real by a consensus of contemporary physicists; what is experienced by way of the five normal senses (and their extension through accepted scientific instrumentation) as existing objectively and independently beyond the observer's own subjective reality.

Possession. The spontaneous and unwanted inhabiting and control of a person's body by a nonphysical being (usually) lacking spiritual development.

Reality testing. The process of "staying in touch" with reality by testing one's subjective reality (beliefs, expectations, etc.) against the objective reality of the physical environment and consensus reality.

Resonance. An oscillating system's tendency to continue to vibrate at a certain rate most natural to it; a state of being in resonance, or being induced into resonance by the rhythm entrainment of another, more powerful or resonant vibrating system.

Self. That which is considered the entire person of an individual, that individual's basic identity—who he or she (or it) really is; a person in his or her (or its) normal state; one's personality considered predominant or typical; having the quality of being an entity (elsewhere in glossary), i.e, "the core identity of any individual existing being;" a psychic center or an energy pattern possessing consciousness; the concept of "Higher Self" (elsewhere in glossary) as an extension of this sense of a normal self; the concept of a self that is construed as a subsystem or off-shoot of a parent self, in the case of self-as-a-personality, as in "sub-personality" or "alter-personality."

Somnambulism. A term often used in the nineteenth century for any sleep- or trancelike state of consciousness and its associated behavior (such as sleep walking or talking); automatism.

Source. The generic term for anyone or anything occupying the transmitting end, or comprising the informational origin, in the channeling process.

"Space Brothers." Alleged beings, some from other physical planets, but most from other planetlike homes existing in higher (etheric) or nonphysical dimensions of reality; possessing advanced technologies, currently unknown to earth scientists, which reportedly allow frequency transformations of matter and energy, space and time, including UFO travel.

Spirit. Sometimes used to refer to any nonphysical being or entity that can be channeled; more specifically, the spirit of a deceased human being; that aspect of a person that is other than the physical body and that survives the death of the body; or beings who have never been human or existed in physical reality; The Universal Being (or God).

Spiritual. The nonphysical; the realm that lies beyond (and some say underlies and is responsible for) physical reality; the realm of the good, the most true, the eternal (or timeless), and the infinite (or immeasurable).

Spiritualism. A religious-type movement inspired by the resurgence of channeling activity in upstate New York in the mid-nineteenth century, which reached international proportions (called *Spiritism* in Europe) and exists to this day; it holds that we survive our physical deaths as spirits who can communicate back to the living through channels, usually termed mediums, and that all spirits, incarnate and discarnate alike, are immortal, ever-learning, and evolving toward the one God of All That Is.

Thoughtforms. Said to be the wave structures created by initiating thoughts within the subtle or nonphysical energy of the mental plane that is shared by all spirits, incarnate or discarnate, and thus provides the one universal tongue that underlies the transmission and reception of all thought on all levels of reality, including telepathy and other paranormal communication.

Trance. A term used by some for any hypnotic-type altered state of consciousness; characterized by conscious attention being turned away from the normal senses and consensus reality.

Trance channeling. Entering a trance state in order to channel; characterized by an unconscious, sleeplike quality in which the channel is said to allow the seat of consciousness to be occupied by another being—the channeled source—who uses the channel's body to speak; afterward the channel returns to normal consciousness with no memory of what occurred.

Universal Mind. All that exists interpreted as mind, or the Mind of all that is; the Mind that is comprised of all other, lesser, minds in the universe, but which is more than the sum of Its parts; the Mind of God.

NOTES

INTRODUCTION: SETTING THE SCENE

1. Quote opening introduction is from Charles H. Hapgood, *Voices of Spirit: Through the Psychic Experience of Elwood Babbitt* (New York: Leisure/Norton, 1975), 196–197. Jeffrey Mishlove, interview with author, 26 August 1986. **2.** Cited in George W. Cornell, "Idea of Hell Loses Its Wallop," *San Francisco Chronicle*, 28 May 1986. **3.** Arthur Hastings, "Investigating the Phenomenon of Channeling," *Noetic Sciences Review*, Winter 1986. **4.** William Kautz, "Channeling: Mediumship Comes of Age," *Applied Psi*, Summer 1985. **5.** Margo Chandley, interview with author, 8 February 1987. **6.** D. Scott Rogo, interview with author, 26 August 1986. **7.** Earl Babbie, interview with author, 9 February 1987. **8.** W. T. Stace, *Mysticism and Philosophy* (London: Macmillan, 1960), 5, 16, 14. See also C. D. Broad, *Religion, Philosophy and Psychical Research* (New York: Harcourt, Brace & Co., 1953). **9.** Ibid. (Stace), 33, 135, 136. **10.** Stanley Krippner, interview with author, 28 November 1986. **11.** Jacob Needleman, quoted in Art Levine, et al., "Mystics on Mainstreet," *U.S. News and World Report*, 9 February 1987. **12.** Margo Chandley, "A Psychological Investigation of the Development of the Mediumistic Process in Personality Function" (Ph.D. diss., International College, 1986), 6. **13.** Tuella, *The Dynamics of Cosmic Telepathy* (Aztec, N.M.: Guardian Action Pubs., 1983). **14.** Marcello Truzzi, interview with author, 27 October 1986. **15.** Earlier quote from Charles T. Tart, interview with author, 27 October 1986. John Searle's quote from a lecture of his at University of California, Berkeley, 6 April 1987. Quotes of Harvey Cox and Eugene d'Aquila from "For Personal Insights, Some Try Channels Out of this World," *The Wall Street Journal*, 1 April, 1987, 1. **16.** In J. S. Morrison, "The Classical World," in *Oracles and Divination*, eds. Michael Loewe and Carmen Blacker (Boulder, Colo.: Shambala, 1981), 106. **17.** C. J. Ducasse, *The Belief in a Life after Death* (Springfield, Ill.: Charles Thomas, 1961), 166. **18.** David Marks and Richard Kamman, *The Psychology of the Psychic* (Buffalo, N.Y.: Prometheus Books, 1980), 200, 176, 186, 193. **19.** In Alan M. MacRobert, "A Consumer's Guide to New Age Hokum," *Whole Earth Review*, Fall 1980, 13. **20.** Michael Murphy, interview with author, 13 September 1986. **21.** Letter to Jeremy P. Tarcher, 8 December 1986. **22.** Mark Plummer and Ray Hyman, quoted in Lynn Smith, "The New, Chic Metaphysical Fad of Channeling," *Los Angeles Times*, 5 December 1986. **23.** In Levine, "Mystics on Mainstreet." **24.** In Carol McGraw, "Seekers of Self Recall 'New Age,' " *Los Angeles Times*, 17 February 1987. **25.** Theodore Flournoy, *From India to the Planet Mars* (New Hyde Park, N.Y.: University Books, 1963; 1st pub. 1900), xxx. **26.** Colin Wilson, *Afterlife* (London: Harap, Ltd., 1985), 159. **27.** Dean Inge, *Survival? Body, Mind and Death in the Light of Psychic Experience* (London: Routledge & Kegan Paul, 1984), 160. **28.** John W. Harrington, *Dance of the Continents* (Los Angeles: Jeremy P. Tarcher, 1983), 36–38. **29.** Truzzi interview. **30.** Huston Smith, interview with author, 9 October 1986. **31.** Murphy interview.

NOTES

1
CHANNELING AS A MODERN PHENOMENON

1. Consecutive quotes are from the following: Jane Roberts, *The Seth Material* (New York: Bantam, 1976; 1st pub. Englewood Cliffs, N.J.: Prentice-Hall, 1970), 302. Jane Roberts, *Seth Speaks* (New York: Bantam, 1974; 1st pub. Prentice-Hall, 1972), 216. Jane Roberts, *The "Unknown" Reality, Vol. I* (Englewood Cliffs, N.J.: Prentice-Hall, 1977), 191. Jane Roberts, *The Nature of Personal Reality* (Englewood Cliffs, N.J.: Prentice-Hall, 1974), 509, 180. **2.** The last two quotes from: *The Seth Material,* 13–14, 18–19. **3.** *Seth Material,* 4–5. **4.** Ibid., 293. **5.** *Seth Speaks*, xv–xvi. **6.** Jane Roberts, *Adventures in Consciousness: An Introduction to Aspect Psychology* (Englewood Cliffs, N.J.: Prentice-Hall, 1975), 131–132. **7.** *The Nature of Personal Reality*, viii. **8.** *The Unknown Reality, Vol. I*, 17. **9.** *Seth Material,* 58–59. **10.** Ibid., 246–247, 250, 252–253. **11.** Jane Roberts, *The World View of Paul Cezanne: A Psychic Interpretation* (Englewood Cliffs, N.J.: Prentice-Hall, 1977), 8. **12.** Ibid., xii. **13.** Jane Roberts, *The Afterlife Journal of an American Philosopher: The World View of William James* (Englewood Cliffs, N.J.: Prentice-Hall, 1978), 13, 16. **14.** Paul Hawken, *The Magic of Findhorn* (New York: Bantam, 1976), 103–104. **15.** Ibid., 258–259. **16.** Eileen Caddy, *God Spoke to Me* (Elgin, Ill.: Lorian Press). **17.** Dorothy Maclean, *To Hear the Angels Sing* (Elgin, Ill.: Lorian Press, 1980), 3. **18.** Ibid., 111. **19.** Last three quotes, ibid., 118, 73, 112–113. **20.** David Spangler, *Conversations with John* (Elgin, Ill.: Lorian Press, 1980), 1. **21.** (Anne Edwards, channel), *A World Within a World: X-7 Reporting; Transmissions from Russia on the Theory and Practice of Solar Light Radiations* (Findhorn, Scotland: Findhorn Pubs., 1981). **22.** Robert Skutch, *Journey Without Distance: The Story Behind a Course in Miracles* (Berkeley, Calif.: Celestial Arts, 1984), 54. **23.** Ibid., 56. **24.** *A Course in Miracles, Vol. 1: Text* (Tiburon, Calif.: Foundation for Inner Peace, 1975), 52–53, 358. **25.** *A Course in Miracles, Vol. 3: Manual for Teachers* (Tiburon, Calif.: Foundation for Inner Peace, 1975), 87. **26.** *A Course in Miracles, Vol. 2: Workbook for Students* (Tiburon, Calif.: Foundation for Inner Peace, 1975), 1, 83, 164, 183, 227, 347. **27.** *Journey Without Distance,* 61. **28.** *A Course in Miracles, Vol. 1: Text*, 6–7, 81, 113; *Journey Without Distance,* 60. **29.** *Miracles, Vol. 3,* 85. **30.** *Journey Without Distance,* 134–135. **31.** Quoted in Alan Vaughan, "Channeling: An Old Phenomenon Goes Modern," *New Realities,* January/February 1987, 47. **32.** Douglass James Mahr, *Voyage to the New World: An Adventure into Unlimitedness* (Friday Harbor, Washington: Masterworks, Inc., 1985), 185. **33.** Other sources mentioned: Douglass James Mahr, *Voyage to the New World: An Adventure into Unlimitedness* (Friday Harbor, Wash.: Masterworks, Inc., 1985); Steven Lee Weinberg, ed., *Ramtha* (East Sound, Wash.: Sovereignty, Inc., 1986); Cindy Black, et al., eds., *I Am Ramtha* (Portland,Or.: Beyond Words Pub., 1986). **34.** In George Hackett with Pamela Abramson, "Ramtha, a Voice from Beyond," *Newsweek,* 15 December 1986, 42. **35.** Craig Lee, "Channeling: Voices from Beyond," *Los Angeles Weekly,* 7–13 November 1986, 20. **36.** All quotes from Kevin Ryerson are taken from Mark Vaz's interview article, "Psychic!—The Many Faces of Kevin Ryerson," *Yoga Journal,* July/August 1986. **37.** In publicity flyer, "Lazaris, the Consummate Friend," from Concept: Synergy, P.O. Box 159(M), Fairfax, Calif. 94930. **38.** Jach Pursel, interview with author, 28 January 1987. **39.** Ibid. **40.** Ibid. **41.** From transcript, "Lazaris on the Merv Griffin Show," 25 July 1986, from Concept: Synergy. **42.** Chelsea Quinn Yarbro, *Messages from Michael* (New York: Playboy Paperbacks, 1979); *More Messages from Michael* (New York: Berkley Books, 1986). **43.** *Messages,* 20. **44.** *More Messages,* 291. **45.** *Messages,* 118. **46.** Ibid., 41, 58. **47.** Ibid., 14. **48.** Robert R. Leichtman, *From Heaven to Earth: Edgar Cayce Returns* (Columbus, Ohio: Ariel Press, 1978), 13. **49.** Last quotes, in order, are from: Robert R. Leichtman, *From Heaven to Earth: Sir Oliver Lodge Returns* (Columbus, Ohio: Ariel Press, 1979), 32, 33, 31; *Edgar Cayce Returns,* 11–12. **50.** Robert R. Leichtman, *From Heaven to Earth: Arthur Ford Returns* (Columbus, Ohio: Ariel Press, 1979), 30. **51.** Robert R. Leichtman, *From Heaven to Earth: Eileen Garrett Returns* (Columbus, Ohio: Ariel Press, 1980), 51. **52.** Ibid., 18–19. **53.** George Adamski and Desmond Lake, *Flying Saucers Have Landed* (London: Werner Laurie, 1953). **54.** In Winfield S. Brownell, *UFO's: Key to Earth's Destiny* (Lytle Creek, Calif.: Legion of Light Pubs., 1980). **55.** In *UFO's,* 74.

56. Tuella/The Ashtar Command, *Project World Evacuation* (Durango, Colo.: Guardian Action Pubs., 1982). **57.** Carla Rueckert and Don Elkins, *Secrets of the UFOs* (Louisville, Ky.: L/L Research, 1977). **58.** J. W./Gloria Lee, *Why We Are Here* (Palos Verdes Estates, Calif.: Cosmon Research Foundation, 1959), 118; Robert Anton Wilson, *Cosmic Trigger* (Phoenix, Ariz.: Falcon Press, 1977), 89. **59.** Djwal Kul, *Intermediate Studies of the Human Aura* (Los Angeles: Summit University Press, 1974), 20. **60.** Ken Carey, *Vision* (Kansas City: UNI-SUN, 1985), vii. **61.** Ken Carey/Raphael, *The Starseed Transmissions: An Extraterrestrial Report* (Kansas City: UNI-SUN, 1982), 2. **62.** Ibid., 3. **63.** Ibid., 68–70. **64.** *Vision,* xvi. **65.** Meredith Lady Young, *Agartha: A Journey to the Stars* (Walpole, N.H.: Stillpoint Pub., 1984), preface, 31, 40–50. **66.** Pat Rodegast and Judith Stanton, *Emmanuel's Book: A Manual for Living Comfortably in the Cosmos* (Weston, Conn.: Friends Press, 1985), iii. **67.** Ibid., xxiv, 4–5. **68.** Maurice Cooke, *The Nature of Reality: A Book of Explanations* (Toronto: Marcus Books, 1979), ix. **69.** Maurice Cooke, *Einstein Doesn't Work Here Anymore: A Treatise on the New Science* (Toronto: Marcus Books, 1983). **70.** Maurice Cooke, *Seasons of the Spirit* (Toronto: Marcus Books, 1980), 99–100. **71.** *Nature of Reality,* ix. **72.** Joey Crinita, *The Medium Touch: A New Approach to Mediumship* (Norfolk, Va.: Unilaw Library/Donning Co., 1982). **73.** Benjamin Creme, *The Reappearance of the Christ and the Masters of Wisdom* (London: The Tara Press, 1980), 229, 235, 239; *Share International* (61 Gloucester Place, London). **74.** *Reappearance,* 21–22. **75.** Carolyn Del La Hey, *Lifeline: Experiences of Psychic Communication* (Surrey, England: Neville Spearman, 1978); *The Revelation of Ramala* (Jersey Channel Islands, England: Neville Spearman/Jersey, 1978). **76.** Gabriele Wittek, *Homebringing Mission of Jesus Christ* (P.O. Box 13, Pelham, N.H. 03076; or Simssee St. 10, D-8200 Rosenheim, West Germany); and *The Christ State* (P.O. Box 3549, New Haven, Conn.: 06525). **77.** William Kautz, "Channeling: Mediumship Comes of Age," *Applied Psi,* Summer 1985, 4–5. **78.** Alan Vaughan, in Nancy Spiller, "They Look for a Channeling Experience," *Los Angeles Herald Examiner,* 12 February 1987. **79.** James J. Hurtak, *The Book of Knowledge: The Keys of Enoch* (Los Gatos, Calif.: The Academy for Future Science, 1977).

2
CHANNELING AS A HISTORICAL PHENOMENON

1. Hans Küng, *Eternal Life?* (Garden City, N.Y.: Image Books/Doubleday, 1985), 52. **2.** Mircea Eliade, *Shamanism: Archaic Techniques of Ecstasy* (Princeton, N.J.: Bollingen/Princeton Univ. Press, 1972). **3.** Nina Epton, "The Black Brotherhoods of Sidi Bilal," in *Trances,* eds. Stewart Wavell, Audrey Butt, and Nina Epton (New York: E. P. Dutton, 1967), 66. **4.** Nina Epton, "Celestial Nymphs of Siva," ibid., 126–127. **5.** Audrey Butt, "A Solitary among Mountains," ibid., 51. **6.** P. Phillips and W. L. MacLeod, *Here and There: Psychic Communication Between Our World and the Next* (London: Corgi/Transworld, 1975), 144–145. **7.** Robert Masters, interview with author, 3 November 1986. **8.** All material in this subsection (through India), unless otherwise noted, is drawn from Lewis Bayles Paton, *Spiritism and the Cult of the Dead in Antiquity* (New York: Macmillan, 1921). **9.** J. D. Ray, "Ancient Egypt," in *Oracles and Divination,* eds. Michael Loewe and Carmen Blacker (Boulder, Colo.: Shambala, 1981), 179. **10.** Ibid., 185–186. **11.** *Spiritism.* **12.** Ibid., 78. **13.** George Luck, *Arcana Mundi: Magic and the Occult in the Greek and Roman Worlds* (Baltimore: Johns Hopkins Univ. Press, 1985), 217. **14.** In *Theagetes.* **15.** One form of open-channeling–type prophecy might involve accessing the Universal Mind, which knows what lies in store; or it might involve information lying in other dimensions which hold possible or probable realities with regard to the physical, as described in various channeled material, such as the "Seth" books. **16.** *Arcana Mundi,* 166. **17.** Henry James Forman, *The Story of Prophecy* (New York: Farrar & Rinehart, 1936), 18. **18.** *Spiritism,* 83. **19.** E. R. Dodds, *The Ancient Concept of Progress in Greece and Rome* (Oxford, England: Oxford Clarendon, 1973). **20.** David C. Knight, *The ESP Reader* (New York: Grosset & Dunlap, 1969), 257. **21.** James Fadiman, interview with author, 26 August 1986. **22.** *Spiritism.* **23.** All biblical quotes from *The Holy Bible,* Red Letter Edition, Authorized (King James) Version (Philadelphia: National Bible Press). **24.** Jer. 1:4–9.

354

NOTES

25. Exod. 22:18; Deut. 18:10–12; Lev. 19:31; Isa. 8:19.   **26.** *Story of Prophecy*, 31–32.
27. Matt. 10:19–20; 17:5.   **28.** Luke 8:21.   **29.** John 1:51; 6:63; 8:23, 28–29, 47; 10:38;
12:50; 14:2, 10; 17:8.   **30.** Rev. 1:10–19.   **31.** Acts 2:2–4; 10:19–20, 44.   **32.** 1 Cor.
2:10, 12; 12:1–7; 14:36–39.   **33.** John Cournos, *A Book of Prophecy: From the Egyptians to
Hitler* (New York: Bell Pub., 1942), 135–136.   **34.** *Story of Prophecy*, 202–204.   **35.**
Hildegarde of Bingen, ibid., 130–131; Richard Rolle, in D. Scott Rogo, *Nad: A Study of Some
Unusual "Other-World" Experiences* (New York: University Books, 1970), 90.   **36.** *Story of
Prophecy*, 134–138.   **37.** Ibid., 194. Also, *A Book of Prophecy*, 140.   **38.** E. Hoffman, *The
Way of Splendor* (Boulder, Colo.: Shambala, 1981).   **39.** Charles E. Ward, *Oracles of
Nostradamus* (New York: Scribners, 1941).   **40.** St. Teresa of Avila, *Interior Castle* (Garden
City, N.Y.: Image/Doubleday, 1961), 72.   **41.** St. John of the Cross, *Ascent of Mount
Carmel* (Garden City, N.Y.: Image/Doubleday, 1958), 242–248.   **42.** George Fox, *The
Journal of George Fox*, ed. Rufus M. Jones (Richmond, Ind.: Friends United Press, 1976),
74–75.   **43.** Emanuel Swedenborg, *Heaven and Hell*, trans. George F. Dole (New York:
Pillar Books, 1976), 12.   **44.** Emanuel Swedenborg, as quoted in Wilson Van Dusen, *The
Presence of Other Worlds: The Findings of Emanuel Swedenborg* (New York: Perennial/Harper
& Row, 1974); (numbers refer to Swedenborg's paragraph numbers) *Arcana Coelestia*, 68;
Spiritual Diary, 1622; *Arcana Coelestia*, 6212; *Heaven and Hell*, 456.   **45.** *The Doctrine of
Tenrikyo*, 2nd ed. (Headquarters of the Tenrikyo Church; printed in Tenri Jihosha, Japan,
1958), 3, 5.   **46.** Geoffrey K. Nelson, *Spiritualism and Society* (London: Routledge &
Kegan Paul, 1969), 51.   **47.** Sir Arthur Conan Doyle, *The History of Spiritualism, Vol. 1*
(New York: Arno Press, 1975; 1st pub. George H. Doran Co., 1926), 25–36.   **48.** Ibid.,
36–41.   **49.** Ibid., 54, 57.   **50.** Nandor Fodor, "The Birth of Spiritualism—The Fox
Sisters and the 'Hydesville Rappings,' " in *The ESP Reader*, ed. David C. Knight (New York:
Grosset & Dunlap, 1969), 23.   **51.** Ibid., 27.   **52.** *History of Spiritualism*, 79.   Ibid.,
84.   **54.** *Spiritualism and Society*, 82.   **55.** "Presidential Reflections," *The National Spir-
itualist*, January 1982, 4.   **56.** Nettie Colburn Maynard, "Seances with Abraham Lincoln," in *The ESP Reader*, 31–46.   **57.** Ibid., 33–36.   **58.** Allan Kardec, *The Spirits'
Book* (privately pub., 1857; modern reprint edition, Anna Blackwell, translator; Starlite,
1982), 88.   **59.** Lord Adare (Earl of Dunraven), "Experiences with D. D. Home in
Spiritualism," in *The ESP Reader*, 52. See also D. D. Home, *Incidents in My Life* (Secaucus,
N.J.: University Books, 1972; 1st pub. London, 1863).   **60.** Trevor H. Hall, *The Spiritual-
ists: The Story of Florence Cook and William Crookes* (New York: Helix Press/Garrett Pubs.,
1963), 170.   **61.** A partial list of such researchers of Palladino and others includes:
Crookes, Carington, Myers, Lodge, Doyle, and the Sidgwicks in England; Hodgson, James,
and Prince in the United States; DeRoches, Richet, Bisson, and Flammarion in France;
Schenck-Notzing in Germany; Lombroso, Galeotti, and Chiaia in Italy.   **62.** William
Stainton Moses, *Spirit Teachings* (London: Spiritualist Press, 1949, 1976).   **63.** OAHSPE:
A New Bible in the Words of Jehovih and his Angel Ambassadors (New York: Oahspe Pub.
Assoc., 1882), 907–908.   **64.** Frederick S. Oliver, *A Dweller on Two Planets* (Alhambra,
Calif.: Bordon Pub., 1952; 1st pub. 1899), x–xii.   **65.** Ibid., xv.   **66.** Alta Piper,
"Professor William James and Mrs. Piper," in *The ESP Reader*, 80. Also, Alta L. Piper, *Life
and Work of Mrs. Piper* (London: Kegan Paul, Trench, Trubner, 1929).   **67.** H. P.
Blavatsky, *The Key to Theosophy* (Pasadena, Calif.: Theosophical Univ. Press, 1972; 1st pub.
1889), 290.   **68.** Ibid., 301–302.   **69.** Theodore Flournoy, *From India to the Planet
Mars: A Study of a Case of Somnambulism with Glossolalia* (New Hyde Park, N.Y.: University
Books, 1963; 1st pub. 1900).   **70.** Robert and Eva Lees, *The Life Elysian* (Leicester,
England, 1905), 129–130.   **71.** F. W. H. Myers, *Human Personality and Its Survival of Bodily
Death*, ed. Susy Smith, abridged edition (New Hyde Park, N.Y.: University Books, 1961),
26–28. (Unabridged 2-vol. ed., New York: Longmans, Green and Co., 1954; 1st pub. 1903).
72. Ibid. (Smith ed.), 407.   **73.** Carl A. Wickland, *Thirty Years Among the Dead*
(Hollywood, Calif.: Newcastle Pub., 1974; 1st pub. 1924), 37, 91–92.   **74.** Levi H. Dowling, *The Aquarian Gospel of Jesus the Christ* (Marina del Rey, Calif.: DeVorss & Co., 1972; 1st
pub. 1907), 14.   **75.** James E. Padgett, *True Gospel Revealed Anew by Jesus, Vol. 2* (Washington, D.C.: Foundation Church of the New Birth, 1972), ii–iii.   **76.** Quoted in
William W. Kenawell, *The Quest at Glastonbury: A Biographical Sketch of Frederick Bligh Bond*
(New York: Helix Press/Garrett Pubs., 1965), 123.   **77.** Major W. T. Pole, "The Death

of Private Dowding," in *The ESP Reader,* 305–308. **78.** W. P. Jolly, *Sir Oliver Lodge: Psychical Researcher and Scientist* (Rutherford, N.J.: Farleigh Dickinson Univ. Press, 1974), 202. **79.** Sir Oliver Lodge, *Raymond, or Life and Death* (London: Methuen, 1916). See also Lodge, *Raymond Revised* (London: Methuen, 1922). **80.** Susy Smith, *The Mediumship of Mrs. Leonard* (New Hyde Park, N.Y.: University Books, 1964). See also C. D. Broad, "The Phenomenology of Mrs. Leonard's Mediumship," *Journal Amer. Soc. for Psychical Research,* April 1955; and Gladys Osborne Leonard, *My Life in Two Worlds* (London: Cassell & Co., 1931). **81.** *The Mediumship of Mrs. Leonard,* 212, 218. **82.** Material on Mina Stinson Crandon/Margery drawn from Thomas R. Tietze, *Margery* (New York: Harper & Row, 1973). **83.** Geraldine Cummins, *The Road to Immortality: Being a Description of the After-life Purporting to be Communicated by the Late F. W. H. Myers* (London: Psychic Press Ltd., 1932, 1967), 123. **84.** Geraldine Cummins, *Swan on a Black Sea: A Study in Automatic Writing: The Cummins-Willet Scripts,* ed. Signe Torsvig (New York: Samuel Weiser, Inc., 1970). **85.** Hugh Lynn Cayce, *Venture Inward* (New York: Perennial/Harper & Row, 1972), 107–108. **86.** Hugh Lynn Cayce, ed., *The Edgar Cayce Reader* (New York: Warner Books, 1969), 140–141. **87.** Ibid., 166–167. **88.** *Venture Inward,* 112–115. **89.** Jess Stearn on Dick Sutphen's audio cassette tape, "Ask the Experts About Channeling" (Malibu, Calif.: Valley of the Sun Pub., 1985). **90.** Creative Age Press, Garrett Pubs., and Helix Press. For example, one of these publications was the exemplary study of Garrett herself by Ira Progoff, *The Image of an Oracle: A Report on Research into the Mediumship of Eileen J. Garrett* (New York: Helix Press/Garrett Pubs., 1964). **91.** Arthur Ford, *Un-Known But Known: My Adventure into the Meditative Dimension* (New York: Signet/NAL, 1968), 48. **92.** *Psychics: In-depth Interviews* (New York: Harper & Row, 1972), 44–45. See also Eileen Garrett, *Many Voices: The Autobiography of a Medium* (New York: G. P. Putnam's Sons, 1968). **93.** Alice A. Bailey, *The Unfinished Autobiography* (New York: Lucis Pub., 1951, 1979), 162–164. **94.** *UnKnown But Known,* 13. **95.** Ibid., 63–64. **96.** Ibid., 68. **97.** Stuart Edward White, *The Betty Book: Excursions into the World of Other-Consciousness* (New York: E. P. Dutton, 1937). **98.** Stuart Edward White, *The Unobstructed Universe* (New York: E. P. Dutton, 1940), 21. **99.** Joan and Darby Grant (pseudonyms), *Our Unseen Guest* (Alhambra, Calif.: Bordon Pub., 1971; 1st pub. 1920). **100.** *Unobstructed Universe,* 56. **101.** Stuart Edward White, *With Folded Wings* (New York: E. P. Dutton, 1947). **102.** Ibid., 80, 87. **103.** *The Urantia Book* (Chicago: Urantia Foundation, 1955, 1981), 1008. **104.** Ibid., 1. **105.** Ibid., 17. **106.** Ibid., 1176. **107.** Maurice Barbanell, *This Is Spiritualism* (London: Herbert Jenkins Ltd., 1959). **108.** A. W. Austen, ed., *The Teachings of Silver Birch* (London: The Spiritualist Press, 1938), 26. **109.** Ena Twigg with Ruth Hagy Brod, *Ena Twigg: Medium* (New York: Hawthorn Books, 1972), 160–169. **110.** Grace Cooke, *The New Mediumship* (Liss, Hampshire, England: The White Lodge Trust, 1973). **111.** Ingrid Lund, *The White Eagle Inheritance* (Wellingborough, England: Turnstone Press, 1984), 25. Other books from the White Eagle Publishing Trust, Liss, Hampshire, England. **112.** Dion Fortune (pseudonym), *The Cosmic Doctrine* (Wellingborough, Northamptonshire, England: The Aquarian Press, 1976), 1–9. **113.** Ruth Montgomery, *The World Before* (Greenwich, Conn.: Fawcett Crest, 1976), 15. **114.** Ruth Montgomery, *A World Beyond* (New York: Fawcett Crest, 1971), 10. **115.** *The World Before,* 178. **116.** Ruth Montgomery, *Strangers Among Us* (New York: Fawcett Crest, 1979), 30–31. **117.** Jean Dixon, *Call to Glory* (New York: Bantam, 1973), 34–35. **118.** Ruth Norman, Vaughn Spaegel, and Thomas Miller, *Tesla Speaks, Vol. 2* (El Cajon, Calif.: Unarius—Science of Life, 1973), 90.

3
WHO DOES IT?

1. Jan Ehrenwald, *Anatomy of Genius: Split Brains and Global Minds* (New York: Human Sciences Press, 1986). **2.** Gertrude Schmeidler, "The Psychic Personality," in *Psychic Exploration,* eds. Edgar Mitchell and John White (New York: Capricorn/Putnam, 1974). **3.** Ibid. Also, Ira Progoff, *Image of an Oracle* (New York: Helix Press/Garrett Pub., 1964). **4.** In Lynn Smith, "The New, Chic Metaphysical Fad of Channeling," *Los Angeles Times,* 5

December 1986. **5.** *Embracing Our Selves: Voice Dialogue Manual* (Marina del Rey, Calif.: DeVorss Pub., 1985). **6.** Margo Chandley, interview with author, 8 February 1987. **7.** Margo Chandley, "A Psychological Investigation of the Development of the Mediumistic Process in Personality Function" (Ph.D. diss., International College, 1986). **8.** Joseph S. Benner, *The Impersonal Life* (orig. pub. 1941; current pub.: Marina del Rey, Calif.: DeVorss Pub.). **9.** Richard Lavin, "The Ultimate Journey" (audio cassette tape U4, San Francisco: Center for Applied Intuition, 17 November 1984). **10.** Alan Vaughan, on Dick Sutphen's audio cassette tape, "Ask the Expert About Channeling" (Malibu, Calif.: Valley of the Sun Pub., 1985).

4
WHAT DO THEY SAY?

1. Some of the earlier researchers already mentioned who have carried out this work include Flournoy, Prince, Myers, Carington, Sidgwick, Hyslop, Wickland, Broad, and Ducasse. **2.** Nora M. Lodor, *Afterlife Communication,* 2nd ed. (Modesto, Calif.: Afterlife Communications, 1978; 1st pub. 1917 as *Letters from Harry and Helen*), 34. **3.** Richard Lavin, "The Ultimate Journey" (audio cassette tape U4, San Francisco: The Center for Applied Intuition, 17 November 1984). **4.** Judith Skutch, interview with author, 11 October 1986. **5.** James Fadiman, interview with author, 26 August 1986. **6.** Charles Tart, interview with author, 11 October 1986. **7.** Aldous Huxley, *The Perennial Wisdom* (New York: Harper & Row, 1945). **8.** Willis Harman and Howard Rheingold, *Higher Creativity* (Los Angeles: Jeremy P. Tarcher, 1984), 153. **9.** Judy Boss, *In Silence They Return* (Saint Paul, Minn.: Llewellyn Pubs., 1972), 98. **10.** Jeanne Walker, *Always, Karen* (New York: Hawthorn Books, 1975), 152. **11.** Charles Hapgood, *Voices of Spirit: The Psychic Experience of Elwood Babbitt* (New York: Leisure/Norton, 1975), 135. **12.** Jasper Swain, *From My World to Yours: A Young Man's Account of the Afterlife* (New York: Walker Books, 1977), 23. **13.** Nils O. Jacobson, *Life Without Death?* (New York: Delacorte/Seymour Lawrence, 1971), 147. **14.** Arthur Ford, *Nothing So Strange* (New York: Harper & Row, 1958). **15.** Raynor C. Johnson, *The Imprisoned Splendour* (New York: Harper & Row, 1953). **16.** Carl Jung, *Memories, Dreams, Reflections* (New York: Vintage/Random House, 1961), 312–313. **17.** Laura Archera Huxley, *This Timeless Moment* (Millbrae, Calif.: Celestial Arts, 1975), 23. Next Mrs. Leonard material from Susy Smith, *The Mediumship of Mrs. Leonard* (New Hyde Park, N.Y.: University Books, 1964), 130–131. **18.** W. Whately Carington, "The Word Association Test with Mrs. Leonard," *Procs. Soc. for Psychical Research,* July 1935. **19.** Dr. Jesse Herman Holmes and the Holmes Research Team, *As We See It from Here* (Franklin, N.C.: MetaScience Corp. Pub. Div., 1980), 110. **20.** Anthony Borgia, *Life in the World Unseen* (London: Corgi Books/Transworld Pubs., 1970), 103. **21.** P. Phillips, *Here and There: Psychic Communication Between Our World and the Next* (London: Corgi Books/Transworld Pubs., 1975), 16–17. **22.** Helen Greaves, *Testimony of Light* (Saffron, Walden, Eng.: Neville Spearman, 1977; 1st pub. 1969), 27, 87, 144. **23.** Jane Roberts, *The Afterlife Journal of an American Philosopher: The World View of William James* (Englewood Cliffs, N.J.: Prentice-Hall, 1978), 162, 164, 176–177. **24.** Marilyn Ferguson, interview with author, 2 September 1986. **25.** ("Dictated to") Mark and Elizabeth Prophet, *Pearls of Wisdom, Vol. 8: Teachings of the Ascended Masters* (Malibu, Calif.: Summit University Press/ Summit Lighthouse, 1965), 41, 39, 41, 46. **26.** Maurice B. Cooke ("Hilarion"), *Seasons of the Spirit* (Toronto: Marcus Books, 1980), 30–31. **27.** Rosemary Brown, *Unfinished Symphonies* (New York: Bantam, 1972). **28.** Ian Parrott, *The Music of Rosemary Brown* (London: Regency Press). **29.** Frank C. Tribbe, "Research Report—Musical Composers," *Spiritual Frontiers,* Spring 1985, 89. **30.** Ibid., 84. **31.** James W. Hyslop, *Procs. Amer. Soc. for Psychical Research.* **32.** Maurice B. Cooke ("Hilarion"), *The Nature of Reality* (Toronto: Marcus Books, 1979), 1, 6, 7. **33.** Walter Russell, *The Secret of Light* (Waynesboro, Va.: University of Science and Philosophy, 1947, 1974), 212, 216. **34.** James J. Hurtak, *The Book of Knowledge: The Keys of Enoch* (Los Gatos, Calif.: The Academy for Future Science, 1977), 116, 515. **35.** Ray Stanford, *Speak, Shining Stranger* (Austin, Texas: Association for the Understanding of Man, 1971). Quote from interview with Stanford in *Psychic,* March/April 1974, 9–10.

5
WHO ARE THEY CHANNELING?

1. Plotinus, quoted in John Randolph Price, *The Superbeings* (Austin, Texas: Quartus Books, 1981), 7.   2. William James, *The Varieties of Religious Experience* (New York: Crowell-Collier, 1961), 394–397.   3. James Fadiman, interview with author, 26 August 1986.
4. Stuart Wilde, on his audio cassette tape set "Channeling," Taos, New Mexico: White Dove International.   5. Ken Wilber, interview with author, 8 December 1986.   6. Judith Skutch, interview with author, 11 October 1986.   7. This and following quotes from Ralph B. Allison, interview with author, 6 February 1987.   8. Lorraine Sinkler, *The Spiritual Journey of Joel Goldsmith* (New York: Harper & Row, 1973), 16.   9. From "Divine Guidance Acceptable as Political, Claims Gallup," Washington Associated Press, *Journal-Courier,* 9 December 1986.   10. Alfred Russel Wallace, *The World of Life* (London: Chapman & Hall, 1910), 392.   11. Huston Smith, interview with author, 9 October 1986.
12. Ceanne DeRohan, channel, *Original Cause: The Unseen Role of Denial* (Sante Fe, N.M.: One World Pubs., 1986).   13. John White, private correspondence with author.   14. Sanaya Roman and Duane Packer, *Opening to Channel: How to Connect with Your Guide* (Tiburon, Calif.: H. J. Kramer, Inc., 1987).   15. Jean Houston, interview with author, 3 November 1986.   16. Valerie Hunt, from the audio cassette tape "The Mind Field" *Residence of the Conscious and the Soul* (Malibu, Calif.: Bioenergy Foundation, 1984).   17. *Cosmic Telepathy,* 3.   18. From the audio cassette tape "Lazaris on Lazaris" (Fairfax, Calif.: Concept: Synergy, 1978).   19. Don Elkins, Carla L. Rueckert, and James McCarty, eds., *The Law of One, Vol. 1* (Louisville, Ky.: L/L Research, 1981), 1.   20. Robert Anton Wilson, *Cosmic Trigger* (Phoenix, Ariz.: Falcon Press, 1977), 25. Gitta Mallaz, ed., *Talking with Angels* (London: Watkins Pub.). H. C. Moolenburgh, *A Handbook of Angels* (Saffron Walden, Essex, England: Saffron Walden/The C. W. Daniel Co., Ltd., 1984).   21. P.O. Box 637, Broomfield, Colo.   22. P.O. Box 4077, Laguna Beach, Calif.   23. D. Scott Rogo, interview with author, 26 August 1986.   24. Quoted in Arthur Hastings, "Investigating the Phenomenon of Channeling," *Noetic Sciences Review,* Winter 1986.   25. Wilber interview.   26. Laeh Maggie Garfield and Jack Grant, *Companions in Spirit* (Berkeley, Calif.: Celestial Arts, 1984).   27. Alice A. Bailey, *A Treatise on Cosmic Fire* (New York: Lucis Pub., 1925, 1962), ix.   28. Allison interview. Edith Fiore, *The Unquiet Dead: A Psychologist Treats Possession* (Garden City, New York: Doubleday, 1987).   29. Stanley Krippner, "Cross-Cultural Approaches to Multiple Personality Disorder: Practices in Brazilian Spiritism" (unpub. ms. provided by Krippner), 20.   30. Maurice B. Cooke, *Dark Robes, Dark Brothers* (Toronto: Marcus Books, 1981), 1–2.   31. Michael Agerscov, *Toward the Light: A Message to Mankind from the Transcendental World* (Copenhagen: Toward the Light Pub., 1920), 104–105.

6
HOW DO THEY DO IT?

1. Stanley Krippner, interview with author, 28 November 1986.   2. Harry Stack Sullivan, *The Interpersonal Theory of Personality* (New York: W. W. Norton, 1953).   3. John Curtis Gowan, *Trance, Art and Creativity* (Buffalo, N.Y.: State University College/Creative Education Foundation, 1975).   4. Stefan Grunwald, *The Renderings of Stefano, Book I: Science and Technology* (Virginia Beach, Va.: Unilaw Library Book/The Donning Company, 1979), 3–4.   5. A "space being" channeled by Tuella, in *The Dynamics of Cosmic Telepathy* (Aztec, N.M.: Guardian Action Pubs., 1983), 79.   6. From "The Robert MacKenzie Case," in *The ESP Reader,* ed. David C. Knight (New York: Grosset & Dunlap, 1969), 125.
7. Gregory Scott Sparrow, *Lucid Dreaming: Dawning of the Clear Light* (Virginia Beach, Va.: A.R.E. Press, 1976). Shafica Karagulla and Viola Pettit Neal, *Through the Curtain* (Marina del Rey, Calif.: DeVorss Pubs., 1983).   8. Alan Vaughan, on Dick Sutphen's audio cassette tape "Ask the Expert About Channeling" (Malibu, Calif.: Valley of the Sun Pub., 1985).   9. Ralph Knight, *Learning to Talk to the World Beyond* (Harrisburg, Pa.: Stackpole Books, 1969), 51–52.   10. *Cosmic Telepathy,* 9.   11. Vincent N. Turvey, *The Beginnings*

of Seership (New Hyde Park, N.Y.: University Books, 1969; 1st pub. 1909), 112–113.   **12.** Ann Rogers, *Soul Partners* (San Jose, Calif.: Abiblical Socety, 1978), 20–21.   **13.** Francine Steiger, on Dick Sutphen's "Ask the Experts" tape.   **14.** This seems similar to the *ganzfeld* in parapsychological research, in which halved Ping-Pong balls are placed over open eyes turned to a light source to create a homogeneous diffuse field of vision; this is said to enhance projection of mental imagery or clairvoyant information reception.   **15.** Graham Bernard, *Why You Are Who You Are: A Psychic Conversation* (New York: Destiny Books, 1985), ii–iii.   **16.** Jane Roberts, *The Seth Material* (New York: Bantam, 1976), 17–18.   **17.** Stoker Hunt, *Ouija: The Most Dangerous Game* (New York: Perennial/Harper & Row, 1985), 9.   **18.** Ibid., 81.   **19.** Susy Smith, *Confessions of a Psychic.*   **20.** *Seth Material,* 21.   **21.** Margaret and Maurine Moon, *The Jupiter Experiment: A Love Story of this World and the Next* (St. Paul, Minn.: Llewellyn Pubs., 1976), 203–209.   **22.** Nils O. Jacobson, *Life Without Death?* (New York: Delacorte/Seymour Lawrence, 1971), 139.   **23.** Marilyn Ferguson, interview with author, 2 September 1986.   **24.** Sir Arthur Conan Doyle, *The History of Spiritualism, Vol. 1* (New York: Arno Press, 1975; 1st pub. George H. Doran Co., 1926), 294–295.

7
PSYCHOLOGICAL EXPLANATIONS

1. Huston Smith, interview with author, 9 October 1986.   **2.** James McClenon, *Deviant Science: The Case For Parapsychology* (Philadelphia: Univ. of Pennsylvania, 1984), 11. Earl Babbie, interview with author, 9 February 1987.   **3.** Karl F. Pribram, interview with author, 15 August 1986.   **4.** Marcello Truzzi, interview with author, 27 October 1986.   **5.** Stanley Krippner, interview with author, 28 November 1986.   **6.** Theodore Troward, *The Edinburgh Lectures on Science* (New York: Filbert, McBride & Co., 1909).   **7.** Alfred Russel Wallace, *The World of Life* (London: Chapman & Hall, Ltd., 1910), 184.   **8.** William James, *The Varieties of Religious Experience* (New York: Crowell-Collier, 1961), 397.   **9.** Thomson Jay Hudson, *The Law of Psychic Phenomena* (Salinas, Calif.: Hudson-Cohan Pub., 1977; 1st pub. 1893; 47th ed. 1925).   **10.** Richard Maurice Bucke, *Cosmic Consciousness* (New York: E. P. Dutton, 1901, 1923).   **11.** Ralph Waldo Trine, *In Tune with the Infinite* (New York: Crowell, 1897), 16.   **12.** Robert C. Fuller, *Americans and the Unconscious* (New York: Oxford Univ. Press, 1986), 197–200.   **13.** M. Scott Peck, *The Road Less Traveled* (New York: Touchstone/Simon & Schuster, 1978), 283.   **14.** Stanislav Grof, *Beyond the Brain: Birth, Death and Transcendence in Psychotherapy* (Albany: State Univ. of New York Press, 1985), 303.   **15.** Quoted in David C. Knight, ed., *The ESP Reader* (New York: Grosset & Dunlap, 1969), 260.   **16.** Dr. Justine Owens, private correspondence with author.   **17.** Sigmund Freud, "Psychoanalysis and Telepathy," in *Psychology and Extrasensory Perception,* ed. Raymond Van Over (New York: Mentor/NAL, 1958), 110.   **18.** Ibid., 109–110.   **19.** Sigmund Freud, "A Case of 17th Century Demoniacal Possession," in *On Creativity and the Unconscious* (New York: Harper Torchbooks, 1958), 263.   **20.** Cited by Robert Ornstein and David Sobel, "The Healing Brain," *Psychology Today,* March 1987, 52.   **21.** Carl G. Jung, *Psychology and the Occult* (Princeton, N.J.: Bollingen/Princeton Univ. Press, 1977), 114.   **22.** Ibid., 114–115.   **23.** Ibid., 117–118.   **24.** Robert Masters, interview with author, 3 November 1986.   **25.** Carl G. Jung, *Memories, Dreams, Reflections* (New York: Vintage/Random House, 1961).   **26.** Carl G. Jung, *Collected Letters, Vol. 1, 1906–1950* (Princeton, N.J.: Bollingen #45/Princeton Univ. Press, 1973), 43.   **27.** Jean Houston, interview with author, 3 November 1986.   **28.** Herbert Silberer, *Problems of Mysticism and Its Symbolism* (New York: Samuel Weiser, 1971).   **29.** Ira Progoff, *The Image of an Oracle* (New York: Helix Press/Garrett Pubs., 1964).   **30.** Ibid., 360.   **31.** Jess Stearn, on Dick Sutphen's audio cassette "Ask the Experts About Channeling" (Malibu, Calif.: Valley of the Sun Pub., 1985).   **32.** E. Mansell Pattison, Joel Kahan, and Gary Hurd, "Trance Possession States," in *Handbook of States of Consciousness,* eds. Benjamin B. Wolman and Montague Ullman (New York: Van Nostrand Reinhold, 1986), 288.   **33.** Masters interview.   **34.** Jan Ehrenwald, *Anatomy of Genius: Split Brains and Global Minds* (New York: Human Sciences Press, 1986), 163.   **35.** Quoted in George Hackett with

Pamela Abramson, "Ramtha, A Voice from Beyond," *Newsweek*, 15 December 1986, 42. **36.** Quoted in B. Debetz and G. Sumner, *Primer on Clinical Hypnosis* (Littleton, Mass.: PSG Pub. Assoc., 1985), 13. **37.** Ernest Hilgard, *Divided Consciousness: Multiple Controls in Human Thought and Action* (New York: John Wiley & Sons, 1977), 205. **38.** Herbert and David Spiegel, *Trance and Treatment: Clinical Uses of Hypnosis* (New York: Basic Books, 1978), 32. **39.** William Kroger and William Fezler, *Clinical and Experimental Hypnosis*, 2nd ed. (Philadelphia: J. B. Lippincott, 1977). **40.** Erickson material taken from: Milton H. Erickson, Ernest L. Rossi, and Shiela I. Rossi, *Hypnotic Realities: The Induction of Clinical Hypnosis and Forms of Indirect Suggestion* (New York: Irvington Pubs., 1976), 144–146, 196–197. Interview: San Francisco Channel 5, CBS affiliate, "The Selling of the Spirits," Wendy Takuda, 11 February 1986, 6:00 P.M. **41.** Charles Tart, interview with author, 11 October 1986. **42.** John and Helen Watkins, "Hypnosis, Multiple Personality, and Ego States as Altered States of Consciousness," in *Handbook of States of Consciousness*, 147. **43.** Morey Bernstein, *The Search for Bridey Murphy* (Garden City, N.Y.: Doubleday, 1956). **44.** Masters interview. **45.** Peter Daniel Francuch, M.D., *Principles of Spiritual Hypnosis* (Santa Barbara, Calif.: Spiritual Advisory Press, 1982), 24. **46.** Ibid., 27. **47.** *Divided Consciousness*, 131. **48.** Ibid., 185–188. **49.** Ibid., 228. **50.** Armand DiMele, interview with author, 20 November 1986. **51.** Houston interview. **52.** *Beyond the Brain*, 297. **53.** Examples: alleged discarnate Drs. Craig Hammersmith (brain surgeon), Thomas Lirtham (heart surgeon), and Charles Boyd (endocrinologist) practicing through channels at Aquarian Center of Universology, Sarasota, Fla.; and discarnate doctors and dentists said to work through channel Joseph Martinez, The Spiritual Healing Center, San Francisco. See also John G. Fuller and Andrija Puharich, *Arigo: Surgeon of the Rusty Knife* (New York: T. Y. Crowell, 1974). **54.** *Diagnostic and Statistical Manual of Mental Disorders, 3rd ed.* (Washington, D.C.: American Psychiatric Association, 1980). All quotes in this *DSM III* section, unless otherwise noted, are from this source. **55.** Truzzi interview. **56.** Quoted in Stanley Young, "Body Doubles," *Outer Limits* (Los Angeles: December 1986), 108. **57.** F. W. H. Myers, *Human Personality and Its Survival of Bodily Death* (New York: Longmans, Green and Co., 1954), 16. **58.** C. Thigpen and H. Cleckly, *The Three Faces of Eve* (New York: McGraw-Hill, 1954); F. R. Schreiber, *Sybil* (New York: Warner Pub., 1974); Daniel Keyes, *The Minds of Billy Mulligan* (New York: Bantam, 1981); By "The Troops for Trudi Chase," *When Rabbit Howls* (New York: E. P. Dutton, 1987). **59.** Ralph B. Allison with T. Schwartz, *Minds in Many Pieces* (New York: Rawson Wade, 1980). **60.** Data from The National Foundation for the Prevention and Treatment of Multiple Personality, cited in "Multiple Personality Disorder: Key Findings," *Investigations: A Research Bulletin; Institute of Noetic Sciences*, Vol. 1, No. 3/4, 1985. **61.** Michael G. Kenny, "Multiple Personality and Spirit Possession," *Psychiatry*, November 1981. **62.** Stanley Krippner, "Cross-Cultural Approaches to Multiple Personality Disorder: Practices in Brazilian Spiritism" (unpub. ms. provided by Krippner), 26. **63.** William James, "Report on Mrs. Piper's Hodgson Control," *Procs. of the Engl. Soc. for Psychical Research*, 23:1–121. **64.** DiMele interview. **65.** Ken Wilber, interview with author, 8 December 1986. **66.** John Beahrs, "Co-consciousness: A Common Denominator in Hypnosis, Multiple Personality, and Normalcy," *Amer. J. of Clin. Hypnosis*, October 1983. **67.** Robert Ornstein, *MultiMind: A New Way of Looking at Human Behavior* (Boston: Houghton Mifflin, 1986), 24, 178. **68.** James Fadiman, interview with author, 26 August 1986. Marvin Minsky, *The Society of Mind* (New York: Simon & Schuster, 1985), 40. **69.** Paul Federn, *Ego Psychology and the Psychoses*, ed. E. Weiss (New York: Basic Books, 1952). **70.** Watkins, 144. **71.** Anita Muhl, *Automatic Writing: An Approach to the Unconscious* (New York: Helix Press, 1963). **72.** Hans Bender, "Mediumistic Psychoses," in *Telepathy, Clairvoyance and Psychokinesis* (Munich: Piper Pubs., 1983). **73.** Trans. Carl Ruthfuss, in Stoker Hunt, *Ouija: The Most Dangerous Game* (New York: Harper & Row, 1985), 127. **74.** *Anatomy of Genius*, 163. **75.** Wilson Van Dusen, *The Presence of Other Worlds* (New York: Perennial Library/Harper & Row, 1974), 117–118. **76.** Ibid., 119, 120–121, 135. **77.** "Psychic Research at a Glance," in *Psychic Exploration*, eds. Edgar Mitchell and John White (New York: G. P. Putman/Capricorn, 1974), 41. **78.** Krippner interview. **79.** Truzzi interview. **80.** Stanley Krippner and Montague Ullman, "Telepathic Perception in the Dream State," *Perception and Motor Skills*, 29 (1969), 915–918. **81.** Gertrude Schmeidler,

"The Psychic Personality," in *Psychic Exploration*, 94–109.   **82.** Iris Owen and Margaret Sparrow, *Conjuring Up Philip* (New York: Harper & Row, 1976).   **83.** Quoted in Adrian Parker, *States of Mind: ESP and Altered States of Consciousness* (New York: Taplinger, 1975), 24.   **84.** Aldous Huxley, *Doors of Perception* (New York: Harper & Row, 1963), 22–24. Roger N. Walsh and Frances E. Vaughan, "What is a Person?" *New Realities*, July 1982, 48.   **85.** Charles Tart, "Science, States of Consciousness, and Spiritual Experiences: The Need for State Specific Sciences," in *Transpersonal Psychologies*, ed. Charles Tart (New York: Harper & Row, 1975), 14–16.   **86.** Houston interview.   **87.** Tart, in *Transpersonal Psychologies*, 39.   **88.** Tart interview.   **89.** Ibid.

8
BIOLOGY AND PHYSICS

1. Julian Jaynes, *The Origin of Consciousness in the Breakdown of the Bicameral Mind* (Boston: Houghton Mifflin, 1976).   **2.** Honegger in Hunt, *Ouija*, 32–35.   **3.** Jacques Lacan, *Ecrits: A Selection* (New York: W. W. Norton, 1977).   **4.** J. A. Hobson and R. W. Mc-Carley, "The Brain as a Dream-state Generator: An Activation-Synthesis Hypothesis of the Dream Process," *Amer. J. of Psychiatry*, 134 (1977), 1335–1348.   **5.** Karl Pribram, *Languages of the Brain: Experimental Paradoxes and Principles of Neuropsychology* (Englewood Cliffs, N.J.: Prentice-Hall, 1971).   **6.** James Olds, "The Central Nervous System and the Reinforcement of Behavior," *American Psychologist*, Vol. 24, 1969, 114–118.   **7.** Sheila Ostrander and Lynn Schroeder, *Psychic Discoveries Behind the Iron Curtain* (New York: Bantam, 1970).   **8.** Arnold J. Mandell, "Toward a Psychobiology of Transcendence: God in the Brain," in *The Psychobiology of Consciousness*, eds. Richard J. Davidson and Julian M. Davidson (New York: Plenum, 1980), 393.   **9.** Stanislav Grof, *Realms of the Human Unconscious: Observations from LSD Research* (New York: E. P. Dutton, 1976), 194.   **10.** Mandell, 405.   **11.** Ibid., 423.   **12.** Wilder Penfield, *The Mystery of the Mind* (Princeton, N.J.: Princeton Univ. Press, 1975).   **13.** Michael Persinger, in Heather Martin, "Voices and Visions: A Guided Tour of Revelation," *Beyond Avalon: A Quarterly Journal* (Bridgeport, Conn.), October 1986.   **14.** DiMele interview.   **15.** D. H. Lloyd, "Objective Events in the Brain Correlating with Psychic Phenomena," *New Horizons*, Vol. 1, No. 2 (1973), 69–75.   **16.** Private communication with Frank Barr; Frank E. Barr (with J. S. Saloma and M. J. Buchele), "Melanin: The Organizing Molecule" (unpub. ms., 820 technical references, Inst. for the Study of Consciousness, Berkeley, Calif., 1981); Frank E. Barr (with Buchele and Saloma), "Melanin and the Mind-Brain Problem" (unpub. ms., 1260 technical references, Inst. for the Study of Consciousness, 1982); Arthur Young, *The Reflexive Universe: Evolution of Consciousness* (New York: A Merlloyd Book; Delacorte Press/Seymour Lawrence, 1976).   **17.** Pittendrig, recent lecture at Stanford University.   **18.** Besides assorted audio cassette tapes of Andrija Puharich's conference presentations, I have for this and later references drawn from the following: Puharich, *Beyond Telepathy* (Garden City, N.Y.: Anchor/Doubleday, 1973); "ELF Magnetic Model of Matter; the Origin of Life; and the Art of Healing: Theory, Experiments and Proofs," unpub. ms. comprised of four long papers (Dobson, N.C.: Essentia Research and Elf Cocoon Corp., copyright February 1987). Also see Robert O. Becker, *The Body Electric: Electromagnetism and the Foundation of Life* (New York: Quill/William Morrow, 1985).   **19.** Besides drawing from assorted tapes from conference presentations by Bob Beck, the following were also used: Beck, "Elf Magnetic Fields and EEG Entrainment, A Psychotronic Warfare Possibility?" and "Bob Beck's ELF Magnetic Field Bibliography," both in *Energy Unlimited: The Nu-Age Science Magazine* (Los Angeles), April-June 1978. See also Jim Hurtak, "Noetic Countermeasures for ELF and Brain Entrainment," *Energy Hotline: The New Age Science Newsletter* (Los Angeles), April 1979.   **20.** James Brown, "Relationships Between Phenomena of Consciousness and Interhemispheric Brain Wave Patterns During Nonordinary States of Consciousness" (Ph.D. diss., Saybrook Institute, 1985).   **21.** Jean Millay, "Brain/Mind and the Dimensions Beyond Space/Time" (paper presented at 2nd Internat. Conference on the Study of Shamanism, Sept. 1985).   **22.** Ibid.   **23.** James Johnston and Jean Millay, "A Pilot Study in Brainwave Synchrony," *The Psi Research Review*, March 1983. See also Jean

NOTES

Millay, "The Relationship Between Phase Synchronization of Brainwaves and Success in Attempts to Communicate Telepathically: A Pilot Study" (Ph.D. diss., Saybrook Institute, 1978). **24.** Robert Monroe, "Hemi-Sync" audio cassette (The Monroe Institute, Route 1, Box 175, Faber, Va. 22938-9749). **25.** In Millay, "Brain/Mind" paper. **26.** John White, "A New Age Fallacy," *Metapsychology: The Journal of Discarnate Intelligence,* Spring 1985. **27.** Wilber interview. **28.** Quoted in Millay, "Brain/Mind" paper. **29.** From an address to joint Math and Physics Depts. Colloquium, Georgetown Univ., September 1985. **30.** Daniel Z. Freedman and Peter Van Nieuwenhuizen, "Supergravity and the Unification of the Laws of Physics," *Scientific American,* February 1978, 126. **31.** From "Lazaris on Lazaris" audio cassette tape (Fairfax, Calif.: Concept: Synergy, 1978). **32.** Dawn Hill, *Reaching for the Other Side* (North Hollywood, Calif.: NewCastle Pub., 1985), 162. **33.** Ruth Norman, *The History of The Universe, Vol. 2* (El Cajon, Calif.: Unarius Educ. Foundation, 1982), 2–3, 152. Elwood Babbitt and Charles Hapgood, *The God Within: A Testament of Vishnu* (Turners Falls, Mass.: Fineline Books, 1982), 13. **34.** Arthur Findlay, *On the Edge of the Etheric; or Survival After Death Scientifically Explained* (London: Psychic Press, 1931), 36. **35.** Gabriele Wittek, *Homebringing Mission of Jesus Christ* (P.O. Box. 13, Pelham, N.H. 03076), 28 December 1980, 2–5; *On the Edge of the Etheric,* 4. **36.** Houston interview. **37.** Elwood Babbitt, in Charles Hapgood, *Voices of Spirit* (New York: Leisure Books, 1975), 194–195. **38.** Sanaya Roman and Duane Packer, *Opening to Channel: How To Connect With Your Guide* (Tiburon, Calif.: H. J. Kramer Inc., 1987). **39.** Babbitt, *Voices of Spirit,* 207. **40.** Jose Stevens, interview with author, 4 December 1986. **41.** William Tiller, "The Simulator and the Being," *Phoenix: New Directions in the Study of Man* (Stanford, Calif.: Fall/Winter 1977), 28–35; "Two Space/Time Mirror-like Universes: Some Consequences for Humanity," *Phoenix,* Summer 1978, 13–21; "The Positive and Negative Space/Time Frames as Conjugate Systems," in *Future Science,* eds. John White and Stanley Krippner (Garden City, N.Y.: Doubleday, 1977), 257–279. **42.** Louis Acker, P.O. Box 81, Chichester, N.Y. **43.** From chapter 4, T. B. Pawlicki, *How You Can Explore Higher Dimensions of Space and Time* (Englewood Cliffs, N.J.: Prentice-Hall, 1984). **44.** Rupert Sheldrake, *A New Science of Life: The Hypothesis of Formative Causation* (Los Angeles: Jeremy P. Tarcher, Inc., 1981). **45.** Rene Thom, *Structural Stability and Morphogenesis* (Reading, Pa.: Benjamin, 1975); Ilya Prigogine, *From Being to Becoming: Time and Complexity in the Physical Sciences* (San Francisco: W. H. Freeman, 1980). **46.** *From Being to Becoming.* **47.** David Bohm, *Wholeness and the Implicate Order* (London: Routledge & Kegan Paul, 1980), 149, 197. **48.** Ibid., 149. 196. **49.** Ibid., 212–213. **50.** Houston interview. **51.** A good presentation of John Bell's proof is chapter 12 in Nick Herbert, *Quantum Reality: Beyond the New Physics* (Garden City, N.Y.: Anchor/Doubleday, 1987), 211. **52.** Eugene Wigner, "Remarks on the Mind-Body Question," in *The Scientist Speculates,* ed. I. J. Good (New York: Basic Books, 1962), 289. **53.** Fred Alan Wolf, *Star Wave: Mind, Consciousness, and Quantum Physics* (New York: Macmillan, 1984). **54.** Brendan O'Regan, "Paraphysics," in *Psychic Exploration,* 494. **55.** Charles Muses, "Paraphysics," in *Future Science,* 280. **56.** Anton Mesmer, *Mesmerism* (London: Macdonald, 1948); Jerome Eden, *Animal Magnetism and the Life Energy* (Hicksville, N.Y.: Exposition Press, 1974); Karl von Reichenbach, *Letters on Od and Magnetism* (New Hyde Park, N.Y.: University Press, 1968); Edwin S. Babbitt, *The Principles of Light and Color* (Secaucus, N.J.: The Citadel Press, 1967; 1st pub. 1878). **57.** See radionics references under note 66, this chapter. **58.** Harold Saxton Burr and F. S. C. Northrop, "The Electrodynamic Theory of Life," in *Frontiers of Healing,* ed. Nicholas M. Regush (New York: Avon, 1977), 233. See also Madeline F. Barnothy, ed., *Effects of Magnetic Fields* (New York: Plenum Press, 1970); A. S. Presman, *Electromagnetic Fields and Life* (New York: Plenum, 1970); Harold S. Burr, *The Fields of Life* (New York: Ballantine, 1973); J. G. Llaurado and A. Sances, *Biologic and Clinical Effects of Low Frequency Magnetic and Electric Fields* (Springfield, Ill.: Charles Thomas Pub., 1974); Ashea R. Sheppard and M. Eisenbud, *Biological Effects of Electric and Magnetic Fields of Extremely Low Frequency* (New York: New York Univ. Press, 1977); Robert O. Becker, *The Body Electric* (New York: Quill/William Morrow, 1985). **59.** Cited in Larissa Vilenskaya, "Some Impressions Concerning Healing in the U.S.S.R." in *Parapsychology in the U.S.S.R., Vol. 1,* Larissa Vilenskaya, compiler (San Francisco: Washington Research Inst., 1981), 22. **60.** Marcel Vogel, *Crystal Knowledge Book,* privately published, 1985. **61.** Peter Tompkins and

Christopher Bird, *The Secret Life of Plants* (New York: Harper & Row, 1973); Julius Weinberger, "Apparatus Communication with Discarnate Persons," in *Future Science,* 465–486. **62.** Konstantin Raudive, *Breakthrough: An Amazing Experiment in Electronic Communication with the Dead* (New York: Taplinger/Lancer, 1971). **63.** George Meek, "Spiricom: Electronic Communications with the 'Dearly Departed,' " *New Realities,* July 1982. Also: George Meek, Metascience Corp., P.O. Box 747, Franklin, N.C. 28734. **64.** Victor Adamenko, in William A. Tiller, "Devices for Monitoring Nonphysical Energies," in *Psychic Exploration: A Challenge for Science,* 488; Hiroshi Motoyama, "The Motoyama Device: Measuring Psychic Energy," in *Future Science,* 445–450. **65.** Valerie Hunt, "Audio Aura Correlation Tapes," Los Angeles: Continuum Montage, 1979. **66.** Albert Abrams, *New Concepts in Diagnosis and Treatment* (San Francisco: Philopolis Press, 1916); Edward W. Russell, *Report on Radionics: Science for the Future* (London: Neville Spearman, 1973); David V. Tansley, *Radionics—Interface with the Etheric Fields* (N. Devon, England: Health Science Press, 1975); David V. Tansley, *Dimensions of Radionics* (Essex, England: C. W. Daniel Co., 1977); Virginia MacIvor and Sandra LaForest, *Vibrations: Healing Through Color, Homeopathy and Radionics* (New York: Samuel Weiser, 1979); Keith Mason, *Radionics and Progressive Energies* (Essex, England: C. W. Daniel Co., 1984). **67.** Jane Roberts, *Seth Speaks* (New York: Bantam Books, 1974; 1st pub. Englewood Cliffs: Prentice-Hall, 1972), 86. **68.** Aldous Huxley, *The Doors of Perception* (New York: Harper & Row, 1963), 22–24. **69.** A "space brother" in Carla Rueckert and Don Elkins, *Secrets of the UFO's* (Louisville, Ky.: L/L Research, 1977). **70.** Ken Carey, *Vision* (Kansas City, Mo.: UNI*SUN, 1985), 12. **71.** "Michael" in Chelsea Quinn Yarbro, *Messages from Michael* (New York: Playboy Paperbacks, 1979), 38. **72.** *Seth Speaks,* 406–407. **73.** Ibid., 451.

9
OPEN CHANNELING

1. Jean Houston, interview with author, 3 November 1986. **2.** Earl Babbie, interview with author, 9 February 1987. **3.** Alan Vaughan, "Channeling: An Old Phenomenon Goes Modern," *New Realities,* January/February 1987. **4.** John White, *Pole Shift* (Virginia Beach, Va.: A.R.E. Press, 1980), 186–187. **5.** Ken Wilber, interview with author, 8 December 1986. **6.** From "Lazaris on Intuition," audio cassette tape (Fairfax, Calif.: Concept: Synergy, 1984). **7.** Alan Vaughan, on Dick Sutphen's audio cassette tape "Ask the Experts About Channeling" (Malibu, Calif.: Valley of the Sun Pub., 1985). **8.** Stanley Krippner, interview with author, 28 November 1986. **9.** Quoted in Philip Goldberg, *The Intuitive Edge* (Los Angeles: Jeremy P. Tarcher, Inc., 1983), 193. **10.** Frances Vaughan, *Awakening Intuition* (Garden City, N.Y.: Anchor/Doubleday, 1979), 3. **11.** *The Intuitive Edge,* 40. **12.** *Awakening Intuition,* 45. **13.** Ibid., 39. **14.** R. A. Durr, *Poetic Vision and Psychedelic Experience* (New York: Delta/Dell, 1970), 140. **15.** Ibid. **16.** *Awakening Intuition.* **17.** Ibid., 24. **18.** In Nel Noddings and Paul J. Shore, *Awakening the Inner Eye: Intuition in Education* (New York: Columbia Univ./Teachers College Press, 1984), 13. **19.** F. W. H. Myers, *Human Personality and Its Survival of Bodily Death,* Susy Smith, abridged ed. (New Hyde Park, N.Y.: University Books, 1961), 74. **20.** *The Intuitive Edge,* 200–201. **21.** Huston Smith, interview with author, 9 October 1986. **22.** Quoted in Arthur Deikman, *The Observing Self* (Boston: Beacon Press, 1982), 46. **23.** Chester Carlson in *New Frontiers Center Newsletter,* Fall/Winter 1986, 9. **24.** Robert Masters, interview with author, 3 November 1986. **25.** Although the term *Pierian spring* is most often historically associated with the muses and the creative arts, I use it in this chapter in the sense of a fount or source of knowledge, which is another way it has been historically depicted. **26.** P. B. Shelley, "A Defence of Poetry," in *Poets on Poetry,* ed. Charles Norman (New York: Collier, 1962), 180, 183. **27.** W. R. M. Lamb, ed., *Plato III* (London: Heinemann, 1925), 423. **28.** In *Poetic Vision,* 11. **29.** Ibid., 15. **30.** Robert Louis Stevenson, *The Works of Robert Louis Stevenson, Volume 16* (London: Chatto and Windus, 1912). **31.** Thackeray quoted in S. Wavell, et al., *Trances* (New York: E. P. Dutton, 1967), 16. **32.** Lowell, in Ghiselin, ed., *The Creative Process* (New York: Mentor/NAL, 1952), 110. **33.** Ibid., 187. **34.** Ibid., 202–203. **35.** Marilyn Ferguson, interview with author, 2 September 1986.　**36.** James Merrill in Stoker Hunt, *Ouija: The Most Dangerous Game* (New York: Harper & Row, 1976), 47.　**37.** Quoted in Willis Harman and Howard Rheingold, *Higher Creativity* (Los Angeles: Jeremy P. Tarcher, Inc., 1984), 46–47.　**38.** In P. E. Vernon, ed., *Creativity: Selected Readings* (Middlesex, England: Penguin Books, Ltd., 1970), 57.　**39.** *Higher Creativity,* 46.　**40.** Ibid.　**41.** In Steven Halpern, *Tuning the Human Instrument* (Belmont, Calif.: Spectrum Research Institute, 1978), 127.　**42.** Ibid., 128.　**43.** Frank C. Tribbe, "Research Report—Musical Composers," *Spiritual Frontiers,* Spring 1985, 83.　**44.** Ibid., 85.　**45.** Ibid., 86.　**46.** Ibid., 87–88.　**47.** Steven Halpern, on Sutphen's "Ask the Experts" audio casette tape.　**48.** Marie-Gabriele Wosien, *Sacred Dance: Encounter with the Gods* (New York: Avon, 1974), 18.　**49.** Wassily Kandinsky, "Reminiscences," in *Modern Artists on Art,* ed. Robert Herbert (Englewood Cliffs, N.J.: Prentice-Hall, 1964), 24.　**50.** In Patrick Waldberg, *Surrealism* (New York: McGraw-Hill Book Company, 1965), 91.　**51.** In Sat Prem, *Sri Aurobindo: An Adventure in Consciousness* (New York: India Lib. Soc., 1904), 145.　**52.** William James, *The Varieties of Religious Experience* (New York: Collier, 1961), 399.　**53.** W. C. McCready and A. M. Greeley, *The Ultimate Values of the American Population* (Beverly Hills, Calif.: Sage, 1976).　**54.** Ralph Metzner, *Opening to Inner Light: The Transformation of Human Nature and Consciousness* (Los Angeles: Jeremy P. Tarcher, Inc., 1986), 179.　**55.** Stuart Edward White, *With Folded Wings* (New York: E. P. Dutton, 1947), 86–87.　**56.** F. W. H. Myers, *Human Personality and Its Survival of Bodily Death,* Susy Smith, abridged ed. (New Hyde Park, N.Y.: University Books, 1961; unabridged 2-vol. ed., New York: Longmans, Green and Co., 1954; 1st pub. London, 1903), 404–407.　**57.** Evelyn Underhill, *Mysticism: A Study in the Nature and Development of Man's Spiritual Consciousness* (New York: Meridian Books/World Pub., 1955), 444–445, 447, 450.

10
YOUR TURN

1. Alice A. Bailey, *Telepathy* (New York: Lucis Pub., 1950), 75–77.　**2.** Joey Crinita, *The Medium Touch: A New Approach to Mediumship* (Norfolk, Va.: Unilaw Library/Donning Company, 1982), 45.　**3.** This rather large notion includes judgment, discretion, self-knowledge, clearness, and so forth.　**4.** Anne Armstrong's tapes from Azoth Institute, 13994 Marc Drive, Sutter Creek, Calif. 95685.　**5.** Laeh Maggie Garfield and Jack Grant, *Companions in Spirit: A Guide to Working with Your Spirit Helpers* (Berkeley, Calif.: Celestial Arts, 1984), 39.　**6.** "Lazaris," in an interview with Craig Lee, *L.A. Weekly,* 7–13 November 1986.　**7.** Judith Skutch, interview with author, 11 October 1986.　**8.** Marilyn Ferguson, interview with author, 2 September 1986.　**9.** "Lazaris" in Craig Lee interview.　**10.** Charles Tart, interview with author, 11 October 1986.　**11.** Ibid.　**12.** Freda Morris, on Dick Sutphen's audio cassette tape "Ask the Experts About Channeling" (Malibu, Calif.: Valley of the Sun Pub., 1985).　**13.** Shakti Gawain, *Creative Visualization* (Mill Valley, Calif.: Whatever Press, 1978).　**14.** Rudolf Steiner, *Knowledge of the Higher Worlds and Its Attainment* (Spring Valley, N.Y.: The Anthroposophic Press, 1947).　**15.** Tuella and her sources in *Dynamics of Cosmic Telepathy.*　**16.** "Kuthumi," through Tuella.　**17.** *Cosmic Telepathy* channeled sources; echoed by dozens of others.　**18.** Ibid.　**19.** Ibid.　**20.** Ibid.　**21.** Anne Armstrong, Tape 12.　**22.** Terrence and Dennis McKenna, *The Invisible Landscape* (New York: Seabury Press, 1975). Andrew Weil, *The Natural Mind: Drugs and the Higher Consciousness* (Boston: Houghton Mifflin, 1986).　**23.** Jon Fox, "States of Consciousness," Tape T3 (San Francisco: Center for Applied Intuition), 13 July 1984, JFK Univ.　**24.** Valerie Hunt, *The Mind Field,* 1984, audio cassette tape.　**25.** Petey Stevens, *Opening Up to Your Psychic Self* (Berkeley, Calif.: Nevertheless Press, 1982), 30–33.　**26.** Rudolf Steiner, *Knowledge of the Higher Worlds and Its Attainment* (Spring Valley, N.Y.: Anthroposophic Press, 1947, 1977), 90.　**27.** Arnold J. Mandell, "Toward a Psychobiology of Transcendence: God in the Brain," in *The Psychobiology of Consciousness,* eds. Richard J. Davidson and Julian M. Davidson (New York: Plenum, 1980).　**28.** Dozens of channels and researchers echo this, from Hereward Carrington to Tuella.　**29.** Annie Besant and C. W. Leadbeater, *Thoughtforms* (Wheaton, Ill.: Quest Book/The-

osophical Publishing House, 1925, 1969).   **30.** Jon Fox, "States of Consciousness" tape.
31. Used widely in self-hypnosis, cognitive therapy, "suggestology," and Neurolinguistic
Programming (NLP).   **32.** Alice A. Bailey and "The Tibetan."   **33.** Elizabeth Clare
Prophet.   **34.** Alice A. Bailey, *Telepathy,* ix (in most Bailey/Lucis Pub. books).
35. *Creative Visualization.*   **36.** Max Freedom Long, *Introduction to Huna* (Cottonwood,
Ariz.: Esoteric Pubs., 1945, 1975).   **37.** Jean Houston and Robert Masters, *Mind Games: A
Guide to Inner Space* (New York: Delta/Dell, 1972).   **38.** Jean Porter, *Psychic Development*
(New York: Random House/Bookworks, 1974), 12—15.   **39.** Itzhak Bentov, *Stalking the
Wild Pendulum: On the Mechanics of Consciousness* (New York: E. P. Dutton, 1977); Steven
Halpern, *Tuning the Human Instrument: An Owner's Manual* (Belmont, Calif.: Spectrum
Research Institute, 1978).   **40.** *Season of Changes: Ways of Response* (Virginia Beach, Va.:
Associations of the Morning Light, 1974), 41, 43.   **41.** "Lazaris on Intuition" audio
cassette tape (Fairfax, Calif.: Concept: Synergy, 1984).   **42.** Leslie LeCron, *Self Hypno-
tism* (New York: Signet/NAL, 1964).   **43.** All quotes from Hal Stone, interview with
author, 11 February 1987.   **44.** Hal Stone and Sidra Winkelman, *Embracing Our Selves:
Voice Dialogue Manual* (Marina del Rey, Calif.: DeVorss & Co., 1985); see also *Voice Dialogue:
A Tool for Transformation* (same authors, publisher, and year).   **45.** All Sanaya Roman and
Duane Packer material from *Opening to Channel: How to Connect with Your Guide* (Tiburon,
Calif.: H. J. Kramer, Inc., 1987).   **46.** Shawn Randall, interviews with author, 18 Febru-
ary 1987, 18 March 1987.   **47.** "Lazaris on Intuition."   **48.** John Curtis Gowan, *The
Development of the Psychedelic Individual* (Buffalo, N.Y.: State University College/Creative
Education Foundation, 1974).   **49.** Stoker Hunt, *Ouija: The Most Dangerous Game* (New
York: Perennial Library/Harper & Row, 1985).   **50.** Andrew Jackson Davis, in Sir
Arthur Conan Doyle, *The History of Spiritualism, Vol. 1* (New York: Arno Press, 1975; 1st
pub. George H. Doran Co., 1926), 58.   **51.** From a letter by James B. DeKome, El Rito,
N.M., in "Debating the Identities of Entities," in *The Common Boundary: Between Spirituality
and Psychotherapy,* September/October 1986, 13.

CONCLUSION

1. Ruth Brandon, *The Spiritualists: The Passion for the Occult in the Nineteenth and Twentieth
Centuries* (New York: Alfred Knopf, 1983), 252—253.   **2.** A good exposition of Paul D.
Maclean's "triune brain" model and related brain evolution theories can be found in Map
21 of Charles Hampden-Turner, *Maps of the Mind* (London: Mitchell Beazley Publishers,
Ltd., 1981), 80—83.

SELECTED BIBLIOGRAPHY

In preparing my study, I worked from more than three hundred books, articles, and tapes about or relevant to the phenomenon of channeling. In addition, I used hundreds more collections of material reported to be channeled. Listed below is a brief exemplary selection.

Afterlife, Colin Wilson; London: Harap, Ltd., 1985.

Agartha: A Journey to the Stars, Meredith Lady Young; Walpole, N.H.: Stillpoint Publishing, 1984.

Altered States of Consciousness, Charles T. Tart; New York: John Wiley & Sons, Inc., 1969. (Also: *States of Consciousness*, Tart; New York: E. P. Dutton, 1975.)

Apparitions and Survival, R. Bayless; Secaucus, N.J.: University Books, 1973.

Applied Psi, quarterly journal of The Center for Applied Intuition, William Kautz, ed.; 2046 Clement St., San Francisco, Calif. 94121.

Automatic Writing: An Approach to the Unconscious, Anita Muhl; New York: Garrett Publications/Taplinger Distrib., 1963.

The Belief in a Life After Death, C. J. Ducasse; Springfield, Ill.: Charles Thomas, 1961.

The Book of Knowledge: The Keys of Enoch, James J. Hurtak; Los Gatos, Calif.: The Academy for Future Science, 1977.

The Case for Psychic Survival, Hereward Carrington; New York: Citadel Press, 1957.

The Case of Patience Worth, Walter Franklin Prince; New Hyde Park, N.Y.: University Books, 1964.

Edgar Cayce. There are dozens of collections of his material, as well as a number of biographies, including *Edgar Cayce—The Sleeping Prophet*, Jess Stearn; New York: Bantam, 1967; and *There Is a River: The Story of Edgar Cayce*, Thomas Sugrue; New York: Dell, 1967.

The College of Mediumistic Studies, London. Numerous tapes, books, classes.

Communication with the Spirit World of God: Personal Experiences of a Catholic Priest, Johannes Greber; Teaneck, N.J.: Johannes Greber Memorial Foundation, 1970.

Companions in Spirit: A Guide to Working with Your Spirit Helpers, Laeh Maggie Garfield and Jack Grant; Berkeley, Calif.: Celestial Arts, 1984.

Conjuring Up Philip, Iris Owen and Margaret Sparrow; New York: Harper & Row, 1976.

SELECTED BIBLIOGRAPHY

A Course in Miracles, anon.; Tiburon, Calif.: Foundation for Inner Peace, 1975.

Divided Consciousness: Multiple Controls in Human Thought and Action, Ernest Hilgard; New York: John Wiley, 1977.

A Dweller on Two Planets, Phylos the Thibetan; Alhambra, Calif.: Bordon Publishing Company, 1952.

The Dynamics of Cosmic Telepathy, Tuella; Aztec, N.M.: Guardian Action Publications, 1983.

Emmanuel's Book: A Manual for Living Comfortably in the Cosmos, Pat Rodegast and Judith Stanton; Weston, Conn.: Friends Press, 1985.

The ESP Reader, David C. Knight, ed.; New York: Grosset & Dunlap, 1969.

Eternal Life?, Hans Küng; Garden City, N.Y.: Image/Doubleday, 1985.

From India to the Planet Mars, Theodore Flournoy; New Hyde Park, N.Y.: University Books, 1963.

From Science to Seance, George W. Meek; London: Regency, 1974.

Future Science: Life Energies and the Physics of the Paranormal, John White and Stanley Krippner, eds.; Garden City, N.Y.: Anchor/Doubleday, 1977.

Here and There: Psychic Communication Between Our World and the Next, P. Phillips and W. L. MacLeod; London: Corgi/Transworld, 1975.

Higher Creativity: Liberating the Unconscious for Breakthrough Insights, Willis Harman and Howard Rheingold; Los Angeles: Jeremy P. Tarcher, Inc., 1984.

The History of Spiritualism, Vols. 1 and 2, Sir Arthur Conan Doyle; New York: Arno Press, 1975.

Human Personality and Its Survival of Bodily Death, F. W. H. Myers; 1st pub. 1903; 1st U.S. unabridged pub. (2 vols.), New York: Longmans, Green and Co., 1954; abridged 1-vol. ed., Susy Smith, ed., New Hyde Park, N.Y.: University Books, 1961.

The Image of an Oracle: A Report on Research into the Mediumship of Eileen J. Garrett, Ira Progoff; New York: Helix Press/Garrett Publications, 1964.

Incidents in My Life, D. D. Home; Secaucus, N.J.: University Books, 1972.

Intuition: How We Think and Act, Tony Bastick; New York: Wiley Interscience/John Wiley, 1982.

Is There Life After Death? Robert Kostenbaum; Englewood Cliffs, N.J.: Prentice-Hall, 1984.

Knowledge of the Higher Worlds and Its Attainment, Rudolf Steiner; Spring Valley, N.Y.: Anthroposophic Press, 1947.

"Lazaris." There are many video and audio tapes of the "Lazaris" material from Concept: Synergy, P.O. Box 159(m), Fairfax, Calif. 94930. At least two books of "Lazaris" material are due to be published in Fall 1987.

Learning to Talk to the World Beyond, Ralph Knight; Harrisburg, Pa.: Stackpole Books, 1969.

Many Voices: The Autobiography of a Medium, Eileen Garrett; New York: G. P. Putnam's Sons, 1968.

Margery (Mina Stinson Crandon), Thomas R. Tietze; New York: Harper & Row, 1973.

A Matter of Personal Survival: Life after Death, Michael Marsh; Wheaton, Ill.: Questbook/Theosophical Publishing House, 1985.

The Medium Touch: A New Approach to Mediumship, Joey Crinita; Norfolk, Va.: Unilaw Library/Donning Co., 1982.

Mediums, Mystics and the Occult, Milbourne Christopher; New York: Thomas Y. Crowell, 1971.

Mediumship and Survival: A Century of Investigations, Alan Gauld; London: Paladin/Granada, 1983.

The Mediumship of Mrs. Leonard, Susy Smith; New Hyde Park, N.Y.: University Books, 1964.

Messages from Michael, Chelsea Quinn Yarbro; New York: Playboy Paperbacks, 1979.

Metapsychology: The Journal of Discarnate Intelligence, Tam Mossman, ed.; P.O. Box 3295, Charlottesville, Va. 22903.

Minds in Many Pieces, Ralph B. Allison with T. Schwartz; New York: Rawson Wade, 1980.

Multiple Man: Explanations in Possession and Multiple Personality, Adam Crabtree; New York: Praeger.

"Multiple Personality—Mirrors of a New Model of Mind?" *Investigations: A Research Bulletin of the Institute of Noetic Sciences,* Vol. 1, No. 3/4, 1985.

My Life in Two Worlds, Gladys Osborne Leonard; London: Cassell & Co., 1931.

Mysticism and Philosophy, W. T. Stace; London: Macmillan, 1960.

The Nature of Reality, Maurice B. Cooke; Toronto: Marcus Books, 1979.

The New Mediumship, Grace Cooke; Hampshire, England: The White Lodge Trust, 1973.

The Occult: A History, Colin Wilson; New York: Random House, 1971.

The Occult in America: New Historical Perspectives, Howard Kerr and Charles L. Crow, eds.; Urbana, Ill.: University of Illinois Press, 1986.

On the Edge of the Etheric; or Survival after Death Scientifically Explained, Arthur Findlay; London: Psychic Press Ltd., 1977 (67th ed., first published 1931).

Opening to Channel, Sanaya Roman and Duane Packer; Tiburon, Calif.: H. J. Kramer, Inc., 1987.

The Other Side: An Account of My Experience with Psychic Phenomena, James A. Pike with Diane Kennedy; Garden City, N.Y.: Doubleday.

Ouija: The Most Dangerous Game, Stoker Hunt; New York: Perennial/Harper & Row, 1985.

Parallel Paths to the Unseen Worlds, Felix J. Frazer; Los Angeles: Builders of the Adytum, Ltd., 1967.

Philosophers in Wonderland: Philosophy and Psychical Research, Peter A. French, ed.; Saint Paul, Minn.: Llewellyn Publications, 1971.

Possession, Demonical and Otherwise, T. K. Oesterreich; New Hyde Park, N.Y.: University Books, 1966.

The Presence of Other Worlds: The Findings of Emanuel Swedenborg, Wilson Van Dusen; New York: Perennial/Harper & Row, 1974.

The Proceedings of the American Society for Psychical Research. This journal has hundreds of research reports spanning more than a century regarding channeling and related psychic communication and survival phenomena.

Psychiatry and Mysticism, S. R. Dean, ed.; Chicago: Nelson-Hall, 1975.

Psychic Experience: An Introduction to Spiritualism, Genevieve Woelfl; Menlo Park, Calif.: Redwood Books, 1976.

Psychic Guide (bimonthly magazine), Paul Zuromski, ed.; P.O. Box 701, Providence, R.I. 02901.

"A Psychological Investigation of the Development of the Mediumistic Process in Personality Function," Margo Chandley, Ph.D. diss., Saybrook Institute, 1986.

Psychology and Extrasensory Perception, Raymond Van Over, ed.; New York: Mentor/NAL, 1972.

Psychology and the Occult, C. G. Jung; Princeton, N.J.: Bollingen/Princeton University Press, 1977.

SELECTED BIBLIOGRAPHY

The Psychology of Anomalous Experience, Graham Reed; Boston: Houghton Mifflin, 1974.

The Psychology of the Psychic, David Marks and Richard Kamman; Buffalo: Prometheus Books, 1980.

"Ramtha." There are at least four books (and many videotapes) about Ramtha, including *Voyage to the New World,* Ramtha, with Douglass James Mahr; Friday Harbor, Wash.: Masterworks Inc., 1985.

Raymond: or Life and Death, Sir Oliver Lodge; London: Methuen, 1916.

Religion, Philosophy and Psychical Research, C. D. Broad; New York: Harcourt, Brace & World, 1953.

The Road to Immortality: Being a Description of the After-Life Purporting to be Communicated by the Late F. W. H. Myers, Geraldine Cummins; London: Psychic Press Ltd., 1967.

The Roots of Consciousness, Jeffrey Mishlove; New York: Bookworks, Berkeley/Random House, 1975.

Jack Schwarz. Aletheia Foundation, 1809 N. Hwy. 99, Ashland, Ore. 97520.

Seances and Sensitives for the Millions, Edward Albertson; Los Angeles: Shelbourne Press, 1968.

"Seth." There are over a dozen Seth books through Jane Roberts, channel (cited in chapter 1). I suggest starting with *Seth Speaks* (New York: Bantam, 1974) and *The Seth Material* (New York: Bantam, 1976).

Shamanism: Archaic Techniques of Ecstacy, Mircea Eliade; Princeton, N.J.: Bollingen/Princeton University Press, 1972.

Spirit Guides: We Are Not Alone, Iris Belhayes; San Diego, Calif.: ACS Publications, Inc., 1985.

Spirit Speaks (A channeling journal), Molli Nickell, ed.; P.O. Box 84304, Los Angeles, Calif. 90073.

Spiritism and the Cult of the Dead in Antiquity, Lewis Bayles Paton; New York: Macmillan, 1921.

Spirit Teachings, William Stainton Moses; London: Spiritualist Press, 1949.

The Spirits' Book, Allan Kardec (privately published, 1857; modern reprint edition, Anna Blackwell, translator; Starlite, 1982).

Spiritualism and Society, Geoffrey K. Nelson; London: Routledge & Kegan Paul, 1969.

The Spiritualist Gazette, the Spiritualist Association of Great Britain, 33 Bell Grove Sq., London.

The Spiritualists: The Passion for the Occult in the Nineteenth and Twentieth Centuries, Ruth Brandon; New York: Alfred Knopf, 1983.

The Starseed Transmissions: An Extraterrestrial Report, Ken Carey/Raphael; Kansas City: UNI-SUN, 1982.

Survival?: Body, Mind and Death in the Light of Psychic Experience, David Lorimer; London: Routledge & Kegan Paul, 1984.

Swan on a Black Sea: A Study in Automatic Writing; the Cummins-Willet Scripts, Geraldine Cummins; New York: Samuel Weiser, Inc., 1970.

"Teach Yourself Mediumship," (cassette tape), Ivy Northage; East Twickinham, Middlesex, England: Ivy Northage School for Mediums and Psychic Studies, 1978.

Telepathy and the Etheric Vehicle, Alice A. Bailey; New York: Lucis Pub., 1950. (Also recommended are the numerous other Bailey books.)

The Theory of Eternal Life, Rodney Collin; New York: Samuel Weiser, 1974.

SELECTED BIBLIOGRAPHY

Thoughtforms, Annie Besant and C. W. Leadbeater; Wheaton, Ill.: Quest/Theosophical Publishing House, 1969. (Also recommended are the other theosophical and H. P. Blavatsky books.)

To Hear the Angels Sing, Dorothy Maclean; Elgin, Ill.: Lorian Press, 1980.

Toward a Contemporary Psychology of Intuition: A Historical, Theoretical and Empirical Inquiry, M. R. Wescott; New York: Holt, Rinehart and Winston, 1968.

Trance, Art and Creativity, John Curtis Gowan; Buffalo, N.Y.: Creative Education Found., 1975.

Trance Mediumship, W. H. Slater; London: Society for Psychical Research, 1950.

Try the Spirits: Christianity and Psychical Research, E. Garth Moore; Oxford: Oxford University Press, 1977.

UFO's: Key to Earth's Destiny, Winfield S. Brownell; Lytle Creek, Calif.: Legion of Light Publications, 1980.

The Unconscious Reconsidered, Kenneth Bowers and Donald Meichenbaum, eds.; New York: John Wiley, 1984.

The Unfinished Autobiography, Alice A. Bailey; New York: Lucis Publishing Company, 1979.

Unfinished Symphonies, Rosemary Brown; New York: Bantam, 1972.

Unity or Multiplicity, John Beahrs; New York: Bruner/Mazel, 1981.

UnKnown but Known: My Adventure into the Meditative Dimension, Arthur Ford; New York: Signet/NAL, 1968.

The Unobstructed Universe, Stuart Edward White; New York: E. P. Dutton, 1940.

The Unquiet Dead: A Psychologist Treats Possession, Edith Fiore; Garden City, N.Y.: Doubleday, 1987.

The Urantia Book, anon.; Chicago: Urantia Foundation, 1951.

The Varieties of Religious Experience, William James; New York: Crowell-Collier, 1961.

Voices of Spirit: Through the Psychic Experience of Elwood Babbitt, Charles H. Hapgood; New York: Leisure/Norton, 1975.

Waking Up: Overcoming the Obstacles to Human Potential, Charles T. Tart; Boston: New Science Library/Shambala, 1986.

What Mediumship Is, Horace Leaf; London: Spiritualist Press, 1976.

A World Beyond, Ruth Montgomery; New York: Fawcett Crest, 1971.

Your Psychic Powers, and How to Develop Them, Hereward Carrington; Brooklyn: Templestar Co., 1958.

INDEX

Glines, Myrtle, 34
Glossolalia, 89, 91, 96, 106, 256–257
God, 10, 85–87, 173, 293–299, 305,
    310, 317
  belief in, 172
  identity with, 150
  pantheistic view of, 173
  as source, 63, 133, 172–174
  universe as, 151
God Spoke to Me (Caddy), 35
Goldberg, Philip, 307, 309
Goldsmith, Joel S., 171
Gospel as Explained by Spirits, The
    (Kardec), 101
Govan, Sheena, 34, 35
Gowan, John Curtis, 187
Grand Unified Theory, 272, 273, 342
"Great Divine Director, The," 161
Greaves, Helen, 159
Greeks, ancient, 82–83
Greeley, Horace, 98–99
Grof, Stanislav, 210, 230, 259
Grounding, 324, 327
Group entities, 176
Guardian angels, 181, 223
Guardian spirits, 180–181
"Guardians of the planet," 177
Guidance, 152–153
"Guides," 126, 180–181, 223

Hail to the Chiefs (Montgomery), 125
Hall, Trevor, 102
Hallucinations, 231–232, 243, 244
Halpern, Steven, 315, 331
Handbook of Angels, A
    (Moolenburgh), 178
Harman, Willis, 151
Harmonial Philosophy, The (Davis), 96
Harrington, John W., 15
"Harvest," 55
Hastings, Arthur, 4
Hauffe, Frederica, 95
Heaven and Hell (Swedenborg), 93–94
Hebrews, 85
Hegel, G. W. F., 271
"Helen," 148
Heraclitus, 82
Here and Hereafter (Montgomery), 125
Heretics, 90
Hidden observer, 227
Higher Aspects of Spiritualism
    (Moses), 103

Higher Creativity (Harman and
    Rheingold), 151
Higher Self, 169–173, 295
Highest States of Consciousness, The
    (White), 174
"Hilarion," 61–62, 64, 160, 162, 164,
    177, 183
Hildegarde, Saint, 91
Hilgard, Ernest, 220–221,
    226–228, 240
Hill, Dawn, 276
History of channeling, 79–128
  modern era, 120–128
Hobson, J. A., 257, 263
Hodgson, Richard, 111
Holmes, Jesse Herman, 158
Holographic model, 286–287, 293, 308
  of brain, 257–258, 272
Holy Spirit, 89
Home, Daniel D., 101–102, 191, 235
Honegger, Barbara, 256
Horus, 56
Houdini, Beatrice, 155
Houdini, Harry, 119, 154
Houston, 229–230
Houston, Jean, 57, 79, 175, 217–218,
    244, 252, 278, 286–287, 303, 330
Howard, Harlan, 315
Hudson, Thomson Jay, 209
*Human Personality and Its Survival of
    Bodily Death* (Myers), 107, 319
Hunt, Stoker, 338
Hunt, Valerie, 16, 175, 290, 327
Hurd, Gary, 219
Hurtak, James J., 66, 165–166
Huxley, Aldous, 150–151, 157, 175,
    251, 298
Huxley, Laura Archera, 157
Hydesville, New York, 97
Hyman, Ray, 14
Hyperspace, 283–284
Hypnosis, 219–228, 259, 329
  age regression and, 223–224
  and channeling, 219–223
  cognitive psychology and, 226–228
  mass, 220
  past life regression and, 224–225
  self-, 223, 332–333
  spiritual, 225–226
Hypothalamus, 263
Hyslop, James W., 163, 217
Hysteria, 220